W9-BVJ-082

ABOUT *COMPARATIVE ECONOMIC SYSTEMS*

"Now that the transition is over, Professor Steven Rosefielde is bringing back a new and improved version of comparative economic systems, one that treats culture, politics, and business misconduct explicitly in a market context. Rosefielde's approach is original and sophisticated, producing a theoretically rigorous text still accessible to the advanced undergraduate student. Students will learn a large amount of economic theory and come to appreciate the variety of economic systems and the sources of that variety. This is a signal accomplishment by a serious scholar and student of comparative economics."

James Millar, George Washington University

"This book is an outstanding text to acquaint students with the differences among the world's major economic systems. Its author is one of the best-informed and most careful scholars in the field."

Quinn Mills, Harvard Business School

"This is an ambitious and innovative work that rigorously and successfully addresses a question that economists often and mistakenly ignore: namely, how do ethics, culture, and politics affect the operation of core economic principles and the relative performance of the major economic systems in the global economy?"

Charles Wolf, RAND

"Rosefielde provides a forward-looking text that is firmly grounded in the fundamentals of comparative economics but that seizes fully the opportunities offered to the field by the end of the cold war. This is a text that can make comparative economic systems a "must-take" course for every undergraduate and a "must-offer" course for every economics department."

Josef C. Brada, Arizona State University

To David, my cherished son.

Comparative Economic Systems

Culture, Wealth, and Power in the 21st Century

Steven Rosefielde

Blackwell Publishers

First published 2002

2 4 6 8 10 9 7 5 3 1

Blackwell Publishers Inc.
350 Main Street
Malden, Massachusetts 02148
USA

Blackwell Publishers Ltd
108 Cowley Road
Oxford OX4 1JF
UK

Library of Congress Cataloging-in-Publication Data

Rosefielde, Steven.
Comparative economic systems : culture, wealth, and power in the 21st century /
Steven Rosefielde.
p. cm.
Includes bibliographical references and index.
ISBN 0-631-22961-2 (alk. paper) — ISBN 0-631-22962-0 (pb. : alk. paper)
1. Comparative economics.   I. Title.

HB90 .R665 2002
330—dc21   2001043234

British Library Cataloguing in Publication Data

A CIP catalogue record for this book is available from the British Library.

Typeset in 10/12 pt Baskerville
by Kolam Information Services Private Ltd, Pondicherry, India
Printed in Great Britain by TJ International, Padstow, Cornwall

This book is printed on acid-free paper.

CONTENTS

FIGURES

TABLES

ACKNOWLEDGMENTS

The ideas in this text have evolved over decades, and my indebtedness to others is extensive. Abram Bergson, Paul Samuelson, Wassily Leontief, Evsey Domar, Oscar Lange, Kenneth Arrow, Jan Tinbergen, Ralph W. Pfouts, Janos Kornai, Gottfried von Haberler, and Alexander Gerschenkron shaped my thinking about the Newtonian core of economics, and the formal correspondences between generally competitive markets and optimal planning in all their capitalist and socialist guises. Their work lead to the realization that if one began with Anglo-American premises about the sanctity of individual preferences, consumer sovereignty, competitiveness, fairness, and the rule of law, then there was a Pareto class of outcomes which appeared to validate the claim that modern micro- and macroeconomic theories were universal. Moreover, imperfect competition derived from the same premises did not contradict this universality; it merely extended the logic to the second best.

The collapse of the Soviet Union, the Yeltsin transition, and a decade of research in Japan were also formative because they compelled me to come to grips with economies that could not be adequately conceptualized with Anglo-American premises. Ruth Benedict's writings and the coaching of the eminent anthropologist Robert Levy showed me how cultures created alternative premises guiding economic activity, and Samuel Huntington's contention that power-seeking was the motor of international relations brought home the conceptual gulf between economic and political perceptions of utilitarian motivation. Their ideas forced me to appreciate that a truly universal theory of economics had to endogenize culture, power, and the sets of systems created when these influences were combined with the Newtonian core.

Sorting all this out has been difficult and I am grateful to all those who critiqued my false starts, and engaged me in fruitful dialogue. In particular, I wish to acknowledge the assistance of Ralph W. Pfouts, Dan Quinn Mills, Stefan Hedlund, Emil Ershov, Valarii Makarov, George Kleiner, Vyacheslav Danilin, Evgeny Gavrilenkov, Alexander Bulatov, Aleksei Ponomarenko, Vladimir Ivanov, Leonid and Inna Lamm, Alyona Kirtsova, Yuri Avvakumov, Maasaki Kuboniwa, Yoshiaki Nishimura, Masumi Hakogi, Ken Morita, Yoji Koyama, Shinichiro Tabata, Sadayoshi Ohtsu, Haruki Niwa, Akira Uegaki, Tamotsu Nakano, Philippe Debroux, Kaoru Nakata, Jim Millar, Gur Ofer, Martin Spechler, Joseph Berliner, Gregory Grossman, Murray Feshbach, John Hardt, Alec Nove, Howard Stein, Edith Terry, Pekka Sutela, Jan Rylander, Andrew Marshall, Patrick Parker, William Van Cleave, William T. Lee, Igor Birman, Joseph Churba, Vitaly Shlykov, Alexander Belkin, Stephen Blank, Lennart Samuelson, Jan Leijonhielm, Bengt-Goren Bergstrand, Wilhelm Unge, and David Rosefielde.

Special thanks goes to Stanislav Gomulka, Stefan Hedlund, and Quinn Mills for their critical comments on the final draft.

Although this text was not directly supported, it could not have been written without the financial assistance or cooperation of many institutions over the years, including the Carnegie Foundation of New York, the Institute for Arts and Humanities (UNC), The Japanese Ministry of Foreign Affairs and Monbusho, the National Research Council, The Peace Institute and Institute for Communist Societies in Transition (Australian National University), the Social Science Research Council, Japan Society for the Promotion of Science, the Erhardt Foundation, IREX, the Abe Foundation, the Japan Foundation, Institute of Economic Research (Hitotsubashi University), Hiroshima University, Ryukoku University, ERINA (Niigata), Fulbright Fellowship, Central European University, National Science Foundation, Hoover Institution, ACLS, the Ford Foundation, Office of the Secretary of Defense, the CIA, DIA, United States Naval Postgraduate School, the Center for Defense and Strategic Studies, FOI (Swedish Defense Establishment), Stockholm Institute of East European Economies, Center for Defense and Strategic Studies (Southwest Missouri State University), and the Council on Foreign and Defense Policy (Moscow).

Nancy Kocher tirelessly and cheerfully prepared seemingly endless drafts of the manuscript.

My wife Susan and daughter Justine gave me support and encouragement, and my brother Alan insights into the strengths and weakness of the American system of commercial and tax law.

To all, I express my deep gratitude.

Steven Rosefielde

PREFACE

The 21st century poses serious challenges to the discipline of comparative economic systems. Until the collapse of Soviet communism on December 25, 1991, comparative economics was primarily concerned with describing the principles of markets and state planning, and assessing the relative merits of capitalism and socialism. During the ensuing years attention shifted toward "transition"; that is, the anticipated transformation of the former communist states from authoritarian command economies to democratic market free enterprise. Comparative economics was perceived as a field headed for extinction, concerned primarily with documenting the final triumph of American capitalism, as "liberalization" swept the globe and managed economies vanished.

The Asian crisis, which began in the summer of 1997 and quickly spread throughout Eurasia and Latin America, provided a useful reminder that post-Soviet optimism should not be overdone. Russia's and China's futures remain precarious, Europe clings to democratic socialism, global economic growth is anemic, and the world is periodically faced with international economic destabilization. Once again there is a need to understand not only the principles which bind the economies of the world together, but those which divide them.

Since most nations today rely heavily on markets, the task of discriminating critical features of economic systems has proven illusive. The old established principles of monopoly, oligopoly, and imperfect competition provide some clues, as do concepts like stages of economic development, but they do not explain why systems like Russia and China perform so differently. This text attempts to fill the gap by explaining how culture in various guises modifies the standard rules of economic engagement, creating systems with properties that differ markedly from those predicted by the theory of general market competition. The analysis is grounded in established principles, but also assumes that individual utility-seeking may be culturally determined; that political goals may take precedence over public well-being, and that business misconduct may be socially detrimental.

These possibilities are not denied by other theorists. Everyone knows that inefficiency, oligopoly, obligation, misgovernance, moral turpitude, and criminality may diminish economic performance, and that positive cultural attitudes toward work and community could be beneficial, but these factors are usually treated as peripheral to the basic laws of supply, demand and their equilibration. The new approach avoids this prejudgment by reformulating the micro- and macroeconomic laws of demand, supply, and equilibration to incorporate culture, politics, ethics, and institutional factors in perfect markets, inefficient markets, anticompetitive markets, obligatory transactions, and state administration. As in the old approach, people are motivated by utility-seeking, but they do not always abide by the rules of free individualist competition. Their actions are modified by social ideals like collectivism and communalism, as well as by compulsion.

Coverage is restricted to highlight how culturally motivated rules of market engagement illuminate the performance possibilities of modern economies, with special attention paid to the great powers, and the widening gap between the rich and poor. Issues of historical interest are touched upon where appropriate, but the text is future-oriented. This should meet the needs of economics and international relations students interested in understanding the systemic forces shaping today's world. Instructors wishing to expose students to a wider range of topics can easily apply the cultural–systemic principles to supplementary readings on other worthy subjects.

INTRODUCTION

I have called this book the *General Theory of Employment, Interest and Money*, placing the emphasis on the prefix *general*. The object of such a title is to contrast the character of my arguments and conclusions with those of the classical theory of the subject, upon which I was brought up and which dominates the economic thought, both practical and theoretical, of the governing and academic classes of this generation, as it has for a hundred years past. I shall argue that the postulates of the *classical* theory are applicable to a special case only and not to the general case, the situation which it assumes being a limiting point of the possible positions of equilibrium. Moreover, the characteristics of the special case assumed by the classical theory happen not to be those of the economic society in which we actually live, with the result that its teaching is misleading and disastrous if we attempt to apply it to the facts of experience.

> John Maynard Keynes, *The General Theory of Employment, Interest and Money*, 1963, p. 3.

Comparative economic systems is the branch of economics devoted to investigating the ways in which production potential and performance are affected by motivational, mechanistic, and institutional forces governing demand and supply. Some people conceive the discipline as a catalog of human economic imagination. They enjoy studying how societies conceptualize and design systems like harmonism, communalism, socialism, communism, and capitalism to construct a better world. Some approach the subject from the standpoint of natural selection, chronicling the evolution of historical systems like feudalism and mercantilism, while others adopt a more pragmatic attitude, trying to discover which institutions and systems work best today.

All are valid, but theorists trained in the classical tradition sometimes view comparative systems research as an exercise in futility because they believe history has shown that free enterprise with minimal state participation is superior to all past, present, and future rivals. It is easy to sympathize with this position. The properties of perfectly competitive economies are extremely desirable, and the postwar successes of liberal capitalism suggest that the more closely real economies correspond with the competitive ideal, the better they perform.

But matters are not really so simple. Textbook models of perfect market competition are not as ideal or complete as they seem. Their attributes depend on special assumptions about technology, information, market access, patentable innovations, and the infallibility of price and quantity adjustment mechanisms (the invisible hand). They disregard government regulation, programs, and transfers, as well as obligation, and of course, the performance of real economies frequently defies classical expectations. Japan's managed system spectacularly outperformed the American liberal model from the early 1960s until the 1990s on most measures.

It is therefore essential to realistically model and scientifically evaluate the performance of different economic systems instead of assuming that globalization will soon render diversity extinct. This is accomplished here by elaborating the core micro- and macroeconomic principles applicable to all economies, and explaining how they are modified by national cultures into distinctive economic systems. The text clarifies conceptual misunderstandings about the comparative merit of free competition and perfect governance, showing in many cases how the same results are attainable using either mechanism, or by combining them. And it illuminates why engineering variables like the quantity and quality of fixed and variable inputs, management, entrepreneurship, technological progress, and economic governance do not adequately explain disorders like the increasing poverty of the world's poorest nations. The alternative approach developed here elucidates how culture, politics, and economic misconduct systemically modify demand, supply, effort, know how, discipline, innovativeness, compensation, income distribution, and social welfare, with special attention devoted to America (as an example of the Anglo-American model), Continental Europe, Japan, China, and Russia. This fresh perspective, which in the spirit of Keynes broadens the scope of general economic utility-seeking behavior, reveals profound global economic trends masked by the old focus. Instead of the universal "convergences" implied by worldwide perfect competition and perfect planning, it points to a reconfiguration of global wealth and power. It shows, as many economists long suspected, that the clarity of ideals like general market competition which purport to encompass the totality of national economic conduct may at times be achieved at the expense of true understanding. In a sense this should be obvious. The cogency of the competitive paradigm rests on the notion that utility-seekers will prefer free enterprise because it allows everyone to pursue prosperity on a level playing field. Rational men and women are expected to utility and profit maximize by producing and consuming the things they most desire. They are supposed to shun unfair anticompetitive practices, including criminal misconduct, and always be efficient. But generally competitive systems are nowhere to be found. People who are assumed to be individually self-seeking, ethically disciplined, and efficient persistently refuse to adhere to their scripts because their actions are culturally constrained, and they are often mismotivated, and unscrupulous.

This problem extends beyond national borders to international economic and security relations. Political scientists like Samuel Huntington conceptualize international affairs as a clash of civilizations, where power, not just competition, is paramount. Anglo-American culture, and the generally competitive principles it espouses, in Huntington's view are unique, not universal; a fact which fundamentally alters the terms of global economic engagement.

Most students and scholars sense these tensions, but like the architects of the transition theory known as the "Washington Consensus" still succumb to rationalist idealism. This is fatal because it always leads back to the misleading inference that all market economies and civilizations are, or soon will be, efficient and broadly alike. The snare is avoided here by elaborating the entire tapestry of systems theory including international relations from first principles.

The details of this new systems theory and its international ramifications are developed step by step in five parts. The first provides the conceptual building blocks connecting principles with systems models. It also addresses thorny matters like the role culture plays in influencing economic behavior. Part II specifies, explains, and evaluates two archetypes: perfect free enterprise (competitive markets) and perfect governance (command), to establish benchmarks for appraising economic performance. Part III delineates the market systems of America, Continental Europe, Japan, China, and Russia, explains their properties, and considers the problem of post-communist transition. Part IV elaborates the postwar economic performance of the great powers, and 169 other countries, and extrapolates trends, qualified by a discussion of the statistical pitfalls clouding comparative analysis of disparate systems. Part V integrates systems and international relations theory. It presents a fact profile of global military capabilities and carries the investigation to conclusion by discussing practical ways to diminish the negative consequences of systems rivalries and global economic engagement.

PART I

SYSTEMS

CHAPTER 1

COMPARATIVE ECONOMIC SYSTEMS

Economics is the study of economic utility-seeking under conditions of scarcity at work and play, and implies rational choice. It tacitly assumes that the utility sought is exclusively associated with consuming goods and services including leisure. Vindictive utility-seeking, which diminishes personal welfare by subordinating rational choice in order to get even with enemies, is noneconomic. People may feel better relinquishing reason for malice or love, and act sensibly on this basis, but their behavior is explained by psychological, physiological, cultural, and ethical principles properly the domain of other disciplines.

The collective outcomes of individual utility-seeking are shaped by people's preferences, technologies, mechanisms, institutions, and rules of personal interaction. These elements are the building blocks of economic systems.

The performance of economic systems can be evaluated "positively" by monitoring variables like the size and growth of the gross domestic product, and "normatively" by making value judgments about matters like income distribution and social justice.

Theoreticians frequently try to assess both the "positive" (technical efficiency), and "normative" (welfare) dimensions of aggregate economic activity by making assumptions about the rules of the game governing utility-seeking. If perfect competition, or perfect planning, is assumed it is relatively easy to interpret economic outcomes and offer policy guidance.

However, perfect competition and perfect planning rarely, if ever, occur. They may apply in some activities, but others will be inefficient, imperfectly competitive (planned), obligatory (force), and state-governed (command, administration and regulation).

Ethics, politics, and culture play important roles in determining the performance of systems. Communal cultures may proscribe or constrain individual utility-seeking, fundamentally altering the rules of the economic game, while competitive societies may over stimulate self-seeking. Ideology may also be a factor, but is usually subsidiary. Real economic systems are governed primarily by specific individual motivations, technology, and the rules of interpersonal utility-seeking, rather than idealistic principles.

ECONOMIC SYSTEMS

Economic systems are sets of self-regulating and culturally regulated "utility-seeking" activities transacted through voluntary exchange, reciprocal or unilateral obligation, and assignment, with scarce resources. A utility-seeking activity may involve work (training, producing, managing, financing, distributing, and governing), or leisure. The utility sought can be any experience consumers desire (demand). A utilitarian experience itself is not "economic," although it usually is the result of "economizing," understood as the rational choice required to achieve higher levels of utility. Scarcity depends on demand and is connected derivatively with supply side sacrifices called "tradeoffs" or "opportunity costs." Most utility-seeking activities are economic, but if resources are free, preferences are inconsistent, or rational choice is overwhelmed by passions like domination, malice, and love, these pursuits are noneconomic. The self-regulating principles, or culturally determined rules of conduct governing patterns of utility-seeking in economic units, or nations, and their corresponding mechanisms and institutions, define and distinguish economic systems.

This broad concept of economic systems as diverse self-regulating or culturally shaped utility-seeking search processes pursued through markets, state governance, and obligation, involving the consumption of goods and services in a world with scarce resources, implies that there may be many ways of achieving goals, and that economizing pervasively affects our lives. However, it is often better to utilize a more restricted framework which focuses on work. Although work and leisure both involve utility-seeking, "work" serves as a proxy for the time people devote to producing, while the remainder of the day is reserved for consuming, including romancing, family building, socializing, politicing, and philosophizing. Materially oriented societies stress work over leisure. Spiritual communities may spend more time on contemplation, working only to secure necessities. Often when people speak informally about economics and economic systems, they have this "work–leisure" dichotomy in mind. Economic activity is perceived as "making a living," as a means to an end (leisure), rather than as a component of a larger economic utility-seeking process which includes leisure. This convention is adopted throughout this text when discussing the gross domestic product, a concept defined exclusively for work activities, but the broader notion of economics as a process covering all scarcity constrained utility-seeking is retained when appraising welfare and comparative economic merit.[1]

MECHANISMS AND INSTITUTIONS

Economic activities can be conducted through self-direction, voluntary exchange (markets), and external regulation (obligation and governance). Individuals can command

---

[1]   The extent to which utility-seeking leisure choice should be considered economic depends on one's attitude toward time. If it is viewed as a scarce factor, then every rational, utility-seeking act is economic. But time cannot be bought and sold, and therefore is scarce in a different sense than labor, capital, natural resources, and land. Some economists therefore prefer to restrict the concept of economic leisure to situations where leisure-time utility-seeking requires the use of conventional scarce inputs, toys, and other paraphernalia.

themselves. They can voluntarily negotiate with others, in which case they are "in the market." And they can be governed by state authority (a supply side imposed transaction) or obligation (custom, or nongovernmental compulsion).

Each mechanism takes many forms. Individuals can use a variety of principles to direct themselves. The rules of market entry and conduct may vary, and obligation and governance may involve mutual support, criminal coercion, edicts, commands, administration, programs, and market regulation by states and private associations.

Organizations which set formal rules of economic conduct and establish compliance mechanisms are called economic institutions. They are distinct from custom, which constitutes an economic mechanism in its own right operating independently, or influencing markets and government, although some economists like Douglas North treat obligation as an aspect of economic institutions. Organizations in this restricted sense vary widely, and sometimes are the defining feature of economic systems. The Yugoslavian economy under Tito was classified as a labor-managed system because managerial decisions were made by workers' councils. The misnomer "Soviet" or workers' council conveyed a similar idea in the early days of Bolshevik rule.

Economic mechanisms also have been employed to classify systems. The classical distinction is between markets and plans; voluntary negotiated transactions (free enterprise) and state command. These concepts seemed to epitomize the distinction between the Soviet and American systems. But they were also a source of misunderstanding because they misleadingly implied that these principles were mutually exclusive; that governance in America and market forces in the USSR were negligible.

These mischaracterizations highlight a deeper problem. Markets, governance, and obligation are almost always complementary because individuals seldom are able to voluntarily agree on and honor rules for conducting business and enforcing contracts. In the real world, some obligation and governance is usually needed to establish markets, and systems are typically mechanistically mixed. Even authoritarian regimes like Stalin's found it expedient to permit a variety of voluntary exchange activities.

UTILITY-SEEKING

The primary force propelling economic activity is utility-seeking. The utility sought applies both to work and leisure, and is conceived as a set of psychic benefits like pleasure, derived from consumption. Economic utility-seeking is considered rational if it is dispassionate and makes people feel better, or enhances their well-being, whether they spend their money on dental care, laundry services, or gourmet delights. Economic utility-seeking, including the pursuit of leisure, always involves choices about what and how much to acquire (work) at prevailing prices. It is usually beneficial, but can be detrimental if reasoned choice is deranged by mania or addiction. And utility-seeking ceases to be economic at all when people act without weighing alternatives. The intensity with which people, groups, and authorities utility seek is often influenced by competition, suasion, and fear.

UTILITARIAN ETHICS

Economic utility-seeking in the most general case is unrestricted. Individuals are permitted to consume goods and services and can employ others for profit, treating people fairly, or manipulating them for their own advantage. Each individual's conduct will depend on his or her utilitarian ethics, and the vulnerability of others. If everyone adheres to the golden rule, doing unto others as they would have others do unto them, all will be treated well,[2] forging social contracts like those advocated by John Locke (1632–1704) to avoid the "war of all against all" which Thomas Hobbes (1588–1679) believed typified human relations. Otherwise scoundrels may victimize the virtuous, restraining trade, domineering, cheating, stealing, and subjugating for their own benefit. "Rational" economic utility-seeking alone thus does not assure good outcomes, and the merit of economic systems often depends heavily on utilitarian ethics.

ECONOMIC MISCONDUCT

Every economic system is vulnerable to four types of economic misconduct. Individuals may be indolent, irrational, and hence inefficient. They may violate the golden rule by engaging in conspiracies in restraint of trade, monopoly, and oligopoly to garner excess profits. The state and private custodians may put their interests before those they are supposed to protect. And they may deprive people of their economic rights. This compulsion is more harmful than imperfect competition because it deprives victims of choice, instead of just adversely imposing unfavorable terms of exchange. Government purpose and rules of conduct are diverse. They may be high-minded, converging to the perfectly competitive goals at one extreme, or corrupt at the other.

Those who control and primarily benefit from particular economic systems are called "sovereigns." Consumer sovereignty prevails when markets are perfect, or workably efficient; otherwise sovereignty may be vested in oligopolists, planners, or elites.

SYSTEMIC MISCONDUCT

Economic misconduct may be ingrained in systems which reject the golden rule. If society condones inefficiencies, imperfect competition, authoritarian governance, and corrupt practices, then these misdeeds will be intrinsic to the system and its outcomes. Since no real-world economy is free of vice, it follows that the performance of all economies is distorted to some degree by crime.

---

[2]   Charlotte Allen, "Confucius and the Scholars," *The Atlantic Monthly*, Vol. 283, No. 4, April 1999, pp. 78–83. The inference does not hold for masochists.

MERIT

There is no consensus about economic right and wrong. Consequently, there is no single standard that can be used to unequivocally appraise the merit of economic systems. Facts can be assembled, and models constructed to explain economic performance, but they cannot prove that any system is best. A few criteria, however, can be used to guide normative assessments, including measures of potential, performance, and ethical worth. Any economic system can be evaluated by the extent to which observed outcomes deviate from their potentials. Inefficient systems are always inferior to efficient ones. Systems can also be appraised relative to the achievements of rivals, and normative issues can be judged with statistics on living standards, income distribution, and unemployment.

ADAM, EVE, AND THEIR DESCENDANTS

These ideas can be restated informally with the aid of an economic parable. Consider the case of Adam, Eve, and their descendants. Once upon a time, when Adam and Eve frolicked in Eden, life was blissful because they did not have to bother with economics. Paradise was a land of plenty, where nothing was scarce, and nothing had to be "economized." Their instincts, drives, and intellectual needs were all completely satisfied with the resources at hand, until the serpent tempted Eve, and the first couple was expelled from Eden into the land of "Economia," where everything was scarce, and they were obliged to work (economic utility-seeking).

Adam and Eve experienced want, and learned that their material welfare depended on mastering four skills: forming transitive preferences, working efficiently, planning, and grappling with the meaning of life. The first skill was critical because work could not be rationally organized if they could not prioritize. The second skill governed supply, the third facilitated coping with the future, and the fourth provided a reference for these plans. Adam and Eve in Irving Fisher's terminology not only had to deal with the present; they had to learn how to trade with the future by working, mastering technology, investing, saving, and sorting out their time pattern of consumption. This necessitated an enormous extension of cognition and will. They had to formulate and expand their set of transitive preferences and act consistently upon them. We know from experience that people do learn, work, master technology, innovate, invest, save, and modify the sequencing of consumption. But there is considerable variation in thoroughness and competence. Often choices are determined by happenstance rather than careful calculation; with people deferring decisions until events are upon them, instead of devising comprehensive intertemporal micro-plans for work and leisure. Given life's imponderables this behavior makes sense, but it also exposes the bounded character of utility-seeking. People can usually improve their lifetime well-being by foresight, search, and calculation, but the benefit if any is not certain because the future is often misenvisioned, critical events misforeseen, forethought is inadequate, rules of thumb are fallible, intertemporal preferences intransitive, and choices made today are perverse from the standpoint of tomorrow's tastes. Consequently there is not a single best knowable way of proceeding, just a series of adaptive steps that allow people some modest control over imponderables.

This ambiguity is increased by the issues of purpose and moral conduct. Enlightenment thinkers believed that any solution to the problem of efficiently getting what you want meant nothing if people failed to harness their powers of higher reason to jointly optimize their material and spiritual potential, and serve the greater social good. The requirement for accomplishing this was a further expansion of Adam's and Eve's preference fields and transitivity, but the complexity of the task raises fresh doubts about whether people's cognitive, intellectual, and analytic faculties are really adequate to assure the efficient supply of things worth desiring.

The cognitive and analytic indeterminism of every aspect of Adam's and Eve's economic utility-seeking is central to understanding comparative economic systems. It reveals that even in rude isolation, better systems of economic action and technique (supply side economics) will not always be discovered, do not guarantee gratifying material outcomes, and even the most efficient material systems may not always be best if they impair Adam's and Eve's quality of existence. What feels good may be harmful to our well-being.

And, of course, matters become further muddled by Adam's relationship with Eve, and Cain's fratricide. A multi-person world creates opportunities and dangers. Every economics student knows that since people have different talents, aggregate productivity can be improved through a division of labor that allows individuals to concentrate their energies on things they do best. Likewise they know that voluntary exchange permits all transactors to be better off. But, in a multi-person world it is also possible for some individuals to augment these opportunities by exploiting others through deception, coercion, compulsion, and subjugation. Slavery, forced labor, theft, unjust taxation, extortion, monopoly, and fraud hurt social welfare, as may inequalities of talent, opportunity, and fortune.

The same kinds of risks extend to other aspects of human relations. People can develop, and share ideas and feelings, or they can dominate, manipulate, and abuse others.

The behavior of any multi-person economy cannot be reliably inferred from first principles of individual and collective economic utility-seeking without a thorough understanding of the temperaments, culture, mentality, criminal proclivities, institutions, and the rules shaping economic interactions. Even if people have well-defined transitive preferences and the mental processing capabilities to act consistently in their own interest within the parameters of bounded rationality, undisturbed by mania or addiction, they may choose to prey on each other instead of utility-seeking in accordance with the golden rule.

The potentials of real economic systems therefore cannot be adequately gauged by invoking axioms which historically exaggerate people's rational and ethical proclivities.[3] Economic systems are not closed sets of reversible, uniquely determinate "Newtonian"

[3]   Martin Hollis and Edward Nell, *Rational Economic Man: A Philosophical Critique of Neo-Classical Economics*, Cambridge University Press, New York, 1975.

relationships. Unlike the law of gravitation, they are also influenced by history, culture, psychology, ethics, politics, and various imponderables, requiring a more complex approach connecting the diversity of motives and disharmonious actions with comparative economic performance.

CULTURE

The structure, purpose, and rules of conduct of economic systems are often shaped by durable ethical, religious, philosophical, and obligational attitudes called culture. Culture affects the behavior of markets, state governance, and obligation. Since these forces are less ephemeral than politics and sociology, culture can be used as a shorthand for explaining distinctive systemic traits, providing insight into their potential, performance, and reform possibilities. Individualist cultures stressing self-reliance over obligation favor golden rule abiding free enterprise, whereas communalist economies dislike individualism, relying instead on obligation to promote community welfare. Culture affects both institutional choices and adaptability. Marxist culture of the 1930s, which associated markets with labor exploitation, obligated Stalin to adopt administrative command planning, and inhibited reform until attitudes softened under Khrushchev a quarter century later. Consistent libertarian cultures should construct ideal, self-regulating economies. But none are known to exist.

Culture typically is complex and inconsistent. It not only shapes people's professed ideals, but the way they act. Whether this double-dealing is due to lapses of logical consistency, intransitive preferences, Freudian repression, or is a cunning device for coping with existential contradictions, culture provides clues as to which misbehaviors are acceptable and which are not.[4] It suggests the thresholds beyond which leaders cannot transgress, or how hierarchy and privilege can be reconciled with communalism. It provides important insights into why nations construct the systems they do; why discrepancies persist between the ideals people espouse and their real conduct (perfect versus imperfect competition); why systems evolve along particular trajectories; why inferior systems are not always swept away by better alternatives; and why leaders resist policy advice from other nations, even when the advice is sound. The concept has its shortcomings. No one today, for example, explains the operation of markets in terms of the Protestant ethic, but if applied judiciously cultural variables are illuminating.

IDEOLOGY AND SCIENCE

However, this judgment does not extend to ideologies which misconceptualize real economic systems in terms of large social forces like the class struggle, instead of motives, mechanisms, and institutions. The appeal of ideology is obvious. It allows people with a metaphysical bent to disregard the complexities of economic utility-seeking, rendering

---

[4]   Vladimir Potanin, an infamous Russian oligarch, recently rationalized his repudiation of his company's Euro debts as "entrepreneurial pioneering."

sweeping misjudgments about comparative merit based on partisan notions of historical, scientific, or ethical "truths."[5]

Economists broadly agree that ideology provides an inadequate conceptual tool for understanding the behavior of real economic systems, although it may provide clues for serious investigations of phenomena like poverty. But there is no consensus about which acknowledged scientific method is best. Positivists pay scant attention to intent, preferring to directly observe correlations and continuities. The "laws" they discover often cannot be generalized, but do suggest how some things work. Rationalists proceed the other way round, conceptualizing how things should operate, while realists try to combine both approaches by empirically discriminating which rationalist theories are best.[6]

The usefulness of each approach depends on its application. Positivist and realist econometrics have shed substantial light on some matters, but rationalism has tended to predominate in the characterization and analysis of systems, because of the complexity of econometrically determining the micro-causality of large systems.

The best known example of this style of analysis is the neoclassical theory of free enterprise which ascribes most inefficiencies to government; but, as our discussion of economic utility-seeking has revealed, this is insufficient. The realist approach adopted in this text takes the neoclassical paradigm as its point of departure, and tries to enhance its explanatory power by incorporating various noncompetitive, anticompetitive, satisficing, and culture-shaped behaviors. When these supplementary factors are absent, and the golden rule prevails, systems are more or less generally competitive; when they are present performance departs from the neoclassical ideal.

Review Questions

1. What are economic systems?
2. When are human activities noneconomic?
3. Can leisure involve economic optimization? Should you choose an assortment of leisure activities within your budget of money and time that maximizes your well-being?
4. Why do economists find it convenient to restrict the term economics to "work" activities, and how does this relate to the problem of computing GDP?
5. Which should society maximize: GDP, or total welfare including leisure utility? Is maximizing statistical GDP a precondition for maximizing welfare? Explain.
6. What are economic mechanisms and economic institutions? How do the two concepts differ?

[5] Economics, like history, is often interpreted by secular scholars such as Karl Marx as having a hidden higher purpose. He believed that utility maximizing combined with the class struggle led to "full communism," in the same way that some advocates of free enterprise assume the markets assure the full realization of competitive welfare. Cf., Harvey Cox, "The Market as God," *Atlantic Monthly*, Vol. 283, No. 3, March 1999, pp. 18–23.

[6] Romano Harre, *The Philosophy of Science*, Oxford University Press, London, 1972; Harre and P.F. Secord, *The Explanation of Social Behavior*, Humanities Press, New York, 1975: Steven Rosefielde, "Post Positivist Scientific Method and the Appraisal of Nonmarket Economic Behavior," *Quarterly Journal of Ideology*, Fall 1979, and Rosefielde, "Economic Theory in the Excluded Middle Between Positivism and Rationalism," *Atlantic Economic Journal*, 4, Spring 1979, pp. 1–9.

7. Do economic systems rely exclusively on a single mechanism like markets, or do they typically encompass obligation and governance as well?

8. What is utility? What is utility-seeking? Why does it serve as a convenient concept for describing human economic motivation?

9. Is utilitarianism compatible with one or many concepts of welfare? Does maximizing utility always come to the same thing as maximizing welfare?

10. How does compulsion differ from monopolistic economic collusion? Hint: consider the scope of individual choice when confronted with the threat of violence compared with monopolistic prices.

11. To what extent may economic misconduct be systemic?

12. What are the three ways economists assess economic merit?

13. The concept of general equilibrium implies that there exists an economic ideal which can be realized for a finite state. Using the case of Adam and Eve, explain why this is unlikely.

14. Does this suggest that economics is inevitably a matter of seeking the "second best"?

15. How do multi-person economies complicate the attainment of "second best" ideals? Could this be important in designing effective economic policy?

16. Socially approved patterns of market behavior, governance, and obligation are determined by culture, not universalist utility-maximizing. Why is this insight fundamental to understanding the diversity of economic systems?

17. How does culture differ from policy?

18. What is ideology? Why is it inevitably a fallible guide to analyzing economic causality?

19. What are the three basic scientific methodological approaches to ascertaining economic causality? Which is best?

CHAPTER 2

CLASSIFICATION AND PRINCIPLES

The universe of economic systems can be divided into two parts: "self-regulating" and "culturally regulated" systems. Self-regulating (category A) systems grant everyone equal rights, voice, and opportunity to conduct themselves as they choose, subject to initial conditions like individual economic utility-seeking, and the golden rule (or their optimal planning equivalents). Their distinctive feature is self-regulating, individualist utility-seeking unencumbered by state or communal intervention; behavioral norms reflecting the enlightenment cultural ideals of the developed West. State or communal regulation and management may be employed from time to time in self-regulating systems to deal with market failure, or adjust income distribution with lump-sum dividends, but must be strictly neutral, without a trace of partisan favoritism. Self-regulation is defined broadly to include competitive markets, democratic governments applying various rules for income redistribution, as well as any cybernetic system including optimal directive planning which replicates these outcomes. Contrary to tradition, perfect competition and perfect planning are not treated as antipodes just because they employ different cybernetic mechanisms. They are viewed as different means to the same end, and are distinguished sharply from culturally regulated systems with other goals. Culturally regulated (category B) systems, their markets, state governance, and obligational mechanisms empower some individuals, groups, the community, or state to establish and routinely intervene in the process of individual utility-seeking, constraining the economic liberty of some for the benefit of others.

Standard microeconomic and macroeconomic principles apply in all category A systems, and shed light on aspects of category B economies. They are useful for understanding how consumption, investment, government, education, and innovational choices should be made in perfectly competitive or perfectly planned systems, and how culture, politics, and ethics modify, restrict, and suppress aspects of individual utility-seeking.

Most of the core axioms of the laws of supply, demand, and equilibration associated with category A regimes hold for category B. The primary differences are caused by the imposition of oligopolist, communal, collectivist, or dictators' utility-seeking on the unconstrained behavior of otherwise autonomous individuals.

These entities disregard the golden rule, and create mechanistic and moral hazards which distort and sometimes destabilize optimization. They affect the micro- and macroeconomic performance of category B systems. Competition and impartial governance, which play important supplementary roles complementing and re-inforcing rational individual utility-seeking, are subordinated to other influences in culturally regulated regimes. The laws of demand, supply, and equilibration modified by culture, politics, and ethics provide a complete theory of micro- and macroeconomic behavior that is more powerful than ideological concepts like capitalism, socialism, and communism.

A CAVALCADE OF SYSTEMS

There are no limits to the number of economic systems that can be imagined. Nonetheless, the universe can be compressed into two archetypes: "self-regulating" and "culturally regulated" systems. Self-regulating systems grant everyone equal rights, voice, and oppor-tunity to conduct themselves as they choose, subject to initial conditions like individual economic utility-seeking, and the golden rule (or their optimal planning equivalents). Their distinctive feature is self-regulating, individualist utility-seeking unencumbered by state or communal intervention; behavioral norms reflecting the enlightenment cultural ideas of the developed West. State or communal regulation and management may be employed from time to time in self-regulating systems to deal with market failure, or adjust income distribution with lump-sum dividends, but must be strictly neutral, without a trace of partisan favoritism. Self-regulation is defined broadly to include competitive markets, democratic governments applying various rules for income redistribution, as well as any cybernetic system, including optimal directive planning which replicates perfect competi-tion. Contrary to tradition, perfect competition and perfect planning are not treated as antipodes just because they employ different cybernetic mechanisms. They are viewed as different means to the same end, and are distinguished sharply from culturally regulated systems with other goals. "Culturally regulated" systems empower some individuals, groups, the community, or state to routinely intervene in the process of individual utility-seeking, constraining the economic liberty of some for the benefit of others. Perfect competition and perfect democratic two-level planning are examples of self-regulating systems; imperfect competition and despotism are different types of culturally regulated regimes.

The behavior of self-regulating and culturally regulated systems depends on their respective potentials and efficiency. The classification scheme presented in table 2.1 illustrates the essentials. It is crowned by a class of complete "social harmonist," conflict free systems where people fulfill every aspect of their personal potential. This category is Utopian (a fairy land that never was) and includes Karl Marx's harmonian vision in the *Grundrisse* and *Communist Manifesto*, which begins with the premise that people are capable of discovering all that is discoverable, and fully satisfying their desires if private property and other sources of disharmony are abolished. And it ends by inferring that if such systems are conceivable, they can be achieved. These and other Shangri-las, remote beautiful imaginary

Table 2.1   Economic systems: main concepts

Harmonist			
		Comprehensive	
		Diverse Utopias	
		Economic	
		Perfect markets	
		Perfect plans	
Scientific			
	Category A		*Category B*
	Self-regulating		Culturally regulated
	Universalistic		National or culturally specific
		Focused on	
	Building approximately perfect markets		Building culturally desirable systems

places where life for ordinary mortals approaches perfection, differ from other visionary ideals like Adam and Eve's paradise in only one essential. They do not assume boundless plenty. Resources are scarce, and activities are economic. This is why they are classified as "economic" Utopias.

Perfect competition and perfect planning are truncated Shangri-las. They promise harmony if people agree to abide by the rules, but only in their economic lives. Proponents of these ideals do not take any consistent position about how other forms of human conflict should be resolved.

The dividing line between utopianism and economic science is the recognition that perfect competition is not a unique, natural state which exists, or is likely ever to be realized. Sometimes economists have a Utopian moment, and speak as if they believe the world's economies are destined to be universally perfectly competitive, but all professionals know better. Their interest is pragmatic. They believe that the concept provides insights for the construction of well functioning, autonomous economic systems, which although imperfect are nonetheless very good. The science of comparative systems begins here, and takes two forms, one universalistic, the other culturally, or nationally specific. The universalistic systems are all self-regulated (or can be reformulated as such using the price "duals" of optimal linear programs; see chapter 6) and are focused on building approximately perfect markets, or less frequently approximately perfect plans (the computational "primals" of perfect competition). Perfect combinations of markets and plans are also conceivable. We shall sometimes refer to these self-regulating systems as category A (individuals in perfectly planned economies are only free to abide by the ideal plan). They form a "Newtonian Core" where causality is immutable, reversible, and determinate – uncomplicated by epochal historical events, culture, will, passion, politics, ethics, or chaos. Culturally and nationally specific systems are shaped by various kinds of privilege, and by obligational mechanisms. They too employ markets and plans, but outcomes always benefit some at the expense of others, and they take explicit account of non-Newtonian elements like the historical emergence of serfdom, and efficiency limiting (or expanding) aspects of culture, psychology, ethics, and politics. The goal of these culturally regulated systems, which we classify as category B, is to build economies that specific civilizations find desirable even though they lack the ethical virtues and atomistic efficiency of general competition.

Many economists, perhaps the large majority, consider category B systems inferior and transitory. Category A systems for them are the only durable ones. They concentrate on the properties of competitive market and planning ideals, explore latent requirements like the transitivity of individual preferences, or the possibilities of destabilizing disequilibria, and examine how modifying assumptions alters results. Transitions of all kinds are studied in the same way. These investigations have led some to conclude that approximately perfectly competitive markets and plans can be realized within the limits of "bounded rationality" by building systems which closely conform with ideal premises. Others see things differently, asserting that oligopoly, or macroeconomic destabilizing forces, are endemic to market economies and have modified competitive theory to take this into account. They have considered every possibility. Keynes assumed that markets were nearly perfectly competitive, but vulnerable to mood shifts (and faulty expectations) in aggregate effective demand. Some have constructed mixed models with elements of perfect and imperfect markets, government regulation, and planning, while others have tried to identify key trans-systemic regularities. Macroeconomic and production function theorists routinely attribute depressions and aggregate economic growth everywhere to factors like consumer confidence and elasticities of factor substitution, assuming that the idiosyncracies of national systems do not matter.

This proliferation of possibilities, where every aggregate model is based on a different conceptualization of the efficiency of market economies, has made it difficult to see the forest for the trees. Most modelers who see economics as a branch of engineering where plans and markets are interchangeable are not really interested in identifying the motivational, mechanistic, and institutional forces shaping the entire array of economic outcomes. They are concerned with discovering simple universalistic relationships that allow them to accurately forecast a few micro- or macroeconomic dependent variables.

These goals are not mutually exclusive. In an ideal fully specified model it should be possible to attribute every outcome to its causes, and ascertain why simple models provide accurate prediction. But the task is not feasible, creating a natural fault line between economists who construct aggregate models on the assumption that most economies are ruled by the same universalistic Newtonian forces, and those who believe that diverse motivations, mechanisms, and institutions matter.

This disjuncture is highlighted in table 2.1 by the division between category A, where utility-seeking promotes everyone's welfare regardless of how transactions are consummated, and category B where ends and means differ from the autonomous ideal. Category A systems are universalistic because they apply to all economies, as long as cultural, political, and ethical factors are not incompatible with key enlightenment axioms. These models are determined by technology and taste. Category B systems by contrast are "heterogeneous" because they depend on diverse culturally, politically, and ethically specific forms of utility-seeking, and control.

Comparativists do not reject universalist theories. They merely take the position that the specification of category A models is often incomplete and misleading, because it ignores demand side variables like culture, politics, and ethics, and the nuances of supply side mechanisms and institutions. The inclusion of these omitted variables shifts the focus of systems models toward the analysis of motivational, mechanical, and institutional factors.

The modeling of comparative economic systems is powerfully affected by judgments about which culturally, politically, and ethically approved motivations are preeminent, and the relative importance of demand and supply side influences. Three distinct tendencies are evident. Some comparativists concentrate on mechanisms; the degree to which economies rely on markets, governance, and obligation. Some stress motivation, while most are concerned with their interplay.

THE CORRESPONDENCE PRINCIPLE

All category B models can be expressed as modifications of some category A system. This correspondence allows us to evaluate category B systems in three different senses: as norms of relative efficiency when category A models are inefficient, imperfectly competitive, and misgoverned; as norms of ideal efficiency when category A models are perfectly competitive; and as norms for comparing different kinds of ideals.

Fortunately, all self-regulating category A models can be subsumed under a single cybernetic archetype: the generally competitive market model, either in one of its pure forms, or modified by notions of "normal" inefficiency, imperfect competition, and misgovernance. This standard is especially serviceable for interpreting the behavior of the Anglo-American system and other individualistically organized economies. Continental European systems which are also individualistic, but display a strong admixture of corporatism, are best appraised with a variant of the perfectly competitive paradigm that allows for optimal big government and transfers (the welfare state). Japan can be handled in the same way, modified to take account of communal sensibilities which encourage people to internalize group priorities.[1] The perfect planning standard, when it mimics perfectly competitive outcomes, provides another useful category A ideal that can be applied to North Korea, and perhaps Russia and China.

The assumption in category A trans-systemic models, that perfect markets and assignments can be interchangeable transactionary mechanisms, allows us to adopt a perfectly competitive benchmark throughout for assessing the potential and performance of all category B systems. Cultural, political, ethical, mechanistic, and institutional factors can either enhance or diminish potential and performance relative to this norm. If collectivist rules of intervention increase production potential, actual potential can be conceived as the combined perfectly competitive and collectivist effects. These correspondences also mean that the key to comprehending the special behavioral characteristics of category B models is identifying precisely which aspects of demand and supply differ from those of ideal competitive exchange and assignment.

DEMAND

The body of concepts which explains why and how people purchase goods and services is called demand theory, and its principles are called the *law of demand.*

---

[1] Groups may or may not hold the same goals as those of the social majority. Communalism usually implies a greater subordination of individualism than collectivism, but this need not always be the case.

This law, which assumes that people know what they want, is often thought to be universal, but may vary from system to system. It asserts that individuals can recognize when the utility of a good they are considering is worth the sacrifice (price), and make their purchases accordingly. More formally, people utility seek by purchasing goods or services to the point where marginal utility is equal to price (the ratio of marginal utilities is equalized with the ratio of product prices), given their preferences, not the desires of others.

The validity of this law depends on four factors:

1. People must possess a faculty for forming consistent preferences which allows them to effectively utility seek. If this faculty is absent, or dysfunctional, people will not be able to maximize their utility.
2. People must possess a faculty for ranking the utility of consumption alternatives, and act consistently on them. If this faculty is absent, or dysfunctional, people will not be able to determine which assortment of goods is best.
3. People must possess a faculty for resolving conflict between their preferences and the advice of others. If this faculty is absent, or dysfunctional, people's preferences may be unstable, or their choices may diminish their utility.
4. The utility people derive from consumption must be diminishing somewhere in the domain of choice. If utility is everywhere increasing, then one good will eventually be preferred to all others and demand will cease being a function of price.

Most economists believe that the law of demand is valid because people seem to utility seek, and have the requisite faculties. Utility appears to diminish beyond quickly attained thresholds, and people's desire to consume as much as they can within their means seems rational. Empirical experiments have been broadly confirming, and mathematical scrutiny has not uncovered any fatal logical flaws.

The familiar graphical methods used to visualize the law of demand and its underlying principles rest on this evidence. Marginal utility is depicted as a negatively sloped curve, with utility diminishing as the volume of any good consumed increases (figure 2.1).

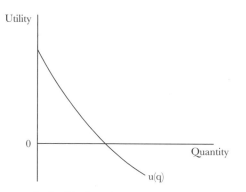

Figure 2.1   Consumer marginal utility function

The demand curve is drawn identically, because the sacrifice (prices) people are willing to make (pay) in foregoing consumption of one good depends on the marginal utility of another. Demand prices fall as the consumption of any good rises in tandem with marginal utilities (figure 2.2).

People's ability to optimize their consumption is illustrated with the aid of utility indifference curves, or as utility functions indicating the compensation required in one product to maintain a constant level of utility when units of another product are sequentially reduced (figure 2.3).

On the assumption that every individual possesses well-defined nested sets of utility indifference curves, it is easily shown that if people utility seek they can utility maximize by choosing the product assortments where their budget constraints are tangent to their highest indifference curves. If people do aspire to utility maximize, figure 2.3 demonstrates that they can succeed by purchasing products to the point where the ratio of product prices is proportional to marginal utilities. The same idea is conveyed in figure 2.2, where only one good is explicitly considered. If the offer price of the product is p, and the price the consumer is willing to pay p*, then the law of demand (utility-seeking) will impel him or her to increase purchases from q* to q.

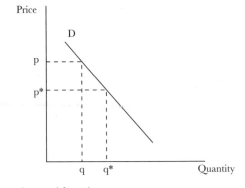

Figure 2.2   Consumer demand function

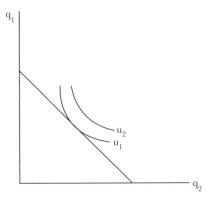

Figure 2.3   Consumer assortment utility optimization

Comparativists accept the logic and evidence for these graphical depictions of the law of demand as plausible descriptions of personal utility-seeking; as characterizations of consumer behavior when the desires of others influence taste, and even as an approximation of collective decision-making. But they strongly distinguish category A cases where individuals attempt to maximize their preferred economic utility states, from situations involving forced substitution where people are compelled to accept the dictates of others, or cases where choice is capricious. While the choice process may be similar in some respects, the implications for personal and social welfare are not. If individuals are swayed by passion, or pressured, outcomes may be detrimental.

SUPPLY

The availability of labor, other scarce factors, and technology are essential ingredients of economic supply, but are not sufficient to assure the efficient production and distribution of goods and services. The body of concepts which explains the goals, conditions, response patterns, and mechanisms by which people fashion things to directly and indirectly satisfy their demands is called supply theory, and the principles which guide them the *law of supply*. This law, like the law of demand is sometimes thought of as being universal, but it too varies from system to system. The law of supply asserts that people are capable of discerning how to design, produce, and exchange (assign) goods to directly meet their own needs, and enhance their ability to acquire goods they may prefer from others. If the law of demand boils down to the assertion that people can and will ascertain which consumption programs are best for them, at diverse terms of exchange, then the law of supply is the complementary belief that people can and will elaborate production programs which allow them to determine best product assortments, for all states of demand. This requires producers to figure out the optimal cost-minimizing and revenue-maximizing requirements for all potential levels of profit-maximizing output, hiring factors until the value they add is equal to their marginal costs, in proportions determined by marginal rates of factor substitution.

The validity of this law and its implications depend on seven conditions:

1. People must possess a faculty for computing the utility generated from alternative forms of self-employment for their own account when there are no possibilities for exchange with others. This knowledge allows them to utility maximize in accordance with the law of demand.
2. People must possess a faculty for computing the utility generated from alternative forms of self-employment for their own account, when product exchange is feasible, but there are no possibilities for hiring others, or purchasing supplies from them. This knowledge allows them to extend their utility-maximizing to include exchange.
3. People must possess a faculty for computing the utility generated from businesses which not only provide them with products to exchange, but augment their command over the goods of others through profit-maximizing. This capacity allows people to increase productivity through scale, organization, management, finance, investment, innovation, and entrepreneurship.
4. People must possess a faculty which allows them to grasp that profit-maximizing, where production costs are minimized everywhere and revenues maximized at the

point where marginal cost equals marginal revenue (price), enables them to maximize their command over the goods of others, given their labor reservation. This capacity implies that people not only understand how to profit maximize, but appreciate that it best enhances their personal utility.

5. People must possess a faculty which allows them to compute optimal supplies when producers decide to abridge profit-maximizing, treating some individuals or groups preferentially.

6. People must possess a faculty for effectively coping with external intrusions into their business by rivals, social organizations, and the state. If they cannot find ways to profit from their endeavors, then it is pointless to act on someone else's behalf.

7. The marginal productivity (cost) of at least one factor, in at least one activity, must be diminishing (increasing) somewhere in the production set. If marginal productivity (cost) is everywhere increasing (decreasing), then all goods will become costless, and there will be nothing to economize.

Most economists believe that the law of supply is valid because people can usually fend for themselves making products, marketing them, and running businesses on a profit-maximizing, or cooperative dividend-maximizing basis. They can invest, finance, master new skills, manage, innovate, pioneer new ventures, and cope with external intrusions. Their behavior is rational from the standpoint of utility-maximizing, and marginal factor productivity (cost) appears to be nearly universally decreasing (increasing) after production reaches a threshold well before demand is satiated. Empirical studies have been broadly confirming, and mathematical investigations have not uncovered any fatal logical flaws.

The familiar graphical methods used to visualize the law of supply, and its underlying principles, rest on this evidence. Factor supply is depicted as a positive function of input compensation (figure 2.4), because the marginal utility of leisure increases as employment expands. Factor prices are set in equilibrium at the intersection of their respective supply and demand curves, and are used by producers to determine the optimal marginal rate of factor substitution, where these factor prices (the wage–rental ratio w/r) are tangent to enterprise isoquants (figure 2.5). Enterprise isoquants are analogous to consumer indifference curves, and show the different minimum input of one factor, for every marginal change in the volume of the other input required to produce a fixed amount of output. The sets of these tangencies for all levels of production determine every firm's marginal cost curve (figure 2.6).

They are initially increasing because empirical studies have confirmed that marginal productivity typically rises and declines in stages, decreasing together with average productivity in the economic region known as stage II (figure 2.7).

Proprietors are able to augment their command over consumption by maximizing profits, producing to the point where the product price is equal to marginal cost in the perfectly competitive case (figure 2.6), or to where marginal cost equals demand when enterprises possess market power. In all these instances, supplies of various sorts are functions of price, just as in the case of the law of demand, but the sign of the functions are reversed. This provides suppliers with the guidance they need for adjusting their behavior whenever they are not momentarily minimizing cost, or maximizing supply. If they are operating at the wrong point on an isoquant, they can easily discover through trial and error that they are losing profits by overpaying for inputs. Or, if they are overproducing, this will quickly become apparent because profits will be less than at the optimum point of production.

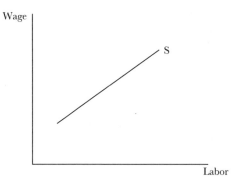

Figure 2.4   Labor supply function

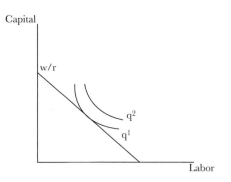

Figure 2.5   Factor mix cost minimization

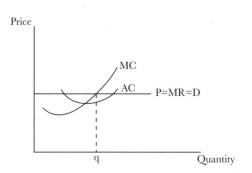

Figure 2.6   Profit-maximizing

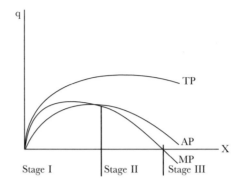

Figure 2.7   Stages of factor productivity

Comparativists accept the logic and evidence for these graphical depictions of the law of supply as plausible descriptions of demand responsive supply optimization; as character-izations of suppliers' behavior when external intrusions modify their production programs, and even as approximations of collective supply decision-making, where insider assess-ments of risk may vary. But they strongly distinguish category A cases, where individuals attempt to freely optimize their supply responses, from situations in which suppliers are primarily swayed by speculative passion, or subordinate their supply programs to the dictates of others. While the process of distinguishing preferred from dispreferred supply programs may be the same in some respects, the implications for personal and social welfare are not. If individuals are impulsive, or forcibly prevented from profit-maximizing, outcomes will be detrimental. The law of supply, when it works, should lead individuals to make rational choices. But this does not settle matters, because their actions may be misguided or coerced by privileged individuals or groups.

DEMAND AND SUPPLY EQUILIBRATION MECHANISMS

The law of demand and the law of supply are each indeterminate in the sense that neither identify ideal consumption and supply programs in isolation, because consumers cannot decide what to buy until they know the sellers' offer prices; and, vice versa, suppliers cannot maximize profits until they find out what people desire, and the terms upon which they are willing to offer their labor services. The existence and attainability of a general equilibrium hinges on the theoretical possibility of constructing one or more mechanisms that can solve this problem by establishing mutually agreeable, voluntary terms of exchange for every transaction, where each participant freely utility seeks within the possibilities of bounded rationality. The body of concepts used to analyze the properties, adequacy, and efficiency of category A economic solution mechanisms is called equilib-rium theory, and its guiding principles are *law of supply and demand equilibration*.

This law is often thought of as universal, but varies from system to system. The law of equilibration asserts that people can ascertain which configuration of goods (consumption program) they desire, and wish to supply (supply program) at any arbitrary set of prices from among their portfolios of feasible programs, and then search iteratively for better solutions by negotiating more agreeable terms of exchange until no one is willing to alter their choices in response to new terms others are prepared to offer. This process can be visualized as movements along fixed demand and supply curves searching for a point of equilibrium,[2] but these curves will also shift as the changing structure of supply affects wage–rental ratios, marginal costs, and the distribution of income. Changes in preferences and technologies provide an additional reason why these schedules may sometimes shift.

The validity of the law of demand and supply equilibration depends on seven conditions:

1. The law of demand must hold as previously specified. People must efficiently compile portfolios of consumption programs for all pertinent sets of prices.
2. The law of supply must hold as previously specified. People must efficiently compile portfolios of supply programs for all relevant sets of prices.
3. People must possess a faculty for discerning whether the assortment and volumes of goods supplied at prevailing prices satisfy their demand (consumption programs).
4. People must possess a faculty for determining how to adjust their consumption programs and price bids when supplies do not meet their expectations.
5. People must possess a faculty for discerning whether the assortment and volumes demanded at prevailing prices are consistent with their supply programs.
6. People must possess a faculty for determining how to adjust their supply programs and price offers when demand does not meet their expectations.
7. People must possess a faculty for effectively coping with external intrusions into their strategies for resolving supply–demand imbalances. If outside factors prevent them from adjusting their demand programs, and altering their bids; or from revising their supply programs, and changing their offer prices as they deem best, then a complete general equilibrium cannot be attained, and potential utility will not be fully realized.

Most economists believe that the law of demand and supply equilibration is valid because demand curves and supply curves as conventionally drawn slope in opposite directions, and always intersect at a price where the quantity demanded is exactly equal to the quantity supplied (figure 2.8).

Even if the slopes of demand and supply functions have the same sign, the curves can still intersect at a point where supply and demand are balanced. Theorists have also shown that disparities between demand and supply are readily perceived, and interpreted in ways that prompt transactors to constructively respond to imbalances. When buyers discover that they want more of a product being offered – that the market is in a state of excess demand – this stimulates them to raise prices to entice sellers into augmenting their supply. And, vice versa, when markets are in a state of excess supply, sellers can discount their prices to reduce their excess inventories. This strategy is called the Walrasian excess demand price adjustment mechanism, and is especially appropriate for resolving distributive disequilibria

---

[2] Every point on conventional demand and supply curves is derived from the consumption and supply programs for the price (and set of prices for other goods) designated on the price ordinate. If the general equilibrium point is in this joint set, then the demand and supply curves will intersect at this equilibrium, and not some transitory partial equilibrium.

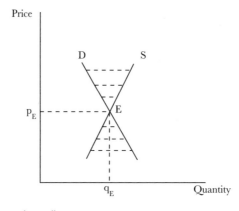

Figure 2.8   Walrasian price adjustment

including labor market imbalances where production of new supplies is unnecessary or infeasible. The hatched lines in figure 2.8 show how price adjustments in either direction sequentially diminish disequilibria as prices converge to the intersection of the supply and demand curves. In any real-world adjustment process, the schedules themselves will also shift around during the equilibration process, but this detail need not be depicted as long as the prices ultimately converge to the final equilibrium at point E.

Transactors can also perceive and respond to disequilibria in another constructive way. If producers sense that buyers are willing to pay more for their products than indicated by the prevailing supply price, then the market is said to be in a state of underproduction (figure 2.9).

Producers under these conditions can augment their profits by expanding output. Each additional unit produced will diminish the excess price gap indicated by the vertical hatched lines to the left of point E, until demand and supply prices are equal and production cannot be profitably increased. The same logic applies in reverse whenever the market is in a state of overproduction. This strategy is called the Marshallian excess price quantity adjustment mechanism, and is applicable wherever disequilibria cannot be resolved by redistributing previously produced goods and factors. Like the Walrasian case, as adjustment proceeds supply and demand curves will shift, but will have the forms depicted when equilibrium is actually achieved at point E.

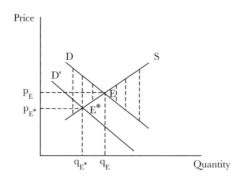

Figure 2.9   Marshallian production adjustment

When disequilibria are due both to maldistributed supply, and under- or overproduction, the ideal response will be for distributive imbalances to be eliminated as swiftly as possible, so that producers can adjust their output to the right global profit-maximizing level with minimal secondary distortion. Once equilibrium is achieved, any subsequent disturbances emanating from changes in preferences, or technology, will shift demand and/or supply curves, triggering another adjustment culminating in a new equilibrium at point E*.

Walrasian and Marshallian adjustment mechanisms are obviously well suited for market economies where people can either negotiate directly by voicing bids and offers, or indirectly by responding to consumption and production price signals. The same solutions, however, are also attainable from a mathematical perspective at arm's length where planners set initial prices, query transactors, and then continuously vary prices until Walrasian and Marshallian results are achieved. An even more direct computer-based solution is conceivable if planners have foreknowledge of participants' general equilibrium consumption and supply programs, but computopia is not a real option.

Comparativists accept the logic and evidence for these graphical depictions of the law of demand and supply equilibration as plausible descriptions of processes which reconcile all individual consumption and supply programs; as characterizations of transactors, behavior when external intrusions modify their programs, and even as approximations of collective disequilibrium response decision-making, where insider assessments of risk may vary. But they strongly distinguish category A cases where individuals attempt to freely optimize their disequilibrium responses, from situations where whims supercede rational calculus, or consumption and supply programs are subordinated to the dictates of others. While the process of distinguishing preferred from dispreferred responses may be similar in some respects, the implications for personal and social welfare are not. If individuals do not utility maximize, or are prevented from maximizing profits, outcomes will be inferior. The law of demand and supply equilibration when it works should lead individuals to make rational choices, but results will be warped if optimization is disregarded or thwarted.

COMPETITION AND ASSIGNMENT

The law of demand and supply equilibration as just explained can generate diverse equilibria depending on the scope of individual freedom. A general equilibrium has been defined as one in which neither dictators nor communities impose their consumption and supply programs on those preferred by others, or group members. This principle holds for criminal activities where some individuals act like "dictators," subjugating others and depriving them of their choice, but an important ambiguity exists in cases where some people exert what others consider undue influence over terms of trade (prices), and hence over their consumption and supply programs. Silver-tongued vendors may oversell the virtues of their wares, and the gullible may overbuy and overpay. Utility-seeking businessmen may strive to acquire oligopoly and monopoly market power by restricting supplies and market access; curtailing production, impeding workers' mobility, preventing new entrants, and even prohibiting retail customers from purchasing goods at wholesale.

Should there be any limits placed on permissible individual utility-seeking in defining an individualistic general equilibrium, or should people be free to tout their products, disinform, collude in restraint of trade, sexually harass, and discriminate? There is a broad consensus in the West that disinformation, sexual harassment, and discrimination should be criminalized, and hence excluded from an unfettered general equilibrium, but opinions about the proper limits of persuasion, consultation, and access vary. It is therefore important to recognize that the law of demand, the law of supply, and the law of demand and supply equilibration have multiple individualistic interpretations in category A models, and corresponding category B systems. This means that unfettered competition and perfect assignment, essential for attaining general equilibria at point E in every market, or planning activity accordingly, have multiple consequences depending on boundaries placed on individual freedom by voluntary social contracts, or informal consensus; and that any socially sanctioned form of anticompetitive conduct like business collusion in category A models can be modified and embellished in category B systems by dictatorial or communal influences on motivation, mechanisms, and institutions.

GOVERNANCE AND OBLIGATION

The coexistence of multiple general equilibria in either category A or category B models is a consequence of the "disharmony" of this class of system, and calls into question the very possibility of achieving any unconstrained individualistic ideal because not everyone may accept, or acquiesce to majority imposed rules of permissible economic conduct, and interpersonal transfer.[3] It is easy to imagine economic regimes in which participants freely negotiate rules and obligations, both state and private, but these conceptions are always descriptively unrealistic and implausible. Few people are ever involved in negotiating laws and unwritten etiquette.

This means that real economic systems invariably have elements of governance and obligation, some of which are compatible with category A systems and some not. The dividing line here is whether state and group consumption and supply programs severely restrict individual options, and are consonant with majority desires. Economies with large state sectors and strong communitarian obligations may still be classifiable as category A systems if the purposes of the state and communities reflect popular individual will and impartially promote everyone's consumption and supply programs, in accordance with the law of competitive demand and supply equilibration. If they do not reflect a popular consensus, the economies are category B.

MECHANISMS AND INSTITUTIONS

These nuances further illuminate the rationale for including planning as a mechanism for attaining category A individualistic general equilibria. While governments by definition

---

[3] Both in economics and diplomacy negotiated rules of conduct are often treated as instruments of influence rather than solemn obligations, declarations to the contrary notwithstanding.

are not competitive for-profit enterprises, and hence invariably violate some efficiency principles of the law of demand, the law of supply, and the law of demand and supply equilibration, nonetheless they may try to achieve the same purposes by administration and a host of planning and assignment techniques. This is why all real economic systems with government sectors are mechanistically mixed, and why familiar distinctions between market and planned economies at best provide only limited insight into their potential and performance. The characteristics and techniques employed by various institutional forms of administration, planning, and assignment often reveal whether motivations are compatible with category A or B systems. Open and transparent institutions which welcome public participation, are responsive to public opinion, and attentive to constituent concerns without falling under the domination of special interests tend to be compatible with category A models; whereas closed and opaque institutions under the thumb of dictators and groups usually are associated with category B systems, whether or not their purposes are beneficent. Comparativists are inclined to believe that open institutions combined with free competition will yield superior results, but openness or closeness by themselves are not sufficient to determine relative potentials and efficiencies. Theory can create a mild presumption in favor of openness, but only practice can settle real comparative merits.

MACROECONOMICS

The equilibrium outcomes of any economy will vary with the system adopted, and serve as indicators of potential. All economies, regardless of system, from time to time fail to attain their potential. Sometimes these inefficiencies are distributive, but often they involve aggregate employment and growth, business cycle fluctuations, price instability including interest, and foreign exchange rate volatility. The study of these phenomena is called macroeconomics, and the principles which distinguish them from other aspects of the law of demand, the law of supply, and the law of demand and supply equilibration are called the *law of macroeconomic equilibration*. Macrotheorists following the lead of John Maynard Keynes accept category A market explanations regarding the way in which individuals devise their consumption and supply programs, and usually assume further that these principles are universally applicable either in perfect or imperfect variants. They also accept the law of demand and supply equilibration, including the Walrasian inventory price and Marshallian production adjustment mechanisms. But they contend that the search for equilibrium initiated when some demand and supply schedules shift runs a high risk of recurrent malfunction. Specifically, Keynes maintains that whenever the production of investment goods as defined in national income accounts rises or falls from an initial point of disequilibrium, this will alter personal disposable income, causing consumption demand curves to shift rightward or leftward in the price–quantity space. These complementary movements called "income effects" are permitted by the law of demand and supply equilibration, but no one before Keynes persuasively argued that they might be dominant. Classical theorists had assumed, using Keynesian terminology, that when the state of business confidence declined, lowering the marginal efficiency of investment (the expected internal rate of return on new productive investment) and inducing a contraction in investment, the resources and money freed in this manner would be immediately reemployed in the consumption sector, because people would have no reason to hold excessive idle cash transactionary balances, and financial intermediaries always would lend deposits if returns exceeded their cost of money. Employment and production from this perspective therefore always should be in the close vicinity of equilibrium because consumption and investment are substitutes. Even drastic fluctuations in the supply of money in circulation should not matter because, as the Fisher money–GDP equation (MV = PQ) indicates, the price level always should be able to adjust reciprocally.[4] Setting aside the further complication that workers and producers might voluntarily withdraw from productive activity when business confidence deteriorates, Keynes argued that these classical expectations were wrong, because business pessimism encouraged individuals and financial institutions to augment their transactionary demand with speculative demand for idle cash balances, while wages and prices adjusted sluggishly to downward pressure. Hoarding and downward wage–price resistance, which normally accompany defensive reductions in aggregate investment, were the facts of life that caused protracted depressions.

Keynes's specification of macroeconomic malfunction has two important corollaries. First, interest rates, understood either in the Fisherian sense as the terms of trading with the future,[5] or in the Keynesian sense as the price of holding idle cash balances, cannot be expected to spark economic recovery as the classical theorists believe, because they are sticky like wages, and are kept excessively high by speculative demand for money, which diminishes the supply of loanable funds. In especially severe circumstances, Keynes described this situation as a liquidity trap. Second, speculative demand for money is likely to negate the efficacy of monetary policy because if these authorities emit additional currency it may be hoarded in anticipation of even worse times to come. This is the reason that Keynes and his early disciples urged governments to emphasize tax relief, investment subsidies, and public expenditure programs (fiscal policy) as the surest method of overcoming the consequences of business pessimism, underinvestment, hoarding, and negative income effects.

Later Keynesians, and post-Keynesian macroeconomic theorists, have filled in details, and clarified the circumstances under which fiscal and monetary policies might assist recovery, stabilization, and the maintenance of rapid economic growth. They have tried to elaborate a menu of joint monetary and fiscal full employment equilibria using LM–IS analysis, and have paid special attention to the impacts of widening and contracting market scope through trade liberalization and protectionism. They have pointed out the magnitude of involuntary workers' income losses caused when risk averse producers exit the market, forcing labor into lower paying forms of self-employment. They have examined a variety of other exogenous shocks, and illuminated the constructive stabilizing role played by government open market operations in regulating interest rates. But the core

---

[4]   These symbols represent money (M), the income velocity of money (V), the price level (P), and all output included in GDP (Q). It is tacitly assumed that when the price level fluctuates, equilibrium wages, capital, and product prices all change proportionately. The classicists believed that this neutrality assured that real output would not be affected by changes in the money supply.

[5]   Irving Fisher, *The Theory of Interest*. Fisher argued that the interest rate was determined by the principle of time preference, where current individual consumption and investment behavior is affected by the size and sequencing of future consumption possibilities. People who care little for the future, and consume intensively today, are said to have high time preferences; whereas patient people have low rates of time preference. Fluctuations in interest rates are demand led in Fisher's conception. Interest rates rise when the community wants to accelerate its time profile of consumption (reducing savings and investment), and fall when it chooses to defer and augment future consumption (increasing savings and investment).

concepts of income effects, wage, price, interest rate, and foreign exchange rate rigidities, and occasional hoarding, remain fundamental. Keynesian macroeconomic theory, and its subsequent embellishments, are broadly compatible with the individualist orientation of category A systems where the state – either in response to the will of the people or on its own initiative – surgically intervenes to keep Walrasian and Marshallian adjustment mechanisms from aggregatively malfunctioning.

The rudiments of the core Keynesian model can be usefully summarized graphically both to clarify various points and to serve as a reference for distinguishing how macro-disturbances might be generated and equilibrated differently in other economic systems. Consider the case of a nearly perfectly competitive category A economy which produces two goods: consumer and investment products that are aggregates of millions of specific items. Achievable full employment GDP is expressed as point E in figure 2.10, and reflects the equilibrium microeconomic supply and demand programs previously described at point E in figures 2.8 and 2.9. Alternative supply and demand points to the right or left of point E can be computed from respective alternative consumption–investment and supply programs at different equilibrium prices which would counterfactually hold if demand shifted in figure 2.9. The sets of these points form an aggregate indifference–demand curve, and a production possibilities supply frontier of the sort derived from contract curves in the Edgeworth–Bowley production space (see chapter 7). A ray from the origin through point E represents alternative bundles of consumption and investment in fixed proportions. Since there are only two aggregate goods in this example, following Keynes each point along the ray except point E can be interpreted as a nonfull employment level of the gross domestic product:

$$GDP = C + I. \tag{2.1}$$

Point E, as previously stated, is the full employment level of GDP. Also, the ratio of consumption to the hypotenuse at all points along the ray shows that there is a fixed average and marginal relationship between consumption and GDP, which can be associated with Keynes's concept of the marginal propensity to consume;[6] the notion that incremental consumption is a fixed share of personal disposable income:[7]

$$\beta = \Delta C / \Delta Y. \tag{2.2}$$

Keynes asserted that depressions are usually caused by a deterioration in business sentiment that reduces aggregate investment in figure 2.10 from I_E to I_A. He illustrates the effects of this pessimism as a downward shift in the marginal efficiency of investment (MEI) curve (expected internal rate of return on prospective investment projects),[8] which he relates to the interest rate construed as the cost of borrowing investable funds (figure 2.11).

---

[6]   If the marginal propensity to consume exceeds the average propensity, this can be indicated by shifting the starting point of the ray to the left of the coordinate axis origin, as is usually done in the simple one-good version of the Keynesian consumption function.

[7]   Via the Pythagorean theorem the hypotenuse is $\Delta Y = [(\Delta C^2 + \Delta I^2)]^{1/2}$, not $\Delta Y = \Delta C + \Delta I$, so that the geometric relationship must be treated only as an approximation of the Keynesian regularity.

[8]   Each point on the MEI (ρ) schedule is computed by comparing the price of an investment product with its stream of expected profits, and solving for the internal rate of return which equalizes both sides of the equations:

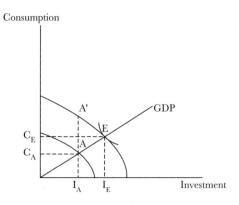

Figure 2.10   Keynesian macroproduction possibilities

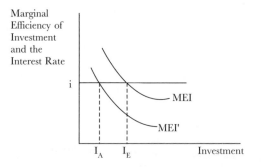

Figure 2.11   Business confidence and Keynesian aggregate investment

Rational investors, he plausibly contends, will never invest in a project with a prospective return lower than the cost of borrowing, and consequently when the MEI shifts downward, investment falls from I_E to I_A, in figure 2.10.

Classical theory, and general competitive category A models, predict that the resources withdrawn from the investment sector will be redeployed in the production of consumption goods, depicted as a leftward movement along the production possibilities frontier in figure 2.10 from E to a new full employment equilibrium at A'. But Keynes, adapting some elementary algebra borrowed from R.H. Kahn, argued that consumption would fall by an amount precisely equal to what he called the income multiplier (k), derived as follows:

$$\Delta GDP = \Delta C + \Delta I$$
$$= \beta(\Delta C/\Delta GDP) + \Delta I$$
$$= \Delta I/(1/1 - \beta)$$
$$= k\Delta I.$$

$$P = \frac{E(\Pi_1)}{(1+\rho)^1} + \frac{E(\Pi_2)}{(1+\rho)^2} + \ldots + \frac{E(\Pi_t)}{(1+\rho)^t},$$

where E is an expectations sign, p is price, π is profit accured in future years $1 \ldots, t$, and ρ is a point on the MEI.

As he defined his terms, the marginal propensity to consume must lie in an interval between zero and one, so that k is always greater than one, except when people fail to spend anything out of an increase (decrease) in their personal disposable income. An autonomous decline in investment should invariably mean that consumption will fall as well, by an amount precisely equal to

$$\Delta C = \Delta GDP - \Delta I. \tag{2.3}$$

Keynes reasoned that any reduction in investment would reduce household incomes of employees, suppliers, and managers by an equal amount. They would respond by cutting consumption expenditure by β (ΔGDP). This decline in consumption in turn would lower household earnings for employees in the consumption goods sector by β^2 (ΔGDP), with the process continuing until the propagation stream ceased at zero.[9] The entire weight of the multiplier effect after the autonomous fall in investment is borne by a curtailment in the production of consumption goods. Other multipliers, and multiplier–accelerator schemes of course, are also plausible, but the important point does not lie in the precise specification, but in the complementarity of sign between consumption and investment which is the essence of the income effect, and the parallel assumption that savings are hoarded in idle cash balances instead of being reallocated to alternative productive use.

Keynes justified this assumption, which violated the old dictum that money was a "veil" serving only as a unit of account and a means of exchange, by arguing that in addition to the convenience value of pocket money, people see money as a store of value and safe harbor from impending financial crises. When the state of business confidence plummets, he contended people defensively withdraw cash from financial institutions to hedge against the risk of bankruptcy, and to capitalize on declining prices. Financial institutions in turn faced with depleted profits, and rising delinquency rates on their loans, raise cash contingency funds and curtail their lending activities. In both cases money which the classical theorists had supposed would be automatically transferred to productive hands via financial intermediation is sterilized.

None of this might matter if the price level, including wages, interest rates, and foreign exchange rates adjusted promptly to restore confidence, raising the marginal efficiency of investment and propelling aggregate economic activity back up to point E with countervailing positive income effects. But Keynes asserted that the Walrasian price and Marshallian adjustments needed would not occur quickly enough, or at all, because wages, some production prices, and interest rates were strongly inflexible on the downside. Workers were prepared to strike, rather than bear the adjustment burden shifted on to them by the moods and machinations of employers, and producers were willing to hold the price line longer than fully informed utility-maximizers, should because they erroneously expected the pessimistic storm to blow over, while interest rates were frozen above the generally competitive level by speculative demand for money.

With regard to this latter point, Keynes acknowledged the merit of the classical position that when businessmen turned cautious they reduced their demand for loanable funds, depicted in figure 2.12 as a leftward shift in the demand curve for borrowing money and credit (e.g., rolling over outstanding loans), causing the interest rate to decline.

---

[9] The power of β increases from $1 \dots, t$ after each income generating round. Since $\beta < 1$, as $\beta^t \to 0$ in the limit, β^t (ΔGDP) $\to 0$.

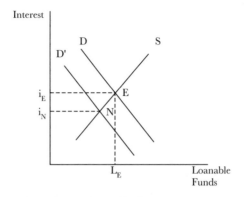

Figure 2.12   The classical market for loanable funds

And he did not try to rebut this inference by pointing out that the supply of loanable funds might also dry up because lending in hard times entailed greater risk. Instead, he claimed that the interest rate was not really determined in the market for loanable funds at all, or at least that speculative demand for idle cash balances prevented the interest rate from declining sufficiently to spark recovery.

The interest rate, he believed, was really set in the money market, by which he meant an invisible space where individuals decide how much cash they want to withhold from circulation (people do not buy and sell contracts for current dollars at a premium). He conceptualized the demand for holding idle cash balances as a function of the foregone rate of return that might be available on other "near money" financial assets. Most people, he reasoned, wished to hold some pocket money, and would be willing to forego a considerable return to do so. But the returns they were willing to forego diminished rapidly as they filled their purses. The money demand curve for transactionary (pocket money) cash balances is illustrated in figure 2.13, designated by the symbols $M^d(T)$.

A family of other curves which add other demands for idle cash balances to pocket money can also be drawn using the same principles, including those which take account of

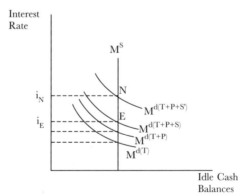

Figure 2.13   The Keynesian market for idle cash balances

precautionary and speculative motives. The equilibrium rate of interest in the market for hoarded (as distinct from borrowable and loanable money) occurs at point E, the intersection of the highest money demand curve and the money supply curve (pool of funds for hoarding) established by the monetary authorities. These hoardable funds, the residual between total cash and money on the table for borrowing and lending, is assumed to be fixed, invariant to changes in the interest rate, and hence vertical.

This conceptualization is unsatisfactory because the supply curve of hoarded money may shift rightward and leftward as the supply of money for other purposes fluctuates, but it does make it clear in a crude way that surges in speculative demand for idle cash balances triggered by fears of a business collapse are likely to offset any leftward shift in the demand for loanable funds in figure 2.11, and thereby prevent the interest rate from sparking a recovery, and perhaps restoring a full employment equilibrium.

Subsequent refinements in Keynes's argument by Sir John Hicks and Alvin Hansen lead to the development of LM–IS analysis; a blend of classical and Keynesian concepts which purports to show how full employment equilibrium can be restored through various combinations of government monetary and fiscal policy at different rates of interest. This "neoclassical synthesis" is accomplished by fixing the prevailing marginal efficiency of investment curve (figure 2.11), and the idle cash balance supply curve (figure 2.13) for all levels of GDP, while assuming that the savings required to implement business investment programs, and the demand for idle cash balances, are positive monotonic functions of income. This respecification adds a family of saving–income schedules to the Keynesian aggregate investment diagram (figure 2.14a) which are only partially compatible with Keynes's principles. Savings increase as household disposable income rises but, contrary to Keynes's fundamental psychological law of consumption, the marginal propensity to save is assumed to be sensitive to the rate of interest. The respecification likewise adds a family of idle cash balance–income demand schedules to the liquidity preference diagram (figure 2.14b). The loci of equilibrium points in both figures are then transformed into derivative schedules in the interest–income space where investment and savings (IS) and liquidity and money (LM) are in equilibrium at various combinations of interest and income (figure 2.14c). The IS curve is interpreted as representing the loanable funds market, and the LM curve the money market (for idle cash balances). The loanable funds and money markets are conceptualized in figure 2.14c as being independently in equilibrium at all points along their respective IS and LM schedules, where $I = S$, and $M^d = M^s$, and in joint nonfull employment GDP equilibrium at point N. This joint equilibrium reconciles Keynes's contention that competitive markets routinely cause significant involuntary unemployment, with the classical view that there only can be one market clearing rate of interest. Full employment in the Keynesian Hicks–Hansen conception requires state monetary and/or fiscal policy to shift the IS and/or the LM schedules until a full employment equilibrium is achieved at Y_E, at any of a number of different interest rates. This discretionary shifting of the IS and LM curves can be conceived as completing the job left undone by the standard Walrasian and Marshallian micro-adjustment mechanisms.

Hicks's and Hansen's synthesis is appealing because it reduces Keynes's extremely complex multi-market disequilibrium theory to a relatively simple policy problem of solving involuntary unemployment by selecting one of many possible joint interest rate equilibria in the loanable funds and money markets. But this goal can only be achieved by doing considerable violence to Keynes's theory of macroeconomic causality, which assumes

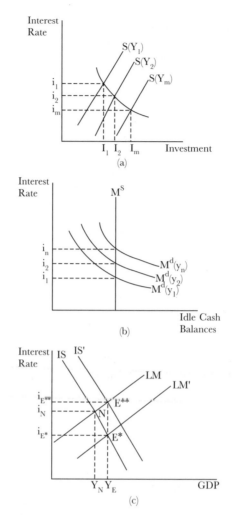

Figure 2.14 (a) Hicks–Hansen partial equilibrium in the idle cash balances market;
(b) Hicks–Hansen partial equilibrium in the market for loanable funds;
(c) nonfull employment and full employment GDP equilibria

that neither the marginal efficiency of investment nor the demand curves for idle cash balances are fixed, fluctuating instead with the vagaries of business confidence, and speculative demand for money. Both these phenomena could easily reverse the sign of the slopes of the IS and LM curves. The Hicks–Hansen neoclassical synthesis is best construed as a device for illustrating the possibilities for fiscal and monetary policy-making under a quasi-Keynesian set of assumptions, rather than as a complete reconciliation of the master's views with those of his disciples.

Another way of looking at the same matter is to recognize that Hicks–Hansen multiple Keynesian equilibria constitute a double set, one containing nonfull employment, the other full employment equilibria, and that only one point in the latter subset is consistent with the generally competitive interest rate. This ideal point can be illustrated with Irving Fisher's geometric methods. Figure 2.15 shows the intertemporal consumption space for an individual like Robinson Crusoe who possesses an initial stock of a nonperishable good such as corn which can be stored, consumed, or planted to create augmented supplies in the next period. This initial endowment is designated as the distance between the origin and the right boundary of the abscissa with the intertemporal exchange line, and production possibilities frontier. Crusoe in this simplified world has three options for trading with the future. He can consume his entire corn stock in any combination for periods 1 and 2 along his linear intertemporal exchange line. He can plant some of the corn, which gives him the option of consuming along a truncated intertemporal exchange line, and obtaining an augmented supply of corn in period 2. And he can set aside a precautionary reserve for possible use in period 3, permitting him the same options as before, but starting from a smaller base.

The intertemporal exchange line can be interpreted as the zero interest rate case because Crusoe obtains one kernel of corn in period 2 for every kernel sacrificed in period 1. The slope of the intertemporal production possibilities frontier, however, is steeper for much of its range, allowing Robinson Crusoe to simultaneously choose terms for trading with the future that correspond to his rate of time preference and the marginal rate of intertemporal transformation (point A). This interest rate will normally exceed zero. And of course, when Friday enters the picture a fourth alternative becomes feasible. If Friday is more patient than Crusoe, and is willing to lend on favorable terms, then Crusoe can profitably expand production to point E, while repaying Friday with interest.[10] Point E

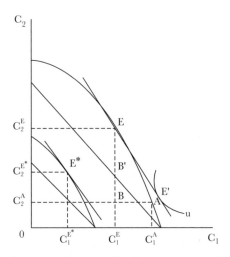

Figure 2.15   The Fisherian general competitive interest rate and GDP equilibrium

[10]   Robinson Crusoe consumes $0C_1^A$ in the first period, and after production $0C_2^A$ in the second. To maintain his current consumption, he borrows an amount equivalent to $C_1^A - C_1^E$ from Friday, repaying this principal, plus interest. The difference between this amount BB′ and the supplementary corn produced BE is Crusoe profit B′E, which together with his pre-borrowing period 2 corn supply $0C_2^A$ constitutes his total augmented period 2 consumption before consideration of additional consumer loans which could bring him to point E′, where he is clearly better off because he consumes more in both periods.

can be interpreted as the equilibrium interest rate in the market for loanable investment funds. This same rate also holds in the market for consumer loans, because Friday is prepared to lend Crusoe corn on the same terms for noninvestment purposes, along the lending line tangent at E (same as the interest rate line) to any point such as E'. Changes in this interest rate associated with variations in Friday's time preference obviously affect the level of aggregate economic activity, just as in the LM–IS model because movements along the intertemporal production possibilities frontier are equivalent to variations in GDP. Moreover, the effect of speculative demand for idle cash balances can also be easily indicated by recalling that Crusoe can at his discretion set aside some of his initial endowment of corn for a rainy day in period 3. The more risk averse he becomes, the further inward his intertemporal production possibilities frontier and GDP decline to point E*. This interest rate in the markets for loanable investment and consumption funds may be the same as the one prevailing in the classical model without hoarding (point E), or may differ due to speculative demand for idle cash balances depending on how the state of business confidence affects Friday's rate of time preference after he establishes his precautionary reserve for period 3. His various decisions will impact the level of economic activity and the universal equilibrium interest rates in all three markets. If these decisions and those of Robinson Crusoe are voluntary, outcomes will be generally competitive, and correspond with the ideal point in the Hicks–Hansen full employment equilibrium set. If Keynesian income effects apply for any reason, including excessive hoarding of idle cash balances, then outcomes will not be generally competitive, and will correspond to some second best Hicks–Hansen nonfull employment equilibrium point.[11]

Contemporary macroeconomics thus is a diffuse body of theories constructed around the concept of income effects, with an equally eclectic body of policy prescriptions. The existence of multiple full employment equilibria in these models is a telltale sign that theorists and policy-makers are less concerned about how government can intervene to assist Walrasian and Marshallian adjustment mechanisms to achieve the (near) general equilibrium solutions in figures 2.8, 2.9, and 2.10 than they are about achieving some other social policy objectives which also happen to be consistent with nongenerally competitive full employment. This provides some insight into why macroeconomists are inclined to believe that their theories and remedies are universal. They are not committed either to any particular set of causes or adjustment processes that trigger and determine the propagation of income effects; appropriate courses of intervention, or unrestricted utility-seeking, and suppose that some of their doctrines always apply. Their attitude is justified if vigorous antitrust enforcement is not enough to rid laissez faire of involuntary unemployment. If markets fail, policy-makers must choose the "second best." Otherwise, as the classical theorists insisted, governments should get out of the business of macro-management.[12]

However, the fact that all economic systems malfunction in ways that may be influenced by monetary and fiscal policy does not mean that the causes, propagation patterns, and optimal courses of intervention are everywhere the same. Economic systems ruled by

---

[11] Speculative hoarding of idle cash balances differs from corn reserves in figure 2.15 because the former are elements of a destabilizing wealth-maximizing game given "sticky" wages and prices, while the latter assume optimally efficient wage and price equilibration.

[12] These arguments are valid in moneyless economies, where defective Marshallian quantity adjustments could cause involuntary unemployment.

governments, communities, or individuals who impose their consumption, supply, and equilibration programs on otherwise free, independent utility-seekers are likely to infect Walrasian and Marshallian adjustments mechanisms with their own peculiar disorders, with unique patterns of contagion that are best addressed with special policies, or a mix of monetary and fiscal policies thought sub-optimal in efficient individualistically oriented economies.

For expository purposes, we can briefly investigate some of these alternative possibilities by revisiting Keynes's core model. The pillar of his entire conception is the fundamental psychological law which states that people have a nonnegative marginal propensity to consume out of personal disposable income, implying that if governments reduce income taxes, aggregate expenditures on consumption will not decline. But when the Japanese government attempted to stimulate aggregate economic activity in 1998 by cutting taxes, households responded by reducing total consumption outlays, because in a communalist society consumer attitudes toward perceptions of increased risk often coincide with those of businessmen. Income effects thus are not always triggered first by shifts in the marginal efficiency of investment as Keynes supposed, and consumer demand does not always place a floor under declining aggregate effective demand as predicted for individualistically organized systems.

This potential source of instability is offset in communal societies by a reluctance either to curtail the production of investment durables, or dismiss employees when the state of business confidence is bearish. Most Japanese workers in large enterprises are hired for life, dampening business fluctuations, but this merely shifts the macroeconomic risk from the present to the future, because cumulative subsidization erodes long-term competitiveness. The same problem exists with respect to speculative demand for hoarding idle cash balances. The communal ethos discourages hoarding in Japan. People are content to park more than a trillion dollars in postal savings accounts at nearly zero rates of interest in order to provide virtually interest free loans to members of the community. But permissive lending degrades the financial solvency of the system, creating the possibility of secular decline, culminating in panic, and hoarding on a scale that might astonish Keynes.

Mechanisms and institutions also matter. While it is true that Keynesian processes can be replicated in category A systems which partly or wholly replace markets with assignment if planners simulate the behavior of individual utility-seekers, in the real world this seldom happens. States, communities, constituencies, and powerful individuals often deliberately repress personal economic freedom disordering competitive Walrasian and Marshallian adjustment mechanisms, and prompting dysfunctional responses to disequilibria. Russian authorities, for example, fostered the development of anticompetitive financial industrial groups (FIGs), and tacitly approved denial of bank credit to most domestic industrial firms in order to augment demand for imports controlled by FIGs. In doing so, not only was assignment substituted for some Walrasian and Marshallian equilibration process, contributing to Russia's sustained hyperdepression, but the government nurtured an institution with vested interests in perpetuating hard times. Motivations, mechanisms, and institutions which distinguish category A from category B systems thus often matter. They not only alter the microeconomic laws of individual utility-seeking demand, supply, and equilibration, but they can profoundly affect macroeconomic causation, intervention possibilities, and aggregate outcomes.

CONVENTIONAL TYPOLOGIES

The classification system elaborated in table 2.1 provides a powerful tool for sorting out the factors which transform the basic laws of micro- and macroeconomic demand, supply, and equilibration into category B models with distinctive systemic characteristics, but these traits do not correspond neatly with traditional concepts. The terms used to describe systems typically have been coined by other social scientists to highlight political, sociological, and ideological principles. Are familiar terms like capitalism, socialism, communism, fascism, anarchism, liberalism, and conservatism useful beyond some vague indication of political–ideological intent? Should category B culturally regulated models be sub-classified under these headings, or should the terms be used only when making some particular political, sociological or ideological point? The dictionary definitions of these concepts are instructive:

1. *Capitalism*:   An economic system characterized by private or corporate ownership of capital goods, by investments that are determined by private decision rather than by state control, and by prices, production, and the distribution of goods that are determined mainly by competition in a free market. Capitalists are people who invest in business, are often wealthy, and by extension are plutocrats.
2. *Socialism*:   Any of various economic and political theories advocating collective or governmental ownership and administration of the means of production and distribution of goods.
3. *Communism*:   A theory advocating elimination of private property; a system in which goods owned in common are available to all as needed.
4. *Fascism*:   A political philosophy that exalts nation and race above the individual and that stands for a centralized autocratic government headed by a dictatorial leader, severe economic and social regimentation, and forcible suppression of opposition.
5. *Mercantilism*:   An economic system developing during the decay of feudalism to unify and increase the power and especially the monetary wealth of the nation through policies designed to secure an accumulation of bullion, a favorable balance of trade, the development of agriculture and manufactures, and the establishment of foreign trading monopolies.
6. *Anarchism*:   A political theory holding all forms of governmental authority to be unnecessary and undesirable, advocating a society based on voluntary cooperation and association of individuals and groups.
7. *Liberalism*:   A theory in economics emphasizing individual restraint and usually based on free competition, the self-regulating market, and the gold standard. A political philosophy based on belief in progress, the essential goodness of man, and the autonomy of the individual and standing for the protection of political and economic liberties.
8. *Conservatism*:   A political philosophy based on tradition and social stability, stressing established institutions and preferring gradual development to abrupt change.

All eight concepts are compatible with core category A models, but none provide any insight into how one system differs from another (remembering that markets and assignments are interchangeable) except by implying that one group or another is likely to fare better under this or that institution or rule. Plutocratic capitalists obviously will be better off under "capitalism," "mercantilism," "anarchism," "liberalism," and "conservatism" than under "socialism" and "communism," but describing market economies as capitalist tells us little about their real technical and welfare potentials. Systems theorists cannot quickly change bad old habits of other professionals, but students should avoid equating broad, politically inspired notions of systems with specific regimes of demand, supply, and equilibration.

Review Questions

1. What are the two archetypical economic systems? Why does the "duality theorem" which stipulates that perfect market and perfect planned outcomes are the same suggest that autonomy and cultural regulation are more fundamental than the dichotomy between markets and plans in classifying systems?
2. How does Marx's economic Utopia differ from paradise?
3. Does perfect competition imply other kinds of perfect harmony?
4. What is the distinction between category A and category B systems?
5. What assumption justifies treating all economies alike, and allows economists to eclectically recommend market and planning solutions to current micro- and macroeconomic problems?
6. Do comparativists reject universalist theories? Under what conditions are category A and category B systems identical? Hint: reflect on culture, politics, and ethics.
7. What is the correspondence principle?
8. Identify and explain the three ways in which comparative economic efficiency can be measured.
9. Why are we able to use a perfectly competitive benchmark for assessing the performance of competitive and controlled economies?
10. What is the law of demand? What are the four factors required for its efficient operation?
11. Why do utility and demand curves have the same slope?
12. Why is utility maximized by choosing the product assortment where the budget constraint is tangent to one's highest indifference curve?
13. Why may outcomes be detrimental, if individuals are swayed by passion or pressured by others into purchasing things they disprefer?
14. What is the law of supply?
15. If the law of demand boils down to the assertion that people can and will ascertain which consumption programs are best for them, what does this suggest about their corresponding supply programs?
16. What are the seven conditions required for supply programs to be efficient?
17. Why must firms produce to the point where their budget line is tangent to their highest isoquant for supply to be efficient?
18. Why is profit-, or dividend-, maximizing essential for efficient supply? Illustrate your response.
19. Demand and supply are both specified as functions of price, ruling out other extraneous influences like obligation and government commands. How does this joint dependency enhance market efficiency, compared with relying on direct binary negotiation?

20. What is the law of supply and demand equilibration?
21. Consumption and supply programs are computed subject to price and income assumptions. The actions of participants, however, affect these initial assumptions. Why does this imply that supply and demand schedules will adjust slightly during the negotiating process?
22. What are the seven conditions required for the law of supply and demand equilibration to be valid?
23. Why do theorists believe that these seven conditions should be satisfied?
24. What is the Walrasian excess demand price adjustment mechanism? In which markets does it best apply?
25. What is the Marshallian excess price quantity adjustment mechanism? How is it related to profit-maximizing?
26. How should the interplay of Walrasian and Marshallian mechanisms be sequenced?
27. How do the terms of the implicit social contract underlying the law of supply and demand equilibration affect the merit of economic outcomes?
28. Under what conditions can economies with large state sectors and strong communitarian obligations still be classified as category A systems?
29. Why are all real economic systems mechanistically mixed?
30. Why is "transparency" an essential ingredient of "self-regulating" category A systems?
31. Are open economies necessarily superior?
32. What is the law of macroeconomic equilibration?
33. Why did classical theorists believe that fluctuations in investment would not have multiplier effects on aggregate economic activity?
34. What is the Fisher equation? Why does it imply that changes in the supply of money will not affect the level of aggregate economic activity?
35. Why did Keynes believe that speculative demand for money could invalidate the implications of the Fisher equation, if wages and prices were "sticky"?
35. Why won't interest rate adjustments automatically reequilibrate the market?
36. Use figure 2.11 to explain how depressions are caused by pessimistic entrepreneurial expectations in the Keynesian model?
37. Use figure 2.12 to explain how deteriorating business sentiment diminishes investment at the prevailing rate of interest.
38. Why did Keynes believe that consumption and investment were complements? How is this related to his concept of the multiplier?
39. What is the Hicks–Hansen "neoclassical synthesis"? How does it re-validate the usefulness of monetary policy? How do its assumptions differ from Keynes's?
40. In what sense can Keynesian policies be considered a third regulatory mechanism, supplementing the Walrasian and Marshallian mechanisms?
41. Using figure 2.15, explain why there is only one Keynesian/Hicks–Hansen full employment equilibrium that is compatible with Fisherian intertemporal equilibrium, and that all other outcomes are second best, even if people are fully employed.
42. Conventional macroeconomic policies often relieve involuntary unemployment and are in this sense second best. Does this imply that they are universal; that they will have positive effects and work the same way in all systems? Explain with reference to Japanese macroeconomic response patterns.
43. Why are ideological terms like capitalism and socialism inadequate for assessing the workings of the laws of demand, supply, and their equilibration? Why are they inadequate for evaluating the roles of government and obligation?

CHAPTER 3

CULTURE, POLITICS, AND ECONOMIC MISCONDUCT

Everyone agrees that culture, politics, and ethics affect behavior, but these factors are seldom taken into account when explaining differences in economic performance. Disparities in comparative levels of gross domestic product, per capita consumption, and growth, for example, are mostly attributed to capital, labor, skill, management, entrepreneurship, and technological progress. International economic organizations appear to believe subpar performance can always be overcome with capital, education, and technology transfer, although in the spirit of globalism they recommend market liberalization, including privatizing, competition, and openness.

These category A attitudes are misconceived. Culture, politics, and ethics profoundly influence the degree to which individual utility-seeking is constrained, subordinated, or replaced by privileged utility-seeking which violates the golden rule, and creates severe institutional and moral hazards. Aspects of the Western cultural heritage are compatible with perfect competition, and even perfect democratic planning. But most often culture, politics, and ethics sustain various forms of imperfect competition, collectivism, communalism, and authoritarianism. In some of these category B cases, they have beneficial effects, but more often productivity, efficiency, growth, and stability suffer compared with the generally competitive standard.

Preferences for category B forms of imperfect competition, collectivism, communalism, and authoritarianism seem perverse from this perspective, but it is important to appreciate that perfectly competitive, perfectly planned, and perfectly mixed systems are Utopian, so that in practice governmental and cultural authorities are compelled to adopt second best stratagems. In an imperfect world, and perhaps even in Utopia, it is easy to understand how some societies may disprefer the competitive, individual self-seeking paradigm lauded in the West, choosing more egalitarian, compassionate, and communal alternatives.

Most economies through the ages have been category B culturally regulated systems. Slavery was widespread among the Greeks, Romans, and Egyptians before the Christian era, and feudalism ruled far and wide for a thousand years until the 20th century. The idea that self-regulating category A economies could be constructed appeared from time to time in the Utopian literature, but it was not until 1776 when Adam Smith married competitive market theory with the rights of man in his *Wealth of Nations* that people grasped the possibilities. The universalism of Smith's approach and its appeal to natural law quickly elevated competitive markets, automatically governed by an invisible hand to the status of science, with all other systems treated as relics of a bygone time.

Proponents of feudalism, slavery, and other category B culture-regulated systems defended their models, but the only persuasive challenges to Smithian free enterprise came from socialists and communists like Count St. Simon, Robert Owen, and Karl Marx, who proposed alternative, self-regulating category A systems featuring egalitarian markets and democratic planning.

For most of the 20th century, the systems debate raged over the theoretic merit of free enterprise, socialist markets, and perfect planning at the "harmonist" level illustrated in table 2.1, and in category A, with advocates criticizing each others' economies as degenerate category B systems. Socialists charged that "free enterprise" was run by the executive committee of the capitalist class; liberals accused the Soviet Union of despotism.

Of course most economists did not see this debate in terms of black and white, and some, like the Japanese, French, and Swedes, insisted that their systems were culturally unique. But when all was said and done, neither balanced assessments of East–West economic performance nor institutional peculiarities mattered. Since most economists and political leaders find it useful to publically embrace Enlightenment values regardless of their cultural preferences, the potential and behavior of the world's economies were primarily evaluated on the basis of universalist category A principles, taking little or no account of culture.

The collapse of the Soviet Union, the eclipse of socialist economic theory, and the triumph of global markets have created an opportunity to examine whether contemporary nonsocialist market economies are self-regulating, universal category A systems, or are better understood as culturally regulated, category B systems with diverse potentials and behavioral characteristics. If modern economies are alike, then living standards throughout the globe should converge toward a common high frontier. If not, comparative global performance will depend on cultural-based systems. Clearly there is more at stake in correctly determining whether culture is important than nuances of classification. Are there good reasons for expecting that national cultures significantly modify the operations of the laws of demand, supply, equilibration, and macroeconomics as they are formulated in self-regulating category A systems?

There is broad agreement that there are. Everyone acknowledges that some societies are more discriminatory than others; that dictatorships intolerant of individual economic freedom often act without regard for productive consequences, and that some cultures severely restrict aspects of utility-seeking. The Dukhobors, an 18th-century Russian religious sect (spirit wrestlers), for example, still discourage acquisitiveness by periodically burning their possessions. But there is considerable disagreement as to whether category B influences are fundamental. Category A theorists prefer to interpret political dictatorship, economic misconduct, and cultural restraints as exogenous, rather than as endogenous influences on the laws of demand, supply, and equilibration. Dictatorship, crime, and even cultural antipathies toward free individual utility-maximizing in their view are subsidiary factors which should be dealt with by political action, law enforcement, and education, not a full-fledged reformulation of utility optimization theory.

Systems theorists concede that cultural factors may be extraneous, but believe that they usually are not because cultural values shape motives, politics, ethics, and utility-seeking. This can be appreciated by reflecting on the golden rule which undergirds virtuous general competition. From both Christian and Confucian perspectives, "doing unto others as you would wish them to do unto you" assumes that everyone has dignity, autonomy, self-restraint, and deserves to be honestly and compassionately treated by others. This is a religious and cultural attitude that upholds righteous utility-seeking, and the rule of equitable commercial law. But suppose culture upheld the dicta that all is fair in love, war, and business, that "supermen" are not bound by social contracts (Nietzsche), and that only the "fittest" should survive (social Darwinism). Then right would be anything anyone could get away with, and the entire logic of just general competition would fall to pieces. Such behavior is corrupt from the standpoint of social welfare optimization, but it is hardly implausible. Continental European culture approves cartels America has criminalized, and in many nations the rule of law scarcely applies.

The assertion that political authoritarianism is atypical or transitory is not persuasive either. Democracy has been the exception, not the rule, since Creation. In 1942 Europe had only two or three democracies, and as late as the 1980s democracy appeared to be an endangered species. Communist authoritarianism and the associated suppression of individual economic utility-seeking under the pretext that ideological duty took precedence over personal well-being only ceased in the former Soviet bloc a decade ago, and persists in China.

And, of course, authoritarians are not alone in curtailing individual utility-seeking. Almost all cultures, societies, and political regimes find reasons for reining personal economic freedom, and empowering privilege. Laissez faire is fine, but everyone prefers that the game be played by his or her own special rules. Culture, politics, and ethics thus are not subsidiary. They collectively influence the values guiding personal behavior, constrain libertarian utility-seeking, and set the rules of acceptable economic conduct. Unrestricted individualist cultures, with well-functioning democracies, and the rule of law will come close to ideal general competition. But other cultures and political and ethical regimes will not.

CULTURES: EAST AND WEST

Eastern cultures (Japan, China, South Korea) which perceive Western libertarian general competition as a threat to group harmony provide insight into why unrestricted individualist utility is not universally accepted as the economic ideal. The structure and character of economic activities in much of East Asia is strongly influenced directly and derivatively by Confucian concepts of bureaucratic societal stratification and governance which subordinate the status and aspirations of the military, security services, entrepreneurs, businessmen, farmers, laborers, craftsmen, and merchants to communalist notions of the good. Rank and obligations of course tend to shift over time. During the Tokugawa shogunate in Japan (1615–1868), the population was rigidly consigned to four estates. The overlord (shogun), his servitor lords (daimyos), and bureaucracy stood at the top, followed in rank by the military (samurai), farmers, and the lowliest of the lot, urban merchants. Individuals were born into a "station" with little upward mobility. The industrial revolution which began with the Meiji restoration and took on a modern democratic form after the Second World War transformed the daimyos into industrial magnates (zaibatsu), farmers into laborers. It reduced the status of the professional military and enhanced mobility. But Confucian notions of deference, competence, honesty, loyalty, and obligation remained, taking new adaptive forms. Political leaders still heavily represented by descendants of the lords and samurai today are viewed as natural authorities, who rule by consensus building. They perpetually consult with business, labor, and agrarian interests to devise policies everyone will tolerate, and then implement their decisions through the state administrative bureaucracy. Although the Japanese, Chinese, and Koreans have a keen sense of their individuality and desire to better themselves, the Confucian residue and other cultural factors (Buddhism, Shinto, Taoism, Legalism),[1] frequently lumped under the rubric of Asian values, obligate them to overexertion, to excessive conscientiousness, and to subordinate personal well-being to duty.

The specifics differ from one Asian society to another, but generally speaking decisions about effort, conscientiousness, self-seeking, terms of compensation, and consumer choice are more strongly influenced by obligation than in the West. Individual preferences, and utility- and profit-maximizing, are often subordinated and constrained by velvet forms of subjugation, coercion, and duty, routinely modifying and countermanding category A economic laws. Transactions are not always based on equivalent exchange of goods. Often poor individuals will give expensive gifts to the wealthy, receiving little or nothing in return, other than some nonbinding obligation to provide protection or other valuable favors. Working long hours overtime without explicit compensation is considered normal. Buying goods for status rather than use value is widespread.[2] And often household's marginal propensity to consume out of personal disposable income is zero, with savings insensitive to variations in the rate of interest. Demand and supply thus frequently are price inelastic, and people may often make choices which are detrimental to their personal interests as they are conceived in the generally competitive ideal.

Western economists observing such behavior tend to deprecate Asian irrationality, but this ignores culture and context. A preoccupation with personal acquisitiveness, unrestrained by duty, is not the only conceivable strategy for pursuing a gratifying life,[3] and many reflective Asians consider the benefits of communality to be worth the abridgment of profit-maximizing.

The pronounced Asian preference for autocracy, station, family, loyalty, diligence, selflessness, obligation, public decorum, and consensus building should not be interpreted as a repudiation of the kind of individualism which undergirds materialist utility-maximizing and the occidental pursuit of equivalent exchange. Asian pleasure-seeking from the sublime to the pornographic is a venerable tradition,[4] and people often keep strict mental

[1] Steven Mosher, *Hegemon*, Encounter Books, San Francisco, 2000, pp. 18–21. Legalism refers to the Chinese governance philosophy of despotic subjugation.

[2] During the 17th century it was illegal for people of one station to buy the status goods of another. The width of merchants' homes, for example, was specified by law, and only samurai could wear two swords.

[3] Tawney, *The Sickness of the Acquisitive Society*, 1919.

[4] This phenomenon was especially pronounced during the Tokugawa period in Kyoto's Gion and Tokyo's Yoshiwara districts, which were the centers of the "floating world" or demi-monde where the Japanese shed their Confucian straitjackets. Paintings by Kano Naonobu "Merrymaking under the Blossoms" (Tokyo National Museum), the "Hanging Scroll of Yuna" (MOA Art Museum) depicting bath house prostitutes, the Hikone Screen (Hikone Art Museum) and pornographic ukiyo-e shunga ("spring pictures") capture the spirit of Japanese hedonism.

accounts of gifts rendered and favors due, even if duty forces them to behave otherwise. And, of course, like their counterparts in the West, some seek refuge from the world in mysticism, asceticism, aestheticism, and naturalism (Shingon Buddhism, Taoism, Confucian scholarship, and the Yamabushi).

Nonetheless, occidental individualism is unique. It is a distinctive reflection of four elite philosophical movements: humanism, the Reformation, the Renaissance, and the Enlightenment. The first of these influences legitimated the pursuit of individual secular well-being independent of Christian religious obligation on the proviso that such actions were virtuous. Precursors of this idea can be found in Socrates (469–399 BC) and Plato (427–347 BC), but philosophers like Erasmus (1466–1536) in the 15th century insisted that such behavior was the defining characteristic of human beings; hence humanism.

The emotional and aesthetic possibilities of humanism were explored during the Renaissance in the 15th and 16th centuries, and are epitomized in the depictions of Albrecht Dürer (1471–1528).[5] But it was not until the Enlightenment of the 18th century that the first two movements were subordinated to the overarching principle of reason. This took many forms under the philosophes, but its primary manifestation in economics was British democratic utilitarianism. Individuals as before were supposed to be guided by virtue, but judgments about the good and determinants of well-being became radically subjective. Each person became the arbiter of "useful virtue" within limits imposed by "natural order," and as rational men and women were supposed to maximize utility in this sense.[6] "*Homo economicus*" was conceived as self-reliant, and responsible for realizing his potential through comprehensive utility-maximizing and democratic political participation. This did not require individuals to be saintly or profane, but did encourage them to be more egocentric, inappropriately self-assertive, aggressive, and ostentatious than East Asians who, under the influence of Confucianism, were more conflict avoiding, deferential, self-effacing, polite, considerate, and community minded under most circumstances. Westerners, of course, also devised ways of curbing interpersonal conflict but, as is readily apparent to any neutral observer, they are much brasher and unabashedly self-serving.

Although personal behavior in the West is tempered by ethics, compassion, altruism, and manners, humanism, the Reformation, the Renaissance, and the democratic utilitarian aspect of the Enlightenment have created a culture that defines virtuous economic activity as self-initiated, unobligated, negotiated equivalent exchange. Rational individuals "ought" to sense their desires, search out the possibilities, evaluate them, and negotiate to maximize their utility without unfairly subjugating or coercing others (the Christian golden rule). Realists, of course, recognize that some individuals may try to dominate other transactors, and often succeed, but Westerners are acculturated to believe that the problem can be democratically alleviated by competition and criminalizing "unfair" business practices, even though (as will be shown in chapter 5) these solutions are insufficient. As a consequence, general competitive theorists tend to conflate real economic behavior with the competitive ideal, and consider other cultural approaches as misguided.

---

[5] Erwin Panofsky, *The Life and Art of Albrecht Dürer*, Princeton University Press, Princeton, New Jersey, 1955.

[6] Post-Enlightenment theories of human motivation and purpose like psychoanalysis, alienation, surrealism, Bohemianism, socialism, communism, and futurism have had little impact on neoclassical theories of rational democratic utility-maximizing, their influence being confined to scholars concerned with political economy.

This attitude is narrow-minded. The Western concept of *Homo economicus* reflects only one facet of the occidental individualist tradition.[7] Its impartiality and efficiency are great virtues, but the fact that real economic behavior everywhere departs from generally competitive category A principles indicates that societies act as if they have other priorities. They create culturally regulated category B systems, that affect national purpose (individual, group, communal, or authoritarian priorities) and the three core mechanisms of all economic systems: their markets, state governance, and customs. Group, communal, or authoritarian goals like the Nazi subordination of individual aspirations to the cause of national socialism modify and sometimes subvert the Enlightenment principles of general competition. Bilateral and multilateral market transactions are deflected from fairly and competitively optimizing. Government services are provided on a partisan basis and are inefficient. And customs obligate people to perform economic functions for reasons that have little, if anything, to do with their free utility-seeking.

PRODUCTIVITY, EFFICIENCY, AND SOCIAL JUSTICE

The effects of culture on economic activity are ubiquitous. They influence all the conventional determinants of productivity: labor time, effort, competence, conscientiousness, factor mobility, technological choice, rates of investment, finance, and hence GDP. Attitudes toward leisure and work, for example, determine the amount of time people devote to occupations included in and excluded from the gross domestic product. Some cultures like the Japanese treat group participatory labor as pleasure, encouraging them to pursue personal welfare through communal activities counted as GDP, whereas Americans seeking the same benefits might work less and play more. The pleasure derived from these alternative pursuits may be the same, but the Japanese gain twice because their excessive labor is not only gratifying but provides income as well.

Obviously, cultures which stimulate effort, competence, and conscientiousness beyond Western norms will tend to have higher GDPs, whether attributable to Japanese communal goal seeking or ideological inspiration. And, vice versa, cultures which discourage factor mobility and restrict technological choice and financial flexibility will diminish GDP, whether due to Continental European corporatism or American collectivism (Glass Steagal Act). These gains and losses usually are caused by the "spotlight" aspects of national cultures, showcased by every society, such as the Japanese institution of lifetime employment. But often the stimulus comes from "shadow" culture, like the collectivist side of American individualism. The main difference between these cultural forces is perception. Americans instantly recognize the connection between their "spotlight" frontier values and entrepreneurship, but are reluctant to acknowledge that "shadow" values like collectivism favor anticompetitive practices. This double standard conceals the importance of disreputable cultural factors, and encourages false explanations of economic causality. Many socialists believed that Soviet production was governed completely by planning,

---

[7]   The association of real behavior with the competitive ideal rests on the Enlightenment belief in natural law. If utility theory had been devised later on the amoral, or even anti-moral, principles of romanticism (Nietzsche) the fallacy of equating real behavior with the competitive ideal would have been obvious.

even though managers bartered inputs among firms. Likewise, America's managed markets are misportrayed as freely competitive.

"Spotlight" values also can be a source of misunderstanding. While American entrepreneurship and Japanese lifetime employment are justly praised from some standpoints, their negative side effects like dysfunctional speculation and factor immobility are too often overlooked. Culture thus not only provides partial explanations for economic behavior; it fosters self-deceptive attitudes.

The same complexities affect other aspects of behavior and their misinterpretation. Cultures not only influence the mobilization of resources; they also codetermine property rights, governance, technical efficiency, demand responsiveness, adjustment mechanisms, income distribution, and transfers. Authoritarian and aristocratic cultures tend to favor private property rights exclusively for the elite. Even in democratic Athenian Greece during the age of Pericles, some segments of society were propertyless and enslaved. The imperial household under the Russian Czars personally owned 40 percent of the nation's assets, while 100 million peasants were dispossessed at the end of the 19th century. By contrast, fully democratic, individualistic cultures like those of contemporary America and the United Kingdom not only permit universal private ownership of the means of production, but they actively encourage individual entrepreneurial enterprise and shareholding. Attitudes toward different varieties of ownership are also culturally codetermined. Collectivistly inclined societies look approvingly on municipal and state ownership, diverse semiprivate proprietary arrangements, and various types of producer cooperatives, including schemes for labor co-management and dividend sharing. Communally oriented cultures go one step further, vesting management and/or ownership rights jointly among group members. In Japan management sharing is emphasized; on Israeli kibbutzim member ownership and control predominate, and in both communal approaches some form of dividend-maximizing tends to displace the profit-maximizing preferred by the competitive market paradigm. Individualistic cultures by contrast are attracted to single proprietorships, or various corporate forms where influence is correlated with the degree of share ownership. Competitive profit-maximizing, with net after-tax revenue distributed in proportion to shareholdings, is a natural accompaniment of this aspect of culturally sanctioned individualism.

Culture also affects the legal or informal juridical mechanisms which determine the relationships between formal ownership and control. Most successful cultures create legal or customary systems which try to assure that formal ownership rights of each particular variety are enforced, but this is not always so. Both contemporary Russia and China are trying to construct economic systems based on individual ownership, but are reluctant to create the kind of individualistically oriented rule of law required for this purpose, making both economies vulnerable to severe inefficiencies and moral hazards.

The impact of culture on remuneration, risk-taking, moral hazard, obligation, job security, management, and income and wealth transfers is also strong. Individualistic cultures reward factors according to their value added (value of their marginal products). They urge people to take risks, to abide by the rule of law, to become proprietors and view income and wealth transfers as charity, or social tranquilizers. Employment is a function of demand, not an entitlement. Collectivists beg to differ. They favor job rights like full employment and equal pay for equal work, even when job rights and equal pay are not competitively justified. They discourage risk-taking, advocate management rights for stakeholders, and equalitarian transfers as a matter of basic fairness. Communalists go even further. They challenge the idea that value is individually added, arguing that the contribution of individuals cannot be separated from the value created by the group. Earnings from their perspective should not be distributed on a preferential basis. They should be distributed to all members equally. Management should be fully group participatory, and there is no need for job rights and income and welfare transfers because group membership is inalienable, and groups are self-sufficient.

No culture is entirely internally consistent. All have "spotlight" and "shadow" aspects. Consequently, no economic system can be adequately described in terms of abstractions like individualism, collectivism, and communalism. Most mix elements from these concepts, or tolerate anticompetitive behavior and various types of economic crime. Each resulting composite reflects a specific balance of cultural, political, and ethical forces, shaping economic systems with a variety of unique features and potentials, some of which will be superior to others. Culture as the matrix for ethical, political, and social values, therefore, is important for a proper understanding of comparative economic systems, not because it allows us to identify some indisputably superior, self-regulating universal category A ideal, but because it illuminates the reasons, both good and bad, why the performance of national economies often defies generally competitive prediction. Russia provides a painful lesson in this regard. Its leaders were urged by foreign advisors to join the Western family of competitive market economies by rapidly abandoning state ownership and planning without considering the anticollectivist and anti-authoritarian cultural requirements for effective transition. Its leaders were assured that "shock therapy" would allow Russia to rapidly recover, modernize, and converge to the material living standards of the developed West. Instead, the nation has not only been bedeviled by a decade of hyperdepression, but the new market economy which has emerged bears little relationship to the generally competitive model, and is likely to be dysfunctional for decades to come.

Review Questions

1. Adam Smith hypothesized that there existed a universal natural law, free competition, which if implemented would maximize social welfare everywhere. Most contemporary economists believe that he was correct, and seek to prove it by rational demonstrations and econometric verification. They are inherently opposed to the legitimacy of comparative economic systems in the long run, because this suggests that there exists not one, but many "natural laws." Apply the lessons developed in chapter 1 about "existence" and culture to assess the plausibility of the claim that there is only one natural economic law.
2. How do some theorists rationalize relegating culture and politics to a secondary role?
3. Is Darwin's concept of the survival of the fittest compatible with Smithian natural law? Hint: Smith insists on the golden rule.
4. What are Asian values? How do they modify individual preferences and utility- and profit-maximizing?
5. What are the four philosophical pillars of Western individualism?
6. How do Asian communitarianism and Western individualism differ?

7. What is "spotlight" culture?
8. Why is American collectivism part of its "shadow culture"?
9. How does culture affect attitudes toward ownership and management?
10. How does culture affect attitudes toward the rule of contract law?
11. How does culture affect attitudes toward obligation?
12. How does culture affect attitudes toward value creation?
13. How does culture affect attitudes toward income distribution, transfers, and state services?
14. Does Russia provide an object example of the dangers of applying transition policies which work in one culture on another?

CHAPTER 4

POWER

Economists are aware that utility-seeking is not always fair; that individuals and nations exert influence and control over others. But the models they build, guided as they are by universalist category A thinking, usually exclude, or marginalize economic power-seeking, engagement, and conflict. This exclusion is useful for highlighting the advantages of unfettered domestic and global commerce, but it misdescribes real behavior and obscures the role of economic and political security in international relations.

In a world comprised of culturally regulated, category B systems, founded on rival civilizations, politics, and ethics, economic power-seeking and security matter. Power-seeking may have a stronger effect on domestic and international economic behavior than global, golden rule abiding competition, and together with dysfunctional culture and misgovernance appears to partially explain the widening gap between the First and the Third World; between the planet's rich and poor nations.

"Global politics is always about power, and the struggle for power, and today international relations is changing along that crucial dimension. The global structure of power in the Cold War was basically bipolar; the emerging structure is very different."
Samuel Huntington, "The Lonely Superpower," *Foreign Affairs*, Vol. 78, No. 2 (March/April 1999), pp. 35–49.

Power is the ability to exert influence or control. It can be conceived of as a means to an end (utilitarian experience), or as a good in and of itself. In either case, when informed by rational choice, power and power-seeking are economic objectives or processes. If power-seeking did not involve scarce resources, or preferences were inconsistent, precluding rational utility enhancement, then these pursuits would be noneconomic. Some philosophers like Arthur Schopenhauer (1788–1860) contend that the domination of others, and the use of power to obtain desirable things on unequal terms, is the best way to utility maximize. This attitude, which subordinates fairness to authority, distinguishes his thinking from that of universalist economists, who favor self-regulating class A systems. Economists recognize that utility-seekers often exert power to gain unfair advantage, but argue that competition, conscience, and the rule of law keep these distortions in check. They believe that rationality drives people everywhere toward universal equitable exchange and away from power-seeking. This is clearly reflected in familiar economic theories of general competition and free international trade, which assume away conflict and exploitation.

Political scientists also disapprove unfair practices, but accept Schopenhauer's assessment of human behavior. They associate power with state governance, and see it as the focal point of international relations. From their perspective, utility-seeking states should not be preoccupied solely with promoting free competition: they should be mindful of the defensive and offensive possibilities of power.

This vision of the world as a process of power-seeking engagement is especially important for systems theorists who acknowledge the role of culture, or more narrowly the rivalry within and among civilizations, in determining economic behavior and potential. Since culturally regulated category B economies differ in goals, politics, and ethics, their actions tend to be influenced by power-seeking; unlike self-regulating, category A systems, where competition is supposed to prevent people from taking advantage of each other. Monopolists, oligopolists, criminals, and governments frequently succeed in dominating other transactors, while some nations do the same abroad. And these efforts are not always restricted to material gain. Fundamentalist societies and authoritarian states often are preoccupied with spreading the faith (including communism), and political domination. Market-oriented democracies care less about empire and more about trade, fair or otherwise. Comparative systems analysis therefore cannot be circumscribed by self-regulating, universalist category A thinking, but must be broadened to encompass utility-seeking that involves power, engagement, and security.

It has to be accepted that competition is not always golden rule abiding and the pursuit of power for its own sake is not always subsidiary. Power-seeking, more often than economists would like to suppose, makes domestic and foreign economic activities Pareto inefficient and sometimes exploitive, and therefore is partly responsible for income inequality, the widening gap between rich and poor nations, and people's desire for economic and military security. Contrary to the widely held belief, "free trade" is not always beneficial for all concerned.[1] Systems which effectively endogenize power-seeking are likely to benefit disproportionately, and may harm those they dominate absolutely.

This poses a large number of interesting problems, two of which merit special acknowledgment. First, some democratic market economies operate with a double standard. They are more or less golden rule abiding at home, but power-seeking abroad. If this behavior is intentional, it reveals that domestic general competition and democracy do not insure that globalization will be universally beneficial. If it is not, then the inconsistency must be acknowledged and corrected. Second, power-seeking raises the spectre that democracies may be vulnerable to authoritarian economic, political, and military aggression if they fail to take the possibility of foreign misconduct seriously. Although democracies, and individual competitors for that matter, will always be able to achieve higher levels of welfare if

[1]   Samuel Huntington, "The Lonely Superpower," *Foreign Affairs*, Vol. 78, No. 2 (March/April 1999), pp. 45–46. Cf. Richard Haass, "What to Do With American Primacy," *Foreign Affairs*, Vol. 78, No. 5 (September/October 1999), pp. 37–49. CIA, Global Trends 2015: A dialogue About the Future With Nongovernment Experts, NIC 2000–02, December 2000 (*http://www.cia.gov/cia/publications/globaltrends* 2015/index.html).

they are not required to divert resources to improving their security, as explained further in chapter 16, good economic systems in the real world must take these kinds of risks effectively into consideration.

Review Questions

1. Samuel Huntington asserts that "power-seeking" is the dominant force in international affairs. Does this mean that liberalization and globalization are about power rather than extending free trade at home to nations abroad? Explain why power and Pareto efficient utility-seeking are mutually exclusive.

2. Utility-maximizing, competitive free-enterprise systems are believed to provide higher social welfare than monopoly regimes. Their leaders shun exploiting other nations. Does this mean that authoritarian societies without these scruples may sometimes achieve higher levels of domestic welfare by exploiting outsiders? In what sense can this be considered a liberal paradox?

3. Do democracies sometimes operate with a double standard: golden rule abiding at home, power-seeking abroad? Give an example.

4. Does power-seeking explain why individuals and nations desire security services which are superfluous under perfect global competition?

PART II

PERFECT ECONOMIC MECHANISMS

INTRODUCTION

Philosophers and economists have long debated whether ideal societies and economies could be conceived and organized. Among those who believe that ideal systems can be constructed, differences of opinion have emerged about their attributes and how they should be ruled. Contemporary theorists for the most part embrace the goal of neutrally maximizing individual utility subject to various distributional rules, but sometimes disagree about how this can be best accomplished. Some of Adam Smith's successors argue that the best way to achieve the ideal is to build a perfectly competitive, self-regulating market system founded on individual utility-seeking and the golden rule. Aristotle's modern disciples, who like Smith accept individual fulfillment as the norm, take the opposite stance, contending that category A perfect governance (planning) is better.

Both schools of thought disregard category B ideals, although these have been considered by others. Both have tried and failed to prove that the category A mechanisms they propose must succeed, but a variety of important points have been clarified. It has been shown that:

1. If the maximization of individual utility is the common goal, it can be achieved under suitable assumptions in the "Newtonian core" with either perfect competition or perfect planning.
2. Neither competition nor calculation guarantee that people will behave as the models require.
3. The merits of competition and governance depend on their operational efficiency, not their theoretical potential, because their potentials by construction are the same.
4. Markets and plans in the "Newtonian core" can be mixed and modified with collectivist, communalist, and authoritarian mechanisms and goals. The merits of these category B systems depend both on their inefficiencies and their potentials.
5. The performance of any system may be affected by non-Newtonian factors like historical shocks, chaos, psychological aberrations, and various imponderable factors.

Part II elaborates these issues and demonstrates that the old systems theory was right in asserting the inferiority of Soviet-type planning and economies with bloated state sectors.

PERFECT MARKETS

Markets provide a natural mechanism for negotiating the exchange of services and goods. They enable utility-seekers on their own initiative to enhance their utility through voluntary production, and trade without the assistance of the state, or other authorities. But of course, it has been apparent from the beginning that markets can be rigged, and sometimes cause severe speculative disorders making them unfair, and inefficient.

One of Adam Smith's important contributions to economic science was the insight that these distortions might be eliminated by competition. He reasoned that as the number of participants increased, the power of monopolists and speculators would diminish so that in the limit the wealth of nations would be maximized, with every individual receiving the value of his or her marginal product. This seemed to imply that ideal competitive markets were both productively efficient and fair, and that government intervention would only diminish social welfare because market outcomes were the best.

Proponents of free enterprise often speak as if these inferences are true. They insist without qualification that competitive markets maximize income, are equitable, and perform better without government assistance than with it. However, it has been known for more than six decades that this is false.[1] When economists set out to identify the assumptions required to achieve "perfect markets" they discovered that under plausible circumstances there were often conflicts between maximizing income and preserving fairness, and that government assistance could sometimes enhance social welfare. Instead of there being a unique perfectly competitive market ideal, there were endless possibilities, and it was essential for utility maximizing societies to choose the alternatives they preferred.

The standard textbook model is the most familiar.[2] It assumes that there is no government, all participants have full access to market information, complete knowledge of market opportunities, that there are no barriers to market entry, people abide by the golden rule, equilibrium adjustment mechanisms never fail, and technology is well behaved. Production functions must be continuous, with diminishing returns to scale in stage II (figure 2.8), so that indivisibilities and increasing returns do not bar equal market access, allowing some participants to receive quasi-rents and monopoly profits. If these assumptions are satisfied, and patents and copyrights do not cause similar distortions, national income will be maximized and everyone will be fairly compensated without government assistance.

Indivisibilities, increasing returns, and socially beneficial patents, however, are commonplace, making it unrealistic to expect that unfettered market competition can be income maximizing and fair. Perfectly competitive models can maximize wealth, if natural

[1]   Abram Bergson, "A Reformulation of Certain Aspects of Welfare Economics," *Quarterly Journal of Economics*, Vol. 52, 1938, pp. 310–34; Bergson, "On the Concept of Social Welfare," *Quarterly Journal of Economics*, Vol. 68, 1954, pp. 233–52; and Bergson, *Essays in Normative Economics*, Harvard University Press (Belknap), Cambridge, MA, 1966. Paul Samuelson, "Reaffirming the Existence of 'Reasonable' Bergson-Samuelson Social Welfare Functions," *Economica*, No. 44, 1977, pp. 81–8; Samuelson, "Bergsonian Welfare Economics," in Rosefielde, ed., *Economic Welfare and the Economics of Soviet Socialism*, Cambridge University Press, Cambridge, 1981, pp. 223–66.
[2]   A truly perfect system must be both micro- and macroeconomically flawless.

barriers to free market information, complete knowledge of market opportunities, and market access are tolerated. They can assure fairness if restrictions are placed on patents and technologies that have indivisibilities, or increasing returns to scale. And these features can be combined, but no option is uniquely and normatively best.

Moreover, a case can be made for limited state intervention where the community democratically hires the government to redistribute initial wealth,[3] redistribute income with lump-sum transfers,[4] and cope with market failure.[5] Perfect markets thus are best perceived not as a guarantee that pure competition is a harmonious Utopia, nor that governmental meddling is always bad. Perfect competition is a strategy for designing optimal economic systems that properly deal with patents, indivisibilities, increasing returns, and the facilitating role of the state where the democratic preferences of the people, not those of the elite, decide what is to be done. This optimal system may be libertarian, as is usually assumed, but surprisingly is also compatible with some forms of socialism including the Lange model, and egalitarian labor-managed regimes.[6]

PERFECT GOVERNANCE

Perfect governance, encompassing every aspect of economic activity by all units of the state and community, also takes many forms. Some simply replicate different kinds of category A perfect markets, but most go further, allowing category B authorities to disregard individual preferences because popular choices are said not always to be wise. Authorities may criminalize marijuana to protect people's health; may require greater charitable transfers than Adam Smith's concept of "imaginative sympathy" warrants; or may even impose segregation to achieve some misguided purpose that rational and enlightened individuals disapprove.

Both category A and B "ideal" models of perfect governance can be achieved using any mechanism including regulation (altering the rules of voluntary competitive exchange), bureaucratic administration, planning, legislation, judicial adjudication, prohibitions, and commands. Perfect governance typically reduces the scope of voluntary exchange, and subordinates some individual preferences to planners' choice. It is compatible with a range of ideologies including communism, socialism, and fascism, and different control concepts stressing planning, command, and market regulation.

---

[3]   Adam Smith argued for private charity, appealing to the principle of "imaginative sympathy." Public charity where individuals voluntarily hire the state as a disbursing agent is consistent with private utility-maximizing and perfect market competition. See Adam Smith, *The Theory of Moral Sentiment*. Cf., Charles Griswold, Jr., *Adam Smith and the Virtues of Enlightenment*, Cambridge University Press, London, 1999.

[4]   A "lump-sum" income transfer redistributes purchasing power without affecting the structure of the economy's aggregate equilibrium demand and supply programs. This assumes that associated income changes are neutral. Also see Paul Samuelson, "Optimal Compacts for Redistribution," in R.E. Grieson, ed., *Public and Urban Economics*, Lexington Books, Lexington MA, 1976.

[5]   Affirmative action is compatible with perfect competition, if policies are supported by the will of the people.

[6]   See Ralph W. Pfouts and Steven Rosefielde, "Egalitarianism and Production Potential in Postcommunist Russia," in Steven Rosefielde, ed., *Efficiency and Russia's Economic Recovery Potential to the Year 2000 and Beyond*, Ashgate, Aldersgate 1998, pp. 269–314. Oscar Lange, "On the Economic Theory of Socialism," in Benjamin Lippincott, ed., *On the Economic Theory of Socialism*, McGraw-Hill, New York, 1964.

The primary weakness of perfect governance is mechanical. While it is easy to assert that the utility- and profit-maximizing motives on which perfect market ideals depend often go awry, advocates of perfect governance have a more arduous task explaining why administration, planning, prohibition, command, legislation, and jurisprudence are not worse. Even if it could be shown that authorities were informed and well-motivated, outcomes should seldom be ideal because planners do not know what consumers want, and cannot be automatically disciplined for their errors.

It can therefore be concluded that there are no easy paths to economic Utopia. Although libraries are filled with books insisting that there is a simple, universally best strategy for constructing an economic system which maximizes human welfare, the assertion is untrue. Instead, there are myriads of category A and B ideals, none of which are really attainable.

Chapter 5 elaborates the perfect market model further, while chapter 6 probes more deeply into the risks and opportunities of administration, planning, and regulation.

CHAPTER 5

PERFECT COMPETITION

Perfect competition is a special theory of markets which specifies the conditions under which Walrasian, Marshallian, and Keynesian adjustment mechanisms generate equilibria assuring that every worker, and asset holder, receives exactly the value of his or her productive contribution, undistorted by privileged access to information, barriers to entry, indivisibilities, returns to scale, product differentiation, or infringements of the golden rule. It constitutes a vision of the ideal outcomes toward which some believe all markets tend, and can be viewed as the antithesis of Karl Marx's market pessimism.

The perfectly competitive ideal is not without its critics. Many assert that it exalts individualism at society's expense, relegates government, encourages inegalitarianism, and fails to protect the needy. Paul Samuelson and others have responded by showing how alternative, socially conscious, perfectly competitive systems can be constructed for any democratically approved income-transfer distribution, and package of government programs. All that is required is for the community to voluntarily set the right rules of the game, and competitive utility-maximizing will automatically generate the ideal.

Unfortunately, these improvements do not suffice either in theory or practice, because it can be shown that competition by itself in the presence of privileged informational access, barriers to entry, increasing returns to scale, indivisibilities, and heterogeneous product characteristics cannot assure utility-maximization, and encourages market power, even if people are inclined to abide by the golden rule. "Perfect" competition by itself in the presence of technical impediments does not lead to any particular virtuous ideal. Competition, as Adam Smith understood, is useful for combating some types of conspiracies in restraint of trade, but it is not a panacea. The merit of general competition therefore should be appraised in this light. It is likely to be beneficial, but it cannot be proven that it is universally superior.

The theory of perfect competition holds a special place in Anglo-American economics because it purports to demonstrate how founding values like personal freedom, equal opportunity, fair play, and even affirmative action through disciplined rivalry can produce an ideal global economic equilibrium. Naive versions dispense with government, giving the impression that private activity is always best, but more sophisticated variants show how perfect private competition can be reconciled with limited perfect democratic governance to voluntarily achieve superior welfare outcomes.

As explained in chapter 2, the notion that personal freedom, equal opportunity, fair play, and affirmative action can be harmonized to create ideal economic outcomes is not novel. Philosophers had long considered the possibility, but usually agreed with Aristotle that ideal economic outcomes for work and leisure required the beneficent hand of a philosopher king (like Aristotle's pupil Alexander the Great) because unbridled freedom usually degenerates into anarchy.

Philosophers of course appreciated that personal liberty was vital because it allowed people to discover and realize their potential. Socrates among others believed that they possessed sufficient intellect, and understood the concepts of justice that make equal opportunity, fair play, and affirmative action desirable, but thought that people left to their own devices could not agree how to live harmoniously.

This judgment stood for more than two thousand years, until Adam Smith recognized that agreement was not necessarily required to achieve ideal equilibrium. It did not matter that people had different tastes, talents, and motives, or that they all coveted the same scarce resources, as long as in seeking to competitively better themselves everyone abided by the golden rule (or Lockean social contract). This insight, if correct, meant that ideal outcomes did not depend on the visible hand of enlightened geniuses, but rather was more reliably achievable through a properly structured competitive game with stunningly simple rules. Players were only required to competitively utility maximize within the limits of bounded rationality on a level playing field. They could seek to win by learning their trades, negotiating, innovating, merchandising, building institutions, and risk-taking, but were prohibited from anticompetitive conduct that denied personal freedom, and equal opportunity to others, or violated the precepts of fair play by cheating or forcing people to act against their will.

The key element in this game was competition. No one doubted that people were self-seeking, or that most obvious forms of unfair behavior, like theft, servitude, and murder, could be criminalized. But could people be aroused to utility maximize, yet still be successfully deterred from circumventing the law by discretely colluding in restraint of trade? Adam Smith's response was guardedly affirmative. Of course he acknowledged that people were often indolent, irrational, and opportunistic, but this might not matter in a competitive environment, because the successes of some would spur the emulation of others, inefficiency probably would be punished by failure, and anticompetitive conspiracies would be dispelled by free entry. Competition would drive people toward being all they could be, while it coaxed firms to act as price-taking profit-maximizers. Businessmen might try to overcharge, but could not count on escaping competitive discipline because rivals were likely to capture their market by offering the same goods more cheaply. Nor could they be certain that markets could be successfully rigged if community sanctions and state antitrust laws prevented the erection of barriers to market entry. As soon as rivals recognized that other firms were making mega-profits, they would be attracted to the business, augmenting supplies and driving returns down toward the equilibrium rate. Yes, Aristotle was right that in the best of worlds people had to be mobilized, exposed to incentives, and disciplined, but this did not mean that they could not be self-regulating. The invisible hand of competition, Smith believed, was sufficient to arouse, guide, and

transform individual utility-seekers into efficient, economy-wide utility- and profit-maximizers, if conscience and law made them golden rule abiding.

The formal requirements for constructing a self-regulating system for generating a
competitive (but not necessarily perfect) general equilibrium have already been elaborated
in chapter 2. Utility-seekers must obey the laws of demand, supply, and their equilibration.
Demand curves normally will be downward-sloping (figure 2.2); supply curves upward-
sloping (figure 2.4); with transitory disequilibria, or shifts in demand and supply curves
being resolved with Walrasian (figure 2.8), Marshallian (figure 2.9), and Keynesian adjustment mechanisms (figure 2.14c) as they variously apply. If competition makes buyers and
sellers utility and profit maximize in the Walrasian case, retailers will always cut prices when
there are gluts, and customers will raise price bids when there are shortages until markets
clear. Likewise with respect to Marshallian production, would-be price-setting firms will be
forced to act as price-taking profit-maximizers by competitive discounting (hence the
horizontal price line in figure 2.6). As a consequence, the factor, production, financial,
and distribution markets for all goods and services, driven by competitive utility-seeking,
will move toward ideal equilibrium individually, and generally for the economy as a whole.
This is illustrated in figure 5.1 by point E, where the community indifference (demand)
curve is tangent to the production possibility frontier (supply curve). Every person in the
ideal case should attain his or her highest utility level, within the limitations properly
imposed by voluntary utility-seeking; a state frequently described as Pareto optimality.

Point E is competitively ideal, just as Adam Smith envisioned, but it might not be perfect
even if players abide by the golden rule because of various natural imperfections. Technology, innovation, asymmetric information,[1] product differentiation, and indivisibilities

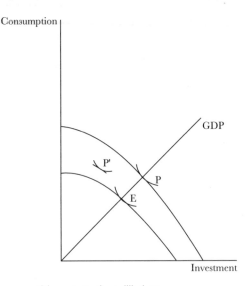

Figure 5.1 Perfectly competitive general equilibrium

[1]   The issue of asymmetric informational access is especially important for patentable innovations. It is often
argued that innovation would be stifled if inventors had foreknowledge that they would not be able to receive
anything more than the riskless, competitive rate of return on their effort. From this perspective societies may be
forced to choose between perfect competition and rapid technological progress.

may create noncollusive barriers to entry which prevent efficiency and productivity from achieving their full conceptual potential. If enterprise production functions exhibit increasing returns to scale, larger firms will have a competitive advantage that cannot be eliminated. Patents granting inventors exclusive market rights to achieve optimal innovation, insider privileged information, heterogeneous product characteristics, and indivisibilities which reduce competition could have the same effect. Perfection therefore requires that technology be pro-competitive, inventors altruistic, informational access non-discriminatory, goods homogeneous, production functions monotonic and diminishing in stage II, and that there be a sufficiently large number of firms in every activity. And, for the sake of realism, it should be added that enterprises must be able to identify their demand curves, and respond effectively to multiple, interdependent disturbances; problems econometricians understand are not easily solved.

Everyone agrees that if these obstacles do not apply, a new and better outcome will prevail at point P in figure 5.1 somewhere on a higher perfectly competitive production possibility frontier, but critics do not consider this credible. They insist that even if people do abide by the golden rule there are no reasons to believe that technology will be pro-competitive; that everyone will have equal informational access, that products will be homogeneous and firms numerous enough to eradicate excess profits. Moreover, perfect competition may not only be infeasible, it may be inferior because if scale and informational economies are present they might be costlessly captured through perfect governmental regulatory intervention.

This possibility does not prove that a mixed regime of nearly perfectly competitive markets and government regulation would actually be better than golden rule abiding free enterprise, but it does cast serious doubt on the comparative merit of private competition, raising a wide range of related normative issues. Does competition really spur initiative, curb price gouging, and guarantee free entry as advocates contend? Does it harm people's well-being by encouraging excessive self-seeking? Is Marx right in alleging that unfettered competition exploits the working class instead of assuring that laborers receive the value of their ideal marginal products? Do market economies abridge the golden rule in other ways? Since some people are invariably born more equal than others in terms of talent, wealth, educational, and social access, is golden rule abiding perfect competition really as just as many claim? Should lump-sum dividends be used to correct injustices of history and nature? Are competitive, utility-driven, self-regulating systems compassionate? Do they take care of the poor, disadvantaged, and needy?

These concerns have led to various refinements, some purporting to show that potential defects in perfect competition can be remedied without significantly infringing free enterprise, and others insisting that the state fix the starting conditions for perfectly competitive games, and impose other solutions when markets fail.

Proponents of free private enterprise have tried to salvage the competitive paradigm by de-emphasizing the selfish aspect of independent utility self-seeking, highlighting the possibilities of compassion and charity, and by developing libertarian alternatives whenever economies of scale, asymmetric information, processing capabilities, product differentiation, indivisibilities, and market size prevent the full competitive attainment of economic potential. The first approach starts from the premise that libertarians might decide on their own volition to charitably alter the existing distribution of wealth and income. This does not completely dispose of the charge that perfect competition is tainted, because the rich alone decide whether the poor should benefit, but it does soften the impression that competitors are heartless. One familiar suggestion obligates asset holders to transfer a portion of their profits, rents, interest, and dividends to propertyless participants in the form of lump-sum (per capita) dividends that minimize effort related side effects.[2] After the transfer, the laws of supply, demand, and equilibration will move the system to a new compassionate perfectly competitive equilibrium P′ on a lower perfectly competitive production frontier (figure 5.1). Production declines because asset holders and dividend recipients have less incentive to supply their services in the new regime, but welfare clearly improves because transfers are voluntary. The same logic holds for voluntary affirmative action, where transfers provide a head start to the disadvantaged. And, of course, libertarians have the democratic right to hire government and shelter some personal activities from the rigors of competition when this increases their utility. Nothing obliges proponents of perfect competition to claim that competition is the best solution for every problem. If perfect competition is applicable to most work activities, and people are permitted to rely on their good sense when it is not, this is enough to maintain that it is very good, and better than the authoritarian alternative.

Other champions of perfect competition, while accepting these premises, have argued for a more visionary approach. They recommend that libertarians agree to establish institutes, or government advisory boards, to formally consider all the ways in which wealth and income can be transferred, and to identify the optimal boundaries of competition, so that the community of independent utility-seekers can wisely select the best options. Some even recommend that the government be empowered to take action to enhance perfect competition without libertarian approval when consultation is impractical.

To appreciate how these types of institutional and government planning can be reconciled with perfect competition, let us reconsider the option of lump-sum dividend redistribution. Imagine that it is possible to conduct a controlled set of experiments where wealth or income is redistributed according to a prescribed algorithm, after which Walrasian, Marshallian, and Keynesian adjustment mechanisms are activated, and the results tallied. Each test will generate a point on a new, modified perfectly competitive production possibility frontier, which together with the best outcomes of further experiments can be used to construct an envelope curve called a grand perfectly competitive production possibilities frontier. Libertarians or administrators can consult this menu to guide their decision-making, or they can ask the technocrats to proceed a step further, transforming the output associated with each point on the envelope curve into an indicator of utility. Post-production transfers generate still more alternatives, culminating in the construction of a grand perfectly competitive utility possibilities frontier illustrated in figure 5.2, which allows the community to select the best welfare outcome for individuals A and B, given decision-makers' preferences at point U.[3] Few of course believe that such calculations are really feasible, even in an approximate

[2]   Paul Samuelson, "Optimal Compacts for Redistribution," in Samuelson, *Collected Scientific Papers*, Vol. 4, Chapter 257, MIT Press, Cambridge 1966; Kenneth Arrow, "Optimal and Voluntary Income Distribution," in Steven Rosefielde, *Economic Welfare and the Economics of Soviet Socialism*, Cambridge University Press, Cambridge, 1981, pp. 267–88.
[3]   Abram Bergson, "On the Concept of Social Welfare," *Quarterly Journal of Economics*, Vol. 68, 1954, pp. 233–52. Paul Samuelson, "Reaffirming the Existence of a 'Reasonable' Bergson-Samuelson Social Welfare Function," *Economica*, Vol. 44, pp. 81–8.

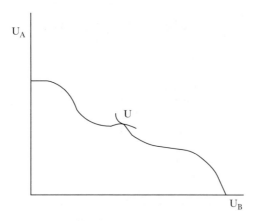

Figure 5.2 The perfectly competitive utility possibility frontier

sense.[4] But the exercise instructively illustrates the possibilities of combining technocratic search methods with bounded libertarian perfect competition to devise better perfectly competitive, private free-enterprise games.

However, opponents do not consider this enough. They counter-argue that these embellishments do not prove that competition, reason, and adherence to the golden rule lead reliably to outcomes where everyone receives the ideal value of his or her marginal product. Indeed, they believe the converse, that natural impediments to perfect competition incline markets toward imperfection, and that this tendency is compounded by inefficiencies, unsuppressed conspiracies in restraint of trade, ubiquitous disregard for the golden rule, and sundry acts of economic compulsion. The perfectly competitive ideal from their perspective not only fails to provide economic justice, but does not even deliver promised efficiencies.

In essence, critics side with Aristotle. With the benefit of modern economic science, they appreciate that individual utility-seeking, guided by competition, disciplined by the golden rule, and softened with higher reason and compassion could yield good, if imperfect, results. They just do not believe that it will either in theory or practice. Our investigation has revealed that their misgivings are not attributable to faulty understanding and cannot be dispelled with refinements and clarifications. Ideal utility-maximizing cannot be guaranteed solely on the basis of a plausibly perfectly designed competitive game, and outcomes therefore must be perceived as inherently second best. This means that sophisticated advocates of optimal competition should not content themselves by pretending that competitive markets are intrinsically superior. They may well be, but if so this is only because directive, administrative, and regulatory alternatives are worse.

---

[4] Abram Bergson, "Social Choice and Welfare Economics under Representative Government," *Journal of Public Economics*, Vol. 6, No. 3, October 1976, pp. 171–90. The algorithm described is impractical because the economy is not a laboratory that permits the required controlled experimentation. The ramifications of lump-sum dividends cannot be impounded, and distinguished from other disturbances. Likewise, it is widely understood that the problem of interpersonal utility comparisons makes it impossible to realistically compute the utilities illustrated in figure 5.2, either ordinally, or cardinally. Nonetheless, Bergson suggests that democratic discourse can provide some guidance on these important matters.

Review Questions

1. Why did Aristotle and his followers believe that the perfect economic order required perfect governance rather than perfect competition?
2. Perfect competition usually excludes government, but does not have to. What assumptions are required to exclude government? Hint: reflect on the concepts of market failure, and the comparative productivity of private and state activities.
3. What makes perfect competition "perfect"? Hint: reflect on the concepts of rent and value added.
4. Why did Smith believe that the invisible hand was not a Utopian conception? Hint: think about competition. Elaborate.
5. What are the formal requirements for constructing a self-regulating system for generating a competitive general equilibrium?
6. Using figure 5.1, explain why the perfectly competitive equilibrium P is greater than the Smithian equilibrium E.
7. Why are critics skeptical about the possibility of attaining point P?
8. Why do they believe that price gouging and restricted market entry call the comparative merit of private competition into question?
9. Do their criticisms imply that Marx is right in alleging that unfettered competition exploits the working class? Explain.
10. How can competition be made more equitable by adjusting the starting conditions of the utility-seeking game?
11. How can affirmative action be reconciled with unfettered competition?
12. With reference to figure 5.2, explain how governance can be combined with perfect markets to identify a "supremely" perfect result at point U. Does this demonstration prove that markets always yield superior outcomes?

CHAPTER 6

PERFECT GOVERNANCE

Governance is a set of control and regulatory procedures employed by governments, communities, agents, and hired managers to direct and guide economic utility-seeking. It can be used to establish the rules of competitive games and in this sense is compatible with various forms of laissez faire, but usually is more intrusive; constraining, regulating, administering, and directing detailed aspects of production and exchange. The essential attribute of governance is the subordination of some individual utility-seeking activities to the will of authorities on the premise that father knows best, including the extent to which the preferences and welfare of other family members should count.

The merit of governance depends on normative judgments about whose preferences matter, and whether the mechanisms employed are as efficient as the market. Perfect governance requires that outcomes be at least as good as those of the competitive ideal, and better whenever increasing returns, informational entry barriers, indivisibilities, adjustment deficiencies, and communalism preclude perfect competitive market equilibrium.

Many economists believe that governance often is superior, and some that it can be made almost perfect because economic activities can be formulated as systems of simultaneous equations with real equilibrium solution values. Advances in computation make such dreams seem almost feasible. But even if it is supposed that econometricians some day have the computational capacity at their disposal to jointly solve every individual's system of simultaneous demand and supply equations, how could they obtain the requisite information, and how could they determine whether it fully reflected potentials?

Planners the world over have striven to find out. The Soviet Union spent vast sums using its economy as a living laboratory. The results were disheartening. Planners, administrators, and regulators were unable to conduct the controlled experiments needed to ascertain potential, or even prevailing demand. Governance was arbitrary, and vulnerable to moral hazards which ultimately proved fatal. Despite high hopes that perfect governance would be better than perfect competition, the Soviet experiment demonstrated that central planning, administration, and regulation were inferior to Western imperfect market competition.

The discovery of linear programming by Leonid Kantorovich in the 1930s,[1] and its subsequent refinement by Paul Samuelson, Robert Solow, and Robert Dorfman in the 1950s,[2] led economists to the insight that under certain assumptions there is an exact correspondence between the output and cost characteristics of perfect planning and perfect market competition, often described as the "duality theorem." This discovery, which showed that category A enlightenment goals could be theoretically attained with market, plans, and their many combinations, should not have been a surprise. Leon Walras had already shown in the 19th century that the problem of computing a multi-product demand and supply equilibrium could be expressed and solved in principle with simultaneous equations if the number of appropriate linearly independent equations were one less than the number of independent variables, subject to an additional balance equation showing that aggregate purchasing power (demand) equaled aggregate cost (supply).[3] Other economists like Gerard Debreu then delved further into the mathematical requirements of production and utility-maximization, to elaborate more powerful proofs that solutions to realistic economic optimization programs existed,[4] even if their attainability by mechanical or market means remained in doubt.[5]

All of these demonstrations begged a variety of questions about whether demand and production functions specified in computable equational systems were realistic, and properly parameterized,[6] but they were treated seriously because real markets demonstrated that good outcomes were possible, indicating that utility and production functions existed, were adequately well-behaved and hence discoverable. If the market found solutions, then it was argued planners could simulate the process, or perhaps find even more powerful techniques.[7]

And, of course, if better methods could be devised, then nothing prevented planners from substituting one set of demand functions for another, manipulating wants, altering technologies, and constraining supplies to generate other solutions, maximizing planners' as distinct from market participants' preferences.[8] The age of feasible "perfect govern-

[1]   L.V. Kantorovich, *The Best Use of Economic Resources*, Harvard University Press, Cambridge, MA, 1965

[2]   Robert Dorfman, Paul Samuleson and Robert Solow, *Linear Programming and Economic Analysis*, McGraw-Hill, New York, 1958.

[3]   Bent Hansen, *Survey of General Equilibrium Systems*, McGraw-Hill, New York, 1970; Leon Walras, *Elements d'economie politique pure*, R. Pichon, Paris, 1926.

[4]   Gerard Debreu, *The Theory of Value*, Wiley, New York, 1959; Kenneth Arrow and Gerard Debreu, "Existence of an Equilibrium for a Competitive Economy," *Econometrica*, Vol. 22, No. 3, 1954; Richard Kuenne, *The Theory of General Equilibrium*, Princeton University Press, New Jersey, 1963.

[5]   Existence proofs depended on the mathematical concept of convexity. The distinction between existence and attainment is fundamental, because it turns out to be impossible to prove that standard adjustment mechanisms culminate in general equilibrium, even though differential calculus can be used to show how this might be achieved if certain conditions are satisfied within designated intervals. Also, similar mathematical difficulties have limited rigorous fixed-point general equilibrium proofs to the exchange of stocks because the starting points of production do not lead in any clearly defined sequence to the optimum.

[6]   Numerically specified simultaneous equation systems can only yield optimal results if parameters are consistent from equation to equation, and with the solution values.

[7]   Ideal solutions are discovered in perfectly competitive market models through trial and error search processes that not only involve the usual double tangency conditions, but also learning.

[8]   Paul Samuelson, "Reaffirming the Existence of 'Reasonable' Bergson–Samuelson Social Welfare Functions," *Economica*, No. 441, 1977, pp. 81–8.

ance" appeared to be dawning. Planners might be able to replicate the perfect market, or do much more without impairing economic efficiency.

Generations of lavishly funded planners throughout the globe, especially in the Soviet Union, strove mightily to prove that technocrats in the service of the state could partly or wholly wrest control over the process of discovering and generating ideal economic outcomes, creating an engineering foundation for perfect governance realized through directives in the case of command planning, or some combination of instruments including selected markets. The Soviets began sensibly enough by decomposing the problem, separating supply from demand in order to concentrate on production technologies thought to be stable, and amenable to rigorous mathematical expression and quantification.

Building on the material balance concepts pioneered by Dmitriev at the turn of the 20th century, and their subsequent formalization into input–output analysis by Wassily Leontief (a matrix of linear production and distribution relationships), Russian economists from the 1930s forward were able to construct four quadrant matrices mapping the aggregate economic process.[9] The table containing a series of linear equations described economic value generation and delivery, from input allocation to intermediate input production, final goods distribution, and transfers, in great detail (figure 6.1).

It clearly showed the fixed proportioned assignment of variable primary inputs arrayed as vectors of capital, labor skills, and other nonlabor factors from quadrant III to intermediate input production sectors (stages of intersectoral fabrication) in quadrant I, their transformation into products of intersectoral use (quadrant I), and final consumption by private purchasers and government (quadrant II) and transfers (quadrant IV). The coefficients for these linear equations were derived from *ex post* GDP data, "from the achieved level." This meant that the matrices had the desirable property of reflecting real relationships. They were not hypothetical. But they were not ideal because observed outcomes were not necessarily optimal. They were not generated by utility-, profit-, or welfare-maximizing. They were merely the result of a state economic governance scheme relying on discretionary directives, rules, and incentives without any clear purpose other than perhaps maximizing output from assigned inputs. Under Soviet arrangements political leaders like Stalin told planners what they wanted. Planners prepared provisional aggregate input commitments and output targets for economic ministers, which were then bureaucratically disaggregated and assigned to enterprises in the form of micro-production and cost plans. They determined managements' actions together with bonus incentives.[10] The only apparent virtue of material balances and input–output analysis given this governance scheme was that they provided an objective basis for estimating output changes caused by variations in input supplies, or reciprocally estimating direct and indirect input needs arising from politically mandated changes in the level and composition of final demand. Both techniques were useful, but did not inform authorities either about the real or ideal marginal productivities associated with alternate input supplies, or about parallel gains and losses which could be attained by improving the existing mechanisms

[9] Wassily Leontief, "Quantitative Input–Output Relations in the Economic System of the United States," *The Review of Economic Statistics*, Vol. 18, No. 3, August 1936; Leontief, *The Structure of the American Economy*, Oxford University Press, Oxford, 1941; Leontief, *Input–Output Economics*, Oxford University Press, New York 1966.
[10] Steven Rosefielde and R.W. Pfouts, "Economic Optimization and Technical Efficiency in Soviet Enterprises Jointly Regulated by Plans and Incentives," *European Economic Review*, Vol. 32, No. 6, 1988, pp. 1285–99.

Industry producing ⇩ Industry producing ⇨	X_1 X_2 X_n	X_f	X_g	X_{f^*}
	Quadrant I Intermediate input processing $\sum\limits_{j=1}^{n} a_{ij}\ (X_j)$	Quadrant II Final demand and gross output		
$X_p = X_f$ $X_o = X_i$	Quadrant III Payments to Primary inputs Gross outlays			Quadrant IV Transfers

X represents the value of an activity.

The subscripts designate:
  j = the jth intermediate sectoral production activity
  i = the ith intermediate sectoral purchaser
  f = the final purchaser of the specified sectoral output
  g = the gross value of the intermediate and final deliveries
  p = input payments by the jth purchasing sector
  o = gross outlay by the jth producing sector

Figure 6.1 A schematic representation of the transactions table of a static, open input–output model

of economic governance, and discovering new opportunities. Planners addressed these additional issues by assuming that fixed input, linear technologies accurately described engineering realities,[11] and that ideal potentials would be gradually discovered through controlled experimentation. Both assumptions were not meant to be taken literally. They were working hypotheses mixing the belief that planning was a sound tool for developing a well-functioning economic governance mechanism, with the acknowledgment that discovering real economic potentials required a continuous, and massive investigative effort.

Some did not understand this, accepting Soviet claims that the achievements of planning proved the superiority of state economic governance, but planners themselves

[11] Paul Samuelson, "Abstract of a Theorem Concerning Substitutability in Open Leontief Models," in T.C. Koopmans, ed., *Activity Analysis of Production and Allocation*, Wiley, New York, 1951; Samuelson, "A New Theorem on Non-substitution," in *Money, Growth and Methodology*, in honor of Johan Akerman, Gleerup, Lund, 1961.

knew better. They recognized that improvements were needed in the supply process requiring managerial incentivization, and socialist entrepreneurship, together with better innovation, technological choices, product design, input acquisition, factor employment, finance, wholesale and retail distribution, and global economic coordination. And, of course, they understood that these steps had to be complemented with enhanced information on consumers' and policy-makers' demands.

The entire post-Stalinist era centered on this search for an acceptable planning regime. In the mid-1950s, a campaign was launched to rationalize production decision-making by directing managers to maximize profits at state fixed input and output prices, instead of filling orders, or maximizing revenues. The Liberman experiment – as it was called, after its principal advocate, Evsei Liberman – is best understood as an attempt to embed an automatic, price-sensitive, Marshallian-type quantity adjustment mechanism in the state directive governance system. Managers under this scheme assumed the role of onsite microplanners responsible for economizing costs, determining activity levels and product assortments both in draft recommendations to their ministerial and planning superiors (*tekhpromfinplany*), and as responses to unforeseen contingencies. Managers had played an analogous role under Stalin, but the quantity adjustment mechanism favored during his era was comparatively inefficient, because it required enterprise decision-makers to maximize the physical volume of output without regard for official prices or costs. Expanding managerial discretionary authority constituted a clear advance, because it provided central planners with a better understanding of production possibilities based on managers, superior knowledge of their production technologies, and gave them an improved first response capability for coping with shocks. The benefit, however, was incomplete and failed to significantly illuminate ideal possibilities, because managers were prohibited from negotiating input and product prices (although there was some informal flexibility), preventing them from truly minimizing cost, or maximizing profit, either for their personal gain, or the state's. Simulated Marshallian adjustments could enhance economic efficiency as it appeared to managers given state-fixed, nonnegotiated wages, and utility insensitive Marxist labor value prime-cost prices, but it could not improve planners' understanding of the latent, unconstrained ideal. And, of course, there were numerous reasons for suspecting that many managers did not base their decisions solely on profit-maximizing criteria, when this was the main factor determining their bonus.

After the initial glow of Libermanism, Soviet planners quickly realized that they needed additional tools for augmenting both technical efficiency (performance evaluated at arbitrary prices) and economic efficiency (ideal supply that maximizes social welfare). The first task led to a series of experiments with more sophisticated quantitative methods. Central planners, design bureau, and enterprise manager/technicians applied linear and nonlinear programming, diverse econometric techniques, cost–benefit analysis, and better accounting, organization, and motivational incentives. The second goal was pursued by developing iterative, computer-based strategies for examining managerial supply responses to hypothetical changes in factor and product prices. Although never seriously applied, planners discussed building a two-level programming mechanism where the center solved an enormous linear production optimization program, and then electronically transmitted the resulting shadow prices to enterprises required to output maximize with this information. The optimal micro-outputs were then sent back to the center, the original linear program revised accordingly, recomputed, and retransmitted to the enterprise until some convergence criterion was satisfied. This kind of iterative play could also be conducted according to less stringent rules, allowing the center to confront enterprises with any other sets of prices it desired, monitoring their responses to better define the system's potential. The approach can be conceptualized as a simulated utility-seeking market search process, where economic actors everywhere are queried about how they would respond to every conceivable choice situation with specified budget constraints, at diverse prices. Answers could either be taken at face value, or checked for consistency if it were suspected that respondents were being deceitful.

Soviet planners to their credit never took this sort of Utopian simulation seriously, although they may have found it institutionally expedient to pretend otherwise. But they did attempt to develop a second best in the form of an "automatic system of management and planning" (ASUP), a grandiose term for modernized, computer-based onsite production planning, information, and knowledge sharing between the center and the periphery, which was supposed to culminate in superior central plans. The effort was not without its technical accomplishments, but to the economic governors' consternation, aggregate economic performance diminished steadily as managerial competency and the technical content of Soviet plans improved. Sophisticated planning techniques, better data, motivational and organizational strategies, and discipline campaigns evidently were not enough to arrest the Soviet Union's gradual deterioration, let alone identify and achieve some elusive economic ideal.

The futility of comprehensive economic microplanning as a surrogate for workable or ideal markets and the quest for perfect governance has not been entirely conceded by its proponents, despite its abandonment by the states of the former Soviet Union, Eastern Europe, China, Vietnam, and Cuba. Attention has merely shifted from directive to regulatory market conceptions of perfect governance, which allow some economic participants to expand the scope of their utility- and profit-maximizing through private, voluntary, negotiated factor and product exchanges. For the sake of continuity, this can be visualized as a generalized form of the Soviet automatic system of management and planning in which the center coordinates clusters of private market activities, instead of relying on onsite agents. Individuals maximize utility, and enterprises profit-maximize under both arrangements, but are less tightly micro-controlled in the regulatory model than under the original automatic system of planning and management. Workers, consumers, and producers can negotiate some factor and product prices, and expand their activities to include product design, technology choice, innovation, entrepreneurship, enterprise organization, management methods, finance, marketing, modernization, growth, acquisitions, mergers, inter-enterprise coordination, and private wealth building. As in the Soviet case, market regulators assume that agents (private actors) can do some things better than central planners for a variety of reasons, involving information, fragmented expertise, and the virtues of hands-on experience. These tasks are delegated, or authorized as legitimate private undertakings. Likewise, continuing the analogy, private individuals may require state assistance in the form of advice (government RDT&E, counseling, information, indicative planning) to maximize social potential. They may need direct financial assistance to generate external economies, or suppress external diseconomies. Perfect governors may also intervene to eradicate conspiracies in restraint of trade, uphold contracts, and transfer incomes directly or through various employment and wage/price preferences.

With the exception of the case where markets are perfect, and public administration is neutral, prospects for activist regulatory success hinge on the ability of the center to conduct controlled experiments that reveal ideal potentials. Western government officials do not have any better *a priori* knowledge of the ideal than their Soviet counterparts. Neither intuition, nor modeling suffice for defining the solution values of ideal general equilibrium. Controlled experimentation in which governors comprehensively vary their regulations, tracking responses, is the only option. But, of course, the task is overwhelming.

The conviction that competent economic governance is a superior strategy for realizing ideal potential therefore is misguided. Sage public policy-making, administration, regulation, legislation, and judicial enforcement are insufficient to realize the ideal, or rectify market inefficiencies and failures. Just as perfect horses cannot fly, economic administration, regulation, legislation, and jurisprudence cannot exceed their own limits. Each mechanism is merely a procedure, which can be carried out with varying degrees of efficiency, not a demand responsive cybernetic technique for discriminating and achieving optimal economic performance. A simple example makes this distinction clear. The American government regulated long-distance telephone rates for more than a half century. Let us assume that they performed this task competently from a procedural standpoint, minimizing administrative costs and adhering faithfully to the rules. Such diligence was commendable, but it did not prevent the community from being over-charged, because the regulators could not figure out the ideal rates. They never dreamed that rates could be reduced by 80 percent, while profits soared, yet this is precisely what occurred when market competition was allowed to ferret out the real potential.[12]

The same principles apply to the notion of competent macroeconomic management. Knowledge of the ideal, and its realization, depend on achieving price stability, full employment, and sustained economic growth through the judicious application of monetary and fiscal policies, assuming that markets in other respects will be in micro-economic equilibrium. This approach appeals to a broad cross-section of planners and policy-makers. Soviet leaders loved it because they had little difficulty concocting statistics indicating that retail price inflation was less than 1 percent per annum, that every citizen who wanted a job had one, and that Soviet GDP grew more rapidly than America's. It is therefore important to appreciate that macroeconomic balance for a nation, or the globe, while being a necessary condition for the realization of ideals, is not sufficient. This is easily grasped by recognizing that full employment, sustainable growth, and price stability can all be achieved with sub-optimal labor allocation, sub-potential production volumes, demand insensitive growth, and repressed inflation. Aggregate effective demand (total purchases of new goods and services), as Keynes theorized may sometimes (but not always) be affected by government expenditures, the level and incidence of taxes (subsidies), and the supply of money and credit, but these actions are seldom competitively neutral, and are never carried out as controlled experiments to discover the characteristics of the ideal. This will not be apparent when the distortion is small, but becomes obvious when misemployment, underproductivity, warped growth, repressed inflation, and inequity are pronounced as they were in the Soviet Union.

---

[12]   Cf. Steven Vogel, *Freer Markets, More Rules: Regulatory Reform in Advanced Industrial Countries*, Cornell University Press, Ithaca, New York, 1996, Chapters 4 and 7.

Perfect economic governance in all its guises thus is a pipe dream, useful only for those wishing to pretend that state programs are as good as they can be. This is not a blanket condemnation of government's role in contemporary economic management. It is a caveat against assuming that state economic governance is infallible, or dependably beneficial.

Review Questions

1. What is the "duality theorem"? Why do socialists find it comforting?
2. How is the "duality theorem" related to the fundamental question of whether a general economic equilibrium exists in principle?
3. Input–output analysis was the touchstone of Soviet economic planning. What is it? What are its strengths and weaknesses?
4. How did the Liberman experiment attempt to overcome the shortcomings of input–output planning?
5. What were the fundamental deficiencies of Liberman's simulated Marshallian adjustment mechanism?
6. What was the Soviet "automatic system of management and planning" (ASUP)? How did it try to overcome the "technical" inefficiencies of Libermanism?
7. How is ASUP related to contemporary Russian authoritarian laissez faire? (See chapter 11).
8. Why didn't the Soviets pursue two-level interactive planning as a device for improving "economic" efficiency?
9. What insight does American telephone deregulation offer regarding the feasibility of perfect governance?
10. How do Keynesian success indicators mask the deficiencies of planning?

PART III

GREAT POWERS

INTRODUCTION

The economies of the world's five leading great powers, America, Continental Europe, Russia, China, and Japan, are all category B systems. They are not generally competitive laissez-faire or perfectly planned economies. They do not attempt to comprehensively maximize individual utility, including individually approved social transfers using markets, plans, and regulation, but instead substitute other cultural norms. Factor allocation, production, retail, income, and wealth distribution are strongly determined by these forces.

Generally competitive, category A utility-seeking is restricted by state and private institutions. The five great power systems can be distinguished not only by the degree to which they infringe category A competitive behavior, but by sources of distortion. All the great powers acknowledge the merit of aspects of the competitive ideal and aspire to realize the efficiency and productivity benefits of competition, but fail in various ways. The American system comes closest to the competitive ideal because its government and culture support pluralist individualism, even though they frequently impair individual liberty, economic efficiency, and productivity, and misdistribute income and wealth. The Continental Europeans deliberately restrict personal liberty more than the Americans because their elites feel that they have an aristocratic right to rule, and their private institutions have a cultural obligation to protect members from harmful competition. The magnitude of state and corporatist intervention is not much larger than in America, but it is more consistently collectivist and protectionist.

Japan in many ways is close to Continental Europe. It allows its citizens to own the means of production, and participate in competitive utility- and profit-seeking, while restricting popular political sovereignty through elite domination and by providing various protections against the distresses of competition. But the primary restraints on individual self-seeking are cultural rather than political. They are based on group obligation and national identity, which makes the Japanese paradigm unique. Japan alone of the five great powers is communally competitive, with a comparatively small government sector, less than half the size of the European norm.

Russia and China, by contrast, diverge more from the generally competitive model than the Japanese because their authoritarianism, reflected partly in state ownership of the means of production, severely distorts other aspects of laissez faire. This has made them vulnerable to moral hazards that threaten their survival.

Since the heyday of Stalin and the Great Depression all the world's economies have been gradually delegating more authority to the market while devising new strategies of regulation and control. This is the sense in which the planet has globalized. The Russian, Chinese, Japanese, and Continental Europeans have each moved toward the American managed market model in their own particular ways, but none have embraced general competition.

Great power economic prospects thus should be diverse. While all five systems rely to some extent on markets, their designs, properties, potentials and vulnerabilities markedly differ.

The performance of all economies differs considerably from their ideals. They are allocationally, productively, and distributionally inefficient. Their comparative merit depends on the magnitude of these inefficiencies and welfare. Neither can be measured precisely, but can be gauged inferentially from systems designs and quantitative evidence. Economic activities in contemporary systems are conducted through markets, government, and obligation (duty, mutual support, and criminal activity), but outcomes vary widely because purposes, institutions, and interplay differ. The propensities which distinguish systems can be likened to "left-handedness." Most lefties can write with their right hands. They just do not want to do it. In the same way, Continental Europeans do not have to preserve their welfare states. They could emulate America, but are uncomfortable with unbridled individualism, and prefer to retain their social democracies. The "human genome" provides another helpful analogy. It recently has been discovered that while humans, bats, and rats are hardly alike, they share 98 percent of the same DNA. Just as differences in only a few genetic codes drastically affect biological potential, so seemingly small differences in culture often radically affect motivation, mechanism, institutions, and the performance of rival economic systems.

The five contemporary systems examined in part III are best understood in this perspective. Leaders can modify the priority they give to markets, government, and obligation. They can reform institutions and revise their goals, but resist fundamental change because of cultural preferences and the realities of political power. It is these enduring regularities that define systems and determine their comparative performance.

This is brought out in the country studies which follow by adopting a common format. Each chapter starts with a general description of national culture, focused on how it determines strategies of market design, state economic governance, and obligation rather than on the anthropology of ritual and values. As economists, we want to understand how economic processes work, more than their symbolic and philosophical meanings.

The mechanisms employed to carry out each system's cultural mission are considered next. These always include the Walrasian, Marshallian, and Keynesian market adjustment processes, supplemented by state governance and obligation. Institutions which shed light on the performance of specific mechanisms are also considered. The operation of these mechanisms is then analyzed from the perspective of the laws of demand, supply, and equilibrium, illuminating the precise ways culture assists or thwarts the attainment of category A ideals.

Next, the inefficiencies of each system are pinpointed graphically by showing how misincentives and constraints distort employment, factor allocation, technology choice, innovation, management, credit, production, investment, retail distribution, and social equity. The geometry of these activities is fully developed in chapter 7. These basics apply to the other country studies, but are not derived anew to avoid repetitiousness. The diagrams in chapter 7 are only replicated for other systems when required for making some important new point.

A capsule summary of each system is provided at the end of every country chapter, followed by a panel outlining how the state tries to respond to inefficiencies caused by national culture and institutions. An impressionistic assessment of the relative importance of culturally regulated markets, state governance, and obligation is presented under the heading "systemic structure." It distinguishes different kinds of markets and state activities. Obligation here takes two forms, custom-guided transactions and crime. Nonnegotiated, ritual exchange activities are disregarded.

Two sets of diagnostics are presented after these panels. The first, labeled "special characteristics," provides subjective judgments about various secondary features of each country's system. No characteristic entirely distinguishes any system, but the assemblage conveys a sense of each system's personality. The second presents a selection of key performance indicators like per capita GDP and per capita GDP growth, which offer insight into national economic performance and merit.

Finally, the reform goals of each system are briefly described and evaluated.

CHAPTER 7

AMERICA

The United States of America is an industrially developed nation, with abundant natural resource wealth, a literate work force, an immense capital stock, and a strong entrepreneurial heritage. It is the world's only economic and military superpower, with expanding multinational interests, and produces nearly a third of global gross domestic product. Its postwar per capita GDP growth lagged Western Europe and Japan until 1993, when the pattern was reversed initially by flagging performance abroad, and more recently by a powerful surge in e-technologies.

The economic system which has produced these results is a "culturally regulated" category B imperfectly competitive market model, founded on individual utility-seeking under the "rule of law," modified by a constituent form of state economic governance. It features private ownership of the means of production, and negotiated price-setting including wages, interest, and foreign exchange rates. The government is a representative democracy, concerned with constitutent special interests, public opinion, and attitude management. The system stresses free enterprise and entrepreneurship, but also possesses a collectivist state which spends about 10 percent of global national income on government programs and transfers. The government intervenes in the economy through legislated programs, micro-regulations, tax incentives and disincentives, subsidies, controls, and transfers; administered by federal and state bureaucracies. Obligation plays a constructive role in preserving support for the rule of law. Its negative aspects, criminality and corruption, abound. They diminish productivity and growth, but do not cause widespread disorder.

American laws of supply, demand, and transaction satisfy the core requirements of the utility-seeking paradigm, mildly distorted by widespread individual infringement of golden rule self-restraint contributing to oligopolistic competition, misgovernance, and the preferential treatment of motivated constituencies. The Walrasian, Marshallian, and Keynesian adjustment mechanisms function adequately within these constraints, but increasing oligopoly concentration caused by "merger mania" may soon have a more adverse impact on economic efficiency.

Opinions about the merit of America's managed free enterprise vary. Some criticize its hyperindividualism and inequality. Real wages for the past quarter century have risen only modestly, and this only during the last five years of the 1990s, while returns on equity have boomed. Critics often advocate larger social spending programs, more progressive taxation, and increased transfers to the needy. Others consider its collectivist government to be a burden on economic efficiency and productivity, and the cause of various social injustices including lavish transfers to undeserving constituencies among the rich, middle, and poor. They counsel downscaling and rationalizing programs, reducing microeconomic regulation and control, replacing bureaucracy with market services wherever cost justified, and reining special interests so that the state serves the public; not the other way round. Both visions are compatible with compassionate governance, but the efficiency and motives of those running the state are assessed differently.

THE AMERICAN ECONOMIC SYSTEM

Culture

America's culture is Western. It is heavily influenced by British individualism, Protestantism, democracy, and common law. Although successive waves of immigration from other parts of Europe, Africa, and Asia have transformed America into a multicultural society, its British roots remain pronounced. This is why specialists frequently classify the American economic system as an Anglo-American model, founded jointly on Adam Smith's pragmatic and charitable principles of free enterprise and the rule of law. Its central features – shared by America, the United Kingdom, Ireland, Canada, Australia, and New Zealand – are individualism, a social contract derived from the Christian golden rule, an obligation to uphold the sanctity of contract law, acquisitiveness, hard work, entrepreneurship, and liberty, complemented with aspects of collectivist state economic governance. The intensity of the Anglo-American cultural preference for the primacy of liberty, entrepreneurship, and the rule of law strongly distinguish it from the Continental European traditions of statism, collectivism, and corporatism, although some contend that this will change in the United Kingdom and Ireland as they integrate into the European Union.[1]

America as an exemplar of the Anglo-American ethos, from the outset of the English industrial revolution in the 18th century, has been one of the world's premier engines of democracy and rapid economic development, outpacing the Continental European achievement for most of the 19th century, and maintaining a preeminent position thereafter, with notable cyclical ups and downs. Although America's per capita GDP growth lagged behind Continental Europe's for most of the postwar period, its standard of living measured on a purchasing power parity basis has remained the highest in the West; a gap which is currently rapidly widening. Americans are individualistic, self-reliant, pragmatic, entrepreneurial, charitable, moralistic, and have a deep faith in technological material progress, despite their own (and the British's) contradictory penchant for infringing golden

---

[1]   Some Anglo-Ameriphiles advocate that the United Kingdom withdraw from the "statist" European Union, federating instead with the United States on a special basis as the 51st state, perhaps in conjunction with Canada, Australia and New Zealand. See Paul Johnson, "Why Britain Should Join America," *Forbes*, April 5, 1999, pp. 84–7. Cf., Johnson, *A History of the American People*, Harper Collins.

rule self-restraint and statist traditions. This optimism has not always been fully justified, but leaders seem to believe that the Anglo-American way which relies heavily on the rule of law rather than the rule of men is best. America is misperceived as a mixed, "self-regulating" category A economy, comprised of relatively micro-efficient, entrepreneurially turbo-charged markets, complemented by a "neutral" form of efficient, democratic state economic governance that includes macroeconomic management, programming, regulation, control, and social transfers. Perhaps the American and British systems will someday realize their generally competitive category A ideal, but it is important to understand that Anglo-American economies are culturally regulated, imperfectly competitive and over-governed.

Motivation

The American economy is a "cultural-regulated" category B variant of the category A state managed "free" private enterprise model which developed as an amalgam of 18th-century constituent democracy, and frontiersmen economic self-reliance, and matured during President Franklin Roosevelt's New Deal. The collectivist aspect of the American system, which partly reflects a rejection of golden rule self-restraint, is downplayed by most theorists, who portray it as an imperfect version of individualistic perfect competition, requiring limited governmental microeconomic intervention to deal with external economies and dis-economies, and conspiracies in restraint of trade. Government scarcely appears in micro-economic textbooks purporting to describe how the American economic works. This concept extends to Keynesian macrotheory, where it is assumed that markets are micro-competitive, but now and then need state assistance to deal with swings in business confidence, sticky wages, speculative demand for idle cash balances, adjustment lags, and crises. These attitudes are affirmed by a political culture which depicts the state as a nonpartisan collection of civil servants, efficiently delivering services to deserving constitu-ents. But such portrayals highlight only one aspect of a complex reality. Anglo-American culture and history are replete with undisciplined self-seeking, as well as statist, corporatist, and communalist influences which often violate the axioms of category A self-regulating systems. From the signing of the Magna Carta at Runnymede in 1215, where the English barons forced King John to grant them a charter of liberties, through the gradual develop-ment of broad-based political democracy in the 19th century, rights and collectivist obliga-tions have been stratified in culturally approved ways that subvert free competition. This has meant privileges for some to dominate others (serfdom, indentured servitude, slavery), but also obligations to restrict some types of predatory and anticompetitive behavior.

   In the 21st century, American indentured servitude and slavery have been eradicated, and the rights and obligations acquired at Runnymede universalized. State restraints on free enterprise are no longer needed to protect serfs from their masters, guilds from amateurs, communes from outsiders, workers from capitalists, or citizens from foreigners. Nonetheless, the collectivist impulse persists. The American government shields some constituencies from competition, and mediates social conflict, but with a different ration-ale. Instead of advocating special rights for professional associations (modern day guilds) and unions, American politicians promote fair competition. They pretend that granting quotas, preferences, subsidies, tax concessions, preferential contracts, and crony transfers is equivalent to assuring everyone equal market access. And while the American and

Continental European welfare states both provide compulsory social security, American politicians claim they are responding to the people's desires, not to social democratic duty as Continental European leaders do.

In some respects, these are distinctions without differences. The nations of Continental Europe, like the United States, are all representative democracies. Their governments pay attention to the wishes of the people. But, invoking the analogy of the human genome, differences of degree and intention often matter. American collectivism is less elitist in dealing with special interest advocacy. Political leaders see themselves as stewards of a pluralist open society without an ideological agenda, and will assist any organized group which can deliver votes, including perhaps the security services of China.[2] But since the high water mark of the New Deal, "fair trade," retail price-fixing, and preferential state aid have become increasingly case specific, as the United States tax code attests.

This specificity makes it difficult to conceptualize how much the governance component of the American economic system is responsive to excessive constituent demands (violating the golden rule), a problem complicated by Arrow's Paradox. Politicians, it has been proven, cannot structure programs consistently with democratic preferences even if they desire to do so.[3] If the special treatment they give motivated constituents is inconsistent with public preferences, politicians can always claim that the fault is a technical shortcoming of democracy, not their mismanagement.[4] On the same grounds, followers of John Rawls[5] and James Meade interpret democratic economic management as an enlightened civic duty.[6] It is therefore vital to grasp that millions of seemingly minor cases of unmerited preferential treatment can cumulate into a serious burden on productivity, efficiency, and economic justice.

[2]   James Risen, "Computer Work is halted at Nuclear Weapon Labs: US Security Fears Heightened by Spy Charges," *New York Times*, April 7, 1999, p. A1. It is alleged that information on America's most advanced, miniaturized nuclear warhead, the W-88, was transferred to China as a consequence of lax standards abetted by lavish Chinese contributions to American political parties. Cf., Harvey Sicherman, "The Inscrutable Americans, Zhu Rongji, and the Deal that Wasn't," Foreign Policy Research Institute, April, 23, 1999.

[3]   Kenneth Arrow, *Social Choice and Individual Values*, Wiley, New York, 2nd edition, 1963. Cf., Abram Bergson, "Social Choice and Welfare Economics Under Representative Government," *Journal of Public Economics*, Vol. 6, No. 3, October, 1976, pp. 171–90; Abram Bergson, "A Reformulation of Certain Aspects of Welfare Economics," *Quarterly Journal of Economics*, Vol. 52, 1938, pp. 310–34; Jan van de Graaf, *Theoretical Welfare Economics*, Cambridge University Press, Cambridge, 1957; Harold Hotelling, "The General Welfare in Relation to Problems of Taxation and of Railway and Utility Rates," *Econometrica*, Vol. 6, 1938, pp. 242–69; M.C. Kemp and Y. Ng, "On the Existence of Social Welfare Functions, Social Orderings and Social Decision Functions," *Economica*, Vol. 43, 1976, pp. 59–66; Abba Lerner, *Economics of Control*, Macmillan, New York, 1944; Ian Little, *A Critique of Welfare Economics*, Clarendon Press, Oxford, 1952; Paul Samuelson, "Bergsonian Welfare Economics," in Steven Rosefielde, ed., *Economic Welfare and the Economics of Soviet Socialism*, Cambridge University Press, Cambridge, 1981, pp. 233–66; Amartya Sen, *Collective Choice and Social Welfare*, Holden-Day, San Francisco, 1971.

[4]   Jan van de Graaf, *Theoretical Welfare Economics*, Cambridge University Press, Cambridge, 1957; Harold Hotelling, "The General Welfare in Relation to Problems of Taxation and of Railway and Utility Rates," *Econometrica*, Vol. 6, 1938, pp. 242–69; M.C. Kemp and Y. Ng, "On the Existence of Social Welfare Functions, Social Orderings and Social Decision Functions," *Economica*, Vol. 43, 1976, pp. 59–66; Abba Lerner, *Economics of Control*, Macmillan, New York, 1944; Ian Little, *A Critique of Welfare Economics*, Clarendon Press, Oxford, 1952; Paul Samuelson,"Bergsonian Welfare Economics," in Steven Rosefielde, ed., *Economic Welfare and the Economics of Soviet Socialism*, Cambridge University Press, Cambridge, 1981, pp. 233–66; Amartya Sen, *Collective Choice and Social Welfare*, Holden-Day, San Francisco, 1971.

[5]   John Rawls, *A Theory of Justice*, Harvard University Press, Cambridge, MA, 1971.

[6]   James Meade, *The Just Economy*, George Allen and Unwin, London, 1978.

The American government infringes the competitive paradigm in four ways. Arrow's Paradox implies that the state produces goods and services it would not if consumers were comprehensively sovereign. It hires others to do the same. It misregulates, and mis-redistributes, national income. Production potential and per capita GDP are impaired because capital, land, and labor are misemployed in state enterprises, and by state contract-ors. Misregulation causes factor misallocation in the private sector, distorting the produc-tion of goods and services. Mis-redistribution of national income depresses effort, skill, and entrepreneurship, diminishing productive rewards and encouraging dependency.

All these shortcomings can be traced to two sources: lack of political self-restraint in shunning state programs that degrade general market competition, and a lack of auto-matic self-regulating bureaucratic mechanisms needed to inform governments about consensus preferences and assure efficient policy implementation. Individuals in the generally competitive private sector do not need coaching. They pursue their personal welfare by maximizing profits and utility, subject to the competitive discipline of the market. But governments cannot mimic these mechanisms. Regulators have no detailed knowledge of the people's preferences, and have no need to maximize profits. They operate in a noncompetitive environment, and cannot help being arbitrary. And even if public officials of all kinds were civically responsive, as social theorists urge,[7] this would not suffice. They still could not determine what people want them to do, and how resources should be competitively economized. This does not mean that all government programs are unworthy. Nor does it imply that representative democracies should discourage constituents from using political means for promoting their special interests. But it does illuminate why free enterprise theorists feel that the burden of proof should be on the state to justify category B market regulation, rather than on the private sector to prove that government programs are cost-ineffective.[8]

The vast majority of Western economists know this, but its impact on their policy recommendations, public attitudes, and government actions is minimal. American culture approves people promoting their personal interests and redressing their grievances through the nation's political institutions, often turning a blind eye toward privilege seeking and petitioners' lack of self-restraint. Although the Republican and Democratic parties disagree about the optimal size and content of various government programs, both appear inclined to increase real aggregate spending.

The structure of these expenditures has no cohesive focus. The government is neither socialist nor capitalist. Its programs may serve both ends, and others but primarily reflect the eclectic desires of an open society. This creates a general propensity to expand the number and size of programs rather than alter their composition, because everyone presumably has an equal right to feed at the state's trough. Government spending has grown relentlessly during the postwar era, with Federal outlays alone, including off-budget credit activities, exceeding 2 trillion dollars (excluding loan guarantees) in fiscal 2000, or nearly 10 percent of the planetary gross domestic product.

---

[7]   Michael Sandel, *Democracy's Discontent: America in Search of a Public Philosophy*, Belknap Press of Harvard University Press, Cambridge, MA, 1996; Robert Levine, "The Empty Symbolism of American Politics," *The Atlantic Monthly*, Vol. 278, No. 10, October 1996, pp. 80–96.

[8]   G.D.H. Cole, British syndicalists tried to solve this problem three quarters of a century ago through elaborate schemes of worker balloting.

The statistics in table 7.1 show that government expenditures are clustered in four categories: human welfare (education, health, medicare, income security and social security), 55 percent; defense (national defense, veterans benefits, and international affairs), 19 percent; interest on the national debt, 13 percent; and other including concealed national intelligence activities, 13 percent. Human welfare outlays primarily involve the direct provision of educational services and health services, medicare and social security insurance operations, and welfare transfers. Defense is principally military and foreign affairs services, while interest on the national debt is an element of the total cost of government programs.

Table 7.1   Federal resources by function 1998 (billions of current dollars)

Function	$ bn
Total Federal government expenditures	1,942.7
Spending	
Discretionary budget authority	530.5
Mandatory outlays	
Existing law	1,137.9
Proposed legislation	2.1
Credit activity	
Direct loan disbursements	37.5
Guaranteed loans	234.7
Tax expenditures	418.9
Agriculture	
Spending	12.3
Credit activity	16.8
Tax expenditures	0.3
Commerce and housing credit	
Spending	4.0
Credit activity	166.6
Tax expenditures	195.9
Transportation	
Spending	15.9
Credit activity	1.1
Tax expenditures	1.4
Community and regional development	
Spending	10.8
Credit activity	4.4
Tax expenditures	2.7
Education, training, employment, and social services	
Spending	57.2
Credit activity	35.8
Tax expenditures	27.9
Health	
Spending	134.7
Credit activity	0.1
Tax expenditures	85.1
Medicare	
Spending	211.4
Income security	
Spending	236.2

Credit activity	0.1
Tax expenditures	86.3
Social security	
Spending	384.2
Tax expenditures	25.3
Veterans benefits and services	
Spending	40.5
Credit activity	31.1
Tax expenditures	3.1
National defense	
Spending	265.3
Credit activity	0.2
Tax expenditures	2.1
International affairs	
Spending	18.6
Credit activity	14.0
Tax expenditures	7.6
General science, space, and technology	
Spending	16.4
Tax expenditures	1.5
Energy	
Spending	1.9
Credit activity	2.1
Tax expenditures	2.2
Natural resources	
Spending	23.4
Tax expenditures	1.7
Administration of justice	
Spending	25.0
General government	
Spending	13.6
Tax expenditures	49.5
Net interest	
Spending	249.8
Tax expenditures	1.3
Undistributed offsetting receipts	
Spending	−52.9

From a competitive category A perspective, these expenditures have two distinct impacts; one on supply, the other on demand. The first involves the diversion of resources from the private sector into state services. Approximately half of government outlays (including interest, treated here as part of the cost of current programs) go for this purpose. The second transfers cash from one group of taxpayers to another. Medicare and social security under the current "pay as you go" system transfers income from the young to the old; income security from the middle class to the disadvantaged.

Assuming that shifting production from the private sector to the state, and income from one group to another, are worthwhile, they are still wasteful to the extent that programs and transfers are inefficiently implemented with bureaucratic methods, and disregard taxpayers' preferences. This squandered national income is compounded by 419 billion dollars of "tax expenditures"; that is, tax breaks of dubious merit from a competitive perspective.

These distortions are aggravated by legislative, administrative, regulatory intrusions into the operation of the private sector. Governmental reach is prodigious. It encompasses contract law, mandates, work conditions (OSHA), employment, immigrant workers, labor management relations, affirmative action, environmental regulation, health and retirement programs, securities and exchange, banking and antitrust regulation, macroeconomic regulations, jurisprudence, arbitration, and – last but not least – the tax code. The legal and administrative costs imposed on businesses and individual workers run well into hundreds of billions of dollars. Some of these compliance costs, incentives, and disincentives are socially justified, but much is "make work" which would never be socially approved if people comprehended the full costs.

The sum of this waste, fraud, and abuse is the economic burden of American category B culturally regulated market management. It constrains the standard of living below the category A competitive potential, distorts income distribution, and creates perverse incentives which diminish the quality of life. The government is viewed either as a patronistic benefactor, or as an albatross in league with special interests.

These attitudes are partly reflected in violent crime, addiction, illegitimacy, licentiousness, civic irresponsibility, and intergroup strife. There are 25 times as many adult rapes per capita in America as Japan, and 125 times as many cases of AIDS. Although this is not news, and is viewed by some as the price of personal freedom, Americans tend to disregard the impact on effort, integrity, competence, and efficiency, which together with technological progress determine economic performance. Labor productivity growth has been declining despite rapid technological change and new capital formation for more than a decade, although there has been some notable recent improvement.[9] Effort, integrity, competence, and efficiency for the most part are lagging improvements in technological potential and may be diminishing, prompting calls for improved attitudes and training.

This problem is compounded from a normative standpoint by sluggish growth in real wages, environmental abuse, and widening inequality. The government has grappled with these disorders, but in America's individualist, adversarial society results have been checkered. Government programs ameliorate, but seldom resolve, social ills because there is no consensus for effective civic action.[10]

These defects are not new, and can be traced back at least as far as the age of Jacksonian democracy, when the White House was symbolically opened to everyone. The nation has flourished despite government misadministration because of the competitive efficiency of its private market sector and its entrepreneurial vigor. Factor allocation, production, and distribution in the private sector have been "workably competitive." Supply has been broadly responsive to consumer demand and factors compensated in accordance with their imperfectly competitive value added. The production of goods and services is determined by profit-seeking and distributed to maximize consumer utility, given purchasers' tastes and incomes.

---

[9]   The Boskin Commission argues that flagging productivity is an illusion because it asserts that the consumer price index understates qualitative improvements and hence growth. But see Thomas Palley, "How to Rewrite Economic History," *The Atlantic Monthly*, Vol. 279, No. 4, April 1997, pp. 20–22. Also, note the Bureau of Labor Statistics has been adjusting American growth statistics based on the Boskin's Commission's recommendations, with the result that reported GDP growth appears to be 0.7 percent higher than it would have been otherwise.
[10]   Robert Levine, "The Empty Symbolism of American Politics," *The Atlantic Monthly*, Vol. 278, No. 10, October 1996, pp. 80–96.

These positives are bolstered by entrepreneurial risk-taking; the remnants of a Puritan ethic that applauds "busy-ness," and a shadow culture that encourages self-advancement. American culture is resource-mobilizing, frenetic, and innovative beyond anything Aristotle might recognize as a golden mean. This vibrancy serves as a powerful counterweight to the deadening effects of excessive taxation, burdensome supervision of business, bureaucratic waste, and misregulation.

American GDP growth has not been slowed to the degree it would have been in a less entrepreneurially aroused society. The postwar rate has been in line with the long-term historical average of 3.2 percent per annum. GDP growth per man–hour has been steady. Entrepreneurship and competition also have positively affected unemployment and consumer welfare. New Deal restrictions on retail pricing, distribution, imports, and labor contracting have been pared, or abolished, and foreign businesses have been encouraged to locate facilities in the United States. These liberalizing initiatives have increased labor mobility, spurred employment, widened choice, and contained inflation. Americans at the beginning of the 21st century are fully employed, and are enjoying a standard of living well above the norm in more controlled and culturally misregulated economies. Advocates of the competitive category A model plausibly insist that further liberalization would make things even better, although some macrotheorists like Paul Krugman worry that liberalization is increasing the risk of another Great Depression. But for the moment at least politicians are content with the state management system they have, delighted that government programs have not killed the goose that lays the golden egg.

They are in a boastful mood,[11] confidently proclaiming a new era of perpetual prosperity co-guaranteed by private entrepreneurship and the "welfare" state. America indeed is doing exceptionally well, judged by the usual macroeconomic yardsticks. GDP per capita is higher, and unemployment is lower than in all of the developed great powers. Inflation and interest rates are low.

But these macro-criteria mask the fact that American economic performance is below its competitive potential, although perhaps not as much as elsewhere. Other great powers could easily eclipse the United States by more thoroughly embracing laissez faire, or even finding alternative ways of empowering their managed markets. America has many virtues, but it has not always been the leader in GDP per capita, life quality, and social justice. This is because the motivations, mechanisms, and institutions that govern demand, supply, and equilibration continue to differ importantly from those assumed in the enlightened classical tradition. Political, bureaucratic, and constituent motivations warp demand and define how the culture distorts micro- and macroeconomic aspects of the Anglo-American system. The American economy can be conceptualized as a two-tier system based on asymmetric access to state assistance. Insiders benefit at everyone else's expense, causing serious collateral, productivity, and efficiency losses.

Mechanisms and Institutions

American economic market, governance, and obligational mechanisms have been crafted over the centuries by politicians, bureaucrats, and constituents to facilitate their aspirations.

---

[11]   Mortimer Zuckerman, "A Second American Century," *Foreign Affairs*, Vol. 77, No. 3, May/June 1998, pp. 18–31; Paul Krugman, "America the Boastful," *Foreign Affairs*, Vol. 77, No. 3, May/June 1998, pp. 32–45.

They have learned that workably competitive, preferentially managed markets under the rule of law suit the bill. The American economic system is conceived as a partnership of business and big government which, together with people's obligation to uphold the rule of law, vouchsafe the energetic entrepreneurial pursuit of prosperity, growth, and economic stability, with benefits skewed toward favored constituencies. America's economic institutions, its lobbies, professional associations, unions, business advocacy groups, corporations, state bureaucracies, and the political organizations are all customized to facilitate the attainment of these goals.

Demand and Supply

A partial transfer of economic sovereignty from individual consumers to politicians, bureaucrats, and constituencies does not void the laws of demand, supply, and equilibration, but may noticeably affect performance and potential. American consumers conduct themselves on the surface like perfect competitors. They form preferences. These preferences appear to be consistent, and they try to minimize the cost of the market baskets selected. Their demand is typically an inverse function of price, given their budget constraints. The assortments they purchase are sensitive to relative prices. But their consumption departs from the competitive paradigm in two striking ways. Consumer choice is strongly affected by political, bureaucratic, and constituent preferences for everything from housing to public recreation. Work, job, and leisure choices are constrained by innumerable regulations and tax considerations, distorting choices and discouraging effort.

The same factors distort the law of supply. The technologies of nearly all American firms exhibit diminishing marginal productivity and increasing marginal cost. Individuals and businesses fully understand that they can augment their utility by trading with others, offering their labor, creating value added, starting entrepreneurial ventures, innovating, hiring factors, economizing costs, improving technology, product design and financing, advertising, and effectively merchandising their products. They grasp the merit of efficient administration and planning. But they are often forced to disregard the law of labor and product supply by government and constituent intervention, or by a desire for monopoly profits. Labor supply is a function of wages, but it is warped by welfare, regulatory, and anticompetitive distortions. Managerial supply curves are also negatively affected, but to a lesser degree.

Americans do not profit maximize in the sense required by "category A, self-regulating" competition, because the state and its constituents insist on preferential market access, refuse to vigorously enforce existing antitrust laws, and create moral hazards preventing proprietors and corporations from conducting business efficiently.[12] To be sure, American managers and businessmen pioneer new ventures, innovate, invest in research, development, testing and evaluation (RDT & E), hire and train the most promising personnel, carefully select technologies, modernize, economize variable input costs including finance

---

[12] Sometimes the government deliberately encourages this behavior, as in the current telecommunications merger mania because, despite its competitive rhetoric, it believes that oligopoly generates compensating public benefits through returns to scale. Brian Gruly, "Why Laissez-Faire Is the Washington Line on Telecom Mergers," *Wall Street Journal*, May 10, 1999, p. 1.

and advertising, conduct market research, set prices, and sell their products to earn sufficient revenue. But none of these activities is carried out solely to maximize the stream of private discounted shareholders' dividends. Business is not just a device allowing individuals to competitively optimize lifetime consumption. It is also a cultural–political process of economic engagement, pitting entrepreneurial and state regulatory ambitions against each other, causing under- and over-employment, depressions, and booms, and corresponding microeconomic distortions. Some state actions underwrite, while others impede, RDT & E and corporate growth. Its deficits maintain high levels of production, but its rules and taxes restrict labor mobility within and among firms. While Americans are hard-working and diligent, the administrative ethos often deflects business from profit-maximizing to political and ceremonial activities, and fosters inter-firm collusion. Many corporate managers are encouraged to evade market discipline if they play by the informal rules and cover their tracks, and are rewarded by oligopolistic rates of return. They seem satisfied with the arrangement, preferring mutual support and collusion to vigorous competition, while consumers and workers pay the bill.

Equilibrium

American-managed markets distort competitive Walrasian, Marshallian, and Keynesian adjustment processes by imposing the demand and supply programs of the government, motivated constituents, and oligopolists for those of free competitors. Politicians, bureaucrats, constituents, and collusive businesses are able to reach agreements, but the equilibria are socially sub-optimal because they do not fully capture opportunities. Equilibria are necessarily second best, and depend significantly on networking skills.

Another way to look at the matter is to recognize that the American economic system has four distinct market equilibration mechanisms; the familiar Walrasian, Marshallian, and Keynesian trio, plus the nexus of government–constituent deal-making and consensus building. The latter sacrifices competitive efficiency for political and bureaucratic ends, and constrains the efficiency of the other processes. The Walrasian mechanism is impaired because factor and product prices are prevented from optimally allocating labor and goods due to job-rights constraints, and collusive marketing practices like those on contact lens, pharmaceuticals, and other regulated products.

The Marshallian adjustment mechanism (which in category A systems depends on profit-maximizing responses to factor and output prices to achieve and sustain equilibrium) is similarly disordered by state regulations, including mandated product characteristics. American firms can and do respond to outside demand, but supplies, influenced as they are by misadministered and misregulated markets, oligopoly, and moral hazard cannot correspond to a full utility-maximizing equilibrium.

The impact of American managed competition on Keynesian adjustment processes is also distortive. State regulation of production and employment mute multiplier effects. It creates jobs that should not exist, discourages dismissals, and encourages business complacency. American corporations expect the state to increase public spending programs, exhort consumer spending, cut business and household taxes, offer subsidies, adjust interest and exchange rates, manipulate nontariff import barriers, augment money supply, and do whatever is required to bolster aggregate effective demand, and promote steady growth.

For the most part they are right. But institutionalization of these practices has a cost. It tends to erode national financial stability, and perpetuate anticompetitive inefficiencies.

Systemic structure

The balance of competitive and anticompetitive forces in the American economy is reflected in its structure. The heart of the American economy is its medium- and large-scale industrial, commercial, and entrepreneurial enterprises, with ready access to politicians and bureaucrats. They are the most dynamic element of the system because they can afford large R&D operations, and often are very entrepreneurial. America has few perfectly competitive markets, and its small-scale ventures, shops and farms, vary greatly in terms of their productivity and efficiency. State regulators assist small underproductive businesses, especially beneficiaries of affirmative action, granting them an array of preferences including assured state contracts, and subsidies in the case of agriculture.

The second largest component is the public sector, which provides regulatory services, and transfer programs like social security on a vast scale. It includes some state ownership of national laboratories, and a large number of nominally private companies dependent on government contracts. Deregulation in the 1990s has reduced aspects of political interference in the airlines, and communications sectors, but this has been partly offset by a burgeoning healthcare bureaucracy and other social programs. America has an officious, often incompetent, and underproductive administrative service bureaucracy, operating without market discipline to the public's detriment. Obligation is a less important component of the American economic system. People do feel some communitarian and civic responsibility, and understand the need to uphold the rule of law. There are institutions which encourage mutual support, but individualism predominates. The American Mafia and other criminals pose a threat to the system that thus far has been successfully contained.[13]

The main feature of America's systemic structure is a consensus-forming game which allows various groups to feed preferentially at the public trough, and the state to fund their programs. It has created a productive, but distorted, over-regulated, and over-taxed market economy peppered with elements of workaholism, rent-seeking, and free-riding. The American system has a bloated public sector compared with Japan, which mollifies some constituencies but alienates others. Nonetheless, the system has stabilized macroeconomic fluctuations, sustained growth, and provided Americans with a first-tier standard of living. Insofar as people feel that the sacrifices in productivity and long-term living standards exacted by the waste, fraud, abuse, and disincentives of state-managed private enterprise are justified as the price for political accommodation, the system must be considered a great success. Most American intellectuals view matters precisely this way, mirroring the attitudes of their Continental European and Japanese counterparts toward their own systems. They argue that the system is better than the "self-regulatory" category A competitive ideal because it: harnesses the mobilizing power of collectivism to inspire competence and effort; mitigates labor–management strife and class antagonisms; nurtures

---

[13]   America is a highly crime-intensive country. This criminal activity diminishes the quality of life, but does not threaten the productive mechanism as it does in Russia because it mostly involves recreation, personal relations, and wealth transfers.

collective knowledge; concentrates attention on entrepreneurship, initiative, modernization, innovation, and competition; coordinates and plans at the administrative level in an environment of trust; takes stakeholder interests including those of the community (environmental concerns) directly into account; risk shares; regulates specific and aggregate effective demand; and promotes cost-efficient delivery of private and public services.

But proponents of individualism, liberalization, and competitive globalization disagree. From their perspective it is tempting to surmise that American market management, like Soviet communism, is inferior; that it makes America underproductive, encourages dependency, free-riding, and an anti-work ethic among large segments of the population, and imposes deeply resented state obligations that diminish social welfare. Moreover, it should be noted that the Continental European corporatist system (the European Union, excluding Britain and Ireland), when evaluated on the basis of GDP per man–hour, performed nearly as well as America for at least a decade until 1993.

THE GEOMETRY OF THE
ANGLO-AMERICAN SYSTEM

To better appreciate the special traits of the Anglo-American system, let us revisit the subject geometrically, starting with its systemic structure. The universal set of economic activities can be divided into five components: (A) generally competitive markets for some generic products, (B) inefficient markets caused by incomplete profit- and utility-maximizing, (C) collusive markets, (D) state administrative bureaucracies which (mis-)regulate and (mis-)command, and (E) obligatory activities where some are induced by custom, or compelled by others to do things they might not on their own volition. These economic mechanisms are illustrated in figure 7.1. The blank spaces separating the subsets refer to leisure activities excluded from conventional definitions of gross domestic product, like hugs and kisses.

The category A generally competitive mechanism is the only efficient market component. It is micro- and macroeconomically self-regulating. The behavioral characteristics of the other mechanisms are less desirable. Profit- and utility-maximizing are incomplete in inefficient markets (B), and discriminatory in collusive exchanges (C). Government (D) which uses a mix of market regulatory and administrative tools is inefficient because there are no automatic adjustment processes disciplining the state to respond to its clients needs, or to cost-effectively provide services. Obligation (E) may be more beneficial when it reflects positive cultural and ethical sensibilities, but also can be more harmful where it involves crime.

Economists influenced by the theory of the second best, believing that all advanced economies are governed by imperfectly efficient markets (BUC), infer that the performance potentials of market systems are alike, paying scant attention to other components. They assume that (BUC) or (AUBUC) is the universal set, and disregard the effects of state bureaucracy (D) and obligatory activities (E). The importance of this oversimplification depends on the size and configuration of all systemic components. America has a small perfectly competitive sector, and large inefficient and imperfectly competitive markets (BUC). It has a large state-managed market [(BUC) ∩ D], and significant customary and criminal activities which affect the way business and government are conducted (E). A

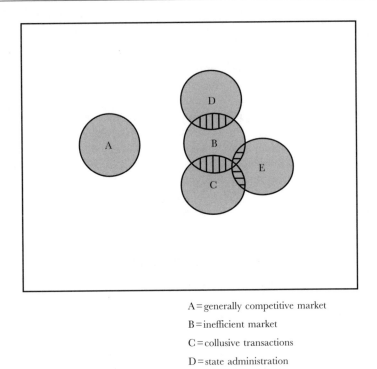

A = generally competitive market

B = inefficient market

C = collusive transactions

D = state administration

E = obligatory activities

Figure 7.1   The universal systems set

and C markets are entrepreneurially vigorous, but the performance of America's bloated government (D) is decidedly mixed.

The distortions associated with this systemic structure and other aspects of American market management can be illustrated further with the aid of Edgeworth–Bowley production and consumption boxes, and diagrams depicting production possibilities and community indifference curves in four core activity spaces: factors, production, finance, and distribution. Supply side relationships shown in the Edgeworth–Bowley production box (figure 7.2) and the production frontier spaces (figures 7.3 and 7.4) take two forms, deviations along the contract curve away from the generally competitive equilibrium (E), and points off this locus. The Edgeworth–Bowley production box shows the geometric relationships between primary factors of production (capital, k and labor l) along the sides of the box; and the isoquants of firms producing two different goods (q_1 and q_2) radiating in increasing order from their respective origins. The locus of joint tangencies of these isoquants represents Pareto efficient allocations and employments of capital and labor, given the wage–rental ratio, and the output price ratios which would hold if the product and input mixes were optimally responsive to different configurations of competitive demand. This nuance is important, because it defines the sense in which every point along the production possibilities frontier is consistent with a "potential" competitive efficiency equilibrium. If other input and output prices were utilized, different frontiers could be generated, but they would not be generally competitive.

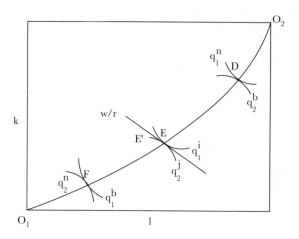

Figure 7.2   American factor allocation

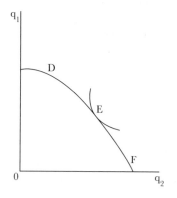

Figure 7.3   American production possibilities

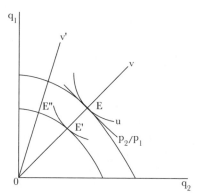

Figure 7.4   American efficiency possibilities

Deviations from the general competitive equilibrium point E on the contract curve thus have very specific meanings. They imply that market participants are lax, demanding a sub-optimal product mix, but otherwise maximize profits and utility in all four core markets. This type of distortion is depicted in figure 7.3 as a movement either to the left (point D) or right (point F) of the universal equilibrium point E along the production possibilities frontier, and is often described as "economic" inefficiency rather than a "technical" shortcoming, because while demand is not optimized, supply is "technically" efficient.

All other lapses of competitive discipline including coercive violations of antitrust law degrade supply efficiency, and consequently necessitate production beneath the production possibilities frontier in figure 7.3. If these inefficiencies proportionally diminish product quality, or the factor productivity of both products, the assortment of goods and services will be the same as the universal competitive equilibrium (assuming demand is efficient), but the amounts produced and distributed will be reduced. The set of these points is illustrated in figure 7.4 as a ray (expansion path) v lying between the origin and point E, and corresponds in the Edgeworth–Bowley production box with a downward renumbering of the isoquants (and a contraction of the box). The larger the numerical reduction in isoquant values, the steeper the shortfall from the production possibilities frontier, and of course any violation of the double tangency requirement may constitute a further proportionate decrease in supply. Just as the points along the production possibility frontier other than E in figure 7.4 are "technically" supply efficient, the points along the expansion path are "economically" efficient, although the term economic efficiency sometimes is reserved solely for point E.

All other inefficiencies which involve both demand and supply will push production off the contract curve in figure 7.2, and off the expansion path between the origin and point E in figure 7.4, implying that the economy is both technically and economically inefficient. This is illustrated by point E″ along expansion path v′ in figure 7.4, which lies on a "production feasibility frontier" constructed analogously with the production possibilities frontier – subject, however, to a set of explicit constraints.

The degree of inefficiency, given these concepts, can be gleaned by considering supply side lapses in competitive discipline. Starting with factors, any irrationality which distorts judgment, effort, and input service time, or regulatory coercion, may cause capital and labor (including management) to be mis-supplied and misallocated. Laziness and unjusti-fied business pessimism may reduce voluntary input supply, and inflict involuntary factor unemployment. Or, in euphoric periods, people may voluntarily overexert themselves, or be pressured into working overtime. In these cases, the size of the Edgeworth–Bowley production box may shrink or expand, and isoquants may be reordered (due to under- or overexertion). Aggregate economic activity in the production space will be sub-optimal because factors are being under- or over-utilized. Any input misallocation, for example, due to preferential pay scales, will further diminish productivity and welfare, as will miseduca-tion and mistraining where growth is taken into consideration.

The degree of distortion in the American factor space is immense. Capital and labor are diverted from competitively determined uses in the private sector into state programs for special interest constituencies, including make-work bureaucracies. This misemployment and waste involves civil servants, but also armies of nominally private sector consultants and agents working primarily for the government. Wage rates and other factor payments are administratively fixed, or are improperly influenced by personal relationships. Prefer-ential job access is given to veterans and other beneficiaries of affirmative action, and similar distortions are imposed on the private workplace by government fiat, contracting requirements, mandated conditions of labor (OSHA), and fringe benefits (retirement, hospitalization, insurance, education, parking, and cafeteria plans), including compulsory unemployment taxes, social security, and medicare "contributions" (FICA taxes), employment subsidies, and an uncountable number of general and special legislative business tax preferences ("tax expenditures"). The government legislates the length of the standard workweek and national paid holidays, and provides unemployment benefits and welfare that affect the supply of labor. It also levies taxes or provides subsidies to specific resources, or nonlabor factor services (energy), instead of neutrally raising revenue on a value added basis. And, of course, since theory teaches that factor supplies depend on real after-tax compensation including transfers, it follows that overtaxation, and over-transfer, mis-taxation, and mis-transfer, further distort factor supply directly, and no doubt indirectly through the encouragement of antisocial behavior.

The inefficiency of American factor markets, however, is not all attributable to government meddling. The state also has taken a lax attitude toward antitrust enforcement, permitting oligopolistic competition with the result that many firms (contrary to competitive assumptions and Locke's social contract) reap excess rates of return by under-supplying and overpricing their goods.

The impact of these cross-distortions on aggregate factor supply has been mixed. Some segments of the population are encouraged to remain outside the work force (including those misled into protracting their education), while others (particularly middle-class women) are driven into it by overtaxation and other governmental misinterventions. And productivity has suffered because government programs have diverted factors from high to low value added activities, and distorted factor allocation in both sectors. This is expressed geometrically in the Edgeworth–Bowley production space in several ways. First, the wage–rental price lines are distorted and segmented because marginal rates of factor substitution are not proportional to marginal factor productivities. Factors are not allocated at point E, the competitive ideal (or its ill-defined "constituent" market counterpart). They are allocated at some other point like F along the contract curve (excess government factor employment) or, more precisely, at F' off the contract curve due to intersectoral factor immobility. Second, these same distortions imply that the isoquants achieved at any points within the space must be lower than their competitive counterparts because factors are not allocated to best use, or most efficiently employed.

American market-managed supply thus is inefficient. It is better than many alternatives, but it falls far below the competitive ideal. Instead of operating at E on the production possibility frontier illustrated in figure 7.4, production actually occurs at E″, below potential on the wrong expansion path.

Moving upstream to the product market, attention shifts to product characteristics, management, technology, and competitive profit-maximizing. A nation cannot realize its full competitive potential unless it produces goods with the right characteristics. The qualitative aspects of q_1 and q_2 must be ideal from the standpoint of equilibrium demand. Misjudgment, irrationality, market power, insider enterprise misgovernance, and communal and state-mandated standards could all cause severe supply inefficiencies where consumers are forced to substitute goods with characteristics they disprefer for those they desire. Forced characteristic and product substitution in the United States is substantial. Not only does the government spend taxpayers' money for constituent programs few would tolerate if they really knew the details, but government-mandated product standards (air bags) burden many consumers with characteristics they would not voluntarily purchase (and handicap competitiveness abroad).

As a consequence, the volume indexes on the isoquants in figure 7.2 have to be adjusted downward by converting goods with dispreferred characteristics into smaller quantities of standard outputs at the competitive marginal rate of transformation. Analogous adjustments are required for the mis-selection of technologies embodied in enterprise isoquants.[14]

Production performance is also impaired by other aspects of government regulation. The communications sector provides a fine case in point. The federal government regulated telephone rates and services for decades, supposedly to protect consumers. However, when ATT was broken up and deregulated not only did rates plunge, but the variety of telephonic services mushroomed and quality improved. The deregulation of television, airlines, and the postal system had the same beneficial effect, indicating the scale of residual suppressed production potential (social security). And, of course, it must never be forgotten that government programs do not profit maximize. Program managers merely assign tasks and spend within their budgets. Hence, they are inherently inefficient. Governmental intrusions into the workplace, including suffocating record keeping and reporting requirements, similarly hamper managerial effectiveness. Scarce management resources are squandered, or diverted from solving problems that could greatly increase productivity.[15] These losses, as well as those attributable to oligopoly and inadequate shareholder influence (insider control), are easily overlooked because American management is dynamic and entrepreneurial compared with many foreign competitors. But they are nonetheless substantial, lowering the isoquant values in the Edgeworth–Bowley production box, driving production off the Edgeworth–Bowley contract curve, and shifting the production possibilities frontier inward.

Laxness and malfeasance in financial markets by lenders, investors, speculators, and governmental regulatory agencies compound the misallocation of factors and productive inefficiencies. If governments misregulate credit, interest, foreign exchange rates, and foreign capital movements, and if bankers exercise unusually poor judgment in evaluating credit risks, and investors and speculators under- or over-borrow, the economy will be more microeconomically underproductive, and may become macroeconomically depressed, or overheated. Contractions and overexpansions of outputs may be intensified, and isoquant levels diminished or augmented in ways that reduce utility, intensify factor misallocation, and worsen product misassortment. These distortions may be persistent or cyclical, amplifying or dampening the familiar boom–bust pattern characterized by intermittent periods of over- and under-full employment, under- and overinvestment, inflation and deflation, prosperity and depression. Supply thus may be gravely inefficient, even in the absence of other impediments.

Chronic governmental deficit budgetary expenditures (understated by various "off book" items) and mammoth loan and guarantee programs have diverted loanable funds from the domestic and global financial markets, increasing the price of credit (interest rates) and diminishing aggregate investment. Governmental provision of credit on pref-

---

[14]   The technologies embodied in the fixed capital stock cannot be radically altered in the short run. The only aspect of technology therefore that bears on efficiency is the degree to which technological improvements correspond with the optimum.

[15]   One of the principal functions of management is preventing avoidable underexertion.

erential terms to various constituents further harms financial efficiency. Likewise, permissive bankruptcy laws have encouraged excessive bad debts, saddling consumers with usurious rates on their credit card debt and other personal borrowing. Efforts at managing foreign currency rates, and international bailouts of Russia, Mexico, Thailand, Indonesia, and Korea, have primarily rewarded speculators.

Any supply side inefficiency, large or small, must degrade social welfare as category A theorists conceive it, because the community will have fewer goods and services in its shops, often with the wrong characteristics, in dispreferred assortments, or with less leisure than it could have enjoyed. And matters will be worse if the distribution of goods produced is inefficient and inequitable, and the utility the people derive from consumption, leisure, and the conduct of everyday life is impaired by other aspects of the system. Restrictions on personal freedom, including health, education, and access to information (government secrecy), constrain people's opportunities for self-improvement, while coercion, compulsion, and subjugation cause pain and suffering. The consequences of all these actions can be highlighted with the aid of community indifference curves overlain on the production frontier space in figure 7.5, the Edgeworth–Bowley consumption box illustrated in figure 7.6, and the social utility frontiers in figure 7.7.

Recalling that the competitive optimum is depicted by the joint tangency of the community indifference curve and the production possibilities frontier in figure 7.5 at point E, demand side inefficiency can be described as any aggregate consumption activity occurring on a community indifference curve lying beneath point E at point E'. This may be due to producers' inability to manufacture products with the characteristics the leaders and consumers desire, in the preferred assortments and volumes, but also to failures of wholesale and retail distribution, including import barriers.[16] If sales taxes make goods prohibitively expensive, goods are inequitably rationed (due to rent controls), are sold on a discriminatory basis to the elite (perks), and if excise taxes are too high, and fall disproportionately on specific groups (alcohol and tobacco), then the level of social utility will fall far

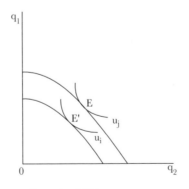

Figure 7.5 American consumption possibilities

---

[16]   In the real world, markets are often segmented in the sense that the same product will be sold at different prices in various locales. Discount stores routinely underprice their full service competitors. Insofar as such differentials are justified by the cost of delivering different levels of shopping experience, they are compatible with competitive principle, but often the price differential is disproportionate because of "velvet" coercion in the form of deceptive advertising and other malpractices.

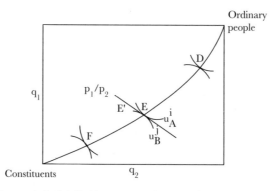

Figure 7.6 American retail distribution

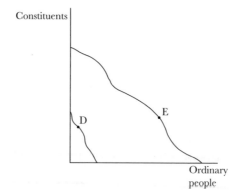

Figure 7.7 American utility possibilities

short of potential. These same distortions likewise may be macroeconomically disequili-
brating to the extent that they cause excess or deficient aggregate effective demand.

The distribution of the gross domestic product may be impaired for other reasons. If some
participants are unusually lax in sensing, searching, evaluating, and negotiating market
consumption opportunities, or are prohibited from effectively communicating their preferences to retailers, consumption will not occur in figure 7.6 (where "constituents" and the
"ordinary people" are depicted respectively on the lower and upper origins) at point E on
the contract curve because purchasing power is misallocated, and will lie off the curve if
Paretian negotiations are incomplete. Also, by analogy with the isoquants in the Edgeworth–
Bowley production box, indifference curve levels may be renumbered downward if the
stresses of state-managed markets diminish the enjoyment of those shouldering the burden.

These distributive inefficiencies are compounded by the concentration of income,
usufruct (state revenues from all sources appropriated for personal use), wealth, and
power in the hands of the elite, making it difficult for ordinary people to get by. This is
illustrated in figure 7.6 by forced movements away from point E toward D (where
constituents receive an unjustly large share of GDP) along the contract curve, or off it at
point E'. It diminishes social welfare by misdistributing goods and services without proper
regard for productivity, need, or merit.

America's record is not as good as it should be. As in other aspects of economic activity, market forces are warped by compulsion and anticompetitive forces giving special constituents disproportionate shares of national income, accompanied by enormous waste and inefficiency. Government misregulation and oligopolistic competition usurp leisure, impede job mobility, misdistribute purchasing power and service access, distort terms of purchase, and constrict choice through forced product and characteristics substitution, and curtail personal liberty.

Figure 7.7, which arrays constituents on the ordinate and the ordinary man on the abscissa, illustrates this outcome by comparing the achieved American social utility frontier with the category A ideal. It indicates that the average quality of American life at point D is far below its potential, with constituents and many deservingly affluent faring well compared with the plight of the common man.

Privileged constituencies have been able to sustain their grip on the American economy because they have successfully persuaded the nation that prosperity depends on treating them preferentially rather than promoting impartial category A general market equilibrium. Until this misconception is dispelled, America's standard of living will remain below competitive potential, and achieved per capita GDP growth will be retarded by the colossal burden of constituent government, despite robust entrepreneurship and aggressive management.

Review

Main Features Of the American Economic System

Culture:	Democratic–patrician/individualist–dependent, historical roots in the Enlightenment idealism of the American revolution, aristocratic notions of governance; the frontier spirit and the inequities of the industrial revolution.
Motivation:	Individual utility-seeking, often constrained by authorities and special interests.
Mechanisms:	Imperfectly competitive markets. Taxable income and wealth partly transferred to motivated constituencies through government programs, tax incentives, subsidies, regulations, controls, and grants.
Institutions:	Private ownership, corporations, antitrust legislation, lobbies, representative democracy, state administration, "rule of law."

Main Inefficiencies

Law of demand:	Individual preferences are often distorted by governmental and special constituency advocacy, government programs, tax misincentives, subsidies, regulations, controls, transfers, and unearned incomes which warp effective demand.

Law of
supply: Labor supply curves are strong functions of compensation and
                 career building, and weak functions of obligation and loyalty.
                 Enterprises respond to these influences, stressing insider profit-
                 maximizing. Entrepreneurship is vibrant.

Law of
equilibration: Markets are imperfectly competitive.
                 The economy is monetized, with little barter.
                 Employment, wholesaling, and retailing are dominated by
                 Walrasian processes.

                 Production is governed by the Marshallian mechanism, and is
                 reasonably effective even though profit-seeking is affected by
                 insider interests and government misregulation.

                 Keynesian macro-stabilization is supposed to be impartial,
                 although monetary and fiscal policies may sometimes be influenced
                 by political, bureaucratic, and constituent interests.

The state manages the market, and provides administrative services.

Rationale for State Economic Management

Topic	Problem	State response
Private property	Sometimes generates unearned quasi-rents	Equal opportunity programs, regulations, transfers
	Disregards community and stakeholders' interests	State regulation, stakeholder advocacy
Insider management	Preference given to insider interests, diminishing shareholder profit-maximizing	Rule of law, enforcement of fiduciary responsibility
Monopoly, oligopoly	Coercive terms of trade, misallocated resources	Antitrust legislation
Representative democracy	Inefficient and inequitable constituent lobbying	Restrictions on campaign contributions and other ineffectual methods

Systemic Structure

	Share of GDP	Productivity	Coercion (Destructiveness)
Markets			
Perfect markets	2	High	None
Inefficient markets	25	Medium	Low
Collusive markets	45	High	Mild
Government	25	Medium	Medium
Obligation			
Criminal disservices	3	–	(Medium)

Systems Characteristics

	Degree/Intensity
State macro-regulation	High
State micro-regulation	
Pro-competitive	High
Elite	Medium
Welfare/security	Medium
State spending programs	
Privileged contracting	Medium
Misappropriation	Low
Cronyism	Medium
Criminal disservices	
Asset seizure and Embezzlement	Low
Addiction/vice	Medium
Repression, extortion	Low
Subjugation and servitude	Low
Causes of macroeconomic disequilibria	
Sticky wages	Medium
Sticky prices	Medium
Pessimistic expectations	Medium
Misinvestment	Low
Liquidity preference	Medium
Insecure property rights	Low
State property rights	Low
Foreign capital flows	Low
Fear of criminality	Low
Anticompetitive business repression	Low
General business repression	Low
Labor subjugation	Low
Judicial risk	Low

State corruption	Low
Macropolicy mismanagement	Medium
Class conflict	Low

Main Performance Indicators

Per capital GDP 1998 (US = 100)	100
Per capita GDP growth 1990–99	
(compound annual rate)	2.0
Per capita GDP growth 1960–1990	
(compound annual rate)	1.5
Inflation 1990–99	3.0
Unemployment 1999	
Share of labor force	4.3
(instantaneous rate: considered over-full employment)	
Retirement burden	Low (growing)
Nonworking mothers and wives	Medium

Recommended Direction of Reforms

Sustaining and increasing prosperity through diminished government programming, micro-regulation, and constituent transfers, while restraining oligopolistic concentration, and narrowing disparities of income and wealth.

Review Questions

1. What is "neutral" macroeconomic management? Give one example of neutral fiscal and one example of neutral monetary policy. Which is likely to be more neutral, a tax cut or a change in the discount rate? Why?
2. What is "fair competition?" Under what conditions can affirmative action be reconciled with "fair" perfect competition? Explain.
3. It is sometimes said that "consumer sovereignty" is a corollary of democracy. What does consumer sovereignty mean? How is it achieved in perfect markets? Given Arrow's Paradox, can consumer sovereignty be achieved through balloting? If not which mechanism better serves people's demand, markets or ballots?
4. What is the relationship between the New Deal policy of "fair trade" and "fair competition"?
5. Make a second best case for government programs, given Arrow's Paradox. How can you tell if outcomes claimed to be second best really are superior?
6. Why do free enterprise theorists believe that market inefficiencies are more easily diminished than governmental inefficiencies?
7. Suppose that the state withdraws from the social security business, requiring people to privately invest a portion of their income, and provides welfare assistance for those falling through the cracks. Analyze the costs and benefits from the perspectives of efficiency and social welfare.

8. Why should there be a correlation between government misadministration and mismanagement and the productive attitudes of the people?

9. In what ways does American culture encourage exertion beyond what Aristotle would have considered the golden mean?

10. Americans criticize "managed trade" and call their private sector free enterprise. Why is this a misnomer? How is "free enterprise" managed?

11. How does the rule of law deter the government from destroying private business through excessive mismanagement?

12. Does obligation play any role in the American system? Why is it less than in Continental European corporatism?

13. How does American state management affect private demand?

14. Explain why American enterprises do not profit maximize in the sense required by general competition.

15. How does "economic engagement" differ from arms-length, golden rule abiding competition? Is the American system one in which the state and business "play" one another?

16. Why is the efficiency of the Walrasian adjustment mechanism impaired in the American labor market?

17. Why is the efficiency of the Marshallian adjustment mechanism impaired in the American production market?

18. Macrotheorists are usually proud of America's post-Great Depression performance. Why are these accomplishments exaggerated?

19. How would America's market structure change if the system were perfectly competitive? Would the role of obligation increase?

20. Why do economists consider the American system a smashing success?

21. Why do critics disagree? Who is right? Why?

22. Why is the locus of joint tangencies in the Edgeworth–Bowley production box (figure 7.2) Pareto efficient?

23. Why do factor and output prices differ at every point along the contract curve?

24. Does it matter if the isoquants are not the highest attainable?

25. How are the dimensions of the sides of the Edgeworth–Bowley production box determined?

26. What is "economic" inefficiency? How does it differ from "technical" efficiency?

27. Why does the American economy operate at point E'' in figure 7.4?

28. How do government "characteristic" mandates diminish market efficiency? How is this expressed in figure 7.2?

29. How does financial inefficiency affect outcomes in the short and long term in figure 7.4?

30. During the New Deal "fair trade" laws prohibited retail discounting. Explain why this was inefficient using figure 7.6.

31. The American system's stress on work and consumerism camouflages its inefficiencies. Explain why welfare would be higher under perfect competition.

CHAPTER 8

CONTINENTAL EUROPE

Continental Europe is an advanced industrial region with a skilled and literate work force, and modern capital stock. It is defined in this text as the European Union, an amalgam of diverse, corporatist-oriented subcultures excluding Great Britain and Ireland, where the rule of contract law and entrepreneurship still takes precedence over corporatism. The region is in the midst of a liberalization and integration wave intended to create an economic union capable of emulating America's entrepreneurially driven high-tech revolution. It collectively possesses strong military capabilities, has extensive multinational economic interests, and produces nearly a quarter of the global gross domestic product. Its postwar per capita GDP growth, although comparatively robust, has been waning for nearly 40 years, falling below the American standard in 1993, despite integration and monetary union. Involuntary unemployment has risen reciprocally to double digit levels, without any clear signs of imminent relief.

The Continental European economic system is an increasingly open category B market economy which blends individualism with corporatism. It features private ownership of the means of production, and negotiated price-setting including wages, interest, and foreign exchange rates. The governments of the region are representative social democracies, concerned with preserving and modernizing the socialist oriented institutions which emerged in the late 19th century. State elites try to balance and harmonize the contending interests of business and labor. The system stresses regulated, socially responsible enterprise at the expense of entrepreneurship, combined with activist government programs costing more than 10 percent of global national income. Egalitarianism is an important goal. Excessive demands by corporatist interest groups for government services violate the golden rule restraint essential for category A self-regulating systems, as do corporatist controls which infringe the rule of contract law. The government participates in the economy through its programs, micro-regulations, tax policies, subsidies, controls, and transfers administered by national bureaucracies and the European Union. Criminality and corruption are widespread, mild in Denmark, pronounced in Italy, but less destructive than in Russia. Although, the Continental European and Anglo-American models remain distinct, liberalization is gradually blurring the boundaries that divide them.

Continental European laws of supply, demand and equilibration are consistent with personal utility-maximizing, distorted by corporatist collusion and state economic harmonization. Collusion generates excess profits, but this is subsidiary. The laws of supply, demand, and equilibration are also warped by misgovernance and elite privilege. The Walrasian, Marshallian, and Keynesian adjustment mechanisms function adequately within these constraints, but not enough to arrest Euro-sclerosis (hardening of the economic arteries).

Opinions about the merit of Continental European social democracy vary. Some laud its mix of highly motivated individual utility self-seeking, business liberalization, elitism, social consciousness, collectivism, environmentalism, social protectionism, and egalitarianism. Others, while acknowledging its humanitarian aspirations, criticize these national systems and the EU for their anticompetitiveness, antientrepreneurial effort suppressing biases which encourage dependency and freeriding, elite privilege, corruption, and egalitarian injustice. They claim that statist systems act as if the people exist to serve the elite, and not vice versa. Both visions are compatible with compassionate governance, but the efficiency and motives of those running the state, and private corporatist institutions, are construed differently.

THE CONTINENTAL EUROPEAN ECONOMIC SYSTEM

Culture

Continental Europe, arguably defined for the purposes of systemic classification as the contemporary European Union excluding Britain and Ireland, has been a principal seat of Western culture and civilization for at least 2,500 years. Its contributions to philosophy, religion, arts, architecture, science, technology, literature, and statecraft from the pre-Socratic Greeks to the present have been impressive, and contemporary living standards are near the global frontier. For almost 200 years after the start of the industrial revolution in England, Continental Europe rapidly modernized, outperforming the rest of the world, producing disparities in economic and military power. Continental Europeans are self-confident. They believe that the European Union assures their continued prosperity, despite symptoms of Euro-sclerosis (devitalizing hardening of the arteries, preceding heart failure), and that integration (centralized European economic governance) and liberalization (freeing business from superfluous government regulation) will solve their economic problems. But they are divided about how this will be accomplished. Liberals hold that the European Union will enable the continent to shed its corporatist legacy, while opponents expect it to empower social democracy.

The Continental European economy today is a culturally regulated category B social democratic market system which combines elements of individualism with corporatist and state strategies of social protection. It arose in the late 19th century and evolved thereafter as an attempt to reconcile individualism (both mercenary and humanistic aspects) with state social protection, professional alliances, managed commerce, national and communal ownership, and socialism. Individualism makes Continental Europeans autonomous, often aggressively self-seeking, materialist, and sometimes anarchistic (anti-state, anti-authoritarian, and even anti-private property) in line with the precepts of 19th-century radicals like Nikolai Bakunin, Pierre-Joseph Proudhon, and Georges Sorel.[1] Collectivism makes them dependent, security minded, and submissive to group authority and obligation. These contradictory tendencies have been harmonized over the centuries by the evolution of corporatism, a set of institutions and relations which permit citizens to privately own the means of production, to utility and profit seek in the marketplace, subject to collectivist controls and obligations. The term corporatism is used to describe the behavior of groups generically called "corporations," and as a shorthand for elite economic sovereignty. Corporations are voluntary associations of individuals seeking to better themselves through mutual support. They include guilds, professional associations, trade union organizations, business corporations, bank affiliates, and cartels. Their role is to discipline members, while promoting their political interest. Members do not submerge their identities in communes; they are only self-interestedly loyal. This solidarity diminishes factiousness, promotes order and skill, enhances authority, and ameliorates societal conflict, while reverence for state authority allows the elites (often descended from the aristocracy) to tax the population more heavily than in America to disregard some constituencies in favor of others, and to meddle in the marketplace. The term statist describes the elites' use of state authority to control social behavior.

State elites and corporatist interest group intervention pervades every aspect of economic activity, subordinating the rule of contract law essential for individualist, self-regulating category A economic systems. Their behavior reflects ethical principles partly at variance with Adam Smith's concept of voluntary, sympathetic charity. The market is managed by government mandates, regulations, wage/price controls, and transfers. These policies are supposed to benefit everyone. Corporations are said to gain from worker enthusiasm, loyalty, legal protections, state contracts, and government macroeconomic regulation, including the erection of nontariff barriers to foreign competition. Workers are supposed to win by gaining improved job security, labor conditions, superior wages, and stakeholder participation, and everyone is expected to be grateful for corporatist promotion of the collective good.

All parties give and take. In return for state assistance, Continental European firms agree to restrictions on the length of the workday, layoffs, and protection against dismissals, and generous vacation, and retirement benefits. They accept affirmative action programs, and relinquish some managerial autonomy to worker participation. They accept excess labor costs of minimum wages, compulsory retirement, heavy medical, and other social insurance costs, as well as bearing the expense of fringe benefits, mandated conditions of

---

[1]   Georges Sorel, *The Illusions of Progress*, University of California Press, Berkeley, 1969; Michael Bakunin, Marxism, *Freedom and the State*, Freedom Press, New York, 1950; P.J. Proudhon, *Idè General de la Revolution Aux XIX Siecle*, Garnier Fères, Paris, 1851.

employment, and compulsory overtime payments. Workers in return are supposed to labor skillfully and energetically for employers, state, and society.[2]

Continental Europeans recognize that these policies may have various negative effects. Job rights and work restrictions impair efficiency, depress effort, and encourage free-riding.[3] But advocates believe that these costs are offset by corporatist solidarity, professional pride, and civic responsibility.

The same rationale justifies intervention in other factor markets. Variable capital, fixed assets, and land are all subject to rationing and regulation, even though this diminishes production potential and efficiency. Likewise, corporatism impairs competitive profit-maximizing. Corporatist enterprises deploy their assets in their members' collective interest, rather than for the benefit of shareholders, subordinating shareholders' equity returns to diverse corporatist purposes. If it suits members they select inefficient technologies, produce obsolete goods, and lavishly support community stakeholders. All these distortions diminish enterprise performance. Supply costs are not minimized, demand is not optimally satisfied, and new capital formation is discouraged by pessimistic investor expectations.

Corporatists try to offset these losses by forming cartels, or using affiliated banks to manage competition. Markets are segmented, and wages and prices regulated for the benefit of affiliated groups. These actions are said to promote stability and facilitate planning, creating healthy companies with deep pockets that are engines of long-term economic growth, despite the high costs of corporatist innovation, and collectivist barriers to entrepreneurship. Corporatists claim that the diminished business risks associated with cartel-managed competition give their firms advantages over competitive rivals in financing research, developing new products, and delivering them to the market, insisting that Continental European growth prospects are superior. This belief is central to the social democratic vision, because it implies that the microeconomic efficiency costs of corporatism and collectivism are recouped by rapid economic development and a high quality of life. Corporations, cartels, professional associations, and trade unions are able to have their cake and eat it. They are not only more dynamic than free enterprise, they are more stable and just as well.

The early postwar economic performance of Continental Europe appeared to justify this optimism, much to the surprise of Anglo-American theorists who believed corporatism was just a rationalization for protectionism. They anticipated that corporatist restrictions and transfers would impair labor mobility and productivity, reduce labor participation, aggravate unemployment, and diminish competitiveness. They expected capital restrictions to harm production potential, and state ownership to depress productivity.

Continental Europe's initial postwar successes, and the convergence of its GDP per man–hour toward the American norm, prompted second thoughts, but then things began

---

[2] Under category A, laissez-faire employment is voluntary and flexible. Workers master skills, choose occupations, and determine the hours they will work based on the wage structure, and what is termed their labor–leisure tradeoff. They will only offer their services up to the point where the utility derived from their last dollar earned is equal to the satisfaction obtained from spending the same time at leisure. Employers for their part only hire workers with specific skills if the revenue generated from their labor equals or exceeds their wages. Management does not "marry" labor. It does not have any extended obligation to employees. When the revenue created by labor dips below cost for whatever reason, some employees will be dismissed. When it rises, employment expands.

[3] American private enterprise suffers from many of these same maladies, but the Continental European manifestations are more virulent.

to fall apart, despite favorable developments like the emergence of the European Union which widened member markets, and the burgeoning of global free trade. As Anglo-American theorists predicted, growth decelerated toward stagnation (although the waning of the postwar catch-up effect may also be partly to blame). Corporatist duty withered, replaced by various forms of free-riding as people discovered that the state would pay them not to work if they were dismissed, could not find a job, or chose early retirement. Unemployment rose to double digits, temporarily exceeding 20 percent in Spain (although this figure is said to be exaggerated by fraudulent unemployment misregistration), partly because of the availability of generous unemployment benefits, but also because corporate costs of dismissal became so high that it was prohibitively expensive to stay fully staffed.

Statesmen have responded by emulating aspects of the Anglo-American model: curbing the growth of public expenditures, cutting marginal tax rates, encouraging liberalized work rules, paring unfunded benefits, denationalizing most industries, welcoming investment from abroad, and pushing ahead with European integration, including monetary union. This has triggered a merger mania driving equities to astronomical heights, but despite the blurring of the boundaries between the Anglo-American and corporatist systems has failed to re-accelerate aggregate economic growth, establish Continental European technological leadership, reduce open and concealed involuntary unemployment, or improve rates of labor participation.

Continental Europe's leftward political drift in the late 1990s suggests that this deteriorating economic performance will not be blamed on corporatism or social democracy, and that reforms will not obliterate the distinctions between the Atlantic and Continental systems. The motivations, mechanisms, and institutions that govern demand, supply, and equilibration will all continue to differ importantly from those assumed in the Anglo-American tradition, creating a system where the statist elite and corporatists are sovereign. Statist–corporatist preferences based on a few universalist shared values dominate at all levels of society from households, to neighborhoods, local communities, voluntary organizations, cooperatives, unions, professional associations, businesses, cartels, government administrative agencies, and the institutions of democratic governance. It is their preferences that shape the broad pattern of effective demand and define the sense in which the Continental European system is micro- and macroeconomically governed. The system can be conceptualized as a two-tier mutual support model integrating state regulation with corporatist protectionism. Elites in both tiers enjoy a life of privilege, while ordinary people make do in their protected niches. European Union institutions add another multinational coordinative tier.

Mechanisms and Institutions

The Continental European economic system is a composite of three primary mechanisms, a competitive market core founded on private ownership, state management, and corporatist obligation. Its markets are imperfect. Government management is social democratic without central planning, and obligations are fixed by local associations and society. Corporatist profit-seeking substitutes for competitive profit-maximizing.

The institutional components of these mechanisms have been crafted to facilitate the achievements of the system's goals. Guilds, professional associations, worker councils, corporatist enterprises, cartels, corporatist friendly laws, indicative planning, semiprivate corporations, occasional state ownership of basic industries, statist social welfare programs, regulation, administration, and the European Union are its key elements. No institution is decisive. They all play an important role.

Demand and Supply

Continental Europeans adhere broadly to the law of demand. They form preferences. Their demand is an inverse function of price, given their budget constraints. The market baskets purchased are price sensitive. Preferences are usually consistent, and they try not to overpay. But, their consumption behavior is also influenced by social democratic economic management and corporatist obligation of everything from housing to banning Russian paper produced under eco-unfriendly conditions. Attitudes toward work and job choice are affected by the same forces. Corporatism instills a pride in workmanship, but Continental European culture also views work as drudgery, prompting its labor force to work significantly less than Japanese and Americans.

The law of supply is modified for similar reasons. The technologies of nearly all firms exhibit diminishing marginal productivity and increasing marginal cost throughout stage II. Individuals and businesses understand the virtues of exchange, offering their labor, creating value added, starting entrepreneurial ventures, innovating, hiring factors, economizing costs, improving technology, product design and financing, advertising, and marketing their products. They appreciate efficient administration, and planning. But corporatist obligations and state economic management often compel them to disregard the law of labor and product supply, distorting production and distribution, and frequently discouraging effort. Labor and managerial supply are only partial functions of wages, altered by corporatist and statist obligations, pride of workmanship, and free-riding.

Profit-maximizing in Continental Europe is imperfect. Proprietors and corporations must accommodate their concern for the bottom line to state and corporatist rules and regulations, and consider oligopolistic coordination a duty and right. This does not stop managers and businessmen from pioneering new ventures, innovating, investing in research, development, testing and evaluation (RDT & E), hiring and training promising personnel, carefully selecting technologies, modernizing, economizing variable input costs, conducting market research, setting prices, and selling their products to earn sufficient revenue. But none of these activities is carried out solely to maximize the stream of private discounted shareholders' dividends. Business is a social process that requires mutual accommodation. Entrepreneurial ambition, innovation, and modernization are tempered to satisfy group, shareholder, and stakeholder risk aversion, partly offset by state subsidies and programs. RDT & E and corporate growth tend to be overemphasized to provide intra-corporate mobility. Enterprise demand for labor is biased by corporatist job rights guarantees and state work management including unemployment assistance. Whether firms circumvent these regulations by underemploying labor, or retaining workers too long to avoid severance costs, managers do not maximize shareholders' profits as market opportunities dictate. And, of course, internal corporatist work rules have the same effect. Reassignment involves complex issues of labor protocol, not merely productive efficiency. While Continental Europeans for historical–cultural reasons can be hard-working, collectivist mutual support often deflects attention from the business of profit-maximizing. Insider control encourages inter-firm collusion to protect the members at the expense of outsiders including shareholders. Corporatist enterprises, and statist policy-makers, evade competitive market discipline, diminishing rates of return and the efficient economy-wide allocation of capital. The extent of these losses, and the moral hazard associated with insider control, are partly offset by oligopoly profits, and government assistance. Returns on equity are not as low as corporatist insider misincentives might suggest. In essence, discrimination against outsiders (including non-EU trade partners) and state assistance financed by high taxes keep Continental European firms financially viable.

Equilibrium

All these convoluted restraints, anticompetitive practices, and tax transfers affect equilibration. Continental European corporatism prevents Walrasian, Marshallian, and Keynesian market adjustment mechanisms from reconciling individual demand and supply programs (including holdings of idle cash balances), given budget constraints at competitively negotiated prices. Guilds, professional associations, unions, companies, cartels, and the statist elite are able to reach agreements, but the equilibria achieved do not optimize utility because the terms of demand and supply are not fully negotiated internally or externally. Equilibria are second best and depend on the completeness of harmonization at every level.

Another way to look at the same phenomenon is to recognize that the Continental European economic system has five distinct market equilibration mechanisms; the familiar Walrasian, Marshallian, and Keynesian trio, plus insider corporatist group negotiation and state intercorporatist coordination. The supplementary mechanisms sacrifice competitive efficiency for group security and the statist social agenda, at the expense of competitive efficiency. The Walrasian mechanism is impaired because barriers like job sharing prevent factor and product prices from allocating inputs optimally to alternative use among occupations and firms, while collusive price-fixing creates shortages and gluts in wholesale and retail supply.

The Marshallian production adjustment mechanism is impaired because competitive profit-maximizing is subordinated to other goals, including protectionism. Continental European firms can and do respond to outside demand, but supplies – influenced as they are by corporatist–statist obligation and moral hazard – cannot correspond to a full utility-maximizing equilibrium either for insiders or outsiders.

The impact of corporatism on Keynesian processes is negative. Corporatist mutual support, accommodation, and collusion in the productive sector, and dependence on state assistance, mutes income multiplier effects by encouraging corporations to honor their collectivist commitments to shelter workers against fluctuations in aggregate effective demand and imposing heavy layoff and severance costs on enterprises. This protects those with jobs, but discourages hiring new job-seekers and the unemployed. Statist institutions create jobs that should not exist, and corporatist solidarity (and statist penalties) make internal enterprise adjustments more attractive than dismissal. Other shocks which could easily destabilize category A competitive macrosystems by diminishing business confidence, the marginal efficiency of capital, and sparking speculative demand for idle cash balances are mitigated by unemployment insurance, and accommodative monetary and fiscal policies, as well as through inter-firm cartel coordination and collusion. Continental European corporatist enterprises, like their Anglo-American counterparts, look to the state to increase public spending programs, encourage consumer spending, cut business and household taxes, offer subsidies, adjust interest rates, stabilize exchange rates, manipulate nontariff import barriers, augment money supply, and do whatever else is required to bolster aggregate effective demand, and promote steady long-term growth. But this entrenches insider inefficiency and moral hazard, preventing the market from realizing its competitive category A potential, and has not solved Continental Europe's chronic unemployment and growth retardation.

Systemic Structure

All of these distortions are reflected in Continental Europe's systemic structure and its special performance characteristics. The heart of the Continental European economy is its medium- and large-scale industrial and commercial corporatist enterprises, which are productive enough to support insider protectionism, stakeholder assistance, and huge tax support to the state. They are the most dynamic element of the system, even though they tend to be anti-entrepreneurial. They generate the largest share of the GDP, because state protection enables them to realize economies of scale. The second largest component of the Continental European economies is their enormous public sectors. Privatization in the 1990s has substantially reduced government production, but other aspects of the welfare state remain, including universal health care, a vast array of municipal and social services, and of course activist government economic regulation. Continental Europe in the monarchical tradition has a relatively well-trained, competent, and efficient administrative bureaucracy, but its diligence is no surrogate for profit-maximizing, and is necessarily underproductive compared with the private sector. Obligation plays a constructive role through corporatist mutual support, while criminal compulsion exerted by the Mafia and others is a serious negative.

Continental Europe has no perfectly competitive markets, and its underproductive small-scale ventures, shops and farms, while relatively inefficient, are stabilized by custom and national corporatist obligation. State regulators assist small underproductive enterprises by granting them zoning and other preferences, and in the case of agriculture heavy subsidies. Entrepreneurship could make the competitive components of this imperfectly competitive sector more dynamic, but is tacitly discouraged. Statism–corporatism thus not only influences the performance characteristics of the components of the Continental European system; it explains the pattern of their interplay and the stability of its structure. Economic activity is predominantly statist–corporatist, rather than individual utility-maximizing. Businesses, the state bureaucracy, and criminal organizations are all enmeshed in the fourth and fifth ways; corporatist accommodation and statist management.

The main effects of Continental Europe's brand of corporatism, balancing individualism with mutual support, are evident. It has created a highly productive, but increasingly effort demobilizing pro-leisure and free-riding ethic, strongly encouraged by egalitarian tax transfers. This differs strikingly from Japan, where the inefficiencies caused by egalitarianism and moral hazard are offset by the communalist work ethic and group ethical obligation. The Continental European system also has a conspicuously bloated public sector compared with Japan, and lacks potent consensus building mechanisms needed to achieve social harmonization. Nonetheless, social democracy in Continental Europe has stabilized macroeconomic fluctuations, promoted growth and provided its people with a first-tier standard of living, and a relatively low level of market destructive crime. Insofar as Continental Europeans feel that the costs of statism–corporatism are justified, the system has succeeded. Many Continental European intellectuals view matters precisely this way, mirroring Masahiko Aoki's assessment of Japan. They argue that social democracy is more efficient than the category A competitive market ideal because it harnesses the power of collectivism to inspire effort; mitigates labor management conflict and class antagonisms; nurtures group knowledge; promotes quality, modernization, and innovation; coordinates and plans in an environment of trust; takes stakeholder interests including those of the community (environmental concerns) directly into account; risk shares; and regulates specific and aggregate effective demand, creating attitudes of civic and social responsibility.

But proponents of individualism, liberalization, and American-style globalization reject this characterization. From their cultural perspective statist corporatism is intrinsically inferior. It makes the Continental Europeans underproductive, encourages dependency, free-riding, and an anti-work ethic; and imposes deeply resented group obligations that diminish the quality of existence. Moreover, they blame Continental Europe's pronounced growth retardation, and intractable double digit unemployment and underemployment, on the cumulating effects of statist–corporatist inefficiencies, including disguised protectionism, and have been urging the Continental Europeans to abandon all anticompetitive corporatist restraints on unfettered profit-seeking.

THE GEOMETRY OF CONTINENTAL EUROPEAN ECONOMIC CORPORATISM

The merit of these contending positions can be evaluated diagrammatically in all activities. Starting with the factor space we find that corporatist constraints and misincentives shrink the Edgeworth–Bowley production box (figure 8.1) and distort factor allocation. The supply of capital and labor are depressed and misallocated by the disincentives of the Continental European corporatist welfare state. Factor incomes are overtaxed, while unemployment, compassionate leave, retirement benefits, and social services are too generous. Factor prices frequently are above the competitive wage and rental rates, discouraging employment, and the rewards for leisure are excessive. Workers and capital suppliers are encouraged to take informal paid holidays by pretending to be unemployed, to take protracted sickness and maternity leaves, and to retire prematurely. Moreover, state wage regulations, including minimum wages and conditions of employment, together with corporatist professional restrictions, skew and segment compensation rates, distorting the allocation of factor services to alternative uses. State ownership of various assets tends to compound these problems because public enterprises have no incentive to maximize profits from current operations, or the present discounted value of the capital stock.

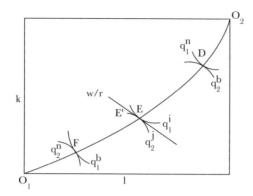

Figure 8.1   Continental European factor allocation

It is therefore hardly surprising that the German labor force participation rate, for example, is only 50 percent, compared with 67 percent in the United States. The number of man–hours labored by employed French workers is only 80 percent of the American norm. And unemployment rates in Continental Europe are double those in the United States.

Continental European corporatist firms and farms operate below their production possibilities because they do not competitively cost minimize, or produce to the point where marginal cost equals marginal revenue (or price when they are price-takers) because insiders are not accountable to outside shareholders. The isoquant levels within the production space have been reduced because capital and labor are misincentivized, misrewarded, and therefore misallocated and undersupplied. Factor prices are in competitive disequilibrium due to corporatist wage- and rent-fixing. These corporatist inefficiencies go beyond those of Anglo-American oligopoly, circumscribing production to a lower feasibility frontier at point R, where output is both technically and economically inefficient (figure 8.2).

The Continental European system is also dynamically inefficient because innovation and industrial pioneering threaten the collectivist social contract, the ability of cartels and the state to provide job security and other aspects of social protection. Unions, professional organizations, cartels, nongovernmental organizations, and the governments themselves create endless legal and administrative barriers, increasing entrepreneurial risk, while low returns to capital associated with insider control reduce rewards. These obstacles have not arrested technological progress and modernization, but they impair the pace and scope of change. The production point R (in figure 8.2) would be significantly higher if Continental European entrepreneurship were more robust.

The excessive involvement of Continental European banking and financial institutions in intercorporate, cartel, and governmental activities is another source of inefficiencies. If finances were competitively optimal, both the size and composition of the GDP would be improved. Continental European social democracy distorts demand in much the same way it does supply. People's purchasing power does not depend solely on their competitively earned wage and asset incomes; it is affected by discriminatory distribution and transfers. Consumers do not compete for goods and services on a level playing field because corporatism is a system of managed competition. This means the GDP (in figure 8.3) is divided between individuals A and B at either point D or F instead of the competitive

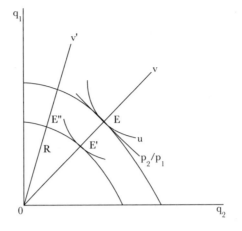

Figure 8.2   Continental European efficiency possibilities

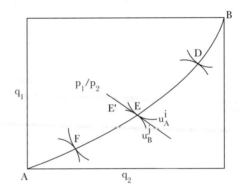

Figure 8.3   Continental European retail distribution

equilibrium E, if there were no price discrimination, or off the contract curve at point E'
due to discriminatory pricing. Some of these transfers may be justified in a category A
competitive welfare model, but the haphazardness of social democratic intergroup bargaining suggests that redistributions are inefficient.

The net effect of corporatist privilege, taxes, transfers, and public services is greater
equality and economic security than provided by free enterprise, achieved at the expense
of "Euro-sclerosis," unemployment, reduced productivity, and slow economic growth. For
those who esteem equality, it is possible to argue that Continental European social welfare
is higher than in a twin category A competitive system even though living standards are
inferior because the outcome is more socially just. But of course, Anglo-American theorists
counter argue that if the people were not bemused by the corporatist elites they would
prefer Pareto optimality.

Continental European elites appear to be broadly aware of the cost and benefits of
corporatism and have been trying to liberalize for more than a half century. They have

augmented the scope of the market and increased its competitive efficiency, using European integration as a device for eliminating intra-European tariffs and other nonprice barriers, and moving toward a currency union. Government and business have tried to alter corporatist culture by encouraging entrepreneurship, streamlining state regulation, and reducing some aspects of social protection. And the people have tried to cope themselves by modernizing their attitudes, expectations, and demands.

The marriage of social democracy and liberalized corporatism, however, has been disappointing. Continental European unemployment levels are double those of a decade ago, and growth has been halved, suggesting that there have been as many negative as positive adaptations even after making allowance for the waning catch-up effect. The possibilities for catch-up should have increased as American growth accelerated during the 1990s. While it is easy to image a perfect integration of free enterprise and corporatism, of individual initiative and elite regulation, apparently it is much harder to achieve. Nominal improvements in the scope and competitiveness of markets do not always amount to real progress, only new and dubious forms of manipulation. If this is so, corporatists, like Soviet communists a decade ago, will be compelled in the not too distant future to commit themselves indefinitely to a system that sacrifices wealth for over-regulation, or opt for free enterprise.

Review

Main Features of the Continental European Economic System

Culture: Democratic–elite/individualist–dependent. The mentality has deep historical roots in the contradictions between enlightened humanism, socialist collectivism, and aristocratic elitism. The class struggle precipitated by the industrial revolution, continuing through the third quarter of the 20th century, is another powerful influence. European socialist collectivism is built on guilt culture. This makes Europeans more autonomous, more entrepreneurial, and less consensual than the Japanese.

Motivation: Private sector individual utility-seeking subordinated to elite collectivist and private corporatist management.

Mechanisms: Corporatist competitive markets provide insider benefits to workers and managers, and taxable income for state programs. Government elites manage these programs and use them together with tax incentives, subsidies, regulations, controls, and transfers to advance social welfare.

Institutions: Private ownership, some state, municipal and cooperative ownership, corporatist enterprises, cartels, limited antitrust, "purity boards" which protect markets by setting special standards, elite institutions, representative democracy, strong trade unions, collectivist political parties, elite bureaucracies, the European Union, and the "rule of law."

Main Inefficiencies

Law of
demand: Individual preferences are often distorted by elite and corporatist
                 influences. Individuals must accommodate themselves to
                 corporatist agendas within firms and the community, and state elite
                 programs. Tax misincentives, subsidies, regulations, controls, and
                 transfers warp the distribution of effective demand. Collectivist
                 influences on demand are imposed from above without Japanese-
                 style consensus and direct participation. Popular opinion affects
                 elite preferences through representative democratic processes.

Law of
supply: Worker supply curves are strong functions of wages, and moderate
                 functions of corporatist obligation. Managerial supply curves are
                 strong functions of compensation, career building, and corporatist
                 obligation. Loyalty is more important on the Continent than in
                 America. Enterprises respond to these influences, stressing insider
                 interest and modified profit-maximizing.

Law of
equilibration: Markets are imperfectly competitive. Distribution is through the
                 market, rather than on an assignment basis. The economy is
                 monetized, with little barter. Marketing outside the state sector is
                 dominated by Walrasian processes, but the labor force is less
                 mobile than in America, partly due to state assistance programs.

                 Marshallian production equilibration is distorted by corporatist
                 and state influences, at the expense of profit-maximizing.

                 Keynesian macro-equilibration is encumbered by corporatist
                 rigidities, microeconomic complications associated with worker
                 protective and egalitarian welfare policies.

The state and corporations manage the market.

Rationales for Managing Free Enterprise and Liberalizing

Topic	Problem	State Response
Private property	Sometimes generates unearned quasi-rents, disregards community and stakeholders' interests	Partial state ownership, state regulation, state support for corporatism, and stakeholder advocacy
Corporatism	Diminishes allocative,	Cooperative partnership

			with state elites
		productive, and distributive efficiency	
	Cartels	Coercive terms of trade, misallocated resources	Cooperative partnership with state elites
	State ownership	Substitutes administrative discretion for profit-maximizing	Privatization initiative to reduce, and perhaps ultimately abolish state ownership
	Insider control	Preference given to insider interests, diminishing shareholder profit maximizing	Left to corporatist decision-making
	Elite-dominated democracy	Over-regulated, misregulated, sclerotic economy	Contradictory policy of elite power consolidation in the European Union, and liberalization

Systemic Structure

	Share of GDP	Productivity (Destructiveness)	Coercion
Markets			
Perfect markets	0	High	None
Inefficient markets	20	Medium	Low
Corporatist markets	42	Medium/high	Medium
Government	35	Medium	High
Obligation			
Criminal disservices	3	(Medium)	High

Systems Characteristics

	Degree/ Intensity
State macro-regulation	High
State micro-regulation	
Pro-competitive	Medium

Elite influence	High
Welfare/security	Very high/medium
State spending programs	
Privileged contracting	High
Misappropriation	Low
Cronyism	Medium
Criminal disservices	
Theft and	
embezzlement	Low
Addiction/vice	Medium
Repression, extortion, and murder	Low
Oppression and servitude	Low
Causes of macroeconomic disequilibria	
Sticky wages	High
Sticky prices	High
Investment risk aversion	Medium
Misinvestment	Medium
Liquidity preference	Medium
Insecure property rights	Low
State property rights	Medium
Foreign capital flows	Medium
Fear of criminality	Low
Business repression	Low
Labor oppression	Low
Judicial risk	Low
State corruption	Low
Macropolicy mismanagement	Medium
Class conflict	Medium

Main Performance Indicators

Per capita GDP 1998 (US = 100)	75
Per capita GDP growth 1990–99 (compound annual rate)	0.8
Per capita GDP growth 1960–99 (compound annual rate)	2.0
Inflation 1990–99	4.0
Unemployment 1999	11
Retirement support burden	Medium (growing)
Nonworking mothers and wives	Medium

Strategy of Economic Reform

Liberals believe that the European Union is supposed to provide a bridge from national corporatism to general competition. Collectivists see it as a strategy for pan-European social democracy.

Review Questions

1. Do liberals and corporatists have contradictory expectations about the European Union? Explain.
2. How does corporatism reconcile the contradictions between individualism and collectivism?
3. What institutions are included in the term "corporation" besides business corporations with unlimited life and limited liability?
4. What are the purported benefits of corporatism? What are its costs?
5. What is "statism?"
6. Do insider concerns take precedence over outside shareholders' interests under corporatism?
7. How does corporatism try to compensate for its microeconomic inefficiencies by forming cartels?
8. Why do social democrats believe that they do not have to curtail the welfare state, and need only pay lip service to improved entrepreneurship and profit incentives?
9. Have postwar economic trends borne out their optimism? Explain.
10. What liberalizing steps have been taken to reverse these adverse trends? Are these initiatives succeeding? If not, could corporatism and social democracy be to blame?
11. Who are the economic sovereigns of Continental Europe?
12. What are the three primary Continental European economic mechanisms?
13. What institutions are associated with these mechanisms?
14. How does corporatism modify the law of demand?
15. How does corporatism modify the law of supply?
16. Do discrimination against outsiders (including non-EU trade partners) and state assistance financed by high taxes keep Continental European firms financially viable? Explain.
17. Why is the efficiency of the Walrasian adjustment mechanism impaired in the Continental European labor market?
18. Why is the efficiency of the Marshallian adjustment mechanism impaired in the Continental European production market?
19. Why is the efficiency of the Keynesian adjustment mechanism impaired in the Continental European macrosystem?
20. How would Continental Europe's market structure change if the system were perfectly competitive? Would the role of obligation decrease?
21. Are inefficiencies caused by egalitarianism and moral hazard offset as they are in Japan by a communalist work ethic and group ethical obligation? Does communalism have an advantage over individualism in this regard?
22. Are the Japanese and Continental European public sectors roughly the same size? If they differ, why?
23. Why do some economists consider the Continental European system superior to America's?
24. Why do critics disagree? Who is right? Why?
25. Why is the Continental European factor space too small?
26. Why are Continental European isoquant levels beneath the competitive norm?
27. Why is the Continental European system dynamically inefficient?
28. If finances were competitively optimal, would the size and composition of the Continental European GDP improve?

29. Does point E' in figure 8.3 indicate that Continental European retailing is inefficient? Explain.

30. Why do Anglo-American theorists argue that if the Continental Europeans were not bemused by corporatist elites they would reject their egalitarianism in favor of Pareto optimality?

31. How does the marriage of social democracy and liberalized corporatism correspond with Chinese authoritarian laissez faire? Does this suggest that the long-term prospects for the Chinese are restricted? Explain.

32. Is it likely that the Continental Europeans will throw in the towel, and embrace free enterprise?

CHAPTER 9

JAPAN

Japan is a highly industrialized nation with a skilled and literate work force, and an immense capital stock. It has embarked on a "big bang" liberalization campaign, opening the economy to foreign investment and deregulating the private sector in order to keep pace with America. Japan's military provides an adequate homeland defense, but it cannot project its forces, and possesses only virtual nuclear capabilities. Its postwar per capita GDP growth, although comparatively robust, has been waning for nearly 40 years, falling below the American standard in 1993, and turning negative 1997–01. Involuntary unemployment has risen reciprocally, but not to the double digit levels that plague Continental Europe. Prospects for imminent relief are uncertain.

The economic system which produced these results is a culturally regulated category B imperfectly competitive market economy, founded on communally constrained individual utility-seeking, private ownership, and negotiated wages, interest, and foreign exchange rate setting. Communal influences are more important than the rule of contract law, subordinating market goals to obligation. Communalist ethics similarly displace the golden rule as the foundation of Japan's social contract. Japan's government is democratic, adhering to parliamentary principles enshrined in the constitution imposed by American occupation forces after the Second World War. The state influences the economy through its expenditure programs, macroeconomic regulation of monetary and fiscal policies, and its microeconomic administration and regulation of domestic and foreign economic activities, including substantial overseas assistance to less developed nations participating in projects with Japanese multinational corporations.

Japanese laws of supply, demand, and equilibration satisfy the core requirements of the utility-seeking paradigm using a mix of market and state regulatory mechanisms. Walrasian, Marshallian, and Keynesian adjustment processes function in the normal ways within these limits, modified by group preferences and communal decision-making. The communalist dimension of Japanese economic activity is pervasive. Communalist motivations, mechanisms, and institutions cause the laws of demand, supply, and equilibration to persistently generate results that depart from individualist, competitive, self-regulating market category A models. This is especially conspicuous in the policy of large Japanese firms employing workers for life, and in workers' willingness to labor long hours overtime without compensation.

Communalism also substantially relieves the state from the obligation of providing transfer income and services to the needy; a burden shifted to families and communities. And it keeps the anti-productive consequences of organized crime (Yakuza) within tolerable limits. Opinions about the merit of Japan's communalist category B strategy are sharply polarized. Some, like Masahiko Aoki, contend that the model is as good, and perhaps better than the individualist competitive market ideal, while others see Japan's current economic woes, including long-term growth retardation, negative growth, anemic entrepreneurship, and its inert response to stimulatory policy initiatives, as proof of its inferiority.

THE JAPANESE ECONOMIC SYSTEM

Culture

Japan has enjoyed a relatively high level of culture and civilization since the rise of the Yamato empire in the 7th century. Although insular, it has been profoundly influenced by Korean and Chinese arts, philosophy, religion, science, and concepts of governance from the founding of Nara to the modern period. Western arts and ideas played a significant role from the early 17th century, filtering into Edo (Tokyo), the seat of Tokugawa power through the port of Nagasaki on Kyushu. Japan's rapid ascent from a comparatively underdeveloped nation at the time of the Meiji restoration in 1868 to one of the world's great economic powers, with a living standard that rivals America's, and exceeds Russia's and China's by more than sixfold, thus did not materialize out of thin air. But it still surprises many theorists, because the Japanese culturally regulated category B system violates all the axioms of general competition.

The uniqueness of the Japanese system does not lie in what is often loosely termed "Asian values," but in the specific way Japan's shame-based communalist culture combines Shinto, Buddhism, Confucianism, Korean, and Chinese values with Western market principles to achieve superior economic performance. Unlike the individualist West, where people cultivate and assert the priority of their own preferences guided by universalist concepts of right and wrong (guilt culture), with little concern for contrary opinion, the Japanese operate the other way round. They actively participate in the formation and inculcation of situational communal values through continual consensus building dialogue with peers and superiors, with only peripheral concern for universal principles of personal conduct. This participatory internalization profoundly affects the Japanese approach to economic activity. The market is not a vehicle for competitively maximizing individual utility potential, or promoting human rights, and entitlements subject to a social contract enshrining the golden rule as a founding principle. It is a mechanism that facilitates the achievement of some communal goals by allowing members limited autonomy. It is a liberalized version of the Tokugawa rice culture, which granted members some discretion in fulfilling their collaborative planting and harvesting obligations, while requiring other aspects of negotiated exchange strictly in conformity with communal custom. Modern production, commerce, and finance, which perpetuate these traditions in new forms, are not just self seeking business activities. They are identity affirming ritual and communal patterns of behavior, that take precedence over the rule of contract law and market efficiency, generating utility as much by process and mutual support as through the goods produced and consumed.

The communality of Japanese market activities is often misunderstood. Many equate it with Continental European corporatism, where professional and business groups collaborate to promote their individual material interests. Some even confuse it with welfare states, misportraying the Japanese government as the guardian of the disadvantaged and providing arms-length aid to the poor. But the Japanese are not primarily concerned with using groups to promote personal advancement, or the state as an agent for the needy. They are more interested in protecting and preserving their community and national culture. This can be seen most clearly in the Japanese propensity to hire employees for life, instead of accepting cyclical involuntary unemployment and cushioning it with unemployment relief. Japanese communalism requires that members' problems be addressed directly; not delegated anonymously to "society," or advocacy groups. Consequently, employees consider themselves team players. They voluntarily work overtime without complaint or extra compensation, whereas in the West the length of the workday and overtime compensation are an integral part of the process of negotiated, individual utility-maximizing.

These and other differences are matters of degree. The Japanese are not completely co-dependent, deferential, self-sacrificing, hard-working, consultative, or anti-entrepreneurial; they just exhibit these traits more strongly than others. Japanese economic activity is not exclusively communalist; it is skewed toward communally guided market, intra-group, and leisure utility-seeking, including communitarian bureaucratic administration and crime (Yakuza), whereas individual self-advancement and pleasure are the guiding light of markets and leisure activities in the West.

The power of Japanese communalism is often unappreciated because observers do not grasp the inner logic of the shame principle, and misconstrue contradiction as a fault. Shame cultures do not have clearly defined universal ethical systems. Right and wrong, good and evil, are not carved in the stone of Mount Sinai. They are situational precepts which depend on group attitudes. The commandments read "thou shall not commit adultery under conditions which could shame the group," not "Thou shall not commit adultery."

When group members violate communal norms or let the group down, they are criticized, censured, and punished for disloyalty, not for committing sins against God or reason. The pain felt from the fear, and reality, of group chastisement is the sting of shame, and its social purpose is to make the group's goals and welfare the arbiter of personal conscience, rather than individual allegiance to universal ethical principles. This has a profound effect on autonomy. Individuals in guilt cultures have independent moral compasses. They can function autonomously according to their precepts of right, heeding or disregarding group attitudes as need be. But personal behavior in shame societies, particularly those continuously reinforced by consensual participation, is much more circumscribed. People can act independently as they believe the group desires, but they are reluctant to act in any way that gives the appearance of challenging communal authority. Unlike Westerners, the Japanese do not rely on confession to disclose and correct their personal and business failings. They shun this corollary of guilt because it often causes needless group conflict. Instead, they are obligated to silently change bad behaviors, and as a last resort, when exposure is inescapable, apologize.

Western individualists, who bristle at the idea of surrendering their rights of independent action to group rules and welfare because it infringes their personal freedom, often assume that others will react negatively in similar situations. They are sometimes right, but these expectations are largely misplaced in the Japanese context because group values are less restrictive than they seem, and people are prepared to accept some curtailment in personal freedom to obtain other benefits.

On the surface, the Japanese are expected to conduct themselves in strict accordance with praiseworthy group values, under close scrutiny from others. During the Tokugawa era five spies were assigned to monitor the behavior of every citizen. Today the Japanese say "walls have ears." But, this rigidity is softened by each group's "shadow culture," complex sets of counter-values and deviant behaviors that are tacitly sanctioned by the group under well-defined circumstances. It is impolite to undermine the self-esteem of others by calling public attention to defects, yet the Japanese from Jomon times to the present have always sought to distinguish themselves with badges of rank in dress, manners, and speech that set them apart from those of lesser stature in the appropriate contexts. Rank and obligation which might seem to contradict communality are inextricable elements of the culture. Modesty, loyalty, and respect for others are prized, but this does not deter the avid pursuit of illicit *ukiyo-e* (floating world) pleasures. And, of course, while it is essential to conceal personal emotion on most occasions, and to avoid offense by telling others what they want to hear (*tatemae*), the Japanese can be as vivacious and frank as anyone else in the appropriate business, social, and personal circumstances.

These flexibilities provide safety valves which soften the burden of Japanese obligation and diminish resistance to group discipline. The secret of personal success and adaptation in Japan's shame culture is to master the situational rules, and adjust effortlessly like bamboo (strong, yet pliable) to the requirements of the moment so that the sacrifice of personal freedom is not too high a price to bear. This skill is not easily acquired. People do not always succeed and are often ridden with anxiety, fearing that they will misread subtle cues and contexts. But these difficulties which tend to make the Japanese cautious, are compensated by an unusual ability to take pleasure in small things, and activities westerners might find distasteful. Japanese know how to enjoy their work, its social context, and the sacrifices they make for collective welfare. Activities and associations that others find tedious provide substantial gratification, and enhance the system's appeal.

Japan's market economy therefore has not, and will not soon strictly adhere to the individualistic utility-seeking principles of the Western category A competitive self-regulating market paradigm or the category B culturally regulated counterparts, despite the claims of some universalists that there are no substantive differences between Japanese and American utility-seeking.[1] The motivation, mechanisms, and institutions that govern demand, supply, and equilibration all differ importantly from those assumed in Western classical theory, creating a system where groups rather than individuals are sovereign. Group preferences at all levels of society from households, work teams, government administrative agencies, parliament, and the emperor are determinative. They govern demand and define the sense in which the economy is micro- and macroeconomically

---

[1]   David Flath, *The Japanese Economy*, Oxford University Press, London, 2000; Magnus Blomström, Bryon Gangnes, and Summer La Croix, *Japan's New Economy*, Oxford University Press, London, 2001; T. Okazaki and M. Okuno-Fujiwara, eds, *Japanese Economic System and Its Historical Origins*, Oxford University Press, London, 2000; R. A. Hart and S. Kawasaki, *Work and Pay in Japan*, Cambridge University Press, Cambridge, 1999.

communal. The Japanese system can be conceptualized as a series of graduated concentric rings, like a Buddhist stupa where the widest element forming the base represents individuals who perceive themselves as active, consensual participants in a family-nation, upwardly linked with neighborhoods, communities, teams, firms, keiretsu, Keidanren, the state administrative bureaucracy, parliament, and the emperor. This arrangement not only shapes attitudes in every ring, but harmonizes actions throughout the hierarchy, making individual, group and community-wide behavior coherent. Control rests in the consultative process which sets group values and agendas, rather than in the hands of individuals. From a Western point of view, communal sovereignty may appear anti-libertarian and oppressive, but for many Japanese the pleasures of group identification and association are ample reward.

Mechanisms and Institutions

Japanese economic mechanisms have been crafted to facilitate its communal agenda. The organization of their markets, obligational exchange, the rules for entry and participation, the style of services, enterprise, and state governance are all group determined. "Time is not money" in Japan. Although aspects of Japanese economic mechanisms, the use of markets, plans, administration, regulation, and production for one's own account have points in common with those in other advanced industrial systems, their character is distinctive in accordance with the requirements of group etiquette and mores. They are inefficient from an individualistic utilitarian perspective, but appropriate for communitarian society.

This is most conspicuous in Japan's signature institutions like the "keiretsu" system of business-affiliated group economic coordination founded on cross-shareholding by related companies and their suppliers, which subordinate individual enterprise competition to the higher communal imperatives of consensus building and conflict avoidance. The Japanese dislike anonymous rivalry, and shun institutions which encourage it. If keiretsu suddenly disappear due to the legalization of holding companies in 1998, business preference for communal accommodation will not vanish. It will only be modified, just as in the past when other institutions like the zaibatsu (dominant firm system) faded into the woodwork.

Demand and Supply

The transfer of economic sovereignty from individuals to groups modifies but does not repeal the laws of demand and supply. Individual Japanese consumers, like everyone else, form preferences. Their demand is an inverse function of price, given their budget constraints. The assortments they purchase are sensitive to relative prices; their preferences are usually consistent, and they try to minimize the cost of their purchases. But their consumption behavior departs from this conventional paradigm in three striking ways. Consumers are unusually prone to substitute group preferences for their own, to find pleasure in things the group decides they should like, and to place a remarkably low value on personal leisure. These tendencies are easily observed in Japanese preference for group travel, company-organized recreation, and local products, and their uncomplaining acceptance of unpaid overtime work obligations.

The impact of communalism on the law of supply is the same. The technologies of nearly all Japanese firms exhibit diminishing marginal productivity and increasing marginal cost throughout stage II. Individuals and businesses appreciate that they can improve their utility by trading with others, offering their labor, working competently, starting entrepreneurial ventures, innovating, hiring factors, economizing costs, improving technology, product design, and financing, touting their products, and marketing them, effectively. They grasp the virtue of efficient administration and planning. But they often disregard the law of labor supply, and seldom profit maximize. Wage differentials in Japan are unusually narrow, and unpaid overtime work is ubiquitous. Labor supply is only a weak function of wages, and a stronger function of obligation. These peculiarities are reflected in statistics on annual person–hours worked, which place Japan at the top of the list of industrialized nations, and more subtly in unreported unpaid overtime, and other work related activities disguised as socializing.

The Japanese do not profit maximize in the competitive sense required by category A competitive systems, because communal obligation deters individual proprietors and corporations from placing personal utility-seeking ahead of group welfare. Japanese businessmen like their American cousins pioneer new ventures, innovate, invest in research, development, testing and evaluation (RDT & E), hire and train the most promising personnel, carefully select technologies, modernize, economize variable input costs including finance and advertising, conduct market research, set prices, and sell their products to earn sufficient revenue. But they do not maximize the stream of private discounted shareholders' dividends. Business is not detached from communal obligation. It is a cultural process that requires entrepreneurs to bridle their speculative ambitions, and to promote conservative RDT & E driven corporate growth in deference to group risk aversion and the need to provide members with internal mobility denied them externally by various aspects of communalism. Enterprise demand for labor cannot be determined solely by the forces of supply and demand in factor and product markets, because group values necessitate that members be protected. Whether firms hold onto workers long after cost minimization requires their dismissal, or employment is granted for life, group obligation thwarts any possibility of maximizing shareholders' profits by adjusting factor demand as market opportunities dictate. And, of course, internal labor use is similarly constrained. Reassignment involves complex issues of group protocol, not merely productive efficiency, and there is no clock set on ritual and consensus building. While the Japanese work hard, enormous amounts of time are squandered on ceremonial obligations, including perfunctory consultation, and teachers sitting idly at their desk when students are on vacation. Insider control also induces inter-firm collusion that distorts the relationship between price and efficient output supply, protecting the group at the expense of outsiders, including unaffiliated shareholders. Communalist enterprises strive to evade market discipline as much as they can without going bankrupt, diminishing rates of return and the efficient economy wide allocation of capital. The extent of these losses, and related costs attributable to insider corruption, is concealed as recent Japan's banking and financial scandals have revealed by imaginative accounting, and a communal code of silence.

Equilibrium

All these distortions of category A laws of demand and supply affect the possibilities, characteristics, and processes of equilibration. Communalism prevents Walrasian, Marshallian, and Keynesian market adjustment mechanisms from competitively equilibrating individual demand and supply programs (including holdings of idle cash balances), by substituting group choices for some individual demand and supply programs, and consensus building and attitude adjustment for competitive negotiations. Members are able to reach agreements, but the equilibria achieved optimize neither individual nor communal utility, because the terms of demand and supply are not fully negotiated with members or outsiders. Equilibria therefore are second best, with the proximity to the communal ideal dependent on the completeness and competence of consultation throughout the order.

Communalism can also be interpreted as a fourth obligational adjustment mechanism supplementing the familiar Walrasian, Marshallian, and Keynesian trio. It relies on insider participatory consensus building instead of impersonal market signals. Supply and demand programs are reconciled through discussion rather than arm's-length market competition. Consensus building sacrifices competitive efficiency for group security and effort mobilizing. It impairs the Walrasian mechanism because factor and product prices are prevented from optimally allocating labor and other inputs to alternative use among occupations and firms due to barriers like lifetime employment, while surplus inventories are not rapidly liquidated because of communally approved collusive price-fixing. And as the international community frequently alleges, Japanese firms sell their excess inventories abroad at excessive discounts.

The Marshallian adjustment mechanism which in category A systems depends on profit-maximizing responses to factor and output prices to achieve and sustain equilibrium is disordered because communalism deliberately circumvents market discipline and subordinates profit-maximizing to others goals. Japanese firms can and do respond to outside demand, but supplies influenced as they are by communal obligation cannot correspond to a full utility-maximizing equilibrium either for members of communal enterprises or outsiders.

Keynesian processes are also distorted by communalism. The insider consensus building mechanism dampens income multiplier effects, over-fully employing the population. Groups create jobs that should not exist, and resist dismissals by making internal accommodations. Other shocks which could easily destabilize category A macrosystems by weakening business confidence, lowering the marginal efficiency of capital, and increasing demand for idle cash balances are mitigated by inter-firm coordination, and collusion, and the belief that government as a full partner in national communalism will provide whatever assistance is necessary. Japanese enterprises expect the state to do whatever is required to bolster aggregate effective demand, and promote steady long-term growth. For the most part, they are right. But the institutionalization of these practices erodes national financial stability, perpetuates anticompetitive inefficiencies, and diminishes economic vitality.

Systemic Structure

The pride of the Japanese economy is its medium- and large-scale industrial and commercial enterprises which provide employment for life. They are the most dynamic element of the system and generate the largest share of GDP, in part because their scale enables them to operate competitively abroad. The state plays an important coordinative role, but is much smaller than in Western industrial economies despite its extensive public health care system.

Japan's public sector is unusual in another way. Tokugawa Confucian obligation and communalist consensus building make it better attuned to social need than Western lobbying.

Japan has no perfectly competitive markets, and its underproductive small-scale ventures and organized Yakuza criminal activities are stabilized by custom in the first instance, and kept in check by shame culture obligation in the second. State regulators assist small underproductive enterprises by granting them zoning, and other preferences, and Japanese consumers patronize them sufficiently even though they have access to better variety and lower prices in supermarkets and discount stores. The influence of communalism thus is pervasive. It is a source of stability, and the key to understanding Japan's unique economic properties. Businesses, the state bureaucracy and criminal organizations are all intertwined in the fourth way; a nationwide process of economic consensus building.

The main effects of communalism are evident. Japanese culture has created a highly mobilized, work-intensive, state-regulated, macroeconomically stable, comparatively egalitarian market economic system, with a first-tier standard of living, and little violent crime. Insofar as the population perceives its excess labor as gratifying communal service, and is content with the obligations imposed by group consensus, the system is a tremendous success. Many Japanese scholars view matters precisely this way. Masahiko Aoki has argued that the Japanese economy is as, or more efficient than, the category A "self-regulating," individualistic competitive market ideal, because it harnesses the power of communalism to mobilize effort, mitigates labor–management conflict and class antagonisms, nurtures and accumulates team knowledge, concentrates team attention on quality, modernization and innovation, coordinates and plans in an environment of trust (in teams, associations of cross-shareholding firms, other business associations, and the government), takes stakeholder interests including those of the community directly into account, risk shares in strategic foreign investment, and regulates specific and aggregate effective demand, all with self-discipline that promotes cost-efficient delivery of private and public services.

But proponents of individualism, liberalization, and American-style globalization disagree. From their cultural perspective, communalism is inferior. It makes the Japanese underproductive, compels them to overwork, and imposes group obligations that diminish the quality of their existence. Moreover, they blame Japan's declining economic vigor on the cumulative effects of communalist inefficiencies, especially protectionism, and have been urging the government to abandon all anticompetitive communalist restraints on profit-seeking.

THE GEOMETRY OF JAPANESE ECONOMIC COMMUNALISM

The validity of these judgments can be assessed geometrically. The degree of communal distortion in the Japanese factor space (figure 9.1) is immense. Capital and labor are oversupplied by communalist obligations, and effort is not reserved to the extent it is in the West by personal drug addiction, alienation, dependency, and crime. Labor force participation is high (except for women, who usually prefer roles as homemakers during their child-rearing years), with large segments of the population continuing gainful employment after they have formally retired. Unemployment, strikes, excess absenteeism, and

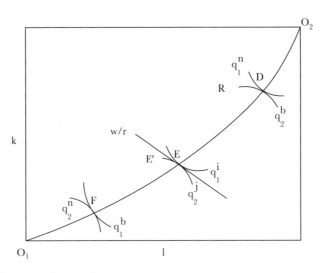

Figure 9.1 Japanese factor allocation

compassionate and medical leaves are low, while the number and quality of person–hours employed is high. The Japanese not only officially work 40 percent more person–hours than the French, logging many more hours informally without compensation; they also labor unstintingly on the group's behalf. Their pay is high by Western standards in absolute terms, but not on a real hourly basis. The extraordinary abundance of labor and other factor supplies therefore cannot be explained by generous rates of hourly compensation. Factors are considered oversupplied in Japan precisely because more services are offered at the going input price than would be forthcoming in a competitive, golden rule abiding, utility-maximizing regime. People do not sacrifice their leisure and utility because they enjoy being drones, but because it would be shameful to do otherwise; behavior illustrated geometrically by expanding the sides of the Edgeworth–Bowley production box. Japanese and American attitudes in this regard are diametrically opposed. For example, American wives complain when their husbands spend too much time at the office; Japanese wives rebuke their husbands if they disgrace themselves by leaving early.

Japanese hard work, however, does not always translate into enhanced factor productivity. The same communal pressures which promote high rates of participation and effort also require endless hours of group affirming ritual from calisthenics to ceremonial consultation. Diligence often has nothing to do with productive activity in a Western sense. Sales personnel are much more concerned with time-consuming details of etiquette than moving merchandise.

Likewise, communalism severs the link between productivity and compensation, while impairing labor mobility through bonds of loyalty and lifetime employment. Japanese workers are relatively unresponsive to competitive offers of alternative employment, and wages are not sufficiently differentiated to serve as a strong lure, even if job-seekers were not burdened by communal obligation. This is expressed geometrically in the Edgeworth–Bowley production space in several ways. First, the wage–rental price lines are distorted and segmented because marginal rates of factor substitution are not proportional to marginal factor productivity. This means that factors are not allocated at point E, the competitive ideal, but at some other point D or F along the contract curve, or more precisely at E′ off the contract curve due to factor immobility. Second, these same distortions imply that the isoquants achieved at points within the space must be lower than their generally competitive twins because factors are not allocated to best use, or most efficiently employed.

Communal factor supply thus can be interpreted as a compensatory process where the inherent inefficiencies of the Japanese input markets are ameliorated and counteracted by over-employment and overexertion, not unlike the strategy adopted by Joseph Stalin to mobilize resources and rapidly industrialize the Soviet Union. Instead of operating an E″ on the normal imperfectly competitive production feasibility frontier illustrated in (figure 9.2), production may actually occur below, or above E″, beyond the production possibilities frontier at point R. In this latter case, GDP exceeds the competitive ideal in physical, and perhaps even in terms of communalist utility, if Japanese workers are gratified by their group service. But if they begrudge their excess labor supply and exertion, and prefer to maximize their individual utility then their welfare is severely diminished below the optimum by forced labor, as was certainly the case under Soviet communism.

Turning to the goods market, attention shifts to product characteristics, management, technology, and competitive profit-maximizing. A nation cannot realize its full competitive potential unless it produces goods with the right characteristics. The qualitative aspects of q_1 and q_2 must be ideal from the standpoint of equilibrium demand. Japanese culture is a powerful asset in this regard. It is perfectionist and attentive to consumer demand. The Japanese disesteem blemishes and poor quality. Goods with the smallest defects are shunned, compelling manufacturers to maintain high production standards attuned both to domestic and foreign tastes. These attitudes have contributed significantly to their economic success, especially in the export of everything from tableware to automobiles. As a consequence, the volume indexes on the export isoquants in figure 9.1 do not have to be adjusted significantly up or down by converting goods with dispreferred characteristics into smaller or larger quantities of superior outputs at the equilibrium marginal rate of transformation. But some adjustments may be required because communal obligation sometimes causes firms to mis-select technologies judged from the competitive standard.

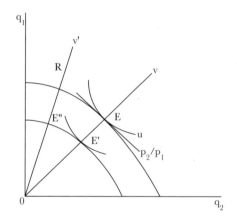

Figure 9.2 Japanese efficiency possibilities

Likewise, when the temptations of insider misgovernance, keiretsu collusion, and communalist pressures cause managers to sub-optimally organize and incentivize their enterprises, and entrepreneurs do not capture rents and pioneer new ventures as fully as they should, realized output will be below competitive potential necessitating a lowering of the isoquant values in the Edgeworth–Bowley production box, and an inward shift off the production possibilities frontier, unless offset by compensatory exertion.[2]

Production inefficiencies in one or both activities also occur because communalist insider control induces firms to incompletely profit maximize by failing to acquire inputs at least competitive cost, or hire them to the point where marginal cost equals price. And, of course, production is driven off the Edgeworth–Bowley contract curve by state and keiretsu market share fixing, and the communal obligation to preferentially buy Japanese products.[3]

Japanese communalism causes other production inefficiencies. Insiders do not always care what they produce, if it promotes communitarian harmony. They do not mind being cost-ineffective, or shun collusion. Most Japanese firms have little reason to competitively cost minimize, or produce to the point where marginal cost equals marginal revenue (or price when they are price-takers) because nonaffiliated outside shareholders as representatives of market forces do not sufficiently control their actions. Consequently, managers incompletely profit maximize and pay non-keiretsu outside shareholders low returns on their equity. Derived demand for inputs likewise is misdirected. Enterprise organization is inefficient and unemployment would be high if it were not for the communitarian obligation to hire for life. And, of course, the system is too tolerant of coordinative planning which entrenches communalist inefficiencies including import protectionism, orchestrated by the Ministry of Foreign Affairs, the Ministry of International Trade and Industry,[4] the Ministry of Finance, the Japanese Planning Agency, and the Bank of Japan. Nonetheless, Masahiko Aoki counter-argues that isoquants do not have to be substantially downscaled because these shortcomings are alleviated by strenuous effort, accumulated team knowledge, the trust associated with lifetime employment, communalist risk-sharing and planning, keiretsu and government coordination, and dampened labor–management conflict and class antagonism. These compensatory effects could be substantial as he suggests, but it is a stretch to infer that they are sufficient to transform losses into gains.

Communalist distortions might warrant only passing concern if entrepreneurship were ebullient, shifting the production possibility frontier in figure 9.2 rapidly outwards. But the Japanese social contract discourages innovation and domestic industrial pioneering. Workers, managers, proprietors, the community, nongovernmental organizations, and the government create legal, administrative, and ethical barriers increasing entrepreneurial

---

[2] Although all individuals in the competitive model independently maximize their utility, managers are permitted to noncoercively negotiate conditions of employment and organizational matters with their employees which may profoundly affect enterprise productivity. Japanese managers have tried to compensate for job right constraints and the lack of flexible renumeration by integrating workers into the management process through devices like "quality circles," but communalism still restricts their degrees of freedom.

[3] In the real world, markets are often segmented in the sense that the same product will be sold at different prices in various locales. Discount stores routinely underprice their full service competitors. Insofar as such differentials are justified by the cost of delivering different levels of shopping experience, they are compatible with competitive principle, but often the price differential is disproportionate because of "velvet" coercion in the form of deceptive advertising and other malpractices.

[4] The acronym MITI was changed to METI in January 2001. METI is the Ministry of Economics, Trade, and Industry.

risk, while low returns to capital associated with insider control reduce anticipated rewards. These obstacles have not arrested technological progress and modernization, but they impair the pace and scope of change, exemplified by 30 years of continuously decelerating per capita GDP growth.

Communalism also has adversely affected investment efficiency and therefore growth by degrading financial efficiency. The excessive involvement of Japanese banking and financial institutions in intercorporate, keiretsu, and governmental promotional activities, together with the virtually interest free, noncompetitive loans provided to local communities by the postal savings banks, has prevented finance from being allocated to best use. The cost of capital is generally too low, and is often squandered, as glaringly reflected in the Japanese government's as yet unsuccessful effort to bail out its banking system from more than a trillion dollars of uncollectible loans. Foreign exchange rates likewise are collusively overvalued in misguided cross-subsidization schemes designed to acquire desired imports cheaply, while over-exporting, in a vain effort to compensate for the limited opportunities of its nontariff barrier protected, communalist domestic economy.[5]

The same story broadly applies to wholesale and retail distribution (figure 9.3). Communalist obligation restricts the range and accessibility of products and keeps prices above the competitive norm, forcing consumption off the contract at point F'. And of course, communalism has a mixed impact on Japanese income distribution. On the one hand, insiders like the business and government elite (including the Imperial family) indisputably benefit from their communal status; an inequity that is aggravated by concealed incomes in kind (perks), corruption, and tax evasion. On the other hand, these inequities are partly offset by high, nearly confiscatory inheritance taxes, communalist income leveling, direct communalist attention to member's special needs, and subsidized public services, especially education, health, and retirement benefits.

It is probably fair to say that the net effect of these contradictory tendencies is greater equality and economic security than should be expected from a competitive regime, achieved at the expense of foregone productivity, growth, leisure, and personal liberty. For those who esteem communalist egalitarianism, it is possible to argue that Japanese social welfare, and certainly communal welfare, is relatively high, despite inferior individual living standards because the outcome is more socially just and communally gratifying. But, of course, libertarians counter-argue that if the people were not ensnared in by communitarian tradition they would not embrace community preferences as their own, choosing to maximize their unique individual wants instead.

Japanese elites appear to be broadly aware of the cost and benefits of communalism and have been trying to ameliorate its negative aspects by liberalizing for more than a half century, both during and after American military occupation. They have tried to

---

[5]   On banking, see Masahiko Aoki and Hugh Patrick, eds., *The Japanese Main Bank System*, Clarendon Press, 1995, and Masahiko Aoki, and Gary Saxonhouse, *Finance Governance and Competitiveness in Japan*, Oxford University Press, London, 2000. According to Thomas Klitgaad, who analyzed Japan's industrial machinery, electrical machinery, transportation equipment, and precision equipment industries, which accounted for 75 percent of the country's exports in 1997, Japanese exporters change profit margins significantly in order to moderate exchange rate fluctuations. They pass on more than half of any changes in the yen price, absorbing the remainder by adjusting profit margins on foreign sales. He also found that the direction of the yen's movement had no effect on exporters' willingness to use profit margins to stabilize prices in foreign markets. See Klitgaard, "Exchange Rates and Profit Margins: The Case of Japanese Exporters," *Economic Policy Review*, Vol. 5, No. 1, 1999.

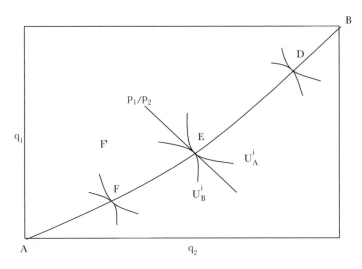

Figure 9.3   Japanese retail distribution

compartmentalize the communalist market, and reduce its sway by gradually expanding the scope of domestic and foreign private competition in all four core markets: factors, production, finance, and distribution. Government and business have tried to attenuate communalist culture by encouraging some individualistic values like leisure, labor mobility, entrepreneurship, and globalism, diminishing the incentives sustaining the keiretsu (by legalizing holding companies in 1998), streamlining state regulation, and reducing some aspects of social protection, especially import tariff barriers.[6] And the people have tried to cope themselves by modernizing their attitudes, expectations, and demands.

---

[6]   "Economic Council's new 10-year economic plan lacks vision for structural reform; Leaving uncertainty about future of tax system, social security," *Nihon Keizai,* July 6, 1999, p. 3. The Economic Council (advisory panel to the prime minister) yesterday released the next 10-year economic plan it worked out with the title "The Ideal State of the Economy and a Policy Outline for Economic Revival." The plan stressed the need to introduce free competition to stimulate economic growth despite Japan's rapidly aging population. The report focused on "individuals." Japan has long aimed at attaining economic growth by mass-producing standardized products. Such an economic society needed the so-called "company men" (those completely devoted to company). But now individualism is required. To this end, the report promises "equal opportunities" through deregulation, and an overhaul of social services. Policy tasks to be considered at early date include the following:

- Reform the entire distribution area.
- Reform the entire telecom area.
- Give greater opportunity in selecting which school to attend.
- Accept foreign workers in special-skill and technology areas in a positive manner.
- Draw up a basic plan for promoting basic technology for manufacturing.
- Work out measures for employment of older workers, including a review of the mandatory retirement age.
- Produce basic policy measures to deal with the declining birthrate and the aging population.
- Introduce reform programs to realize a recycling society.
- Work out programs to dispatch information to other countries.
- Clarify the nation's prospects for international economic cooperation.
- Produce specific programs for fiscal reconstruction after turning around the economy.
- Consider prefectural governments' functions and the significance of the local autonomy system.

The marriage of shame culture bred communalism and individualism, however, has been disappointing. Japanese growth ceased, the worth ethic is eroding, unemployment and crime are rising, and codes of communal conduct have been degraded judged by phenomena like urban blight. There appear to have been as many negative moral and efficiency hazards created as positive adaptations.

While it is easy to imagine a perfect integration of communalism and individualism, community-guided economic activity, and individual initiative, it is much harder to achieve. Nominal improvements in competitive utility-maximizing do not always amount to real progress, only new and dubious forms of communalist regulation. The replacement of the keiretsu by communalist holding companies may merely constitute a change in form, not substance, and it is not clear why people should accept the values and authority of groups that preach the superiority of individualism, or that a well-functioning guilt culture can quickly replace a shame culture that has stood the test of time for more than a thousand years. If this is so, Japanese may not ultimately be able to construct the ideal mixed system toward which their consensus-driven culture is driving them. They may have to content themselves with a communalist order that is less materially productive, but more culturally satisfying.[7] There is no doubt that all this activity is a sign of Japanese adaptive health, which combined with cautious pragmatism bodes well eventually for a successful outcome. But, just as in Continental Europe, adverse aggregate economic

---

[7]   Philippe Debroux contends that the relative weights of the government bureaucracy, financial institutions, and market investors in the communalist governance mechanism have never been fixed, adjusting effectively to changing requirements. From 1945 to the 1960s, MITI and main banks continued the directive methods of Japan's wartime economy by firmly guiding a structural shift from light to heavy industrial manufacturing. Once this was accomplished, the emphasis was redirected toward deregulation, weakening the influence of MITI and the banks; a process accelerated during the 1980s by the globalization of capital markets and the internationalization of the Japanese economy. Domestic stakeholders, suppliers inside the keiretsu, the Keidanren, Nikkeiren (association responsible for wage negotiations with unions), and their clients all increasingly have fallen under the sway of global economic forces. The change is especially visible in shareholder and stakeholder influences on management, a phenomenon reinforced by increased foreign ownership of Japanese firms (which pay higher dividends and have higher rates of return on equity), and the internationalization of indigenous companies, although it should also be noted that shareholders played a significant role in the 1930s, when companies paid high dividends that were proportional to profits. Foreign investors' presence on the boards of large companies is growing rapidly. They monitor their investments very closely, imposing strong discipline on management, pushing them to cultivate investor relations. Parenthetically, the Keidanren took the initiative to establish the Japan Investor Relations Association in 1993. Communalism therefore does not preclude strong external Japanese corporate governance. The same point holds with respect to main banks which are providing smaller and smaller shares of large firms' financing since the mid-1980s. These firms not only tapped the Euro–dollar market, but issued an enormous amount of convertible bonds, which ultimately improved their debt–equity ratios. The tendency for communalistic firms to underperform has come under pressure from other sources as well. Japanese insurance companies are pressing for improved performance on their equity portfolios, recently releasing a report on corporate rates of return on equity and accounting disclosure practices. While it is possible to reconcile these changes with communalist national coordination, the increasing influence of outside shareholders runs counter to cultural reflexes because the Japanese do not like unpredictability, and from this perspective testifies to the earnestness of deregulatory reforms. Of course, sometimes market adaptations are a double-edged sword. In response to competitive pressures, the keiretsu have moved away from rigid structures toward networks, and are pruning weak members from its ranks to improve collective rates of return. While the addition of these weak firms to the noncommunalist market expands the scope of competition in this sector, it also strengthens the keiretsu's coercive market power *vis-à-vis* outsiders, and the predominance of long-term concerns over short-term returns on equity. Keiretsu organization therefore will continue to adhere to traditional policies of employment security, sales growth, and market share. Debroux characterizes these cross-tendencies as

growth and employment trends associated with this constructive experimentation are not reassuring. Apparently communalism in Japan and corporatism in Continental Europe coalesce in new, underproductive forms when "allocative efficiency" and "X-efficiency" are mixed, or the net effect of hybridization is negative. This confirms the evidence from Gorbachev's and Yeltsin's experiments, where the idea of mixing seemed so seductively simple, but the reality left much to be desired.

Review

Main Features of the Japanese Economic System

Culture: Consensus building communalism with deep historical roots founded on the shame principle.

Motivation: Communalist-dominated individual utility-seeking.

Mechanisms: Markets are communalistically regulated. They are internally protectionist and externally mercantilist. State economic governance is communally conscious, performing a wide range of activities including procurement programs, bureaucratic assignments, controls, some state ownership and extensive micro- and macroeconomic regulation of the laws of demand, supply, and equilibration.

Institutions: Keiretsu, Keidanren, Gaimsho, METI, Japan Planning Agency, Ministry of Finance, Bank of Japan, parliamentary democracy, communalist firms, lifetime employment, and communalist legal system.

---

a manifestation of a larger global process in which communalist (Japan) and social democratic corporatist societies (Continental Europe) are trying to synthesize their non-Smithian mechanisms with individualistic, noncoercive, negotiated (market) utility-maximizing, which he describes as an attempt to mix "allocative efficiency" with Leibenstein's "X-efficiency" (a phenomenon of course which can also be endogenized in the Smithian paradigm with innovative management that pays attention to issues like trust and accumulated associative knowledge when making decisions about hirings and dismissals). The success of such initiatives, as he recognizes, depends in part on an acceptance of new rules of the game, or cultural revolution, and offers some examples. Rengo, the trade union confederation, is pushing for more direct union participation in management, a step toward German-style "*Mitbestimmung*," and a step away from collective bargaining. This could improve worker–management relations, but also may threaten returns to outside shareholders. Likewise, sight should not be lost of the fact that holding companies were legalized in 1998, which could prove to be a more flexible and efficient mechanism of intercorporate collaboration than the keiretsu, and might lead to the termination of lifetime employment (at a significant cost to labor–management relations, especially regarding wage compensation), although some neo-liberal unions like Rengo support efficiency reforms. These cross-currents complicate transition. Witness the growing disagreement between industries and the mounting difficulties of maintaining a common front during the spring wage offensive. They are compounded by defects of the educational system which make it difficult for Japanese workers to function outside of a what Eduard Hall calls a "high context" environment, and deal with some aspects of entrepreneurship. Debroux believes that Japan is still probably best in the manufacturing aspects of information age hardware, due in part to the adaptive success of its multinationals, but much still needs to be done.

Main Inefficiencies

Law of
demand:

Individual preferences are inordinately influenced by groups and communalist culture. People are expected to prefer Japanese products, especially local crafts and group leisure. People are expected to place group obligation above personal interest, and adjust attitudes when the communal consensus changes.

Law of
supply:

Worker and managerial supply curves are weak functions of wages, stronger functions of obligation. Enterprise supply functions give priority to group obligation over profit-maximizing. Marketing supply functions give priority to communal coordination over unfettered profit-maximizing.

Law of
equilibration:

Walrasian distributive equilibration in factor and product markets gives priority to communal obligation over individual utility-maximizing; exemplified by the labor immobility associated with employment for life, extraordinary labor exertion, and a mercantilist export strategy. Marshallian production equilibration gives priority to communal obligation over profit-maximizing, both for individual firms and various affiliations of enterprises. Keynesian macro-equilibration is tied to the government's communally influenced micro-coordinative procurement programs, bureaucratic administration, and regulation. Both the causes of macro-disequilibria and the state's responses often differ significantly from conventional Keynesian diagnoses and prescriptions.

Japan relies heavily on communal regulation.

Rationale for Communal Economic Management

Topic	Problem	Cultural response
Private property	Sometimes generates unearned quasi-rents	Communalism, including lifetime employment
Employment for life	Weak motivation	Group obligation, worker participation, including management, consensus building, egalitarian wages, group fringe benefits

	Immobility	Internal transfers, enterprise growth, superior human capital, early retirement
Management	Low compensation	Group obligation, large fringe benefits, early retirement
	Immobility	Internal transfers, enterprise growth
Enterprise	Insider control, no profit-maximizing, (group welfare constrained net revenue-maximizing), sheltered competition	Group obligation burden sharing, no jurisdictional barriers, superior human capital, external keiretsu and governmental support
Keiretsu	Price-fixing, market sharing	Shared knowledge, burden-sharing
Keidanren	Anticompetitive protectionism	Coordination, risk-sharing
Government	Protectionism, paternalism	Communal legitimization, shared knowledge, coordination, burden-sharing, risk-sharing
Community	Rule of obligation, not rule of law	Strong communal justice, strong communal services

Systemic Structure

	Share of GDP	Productivity (Destructiveness)	Coercion
Markets			
Perfect markets	0	–	–
Inefficient markets	17	High	High
Coercive markets	65	High	Medium

Government	15	High	Medium
Obligation			
Criminal disservices	3	(Low)	–

Systems Characteristics

	Degree/ Intensity
State macro-regulation	High
State micro-regulation	
Pro-competitive	Medium
Local constituent	High
Elite	High
Welfare/security	High/medium
State spending programs	
Privileged contracting	High
Misappropriation	Low
Cronyism	Medium
Criminal disservices	
Asset seizure and embezzlement	Low
Addiction/vice	Medium
Repression, extortion, and murder	Low
Subjugation, servitude	Low
Causes of macroeconomic disequilibria	
Sticky wages	High
Sticky prices	High
Investment avoidance	High
Liquidity preference	High
State of confidence	High
Foreign capital flows	Medium
Insecure property rights	Low
Fear of criminality	Low
Anticompetitive business	
Repression	Low
Labor subjugation	Low
Judicial risk	Low
State corruption	Low
Macropolicy mismanagement	Low
Business repression	Low
Class conflict	Low

Main Performance Indicators

Per capita GDP 1998 (US = 100)	84
Per capital GDP growth 1990–99 (compound annual rate)	0.5

Per capita GDP growth 1960–99
    (compound annual rate)   3
Inflation 1990–99
    (compound annual rate)   1
Unemployment 1999
   Share of labor force
      Domestic definition   4.5
      International definition   7.3
Length of work year
   Person–hours (US = 100)
      Excluding unpaid overtime   115
      Including unpaid overtime   130
Retirement support burden   High
Nonworking mothers and wives   High

Present Attitude Toward Reform

Japan wants to reinvigorate communalism. If it fails, opinion is divided about whether it would be better to embrace Western individualism and Western-style state market management, or retain communalism with its shortcomings and strengths.

Review Questions

1. Does the uniqueness of the Japanese system lie in its "Asian values?"
2. What is shame culture? Does it require consensus building?
3. What are situational ethics? Are they compatible with universal ethics? Are they likely to be better developed in shame cultures? Why?
4. Is the Japanese market a vehicle for competitively maximizing individual potential?
5. Is the Japanese market a vehicle for facilitating the achievement of some communalist goals? Explain.
6. How does the Japanese community's use of limited individual utility-seeking and markets differ from Chinese authoritarian laissez faire and American managed markets?
7. It is often said that Japanese communalism is a consequence of its rice culture. Russia too has an agrarian communalist heritage. Why do you think that the Japanese were able to successfully transfer communal control to industrial and post-industrial society, while the Russians failed despite 73 years of Soviet communism?
8. Japanese communalism is not encumbered by socialist universalist ethics. Is this an important ingredient of its adaptive success?
9. How does Japanese communalism differ from Continental European social democracy in terms of cultural goals?
10. How does shame affect individual autonomy? Could this be economically significant? Explain.
11. What is "*tatemae*"? How does it differ from sycophancy?
12. How does the Japanese ability to find pleasure in fulfilling situational obligations affect their capacity to work?

13. Who is economically sovereign in Japan?
14. Does obligation play a stronger role in Japan than the West? Explain. Discuss employment for life.
15. What is "keiretsu"? How does it relate to obligation? How does this differ from cross-shareholding in the West?
16. How does communalism affect Japanese demand?
17. Why do not the Japanese profit-maximize as prescribed by generally competitive theory? Elaborate.
18. Graph the Japanese labor supply function, taking account of unpaid overtime. Is this normal? How does it affect profit-maximizing?
19. What are the micro-inefficiencies of Japanese communalism?
20. Why is Japan's Walrasian adjustment mechanism competitively inefficient? Is it also welfare inefficient?
21. Why is Japan's Marshallian adjustment mechanism competitively inefficient? Is it also welfare inefficient?
22. Why is Japan's Keynesian adjustment mechanism competitively inefficient? Is it also welfare inefficient?
23. Is communalist consensus building a fourth adjustment mechanism based on "voice"? Explain.
24. What are the special features of Japan's system structure? Why is the government sector so small?
25. Why do inefficient mom and pop operations thrive in Japan?
26. Why does Masahiko Aoki consider the Japanese system successful?
27. Why do critics disagree?
28. Are Japan's factor supply and allocation Pareto efficient? Use the Edgeworth–Bowley production box in figure 9.1 to explain.
29. How does Japanese perfectionism affect the numbering of the isoquants in the Edgeworth–Bowley production box?
30. Is Japan's production Pareto ideal? Use figure 9.2 to explain.
31. How does communalism mitigate the dangers of insider control which are destroying Russia's productiveness?
32. How does communalist finance affect savings, the allocation of loanable funds, and growth?
33. Is Japan's retailing efficient in either a Paretian or communalist sense? Use figure 9.3 to explain.
34. Is Japan's system socially just? Explain, taking into account other aspects of communalist welfare.
35. Why have the Japanese had difficulty liberalizing; integrating Western utilitarianism and communalism?

CHAPTER 10

CHINA

China is an underdeveloped nation with a three million man army and expanding intercontinental ballistic missile nuclear capabilities. Its standard of living is approximately one tenth Japan's and America's but grew rapidly during the 1990s, despite transitioning from a Soviet-style command economy. This striking success has been attributed to the retention of state ownership of the means of production, to liberalization, wise Communist party macroeconomic management, and massive capital and technology transfers by the overseas Chinese. The economic system is a "culturally regulated," Eastern category B market economy, founded on restricted individual utility-seeking, state ownership of the means of production, and negotiated prices including wages. The foreign exchange rate is fixed by the state. The government is authoritarian, with Soviet-style Leninist "democracy," controlled by the Communist party. The regime officially classifies itself as a "socialist society." The Communist party is the supreme authority, and it uses the state to influence the economy through its ownership, executive, legislative, and judicial powers. The Communist state operates its enterprises both as proprietor and guardian of the public interest. These powers are diluted where ownership is mixed, communal, or private, but remain formidable. The party also manages the economy, with huge state military and civilian expenditure programs, selected price controls, wage repression, stern macroeconomic regulation of monetary and fiscal policies (especially credit and foreign capital) controls, and microeconomic administration and regulation of domestic and foreign activities. Its decisions supercede all judicial precedent, and preclude the rule of contract law essential for establishing a self-regulating category A system. Although Confucius formulated a variant of the Christian golden rule, the ethics of Chinese communist economic management is founded more on the authoritarian exercise of power than individual economic empowerment and fairness.

Chinese laws of supply, demand, and equilibration satisfy the core requirements of the utility-seeking paradigm using a mix of markets and state command, with relatively little transparency. Walrasian, Marshallian, and Keynesian adjustment mechanisms function in the normal ways subject to these limits, modified by the public and private interests of the Communist party elite. The reach of the Communist party is pervasive. Its motivations, mechanisms, and institutions, especially state ownership of the means of production, cause the laws of demand, supply, and equilibration to persistently generate results that depart markedly from individualist, competitive category A models with private ownership of the means of production. This is especially conspicuous in the repression of wages, other controls on labor, the underproductivity of the traditional industrial sector, and the insider corruption rampant in newer ventures.

Opinions about the merit of China's Communist party managed state laissez-faire strategy are sharply divided. Some interpret the system as a device for mobilizing competitive profit-driven effort, with the assistance of overseas Chinese venturers, to achieve rapid economic development, while protecting the population from the worst abuses of private coercion and criminal exploitation. Some see it as a transitory phase in China's march to an unrestricted category A multi-party democratic, market economy with universal private ownership of the means of production, while others foresee the possibility of more destructive outcomes, where growth succumbs to the intrinsic inefficiency of Communist party controlled authoritarian laissez faire, or degenerates into some variant of Russian market kleptocracy. These issues are further complicated by China's low stage of economic development. It can be argued that "socialist" laissez faire suits China's needs today, but will be detrimental tomorrow.

THE CHINESE ECONOMIC SYSTEM

Culture

China has been one of the world's great civilizations for five thousand years. Its contributions to the arts, architecture, science, technology, literature, and statecraft are impressive, and its living standards were probably on a par with Europe's until the industrial revolution allowed the West to excel. China's response to this challenge over the ensuing two hundred years, unlike Japan's, was inadequate. The Ching emperors resisted democratic modernization, and tried to insulate themselves from the threat of Western imperialism, while their successors, from Sun Yatsen and Chang Kaishek to Mao Tsetung, found it difficult, for political, ideological, and economic reasons, to close the gap. In 1976, after the human and material catastrophe that was the Great People's Proletarian Cultural Revolution, China's standard of living was substantially less than one tenth the American level, with little prospect for rapid improvement. This pessimism was well-justified, because even as both the pandemonium of Mao's "red" zealotry against "experts" and the command economy receded, China still found itself saddled with a primitive category B Soviet-style administrative control system. As with other communist leaders, Deng Xiaoping responded to this challenge by experimenting with a variety of market reforms designed to reinvigorate and enhance the efficiency of the state economic control mechanism, without exposing the population to the perceived dangers of capitalist exploitation. At first progress was slow, but momentum picked up toward the end of the 1980s, culminating in the mid-1990s with a variant of market socialism first suggested by Oskar Lange in the 1930s, where the state retained ownership of the means of production, while producers were allowed to freely maximize profits, and consumers utility, at competitively determined market prices.[1] As in the past, this model may turn out to be just another phase in the evolution of China's economic system. Jiang Zemin and Zhu Rongji have often stated that they desire to ultimately fully privatize state-owned assets, creating a socialist market system similar to Continental Europe's, stewarded by the Chinese Communist party. Perhaps they will succeed like other one-party systems such as Mexico, or still better the Communist party will relinquish its political dictatorship, ushering in an era of democratic socialism, but this is speculative.

The Chinese economy today is a "culturally regulated" category B, authoritarian laissez-faire variant of a "self-regulating," category A Langean socialist market model.[2] It is distinguished by widespread state (communal) ownership of the means of production, enterprise control vested at the state's discretion in the hands of appointed directors, and Communist party economic regulation codetermined by Marxist principles and traditional Chinese culture.[3] The state, controlled by the Communist party, claims a legal entitlement to the assets and incomes derived from the nation's mineral wealth, land, and most of its medium- and large-scale capital stock, and asserts the right to administer, tax, subsidize, price-fix, transfer, regulate, and control economic activities at its sole discretion. The state, or more precisely the upper crust of the Communist party, is economically sovereign. As sovereign, the Communist party permits provincial authorities to treat agrarian assets as communal property. Municipalities have been granted revocable autonomy and state-owned enterprises have been allowed to form joint ownership venturers with foreign private entities. Managers and workers in primarily state-owned enterprises are seldom co-owners as in the Russian model. Enterprise directors broadly operate like their Russian counter-

---

[1]   This was Lange's intent, but his model would not have worked as he desired because the rules for setting competitive prices he imposed on the "State Price Board" were not sufficient to achieve a general competitive optimum. See Steven Rosefielde, "Competitive Market Socialism Revisited: Impediments to Efficient Price-Fixing," *Comparative Economic Studies*, Vol. XXVII, No. 3, Fall 1986, pp. 17–23.

[2]   Oskar Lange and Fred M. Taylor, *On the Economic Theory of Socialism*, University of Minnesota Press, 1938.

[3]   In Lange's market socialist model the state owns the means of production, but requires enterprise managers to profit maximize (literally produce until marginal revenue equals price). The state protects society by policing managerial compliance and regulating prices. The Chinese model differs from Lange's because the state regulates firms more comprehensively than in the pure model, and because ownership in China is much more heterogeneous and changing. Jean-François Huchet and Xavier Richet list the following main types:

1.   The major financial holding companies in the public sector (financial, transport, trade) dependent on central or provincial government, and traded on the Hong Kong Stock Exchange as "Red Chips" (CITIC, COSCO, China Resources, Beijing Enterprise).
2.   The major state groups controlled by the central government and operating in the protected sectors.
3.   The state sector and collective groups operating more autonomously from the central administration because they are leaders in competitive fields.
4.   Joint ventures controlled by, or wholly owned by, foreign multinationals like Alcatel, Motorola, and Volkswagen.
5.   Small groups in the state and collective sector controlled by local governments.
6.   Private groups in the competitive sectors that increasingly act like conglomerates.
7.   Small private and family collective commercial firms in the service sectors in urban and rural areas.

Collective firms discussed in the literature on "hybrid" property rights are classified under categories 3 and 5. Huchet and Richet see most of these firms (TVE, or town village enterprises) as transitioning to a wholly private category, albeit under the scrutiny of local officials. Only 40 percent remain collectively owned, compared with 80 percent in 1990.

parts under the principle of one-man rule, but this is a privilege granted by the state to agents, not a legislated entitlement or a right of co-ownership. Furthermore, individual entrepreneurs recently have been authorized to form their own private businesses, as Soviet venturers had before them in the 1920s under the New Economic Policy (NEP), which eventually could lead to an orderly privatization through acquisitions and mergers.[4]

These complexities have given rise to different interpretations of China's ownership structure. It can be argued that private ownership predominates by treating joint ventures and communes as private enterprises, together with mom and pop proprietorships. But this is misleading because the state is the majority owner of most joint ventures, and has ultimate authority over communes and natural resources, operating in an environment similar to the Soviet experience during NEP (1921–29), or of the type Gorbachev envisioned under "*arenda*" (leasing).[5]

Despite its enormous formal powers, the Communist party has chosen to treat state managers (directors) and private entrepreneurs as independent state agents, while subjecting state workers and peasants to strict party discipline. The discretionary powers granted to the state's "business agents" were initially circumscribed, but now replicate those of category A proprietors, at least on paper. Profit incentives were introduced in 1978, followed shortly thereafter by the "contract responsibility system" granting enterprises expanded autonomy. After Tiananmen Square, Deng allowed suppliers to competitively satisfy buyers' demand (instead of compelling consumers to choose among whatever nonrationed goods they were offered). He decontrolled price and wage-fixing, pared the authority of the planners and ministries including prime contractors, expanded managerial powers at all levels, and adjusted the focus of party supervision to deter embezzlement, misuse, and misappropriation instead of stressing plan compliance. Enterprises were free to

---

The most important point, however, is that 95 percent of the top 100 operating firms in China in 1997 are SOEs (state-owned enterprises). This suggests the strong Langean character of the Chinese model, despite its many special complexities. See Jean-Francois Huchet and Xavier Richet, "Between Bureaucracy and Market: Chinese Industrial Groups in Search of New Forms of Corporate Governance," paper presented at the American Economics Meetings, New Orleans, January 6, 2001; V. Nee, "Organizational Dynamics of Market Transition: Hybrid Forms, Property Rights and Mixed Economy in China," *Administrative Science Quarterly*, No. 37, 1992, pp. 1–27; M.L. Weitzman and Chenggang Xu, *Chinese Township Village Enterprises as Vaguely Defined Co-operatives*, London School of Economics, London, 1993; Gary Jefferson, Thomas Rawski and Yuxin Zheng, *Institutional Change and Industrial Innovation in Transitonal Economies*, World Bank, Washington DC, 1994; Jean Oi, "The Evolution of Local State Corporatism," in A. Walder, ed., *Coping in Transition*, Harvard University Press, 1998, pp. 35–61; Samuel Ho, Paul Bowles, and Xiao-Yuan Dong, "Privatization and Enterprise Wage Structure During Transition: Evidence From Rural China," paper presented at the American Economics Meetings, New Orleans, January 6, 2001.

[4] The Chinese have avoided minority co-ownership while semiprivatizing in part by selling shares in some otherwise wholly owned state enterprises in the open market. Until now, enterprises have listed just 20 percent to 30 percent of their shares, insulating managers from market pressures. The Communist party is now considering allowing more than 50 percent of shares to be listed, but leaving the state as the largest shareholder. Ian Johnson, "China's Leaders Meet for Annual Strategy Session," *Wall Street Journal*, July 27, 1999, p. A19. Also, see note 76.

[5] Ian Johnson, "China Takes Steps to Protect Private Property, Breaking With Its Past to Revise Its Constitution," *The Wall Street Journal*, February 1, 1999, p. A18. The goal is to give China's mostly tiny, family-run companies a chance to develop into large companies or even conglomerates. The constitution will have four revisions calling for protection of private enterprise, adherence to the rule of law, recognition of multiple forms of ownership, and implementation of the pragmatic ideology of Deng Xiaoping. Louis Putterman, "The Role of Ownership and Property Rights in China's Economic Transition," *The China Quarterly*, Vol. 144, 1995, pp. 1047–64.

select input suppliers, and allowed to invest directly in their own firms, subject to stringent credit restrictions imposed by the state bank, operating as an instrument of state directive control.

The expanded powers of the firm were codified in "The Regulations on Transforming the Management Mechanism of State-Owned Industrial Enterprises," issued July 1992. This document granted managers 14 control rights over: (1) production, (2) pricing, (3) sales, (4) procurement, (5) foreign trade, (6) investment, (7) use of retained funds, (8) disposal of assets, (9) merger and acquisitions, (10) labor, (11) personnel management, (12) wages, (13) bonuses, and (14) internal organization, and refusal to pay unauthorized charges by the government.

These sweeping powers theoretically permitted Chinese managers to act as if they were capitalist owners, choosing location, facilities, and technologies; designing products, selecting least cost input suppliers, hiring and firing labor, negotiating wages, producing and distributing goods in assortments that maximize enterprise profits (for the state), and determining their own compensation. Managers were also permitted to form joint ventures with foreign companies which afforded them numerous perks.

Each of these 14 rights relaxed a restriction on free enterprise increasing economic efficiency. As the state sector began producing things people wanted at lower cost, the economy built up considerable transformational momentum that attracted foreign investors, who found the combination of enterprise adaptivity and disciplined cheap labor irresistible. China increasingly came to be perceived as an inexhaustible low-cost platform for foreign multinationals, sustained by a supportive Communist government. And, of course, the prospect of 1.25 billion mass consumers of Western exports was lost on no one.[6]

But these rosy expectations disregard the inherent contradictions of a system which retains Communist party economic sovereignty, including remnants of Soviet-style enterprise management, while urging laissez faire. The first contradiction involves insider control and the preferential treatment of "business agents" (Red directors, private managers, and entrepreneurs), which permit the Communist party elite to prosper at the expense of the state and productive labor. The delegation of authority always entails moral hazard because it allows agents to act in their own interests at the owners' expense. In the Chinese case, the separation of ownership from control creates the possibility of three kinds of moral hazard. The Communist party itself, in its capacity as steward–agent of the state, and its "business agents" can misappropriate wealth and income by diverting public revenues and/or assets to personal use. The Communist party elite in its stewardship role tends to feather its nest by charging lavish personal expenses to the state budget, and obtaining other perks, while "business agents" including the Communist elite charge similar personal expenses to enterprise revenues, and as is now possible by "privatizing" lucrative pieces of state assets to themselves through a variety of devious stratagems. For example, Chinese managers may sell state assets to foreign joint ventures at steep discounts, receiving under-the-table personal payments in cash or shares in foreign companies' holdings in China or abroad. All these forms of supplementary compensation diminish social welfare to the extent that transfers exceed value added, but they may become especially destructive if the Communist party and state "business agents" disregard worker welfare and make stealing their primary occupation, neglecting current operations, and thereby causing productivity and the GDP to decrease as they have in Russia.

---

[6]   Robert Kaplan, "China: A World Power Again," *Atlantic Monthly*, Vol. 284, No. 2, August 1999, pp. 16–18.

The degree of moral hazard in these aspects depends fundamentally on political discipline and culture. In the Chinese case, where guilt culture predominates over shame, this means that Confucian discipline (based on the Chinese version of the Christian golden rule),[7] communist idealism, or some other set of universal moral principles must inspire rulers, "business agents," workers, and peasants to exert themselves, and take initiative in a disciplined manner. The evidence is mixed, and unencouraging. Although Chinese everywhere are energetic, purposive, and productive, this has not always been enough to overcome the moral hazard created by the radical separation between ownership and control engineered by Deng. China has had difficulty with corruption and disorder even when ownership and control were relatively unified under Maoist and imperial rule, and socialist idealism or Confucianism were strong moral influences. Prospects today, when insiders have been given carte blanche, and socialist idealism and Confucianism are in decline, can hardly be considered promising, despite China's enormous development potential.[8]

It is therefore reasonable to infer that China's "Eastern" market system where the Communist party uses the proprietary, regulatory, and delegatory powers of the state to further personal ends, and perform the normal tasks of socialist governance, will not operate strictly according to the morally hazardless Western competitive ideal. The motivation, mechanisms, and institutions that govern demand, supply, and equilibration all differ importantly from those assumed in the Anglo-American market model, where the golden rule and the rule of contract law are indispensable, creating a system where the Communist party elite rather than individuals are sovereign. It is the Communist party elite's preferences that govern demand and determine how "laissez faire" is managed. The model can be conceptualized as a two-tier system where those with privileged access to the state prosper, while workers, peasants, and small proprietors toil for subsistence incomes and diminishing social protection.

Mechanisms and Institutions

The main economic mechanisms used by China's communist sovereigns are state administration, management, and delegation; "socialist" markets; and communist/Confucian bureaucratic obligation. China's leaders have retained the "worker and peasant political dictatorship," state ownership of the means of production, authoritarianism, and pervasive powers of economic governance which allow the leadership to rule by decree while enhancing the system's potential with what it claims are socialist markets, operating without benefit of rule of law. They have also relied on cultural traditions of subservience and obligation to reduce moral hazards and sustain effort.

The Chinese Communist party is the defining institution of state power. It not only is the supreme directive authority, it is the sole source of authoritarian law which takes precedence over all commercial and individual rights. The Communist party alone determines the legality of socialist market institutions. Joint ventures, liberal state supervision, one-man-enterprise rule, peasant control over their plots, price decontrols, and

---

[7]   Charlotte Allen, "Confucius and the Scholars," *The Atlantic Monthly*, Vol. 283, No. 4, April 1999, pp. 78–83.
[8]   Angus Maddison, *Chinese Economic Performance in the Long Run*, OECD, Paris, September 1998. Cf. Steven Mosher, *Hegemon*, Encounter Books, San Francisco, 2000.

expanded legalization of private exchange are specific institutional aspects of the authoritarian laissez-faire mechanisms the Communist party has approved. Their merit is not intrinsic. It depends entirely on how they contribute to the achievement of communist goals by stimulating effort, making supply responsive to demand, augmenting elite compensation, and limiting "business agent" misconduct.

Supply and Demand

The sovereignty of the Communist party has not repealed the basic laws of negotiated utility- and profit-seeking. But it has modified some fundamental aspects. Chinese consumers form preferences. Their demand is an inverse function of price, given their budget constraints. The assortments they buy depend on relative prices. Their preferences are usually consistent, and they try to avoid overpaying. But their choices are restricted by prohibitions on goods and assets, preferential market access, state production, and import controls. Similarly, workers and peasants are compelled to overexert themselves (underconsume leisure) at prevailing wage rates by draconian administrative discipline including protracted penal forced labor. These curtailments of economic liberty are amplified by quotas placed on things consumers clearly desire, like domestic automobiles.

The law of supply holds with similar qualifications. The technologies of Chinese firms seem to exhibit diminishing marginal productivity and increasing marginal cost throughout stage II. Individuals and managers know that they can improve their welfare by trading with others, working, starting entrepreneurial ventures, hiring factors, economizing costs, innovating improving technology, borrowing and lending, advertising, and marketing their goods. They understand the virtues of efficient administration and planning. But their discretion is restricted by the Communist party. Labor supply is only a weak function of wages, and a stronger function of state discipline. Managerial supply curves depend on compensation, but are distorted by anti-productive insider self-seeking, frequently causing misinvestment, and oversupply.[9]

The Chinese do not profit maximize from the standpoint of the Communist party sovereign, or Anglo-American market competition because the separation of state ownership from "business agent" control, the suppression of wages, other government intervention, and collusion between Communist party officials and agents for personal gain discourage managers from maximizing returns to state and private equity. This does not stop some Chinese businessmen from pioneering new ventures, innovating, investing in research, training promising personnel, adopting best technologies, and otherwise increasing net revenues. But none of these activities maximize state dividends, and derivatively competitive national welfare. It is a control process through which the Communist elites pursue their antilibertarian sovereign objectives. Entrepreneurial ambition, innovation, and modernization must all be modified as the Party commands. Enormous amounts of

[9] The Chinese Model?" *Wall Street Journal*, October 23, 1998, p. A14. "Despite the development of the contract responsibility system since the early 1980s, governing relations between the managers of State-owned enterprises and the overseeing administration, and the spread of practices such as an auctioning off to the highest bidder of the job of CEO of State-owned enterprises, Chinese firms are still far from taking advantage of a market in chief executives comparable to developed industrial economies. Appointment of managing directors in the State-owned enterprises are more the result of a political and bureaucratic compromise between a host of local and

time are squandered working to rule in traditional state enterprises, or in unproductive collusive activities where moral hazard is a serious problem. Insider control also entrenches resentments and anti-productive attitudes among workers who cannot help recognize that, despite the state's nominal protection, they are being underpaid.

The extent of these losses is disguised by the benefits of massive foreign investments primarily by overseas Chinese, selected statistical disclosures, and by emphasis on macroeconomic statistics which gloss malfeasance, and do not adequately account for misinvestment and reporting fraud. In essence, the advantages of relative backwardness and overseas ethnic loyalties are concealing the flaws in the Langean model, while aggregate data hide distributive inequities.

Equilibrium

Chinese state mechanisms and socialist/Confucian bureaucratic obligation diminish and distort the efficiency of the Walrasian, Marshallian, and Keynesian adjustment mechanisms. Chinese communism substitutes party choices for individual demand and supply programs, and discipline, collusion, and compulsion for competitive negotiations, without consistently seeking to maximize social welfare. The Communist party elite, its "business agents," state functionaries, small private venturers, workers, and peasants are able to reach agreements, but the equilibria do not optimize individual, or authoritarian, welfare because the terms of demand and supply are not fully and fairly negotiated. Equilibria are second best, and subject to the vagaries of power and corruption.

The Chinese economic system alternatively can be conceptualized as a model with five market adjustment mechanisms: the familiar Walrasian, Marshallian, and Keynesian trio, socialist insider economic governance, and obligation. Communist policies sacrifice competitive efficiency for party power, and obligation bolsters work discipline and keeps some abuses within bounds. The Walrasian mechanism is impaired by communist governance because factor and product prices are prevented from optimally allocating labor and other inputs to alternative use among occupations and firms by mismanagement, regulatory barriers, and corruption, while surplus inventories may not be rapidly liquidated because of price-fixing and other collusive practices.

The Marshallian adjustment mechanism which in category A systems depends on profit-maximizing responses to factor and output prices to achieve equilibrium is similarly disordered because "business agents" subordinate profit-maximizing to other goals, and

---

central government agencies that have a say in the way the firm is run. Moreover, still with respect to large companies, the border between a political career and one as manager continues to be a hazy one, as in the former centrally-planned system." Huchet and Richet, "Between Bureaucracy and Market: Chinese Industrial Groups in Search of New Forms of Corporate Governance," paper presented at the American Economics Meetings, New Orleans, January 7, 2001. Cf. T. Groves, Y. Hong, J. McMillan and B. Naughton, "China's Evolving Managerial Labor Market," *Journal of Political Economy*, No. 103, pp. 873–92; Barry Naughton, *Growing Out of the Plan: Chinese Economic Reform 1978–1993*, Cambridge University Press, Cambridge, 1995. Also see, Xiao-yuan Dong and Louis Putterman, "Investigating the Rise of Labor Redundancy in China's State Industry," paper presented at the American Economics Meetings, New Orleans, January 6, 2001; Xin Meng, "Unemployment, Consumption Smoothing, and Precautionary Saving in Urban China," paper presented at the American Economics Meetings, New Orleans, January 6, 2001.

the Communist party distorts market equilibration with regulations including price, wage, and foreign exchange rate fixing, and tight foreign capital controls. Chinese firms can and do respond to outside demand, but supplies do not correspond to a utility-maximizing equilibrium because of party-dominated state governance and corruption.

Communism also distorts Keynesian adjustments by dampening or intensifying the income multiplier, under- or over-fully employing the population, and imposing barriers to internal mobility. The party–state creates jobs that should not exist, or fires workers on mass. Shocks affecting business confidence, the marginal efficiency of capital, and speculative demand for idle cash balances such as labor militancy are mitigated or aggravated by labor repression and activist monetary and fiscal policies, especially credit and foreign exchange controls. The party elite provides "business agents" with privileged contracts, exhorts consumer spending, cuts business taxes, offers subsidies, adjusts interest rates, augments credit, or forgives debt to bolster aggregate effective demand and long-term growth. These practices are sometimes beneficial in the short run, but erode national financial stability, and perpetuate anticompetitive inefficiencies that gradually devitalize the system.

Systemic Structure

All of these distortions are reflected in China's systemic structure and performance characteristics. The heart of the Chinese economy is its relatively closed party–state, "business agent" industrial and commercial enterprises, which provide a lavish life for a few and a meager living standard for everyone else. The foreign joint venture, and domestic construction and financial, sectors generate the largest hard currency contributions to GDP because they are portals to the global economy. Party–state control also extends beyond this into communally dominated agriculture, and public services which are extremely underproductive. These two mechanisms account for most of China's gross domestic product. There are no perfect markets, and a small criminal sector which commands, controls, and subjugates, much like some activities of the party–state, but without its legal sanction. The rest of the GDP is produced by miscellaneous inefficient agrarian, industrial, and commercial small proprietors aspiring to become a greater economic force.

Communist party power and purposes, and the activities of the elite's "business agents," thus explain most of the performance characteristics of Chinese systems; the stability and interplay of its mechanisms. Category A market economies are equilibrated through Walrasian, Marshallian, and Keynesian mechanisms. But in China economic activity throughout facilitates the Communist party elite's personal and political objectives, with government and obligation guiding markets and dominating outcomes.

The main effects of China's authoritarian laissez faire are evident. It has created a highly mobilized, work-intensive, party–state-dominated, macroeconomically volatile, corrupt, inegalitarian, "business agent" market economic system, with a fourth-tier standard of living, and a low level of crime. Insofar as the Communist party elite, "business agents," foreign investors, small proprietors, workers, and peasants are satisfied with these arrangements, the model could continue generating high growth and mixed welfare outcomes for many years, perhaps decades. But authoritarian laissez faire is contradictory.

It is a market model without the effective rule of contract law, which few, believe is viable in the long run. The Communist party elite, "business agents," and foreign investors want to enhance their positions, and gain clear title to the benefits they currently enjoy by privatizing much of the means of production, but China's leaders are concerned about the loss of their political authority, and the Russian disease. They know that the creation of unrestricted free enterprise de-legitimatizes the vanguard role of the Communist party, and that if privatization turns into a crazed scramble for wealth, the economy could nose-dive into hyperdepression and political disorder. Likewise small proprietors, workers, and peasants want political and economic freedom, but are concerned about losing what is left of the state's social protection. The leadership also recognizes the danger of temporizing. If it maintains the status quo, the system is likely to become dyspeptic, like the Soviet Union after 1968, as insider corruption proliferates, and those excluded from the magic circle become increasingly disgruntled. This suggests that while Langean category B models do provide a temporary institutional strategy for harnessing state control and markets, China will soon have to choose transitioning to a Western market model or reining its "business agents" and entrepreneurs. All options are risky. Privatizing does not guarantee the creation of viable free enterprise. There is always the Russian disease. Tightening discipline will alleviate some inefficiencies and grievances, but foment others. And staying the course may be worse.[10]

THE GEOMETRY OF CHINESE AUTHORITARIAN LAISSEZ FAIRE

The performance characteristics of Chinese authoritarian laissez faire can be formally examined with the aid of Edgeworth–Bowley production and consumption boxes, and diagrams depicting production possibilities and community indifference curves.

Employment opportunities and resource allocations in China are distorted by regulations, and factor price-fixing. Factor supplies are responsive to disequilibrium input prices, and derived factor demand is warped because state "business agents" do not competitively

[10]   There is growing skepticism about the Chinese model. See Louis Kraar, "Five Chinese Myths," *Fortune*, May 10, 1999, p. 30. The five myths he identifies are: (1) the PRC is a huge market (its per capita income computed at the exchange rate is only $800), (2) China will become the world's largest economy (claims that per capita growth in 1998 was only 3–4 percent), (3) the key to modernizing China is foreign investment (investment has been low tech), (4) China is immune from the Asian crisis (not so), and (5) market forces have taken over the Chinese economy (the economy is dominated by state corporations and collectives; only some 40 percent of industrial output comes from private ventures – a big increase from 1979, but still a minority). Regarding the danger of the Russian disease, see P. Boone, S. Gomulka and R. Layard (eds.), *Emerging from communism: Lessons from Russia, China and Eastern Europe*, MIT Press, Cambridge, 1998. Concerning corruption, see Julia Kwong, *The Political Economy of Corruption in China*, M.E. Sharpe, Armonk, 1997; and Biyan Liu and Perry Link, "A Great Leap Backward?" in *The New York Review of Books*, XLV, No.15, October 8, 2000, pp. 19–23. On asset-stripping, see Yanzheng Chao, Yingyi Qian and Barry Weingast, "The Sale Goes on: Transforming Small Enterprises in China," in *Transition*, February 1998, pp. 5–7; and X.L. Ding, "The Illicit Asset Stripping of Chinese State Firms," in *The China Journal*, No. 43, January 2000, pp. 1–28. For the possibility that the Russian contagion may spread to China's macro-economy, see Nicholas Lardy, *China's Unfinished Economic Revolution*, Brookings Institution Press, Washington DC, 1998; Lardy, "The Challenge of Bank Restructuring in China," China Research CLSA Emerging Market, 27.04.2000, and Lardy, "Fiscal Sustainability: Between a Rock and a Hard Place," *China Economic Quarterly*, No. 2,

profit maximize. At times during the Maoist period, corresponding inefficiencies were partly mitigated by managerial bonuses which restricted managers' room for maneuver, and a fervid sense of communist obligation (causing individuals to work harder in accordance with group expectation), but insiders now are encouraged to pay more attention to spurring growth through entrepreneurial rent-seeking, than protecting their employees and preserving the state's assets. This not only is eroding employee trust and loyalty and undermining productivity, but impairs labor allocation, with some workers being needlessly retained and others arbitrarily dismissed. Collectivized control and ownership in the agricultural sector have the same adverse impacts. Under Mao it could have been argued on ideological grounds that "redness" (devotion to the spirit of communism) transformed toil into pleasure, prompting a higher voluntary labor supply than in a category A system, but the decay of socialist idealism (and communality) suggest that this is no longer applicable. The net result of these forces has been a contraction of the labor axis of the Edgeworth–Bowley production box (figure 10.1), and expansion of the capital axis. The isoquant levels within the production space are lower than the competitive ideal because capital and labor are misincentivized and workers inadequately rewarded. And, of course, factor prices are in acute disequilibrium due to wage- and price-fixing, entry barriers, crony authoritarian laissez faire, and insider control. Thus instead of operating at E'' on a relatively efficient "authoritarian," production feasibility frontier illustrated in figure 10.2, production occurs on a lower feasibility frontier at point R.

The composition and characteristics of China's goods are also marred by forced characteristic and product substitution. Consumer demand has less influence over managerial supply decision-making in Jiang's market than in the West. As a consequence, the volume indexes on the domestic good isoquants q_A^1 in figure 10.1 have to be adjusted downward by converting goods with dispreferred characteristics into smaller quantities of standard outputs at the competitive marginal rate of transformation. The situation for exports is similar, but less serious because of the competitiveness of the global marketplace. Analogous adjustments are required for the mis-selection of technologies,[11] mismanagement, and faulty entrepreneurship, all lowering isoquant values in the Edgeworth–Bowley production box, and causing an inward shift off the production possibilities frontier.[12]

Many state firms, however, have prospered. But unfortunately they are exceptions that prove the rule. Collusive contracting between the party elite and state managers, easy credit, and creative accounting have become preferred paths to prosperity for the fortunate

---

2000, pp. 36–41. Chinese leaders have responded by trying to improve governance. See Harry Broadman, "China's Membership in the WTO and Enterprise Reform: The Challenge for Accession and Beyond," Discussion Paper, The World Bank, 2000; Joseph Chai, *Transition to a Market Economy*, Oxford University Press, London, 1998; Ross Garnaut and Yiping Huang, eds., *Readings on the Chinese Economy in the Era of Reform*, Oxford University Press, London, 2000.

[11] The technologies embodied in the fixed capital stock cannot be drastically altered in the short run. The only aspect of technology therefore that bears on efficiency is the degree to which technological improvements correspond with the competitive optimum.

[12] Although all individuals in the competitive model independently maximize their utility, managers are permitted to noncoercively negotiate conditions of employment and organizational matters with their employees which may profoundly affect enterprise productivity.

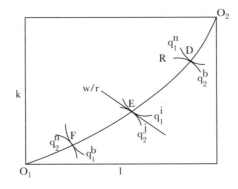

Figure 10.1   Chinese factor allocation

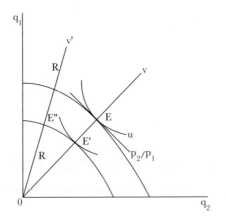

Figure 10.2   Chinese efficiency possibilities

few. Asset-stripping (looting, scrapping, and sale of otherwise useful collectively owned assets for personal gain) is becoming troublesome, and oligopoly provides a lucrative alternative to competitive profit-maximizing. Chinese entrepreneurship has counteracted these static inefficiencies by raising productivity from wretchedly low levels, but entrepreneurship is also a source of concern because managers gamble recklessly with the state's money, too often resulting in staggering losses (a phenomenon disguised in the GDP growth statistics by under-reporting capital depreciation). Misallocation of investment credit by the state banking monopoly, and the underdevelopment of the consumer credit markets are additional sources productive inefficiency.

The welfare characteristics of authoritarian laissez faire are similarly defective. Jiang's reforms have unleashed a spate of revenue-grabbing, asset-stripping, rent-seeking, and financial malfeasance which concentrates control of wealth and income in relatively few hands, mostly protégés of the Communist party, while repressing wages and preserving low incomes in the countryside. This is illustrated in figure 10.3 by forced movements away from point E toward D (where the Communist party receives an unjustly large share of GDP) along the contract curve, or off it at point D′. This diminishes social welfare by misdistributing goods and services without regard to value added, need, or merit. The system

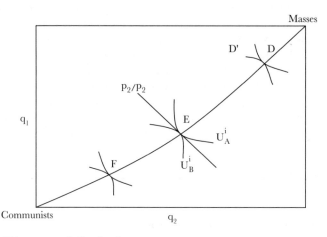

Figure 10.3   Chinese retail distribution

has proven to be doubly unjust because wealth, income, and access to governmental services have been usurped, not earned causing severe distributional inequities. It has reduced welfare further by impeding job mobility, distorting terms of retail trade, and constricting choice through forced product characteristic substitution and restricted personal liberty. Despite the ostentatious display of the nouveaux riches, the standard of living for most is poor because supplies are inadequate, and the retail sector is not responsive enough to the demands of ordinary people. Figure 10.4, which arrays the Communist party elite and other state "business agents" on the ordinate and workers and peasants on the abscissa, illustrates this inequity by comparing the achieved Chinese social utility frontier (which takes account of all infringements of personal liberty) with the competitive ideal. Point D shows that the

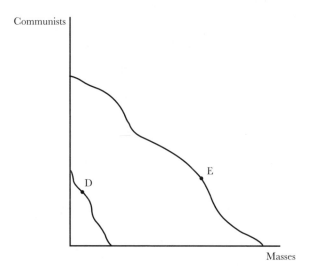

Figure 10.4   Chinese utility possibilities

average quality of Chinese life is a small fraction of potential (E), with the Communist party elite and insiders faring well compared with the plight of the masses.

Jiang's communist laissez faire thus is comprehensively inefficient. But China's market is paradise compared with Russia's, because "business agent" energy has been channeled into revenue-maximizing by the state's refusal to radically privatize, and by the massive inflow of foreign know-how, technology and capital. As long as the Chinese Communist party keeps a lid on labor costs, and retains state ownership,[13] GDP may continue to grow rapidly, but the strategy also may come unglued if labor becomes restive, or Jiang throws the doors open to insider individual privatization, precipitating a spate of asset grabbing of the sort destroying Russia.[14]

Review

Main Features of the Chinese Economic System

Culture: Communist authoritarian/family-centered guilt-based individual self-seeking. Communist authoritarian development mentality, overlain on Confucian social ethos marked by strong autonomous values, and extended family obligation.

Motivation: Communist elite preservation of party power and self-seeking privilege.

Mechanisms: Natural resources, land and a substantial share of the industrial means of production remain partly or wholly state (communally) owned, providing a basis for Communist party regulated and controlled, markets. Workers are repressed, while managers are given broad discretion in operations, investment, entrepreneurship and finance.

   State economic governance partly serves the public interest and partly the venal purposes of the Communist party elite through a wide range of activities including procurement programs, bureaucratic assignments, controls, state ownership, and extensive

---

[13]   State ownership is not intrinsically desirable, but it may be a second best if alternative privatization programs are inconsistent with general competition.

[14]   Shan Li and Tian Zhu, "China, Too, Faces Financial Perils," *Wall Street Journal*, October 28, 1998, p. A22; "The Chinese Model?" *Wall Street Journal*, October 23, 1998, p. A14; Erik Eckholm, "Not (Yet) Gone the Way of all Asia: China Holds its Ground, Despite the Economic Warning Signs," *New York Times*, November 15, 1998, p. 6; Edward Steinfeld, *Forging Reform in China: The Fate of State-Owned Industry*, Cambridge University Press, New York, 1998; Jean-Francois Huchet, and Xavier Richet, "Between Bureaucracy and Market: Chinese Industrial Groups in Search of New Forms of Corporate Governance," paper presented at the American Economics Meeting, New Orleans, December 7, 2001. For more information on contemporary governance rules, see OECD, *Reforming China's Enterprises*, Paris, OECD, 2000; John Knight and Linda Song, *Economic Disparities and Interactions in China*, Oxford University Press, London, 1999; Azizur Rahman Khan and Carl Riskin, *Inequality and Poverty in China in the Age of Globalization*, Oxford University Press, 2000. See also Randall Morck, Bernard Yeung and Wayne Yu, "The Information Content of Stock Markets: Why Do Emerging Markets Have Synchronous Stock Price Movements?" *Journal of Financial Economics*, No. 58, 2000, pp. 215–60 (this paper demonstrates the inefficiency of China's financial markets).

micro- and macroeconomic regulation of the laws of demand, supply and equilibration. Public administration and markets are distorted by moral hazard and adverse selection.

Institutions: Authoritarian state governance, joint ventures, and some industrial collectivist shareholding, one-man-rule by state agent enterprise managers, communal ownership, and the Communist party apparat.

Main Inefficiencies

Law of
demand: Individual preferences are influenced by the directives, programs, controls, regulations, moral hazards, and the property right policies of the Communist party. There are also some communalist influences operating parallel to Communist party ideals, but they are not as strong as in Japan.

Law of
supply: Worker supply curves are weak functions of wages; stronger functions of communist discipline policies. Managerial supply curves are increasingly functions of compensation. Enterprise supply functions in traditional firms are subservient to party guidance; those under the authoritarian laissez-faire regime while profit-seeking are strongly influenced by insider self-seeking. Marketing supply functions give priority to the Communist party elite, and special institutions like the military, while the rest of the economy is dominated by Walrasian processes.

Law of
equilibration: Markets are imperfectly competitive. Distribution to the Communist party elite and privileged institutions like the People's Liberation Army tend to be on an assignment basis. Marketing to the rest of the economy is dominated by Walrasian processes. Labor mobility, especially migration from the countryside to the cities, is partly controlled by state. The labor productivity losses associated with immobility are not offset by obligation as in the Japanese case.

Marshallian production equilibration gives priority to Communist party policy and insider self-seeking over competitive profit-maximizing.

Keynesian macro-equilibration is tied to Communist party policy, which takes account of regional and local political interests, and to insider self-seeking, not to worker aspirations and nonparty interest groups. Wage repression, worker discipline, credit and foreign capital controls, and fixed exchange rates greatly affect macroeconomic causality.

Authoritarian Laissez-Faire
Rationale for Liberalizing the Command System

Topic	Problem	Party Response
State planning, command, and enterprise control	Suppress individual autonomy, curtail utility-seeking, depress initiative, diminish competence, promote apathy and corruption	Discipline, exhortation, "authoritarian laissez faire" but retaining substantial state ownership
State ownership	Administrative managerial mentality unconcerned with profit-maximizing, efficiency, consumer satisfaction, and entrepreneurship	"Authoritarian laissez faire" granting managers autonomy and rights over the use of state funds
"Authoritarian laissez faire"	Rent-seeking, asset-grabbing, elite-collusive, anticompetitive, worker exploitive insider control	Admonitions to uphold communist ethical principles
Foreign joint ventures	Vehicle for transferring embezzled state funds abroad	Nominal controls
Communist party	Subordinates public interest to elite self-seeking, and ideological imperatives	Token democratization

Systemic Structure

	Share of GDP	Productivity (Destructiveness)	Coercion
Markets			
Perfect markets	0	–	–
Inefficient markets	18	Very low	Medium
Business agent markets	55	Medium	High
Government	25	Very low	High

Obligation
   Criminal disservices   2   (High)   –

Systems Characteristics

	Degree/Intensity
State macro-regulation	High
State micro-regulation	
Pro-competitive	Medium
Elite	High
Welfare/security	Medium/high
State spending programs	
Privileged contracting	High
Misappropriation	Medium (growing)
Cronyism	Medium
Criminal disservices	
Asset seizure and embezzlement	Low
Addiction/vice	Low
Repression, extortion, and murder	Low
Subjugation, servitude	Low
Causes of macroeconomic disequilibria	
Sticky wages (upward)	High (overproduction)
Sticky prices	Medium
Investment avoidance	Medium
Misinvestment	High
Liquidity preference	High
Insecure private property rights	High
State property rights	Medium
Foreign capital flows	Medium
Fear of criminality	Low
Anticompetitive business repression	Medium
General business repression	Low
Labor subjugation	High
Judicial risk	High
State corruption	High
Macropolicy mismanagement	Medium
Class conflict	Incipient

Main Performance Indicators

Per capita GDP 1998 (US = 100)	11
Per capita GDP growth 1990–99 (compound annual rate)	9
Per capita GDP growth 1960–99 (compound annual rate)	?

Inflation 1990–99	10
Unemployment 1999	
Share of labor force	
Domestic definition	1
International definition	?
Length of work year	
person–hours (US = 100)	?
Retirement support burden	low
Nonworking mothers and wives	low

Main Direction of Reform

Glacial transformation to a multi-party democracy; gradual development of private enterprise, with strong cronyist state management.

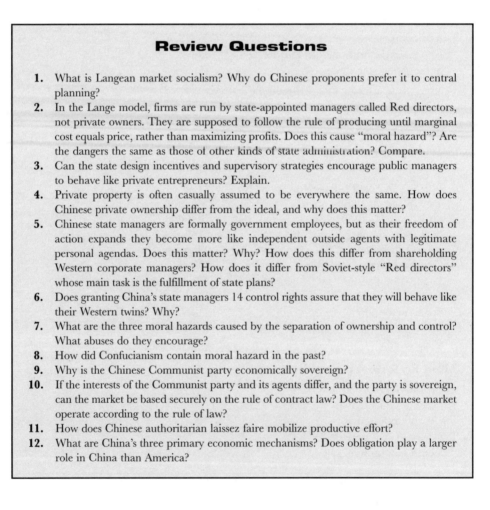

Review Questions

1. What is Langean market socialism? Why do Chinese proponents prefer it to central planning?
2. In the Lange model, firms are run by state-appointed managers called Red directors, not private owners. They are supposed to follow the rule of producing until marginal cost equals price, rather than maximizing profits. Does this cause "moral hazard"? Are the dangers the same as those of other kinds of state administration? Compare.
3. Can the state design incentives and supervisory strategies encourage public managers to behave like private entrepreneurs? Explain.
4. Private property is often casually assumed to be everywhere the same. How does Chinese private ownership differ from the ideal, and why does this matter?
5. Chinese state managers are formally government employees, but as their freedom of action expands they become more like independent outside agents with legitimate personal agendas. Does this matter? Why? How does this differ from shareholding Western corporate managers? How does it differ from Soviet-style "Red directors" whose main task is the fulfillment of state plans?
6. Does granting China's state managers 14 control rights assure that they will behave like their Western twins? Why?
7. What are the three moral hazards caused by the separation of ownership and control? What abuses do they encourage?
8. How did Confucianism contain moral hazard in the past?
9. Why is the Chinese Communist party economically sovereign?
10. If the interests of the Communist party and its agents differ, and the party is sovereign, can the market be based securely on the rule of contract law? Does the Chinese market operate according to the rule of law?
11. How does Chinese authoritarian laissez faire mobilize productive effort?
12. What are China's three primary economic mechanisms? Does obligation play a larger role in China than America?

13. How does China's state management affect private demand? How does the derived demand for forced labor differ from ordinary derived demand?

14. Explain why Chinese enterprises do not profit maximize in the sense required by general competition.

15. Do the Communist party and its agents play each other in the same way that the state and business do in America?

16. Why is the efficiency of the Walrasian adjustment mechanism impaired in China?

17. Why is the efficiency of the Marshallian adjustment mechanism impaired in China?

18. Chinese macrotheorists are proud of the People's Republic's performance. Why are these accomplishments exaggerated?

19. How would China's market structure change if the system were perfectly competitive? Would the role of obligation increase?

20. Why do some economists consider Deng's system a success?

21. Why do critics disagree? Who is right? Why?

22. Is China's factor supply and allocation Pareto efficient? Use the Edgeworth–Bowley production box in figure 10.1 to explain.

23. Is China's production Pareto ideal? Use figure 10.2 to explain.

24. How do Chinese financial inefficiencies affect outcomes in the short and long term in figure 10.2.

25. Is Chinese retailing efficient? Use figure 10.3 to explain.

26. Is the Chinese system socially just? Use figure 10.4 to explain.

27. The priority given to work, development, and consumerism in the Chinese system camouflages its inefficiencies. Explain why welfare would be higher under perfect competition.

CHAPTER 11

RUSSIA

Post-communist Russia is a mis-industrially developed nation, with enormous natural resource wealth, a literate work force, and a huge, but obsolete capital stock. It is a Eurasian power, with territories stretching from the Baltic Sea to the Pacific Ocean, which holds sway over much of the Commonwealth of Independent States, the federated successor of the USSR. Moscow possesses the world's largest nuclear stockpile, complementary intercontinental ballistic missile (ICBM) delivery systems, and antiballistic missile (ABM) capabilities of dubious worth.

As late as 1991, the American Central Intelligence Agency (CIA) considered the Soviet Union to have the world's second largest GDP. The Russian republic within the USSR was said to enjoy a standard of living at the West European mean. A succession of reappraisals, following the collapse of the Soviet Union, and the Russian Federation's precipitous economic decline have drastically altered this impression. Estimates by the state statistical agency (Goskomstat) placed Russia's per capita GDP just above China's in 1998.

This downgrade, which may understate its living standard, is partly explained by the hyperdepression engulfing Russia in the wake of the USSR's dissolution, and the abandonment of Soviet command planning, which has made Russia the "sick man of Eurasia." Neither former Soviet President Mikhail Gorbachev nor his Western advisors thought anything like this post-Soviet debacle would happen, assuming that it was just a hop, skip, and jump from a system of complete centralized state control to some attractive variant of European social democratic free enterprise.

Unfortunately, Russia has landed in another place somewhere between the hop and the jump. The economic system which has taken root is a culturally regulated category B variant of an imperfectly competitive Eastern authoritarian market economy, founded on individual utility-seeking, opportunism, mixed ownership of the means of production, and negotiated prices, including wages, interest, and foreign exchange rates. The government is formally democratic, with an authoritarian executive focused on building new structures of post-communist privilege. Putin's grip on the regions, and on operational aspects of the economy, is feeble compared with prior Soviet leaders, or Jiang Zemin's Communist party controlled China. The state's primary power lies in its ownership of natural resources, land, and some valuable industrial assets. It also wields authority through control over money emission, credit, and the disbursal of tax revenues for legitimate public programs and cronyist ventures. Russia's micro- and macroeconomic regulatory and contract enforcement mechanisms are inefficient and sometimes dysfunctional. Its markets are not disciplined by the rule of contract law, as they must be in well-functioning category A self-regulating market systems, and authoritarian economic governance is not rationalized by the golden rule.

Russian laws of supply, demand, and equilibration satisfy the core requirements of the utility-seeking paradigm, but are disordered by a widespread refusal to adhere to the golden rule, with some segments of society exploiting others in free-form criminal games with few signs of normalization. The dominant players are motivated by asset-grabbing and rent-seeking, rather than productive profit-maximizing. They are anticompetitive, and protect their misacquired wealth by exporting it to safe havens abroad. The Walrasian distributive adjustment mechanism functions constructively within these constraints, but the Marshallian and Keynesian adjustment mechanisms are dysfunctional. Russia has managed to extricate itself from an earlier bout of hyperinflation, but the real economy continues to operate at less than 50 percent of its pre-Soviet industrial capacity.

Opinions about the merit of Russia's klepto-authoritarian liberalization depend on whether the system is viewed as a permanent model or a way station to free enterprise. No one has anything good to say about kleptocratic laissez faire (a variant of the Chinese model with private ownership, and weak executive economic control) except perhaps by comparison with Stalinism, but many remain optimistic that Russia will achieve a successful competitive market system within a decade.

THE RUSSIAN ECONOMIC SYSTEM

History

Russia has been a great, but turbulent, nation since the founding of Kievan Rus in 864 AD.[1] It was conquered and ruled by the Tatars (Mongols) from 1240 until the reign of the Muscovy Czar Ivan III in 1480. Thereafter, it began a slow, steady expansion of its dominions, sprawling south, west, and east under Alexei, Peter the Great, Catherine the Great, Alexander III, Lenin, and Stalin, until it absorbed the Ukraine, Siberia, Far East, Byelorussia, Moldavia, and the Baltic States, as well as Kazahkstan, Kirghizia, Uzbekistan, Tadzhikistan, Georgia, and Armenia, and a large portion of Poland. The dissolution of the Soviet Union stripped Russia of many of these territorial acquisitions. Latvia, Estonia, and Lithuania appear to have permanently left the Russian orbit, but Byelorussia has recently deepened its links with the Russian Federation, and the rest of the former member states

---

[1]   This date marks the Swedish Viking Rurik's (legendary) founding of Novgorod. The beginning of the Viking Oleg's (Helge in Swedish) rule over Kiev as Grand Prince in 882 AD is an alternative starting point. He was followed by Igor in 912–45, and Olga (Swedish Helga) in 945–62. Kiev and Novgorod were united under Oleg.

remain affiliated in the Commonwealth of Independent States, the successor institution to the USSR, with a military organization under the control of the Russian Ministry of Defense. Russia possesses the world's largest territory, with vast mineral wealth, and armed forces including nuclear, ballistic, and antiballistic missile assets to match. This makes it a nuclear superpower, but the nation has fallen on hard times following the collapse of the Soviet Union. It lost roughly 40 percent of its population and a third of its GDP as a direct consequence of disunion, and then swooned into a hyperdepression (1989–98) that is now estimated to have reduced GDP by 30 to 50 percent. In 1992 the American Central Intelligence Agency estimated that the Soviet Union's GDP was the world's second largest; that Russia's per capita income placed it in the first development tier (United Nations five-tier classification system), at the European mean. All this has changed. According to the Russian statistical agency (Goskomstat), Russia's per capita income in 1998 was only a little higher than China's, in the fourth development tier, with an aggregate GDP approximately one tenth of the People's Republic. This downgrade is explained partly by Russia's depression, and partly by a sharp cut in estimated dollar purchasing power parities. A revised estimate gives a more favorable impression, but is still far below the old level.

Although Russia and China shared a similar Soviet-type, Communist party dominated command economic system for 40 years, and both subsequently adopted radical market reforms, Russia's per capita GDP has declined at a compound annual rate of approximately 5 percent per annum for much of the 1990s, while China's has surged forward at a 9 percent clip, despite many lingering similarities of system and hegemonic culture. Both states retain substantial ownership stakes in their respective industrial means of production, have sole title to mineral wealth, place strong restrictions on the ownership of land, and have agrarian sectors with communal legacies, and regulated private farming. Both have largely abolished command central planning (although indicative planning persists), and have granted producers and consumers wide discretion in transacting their business through the market. Producers, who are accustomed to operating in an authoritarian cultural environment, have considerable freedom in determining all aspects of supply, and most aspects of distribution, and consumers are permitted to customize their purchases and competitively negotiate price, including wage rates and other compensation. But neither country's markets nor government sectors are competitively self-regulating under the "rule of law" as required in category A consumer sovereign systems. Russia and China are both authoritarian "culturally regulated" category B market/administrated systems which combine imperfect competition, planning, administration, government regulation, and controls. They differ from each other only by the degree to which state agents are allowed to subordinate their productive obligations to personal enrichment. Russia's leaders have permitted ministers, state agents, and cronies to disregard their official duties, channeling their energies into acquiring denationalized assets and misappropriating state revenues, whereas the 55 million strong Chinese Communist party has maintained administrative discipline.

Both models are collectivist with partial state ownership, managerial profit-seeking, and consumer utility optimizing. But in the Russian version, the leadership has abandoned its economic oversight and stewardship in favor of self-enrichment and new forms of privilege, while the Chinese Communist party continues to restrain managerial abuses, and advance its domestic and global aspirations. As in the past, Moscow's model may be just a passing phase. President Vladimir Putin's declared intention is to ultimately privatize Russia's remaining state-owned industrial enterprises, and all land, although he has been less forthright about mineral ownership, creating a "self-regulating" category A generally competitive market system, without the stewardship of this or that political party (including the Communists) under what he calls "the dictatorship of law." Perhaps he will succeed, breaking completely with Russia's thousand year authoritarian legacy.

Culture

The Russian economy today from a formal standpoint is a dysfunctionally authoritarian "culturally regulated" category B Eastern market system. Both its authoritarianism and dysfunctionality have deep cultural roots reflecting Russia's position on the periphery of Europe and Asia. It inherited a Christian guilt culture from the West, but failed to assimilate the ethical refinements of humanism and the Renaissance because of the Mongol occupation and the despotism of Ivan the Terrible. This could have been offset by Confucianism or Taoism, but the East's primary legacy was almost entirely negative. During the Mongol occupations the Kremlin was servile, fatalistic, and passively resistive when the horde passed through, and despotic when it was absent. Russians of all strata learned to live opportunistically. They disesteemed productive labor and investment because the future was too problematic, and rulers simply took what they wanted. And of course, misery loved company, the poor begrudged their neighbors' self-advancement, and the aristocracy had little sense of social obligation. Russia under the Czars was a Hobbesian world; a war of all against all without scruples or communitarian purpose, despite the usual "sunshine" cultural idealism. Serfdom, as Alexander Gerschenkron showed, was virtual slavery with people being bought and sold, shunted hither and thither, and families broken apart at the lord's whim despite legal prohibitions. It was the most despotic form of peasant subjugation in Europe, lasting formally until 1861, and informally well beyond. The Russian brand of authoritarianism associated with these cultural values displays a distinct split personality. Strong rulers like Ivan the Terrible, Peter the Great, Catherine the Great, and Stalin, with expansive imperial aspirations, found that they could easily overcome cultural gravity with an iron fist. They could mobilize effort and suppress dissent. But whenever the state was weak, Russia became indolent, polarized, and corrupt in ways that precluded either free enterprise under the rule of law, or authoritarian dictate from forging an effective economic system.[2]

Contemporary Russian authoritarianism stems from this heritage, reflected in the constitutional powers of the president, and the ease with which privileged members of closed state and private circles impose their will on the market and other economic processes. It is reflected in executive domination of the media, the use of tax police

---

[2]   Geoffrey Hosking, *Russia and the Russians: A History*, Harvard University Press, Cambridge, MA, 2001. Hosking leans on an insight borrowed from the Soviet semiotician Yuri Lotman: "In Russia, the most radical changes, despite appearances, actually reinforce the traditions of the society they are meant to change." Cf., Vladimir Maliavin, "The East, the West and the Russian Idea: A New Approach to Comparative Civilizations," *The Stockholm Journal of East Asian* Studies, Vol. 10, 1999, pp. 125–42.

for business and regional tax enforcement,[3] majority state and worker ownership of substantial portions of the means of production, the "one-man rule" of minority co-owner managers, and economic collusion among state officials, managers, the Red Mafia, and oligarchs (a few tycoons who have cobbled together private financial empires from denationalized and semi-denationalized properties). The state, controlled by the president, claims proprietorship of the assets and incomes derived from the nation's mineral wealth, land, and a significant portion of the medium- and large-scale capital stock, and additionally asserts the right to administer, tax, subsidize, price-fix, transfer, regulate, and control any and all economic activities at its discretion. But neither Russia's presidents nor its bureaucracy have chosen to uphold the golden rule, to responsibly exercise these powers on the people's or the state's behalf.[4] Instead, they have engaged in macroeconomic misconduct for their personal benefit and delegated unsupervised micro-economic autonomy to state-appointed managers where majority ownership is still vested with the government, to co-shareholding managers in state minority-owned firms, and to entrepreneurs in wholly privately owned ventures, without taking adequate measures to assure fair compensation and protect assets and proprietary income. These agents and privileged parties have embezzled state funds from the central bank, including IMF monies, pocketed money from the state budget, and participated in schemes for personal gain that would have been criminally prosecuted in the West.[5]

This rogues' gallery of politicians, officials, bureaucrats, oligarchs, managers, new entrepreneurs, security police, and professional criminals, many survivors of the Soviet Communist party apparat, collectively can be described as kleptocrats; a coterie that has usurped the economic sovereignty of the state, and of consumers. They have created a Byzantine set of property and market rights which reflect the ever changing, free-form struggle within Russia to control the divestiture of the people's assets, and to institutional-ize privilege. Private ownership in Russia is not the transparent and familiar concept Westerners often mis-suppose. Much of what passes for private property is actually semiprivate, with various degrees of state participation, and nonstate ownership dispersed among three groups: workers, managers, and outsiders. Overall, the largest shareholders in the nation's assets are workers (including managers) and the state, with proportions varying greatly both within and among classes of assets. The state is majority owner in a significant number of industrial and commercial enterprises, and nearly all of agriculture since it continues to own the land. Despite the rhetoric of privatization, it retains a huge proprietary stake throughout the economy, which could easily allow the government to

[3]   Theodore Karasik, *Johnson's Russia List*, No. 4533, 2000.
[4]   Peter Reddaway and Dmitri Glinski, *The Tragedy of Russia's Reforms: Market Bolshevism Against Democracy*, US Institute of Peace Press, Washington, DC, 2001. They argue that Yeltsin's "authoritarian modernization ruined the nation and despoiled the idea of democracy in the popular mind."
[5]   Christopher Cox (Chairman House Policy Committee), *Russia's Road to Corruption*, US House of Representatives, Washington DC, September 2000. Andrew Higgins and David Cloud, "Senior Russian Official is Arrested in New York," *Wall Street Journal*, January 19, 2001, p. A11. Pavel Borodin, a senior official and patron of President Vladimir Putin, was arrested and held for extradition to Switzerland to face money laundering charges involving 25 million dollars in kick-backs from Swiss companies that renovated the Kremlin. Borodin is immune from prosecution in Russia. Also see Anders Aslund, "Russia's Collapse," *Foreign Affairs*, Vol. 78, No. 5, September/October 1999, pp. 64–77, and Jeffrey Taylor, "Russia is Finished," *The Atlantic Monthly*, Vol. 287, No. 5, May 2001, pp. 35–53.

exercise operational control, especially if it dilutes the equity of other owners by arbitrarily issuing supplementary shares (velvet expropriation).

The public also has equity stakes in largely moribund industrial firms (valuable assets being reserved, or given to the oligarchs) as a result of a voucher scheme which gave each citizen a token share in the means of production. These shares were mostly deposited in mutual funds, partly embezzled, and are now concentrated in relatively few hands, but they do not provide owners with assured dividends or influence. They may be important from time to time in acquisitions and various speculative ploys, but otherwise do not significantly affect enterprise operations.[6]

The smallest primary shareholding class is arguably management. The state granted this group approximately 20 percent of the insider stock, but through various means their share has risen to 15 percent of the total. The pattern of managerial ownership varies widely, seldom exceeding the combined weight of the state and workers, but managers nonetheless enjoy effective control thanks to legislation granting them one-man rule, and the state's aversion to governmental micro-supervision. This decision, which replicates Soviet arrangements where worker collectives nominally co-managed production but managers directed operations, has brought about a radical separation of ownership and control, encouraging managers to pursue their personal interests at the expense of other co-owners through adverse selection.

The official rationale for Yeltsin's privatization strategy was much like Deng Xiaoping's. Both blamed the underperformance of their command economies on the constraints placed by planners and ministerial administrators on managerial discretion and entrepreneurship. These had been gradually relaxed since Stalin's death, but it was believed that

---

[6]   The initial book value of vouchers was approximately 50 dollars. A. Radygin, "Pereraspredelenie pravsobstvennosti v post-privatizatsionnoi Rossii,"(The Redistribution of Property Rights in Post-Privatized Russia), *Voprosy ekonomiki*, Vol. 6, June 1999, pp. 54–75, provides data on the evolution of insider and outsider shareholding for private corporations. According to the latest estimates by S. Aukutsionek, R. Kapliushnikov and V. Zhukov, "Dominant Shareholders and Performance in Industrial Enterprises," *The Russian Economic Barometer*, 1998, No. 1, pp. 8–41, insiders held 58.5 percent and outsiders excluding the state held 31.7 percent of industrial corporate shares in 1995. The state retained a 9.5 percent stake. Workers owned 48.5 percent of the total, directors 10 percent. Outsiders respectively held the following positions: banks 1.6 percent, investment funds 7.2 percent, holding companies and FIGs 8.1percent, individuals 9.6 percent, and foreigners 1.7 percent. Others accounted for 0.3 percent. The authors forecast a decline in workers' ownership to 36.3 percent and the state's share to 2.7 percent in 1999, with the primary gainers being managers (15 percent), FIGs (11.8 percent), and individuals (15.6 percent). Separately, John Earle believes that there has been little change in ownership structure since 1994. Cf. John Earle and Saul Estrin, "After Voucher Privatization: The Structure of Corporate Ownership in Russian Manufacturing Industry," paper prepared for the American Association for the Advancement of Slavic Studies meetings, Seattle, WA, November 22, 1997. Radygin concludes that the structure of ownership is not as important as the corrupt control of managers. For a contrary view about the positive effects of privatization, see Iu. Perevalov, I. Grimadi and V. Dobrodei, "Vliiaet li privatizatsiia na deiatel 'nost' predpriiatii?" (Has Privatization Affected Enterprise Performance?), *Voprosy ekonomiki*, No. 6, June 1999, pp. 76–89. Saul Estrin and Mike Wright, "Corporate Governance in the Former Soviet Union: An Overview," *Journal of Comparative Economics*, Vol. 27, No. 3, September 1999, pp. 398–421; Trevor Buck, Igor Filatotchev, Mike Wright and Vladimir Zhukov, "Corporate Governance and Employee Ownership in an Economic Crisis: Enterprise Strategies in the Former USSR," *Journal of Comparative Economics*, Vol. 27, No. 3, September 1999, pp. 459–74. J. David Brown and John Earle, "Privatization, Competition, and Transition Policy Strategies: Theory and Evidence from Russian Enterprise Panel Data," paper presented at the American Economics meetings, New Orleans, January 5, 2001; Saul Estrin and Mike Wright, "Corporate Governance in the Former Soviet Union: An Overview," *Journal of Comparative Economics*, Vol. 27, No. 3, September 1999, pp. 398–421.

liberalization hadn't gone far enough, even under Gorbachev's program of radical economic reform. Managers were given restricted authority to modernize enterprise capital,
redesign standard products and innovate new ones, vary product mixes, violate some plan
targets, bonus maximize with respect to output and profit, market products outside the
state material technical supply system, and start new ventures. But wages, prices, interest,
and foreign exchange rates remained fixed, and access to credit and money were tightly
controlled. Enterprises for the most part did not sell their products for cash in the open
market. They received credit entries in their accounts in the state bank as soon as goods
were manufactured and delivered to the state wholesale network, Gossnab. Wages and
other input costs were debited in the same way. These procedures deterred embezzlement
and other misuse of state funds, and provided managers with the luxury of assured
demand for everything they produced. But they also tied managers hands, and prevented
the competitive allocation of resources and product distribution.

Within weeks after the dissolution of the Soviet Union on December 25, 1991, urged by
Western advocates of shock therapy, Yeltsin attempted to free managers from these
restraints, command planning, and ministerial supervision with one bold stroke. He can-
celed all nonessential state contracts, effectively terminating assured government purchase,
and compelled enterprises to fend for themselves. To assist them, firms were relieved of the
burden of state bank financial controls, central plans, ministerial micro-production and
distribution directives, and state-fixed wage rates and prices. They were empowered to
conduct their businesses with all the theoretical rights of category A competitive transactors.

These included unfettered control rights overproduction, pricing, sales, procurement,
foreign trade, investment, use of retained funds, disposal of assets, merger and acquisitions,
labor, personnel management, wages, bonuses, and internal organization. Russian managers could act as if they were capitalist owners, choosing location, facilities, and technologies, designing products, selecting least cost input suppliers, hiring and firing labor,
negotiating wages, producing and distributing goods in assortments that maximized
enterprise profits (for all shareholders including the state), and determining their own
compensation. They were also permitted to form joint ventures with foreign corporations
and hold assets abroad.

Each of these rights had the effect of relaxing a restriction on free competition, which –
other things being equal – should have, and in some instances surely did, increase economic
efficiency. As the newly fashioned state, semiprivate, and private sectors began producing
things people wanted at lower cost, it seemed reasonable to suppose that the economy would
build up considerable transformational momentum, attracting foreign investors lured by
new opportunities and cheap, skilled labor. But these expectations were dashed. Instead,
Russia's economy began to sink like a stone, plunging into hyperdepression (perhaps as
much as twice as deep as the American Great Depression of 1929), accompanied by spiral-
ing hyperinflation (2,500 percent per annum) because the state had not prepared adequately
for the transition, and the strategies it adopted were destabilizing and destructive.

The most glaring defect of "shock therapy" (some dispute the therapeutic intent), lay
in the impossibility of rapid transition from the command to the competitive model.[7] Even

[7]   The Debate over "shock therapy" continues to rage. See Joseph Stiglitz, "Wither Reform? Ten Years of
Transition," *Annual Bank Conference on Development Economics*, edited by Boris Pleskovic and Joseph Stiglitz, World
Bank, Washington, DC, 2000, pp. 27–56; Marek Dabrowski, Stanislaw Gomulka, and Jacek Rostowski, "Whence

if property somehow had been transferred into honest and competent hands, managers had no practical knowledge of redesigning products to suit consumer tastes, and effectively marketing them. Nor did they have access to credit to finance the transition as they learned by doing, after the state terminated its Soviet-era commercial banking commitments. Managers found themselves in the exasperating position of not being able to continue traditional operations or move forward, a predicament which had severe consequences. Not only did production plummet, but managers began selling enterprise assets for scrap as a survival strategy, diminishing the economy's capacity to recover. Worse still, they quickly succumbed to corruption, asset-stripping, and privatizing valuable properties to themselves, leaving their firms with the debt baby. Shock therapy in this way became an incubator of managerial misconduct and destabilization. Western advisors and domestic liberals seem to have tacitly misassumed that managers would not violate their trust, fearing state discipline. But this category A thinking was naive. Russia had difficulty with corruption and disorder even when ownership and control were relatively unified under the Bolsheviks and the Czars, when communist idealism and Christian virtue were significant moral influences. Shock therapists sincerely concerned with social welfare, who did not see primordial chaos as an opportunity for personal enrichment, should have known better, but did not.[8] As a result, Russia was not only submerged by a wave of criminality, but its markets were internally corrupted by the adoption of an implicit social contract that encouraged anyone in authority to violate others' rights and suppress competition. Russian kleptocrats embraced W.C. Field's dictum: "Never give a sucker an even break!" Politicians and state officials quickly chose to use the proprietary, regulatory, and delegatory powers of the state to further personal ends, contemptuous of their civic responsibilities, colluding with managers at the expense of other shareholders including the state, creating a system where privileged authorities rather than consumers are sovereign. Their preferences define the sense in which the Russian system is micro- and macroeconomically controlled. The system can be conceptualized as a two-tier model where those with privileged access to the state (its authority, budget, and property), including favored managers, provincial authorities, and the Red Mafia, are in a position to prosper disproportionately, while managers of valueless Soviet-era industrial assets, workers, peasants, and small proprietors are obliged to fend for themselves in an intensely hostile environment.

Mechanisms and Institutions

The mechanisms employed to realize these objectives are consistent with klepto-authoritarian motivation. Russia's leaders have learned through experience that the Stalinist command model, Brezhnev's cautious reformism, and Gorbachev's iconoclastic radicalism do not deliver the material benefits desired. They are wary of each other, managers, entrepreneurs, workers, peasants, and foreigners. Yeltsin and Putin therefore have retained

Reform? A Critique of the Stiglitz Perspective," *Policy Reform*, 2001, pp. 1–34; and Stanislaw Gomulka and John Lane, "The Transformational Recession under a Resources Mobility Constraint," *Journal of Comparative Economics*, September, 2001.

[8] Janine Wedel, "Rigging the US–Russia Relationship: Harvard, The Chubais Clan and Russia's Ruin," *The National Interest*, Spring 2000, pp. 23–34.

those elements of authoritarian power including state contracting, finance, and regulation which further their purposes, coupling this with property and market rights which violate the rules of self-regulating, category A general market competition, but allow them to craft a hierarchy of privileged market and administrative relationships that suit their purposes. Constructive state and private obligation have almost no role in the new regime. The era of socialist self-sacrifice and mutual support is a faded memory, and criminal compulsion is the only aspect of obligation that has flourished. Russia's state economic programs and administration as well as activities "outsourced" to the market are undisciplined by competition, duty, or the golden rule.

The same principles apply to Russia's new institutions. Semiprivatization, worker ownership, the separation of majority shareholder ownership from managerial control, kleptocratic economic governance, financial industrial groups (FIGs), and the absence of the rule of law are specific institutional aspects of the authoritarian laissez-faire mechanisms Russia's leaders approve.

Demand and Supply

The power and criminality of Russia's state authorities, their agents, cronies, and tycoons does not alter many aspects of the law of demand. Individual Russians from all walks of life form preferences. Their demand varies inversely with price, given their budget constraints. The assortments they purchase are sensitive to prices. Their preferences are consistent, and they try to minimize the cost of the market baskets they select, when they are not trying to awe friends and foes. But their consumption and employment are inefficient from a self-regulating category A perspective because individual utility-seeking is distorted by forced substitution. Household demand for public collective goods is mostly disregarded by state authorities, and consumers are compelled to purchase items the system supplies, not those they desire. Likewise, Russia's dysfunctional markets prevent workers from finding preferred employment and earning the higher incomes they would under general competition.

Putin's system does not repeal all aspects of the law of supply either. Technologies mostly exhibit diminishing marginal productivity and increasing marginal cost throughout stage II. Individuals and businesses are aware that they can gain by offering their labor, creating value added, starting entrepreneurial ventures, innovating, hiring factors, economizing costs, improving technology, product design and financing, and advertising their goods. They appreciate the virtues of efficient government. But the personal gains from defrauding other shareholders and taxpayers, misappropriating the state's natural resources, exerting market power, and suppressing competition are irresistible. Derived labor demand therefore is only a weak function of wages, and a stronger function of authoritarian market dysfunction. Derived demand for outside management recruits is increasingly a function of compensation, but is also distorted by insider management rent-seeking. Just as in the case of egalitarian labor-managed firms, insiders may hire too few managers if they feel obliged to share asset rents with them. Managerial supply curves are becoming more sensitive to compensation, but are also distorted by anti-productive co-owner self-seeking.

Russians do not profit maximize as they should because the separation of majority shareholder ownership from minority co-owner managerial control, official collusion with managers, and other forms of government intervention discourage executives from maximizing returns to shareholder equity. Of course, Russian managers do things which generate revenue and control costs. They update their products and economize variable input expenses. But they do not comprehensively maximize the stream of shareholder dividends. Business is not just a device allowing utility-seeking individuals to optimize lifetime consumption, detached from moral hazard. It is a control process through which privileged authorities pursue their sovereign objectives to society's detriment. Enormous amounts of time are squandered idling and working to rule in conflict-ridden, semiprivatized firms where Soviet-era attitudes continue to prevail in an environment of disillusionment and corruption. Shareholder conflicts and a sense of social abandonment also feed resentments and encourage labor reservation.

Equilibrium

Russia's klepto-authoritarian markets disorder its Walrasian, Marshallian, and Keynesian adjustment mechanisms by allowing privileged insiders to manipulate demand and supply, preventing rivals from responding to market signals, and applying force instead of voluntary negotiation. Agreements reached in all negotiated transactions among political leaders, officials, minority co-owners, state functionaries, private venturers, workers, peasants, and the Red Mafia are inferior because the terms of demand and supply are not fully and fairly determined, depending as they do on the vagaries of power and corruption.

Looked at from another angle, the Russian economic system has five distinct equilibration mechanisms; the familiar Walrasian, Marshallian, and Keynesian market trio, plus state misregulation, and various forms of criminal conduct involving state authorities, their agents, enterprise co-owners, and tycoons which sacrifice competitive efficiency and the state's social welfare agenda for personal gain and privilege. The Walrasian mechanism is impaired because price-fixing and other collusive practices interfere with the equilibration of shortages and gluts in factor and inventory markets.

The Marshallian adjustment mechanism is disordered by the subordination of profit-maximizing to other goals, including asset-stripping (spinning off valuable assets to themselves), and asset-grabbing (using illegal means to dilute other shareholders assets, and to seize properties of other companies). Soviet industrial firms are denied credit and retail shelf space by Russia's privileged monopolists, preventing them from responding to consumer demand. And the state weakens market discipline further by applying preferential controls, taxes, and regulations, including price, wage and foreign exchange rate manipulation, and foreign capital controls.

The impact of Russia's authoritarian market on Keynesian processes is also detrimental, regardless of whether Putin heeds the IMF's monetarist advice. State and managerial misconduct severely depress aggregate economic activity. Many Russian manufacturers are unable to adequately respond to increases in aggregate demand because they lack credit for operations, are excluded from retail outlets, cannot produce desirable goods, or are otherwise inert. The adversarial and predatory business environment also drastically depresses the marginal efficiency of investment, and increases speculative demand for idle cash balances, preferably in the form of hard currency deposited abroad, repressing aggregate effective demand, and creating conditions of persistent hyperdepression that have been the hallmark of the Russian transition system. And, of course, these problems are compounded by irresponsible monetary and fiscal policies fashioned to rob the treasury, and promote speculative opportunities for personal enrichment. In the early 1990s, Yeltsin was in the habit of ordering the treasury to print money without collateral, and then distributing it as he saw fit. In the mid-1990s, money emission was tied to the excess sale of government bonds; a strategy which temporarily reduced inflation, but then led to the government simply defaulting on its debts in August 1998.

Systemic Structure

The balance of these competitive, anticompetitive, and criminal influences on Putin's economy is discernible in its structure. The centerpiece of the Russian economy is its state–agent–crony–tycoon network, which prospers from the sale of the nation's natural resources, rent-seeking, asset-stripping, and asset-grabbing, including defrauding foreign investors and assistance-givers like the International Monetary Fund, the World Bank, and the European Bank for Reconstruction and Development (acknowledged, and then later denied, by the former American Secretary of the Treasury, Robert Rubin). It has two components. The first is the traditional Soviet-type public sector which provides basic military, security, health, education, administrative, and regulatory services, together with the foreign sale of natural resources and weapons. The second is the transfigured Soviet state industrial, commercial, and agricultural sector, divided into a small cluster of favored enterprises and a large group of disregarded bankrupt firms. The productivity of both components is extremely low, disguised in the eyes of some by the opulent lifestyle of those living lavishly off the system. It relies for the most part on anticompetitive methods of all sorts that are incompatible with category A models.

Russia of course has no perfectly competitive markets, and the productivity and prospects of most private "hole-in-the-wall" operations is problematic, even though they are perceived by some as the vanguard of e-age entrepreneurial capitalism. The outlook for the Red Mafia is brighter. They are ruthless criminals, many hardened in gulag, who provide the usual assortment of disservices including prostitution, gambling, narcotics, "adult" entertainment, extortion, and murder. They prey on those who have revenues and assets worth protecting, and are actively involved in banking, upscale hotels, the luxury goods trade, and in the exploitation of illegal residents. Their affluence is another indication of the system's disorder.

The overriding logic of Russia's economic structure is clear. Its mechanisms are designed to promote economy-wide webs of privilege that enrich elites with state resources and benefices without advancing the country's productive capacity. Small-scale entrepreneurship is tolerated only if it is not a competitive threat, or provides an opportunity for extortion.

The main effects of this anti-productive system are a demobilized, work-suppressing, depressed, corrupt, and inegalitarian Eastern market system with a low standard of living,[9] and limited prospects for sustained development. Insofar as authorities are satisfied with

---

[9]   Iu. Ivanov, "O mezhudunarodnykh sopostavlenniiakh VVP," (On International Comparisons of GDP), *Voprosy ekonomiki*, No. 3, March 1999, pp. 112–27, argues that dollar purchasing power parities "experimentally" derived according to methods employed in a 1996 OECD study indicate that Russia's per capita GDP in 1996 is

these arrangements, the model could endure for decades.[10] But many observers do not believe that the system will survive in its current form. The winners want their privileges consolidated and enhanced under a suitably supportive, authoritarian friendly rule of law. There is ample precedence for this in Russia's Czarist past, where the nobility found it convenient to subjugate and exploit most of the population. But Russian liberals, small businessmen, segments of the working class, and peasants desire greater economic opportunity and security. The lure of prosperity inclines them toward category A markets systems, and their insecurities toward a better form of authoritarianism, perhaps like China's where the Communist party has done a superior job disciplining agents, cronies, and would-be tycoons.[11]

THE GEOMETRY OF RUSSIAN AUTHORITARIAN FREE ENTERPRISE

Geometric analysis provides a deeper appreciation of the systemic deficiencies of Russia's authoritarian "free enterprise." Starting with the factor space illustrated in figure 11.1, we find that the Edgeworth–Bowley production box has drastically contracted because factors are underemployed. Managerial insiders do not maximize shareholder profits from current operations, or the present discounted value of the capital stock, because of the moral hazards and adverse selection associated with Russian co-ownership and the restrictive effects of oligopoly. They prefer to asset-strip, rent-seek, and anticompetitively collude. During the Soviet period similar disorders were contained by state ownership, managerial bonuses, and centralized investment, but insiders now are left to their own devices. More than half Russia's industrial capital capacity is idle (judged by prior achieved production

27 percent of the US figure. This estimate is 35 percent greater than the figure derived in a Goskomstat RF study, undertaken in conjunction with the OECD in 1993, and places Russia in tier 3, the mid-range of the United Nations five-tier development classification. Alternative estimates for 1995 by Aleksei Ponomarenko, Deputy Chief of the Department of National Accounts (Goskomstat RF), presented in 1998 based on regional data place per capita GDP at about 52 percent of Ivanov's estimate, implying a standard of living in tier 4 (underdeveloped), in the vicinity of Thailand. All these various estimates can be instructively compared to the CIA's and Goskomstat SSSR estimates circa 1991, which placed Russia (not the Soviet Union) in the tier 1 with a per capita income of $13,137 in 1991 prices. Obviously, results depend on the underlying conventions used to form purchasing power parities. If a "composite good" cost basis (including cost estimating relationship and engineering studies) is employed in line with CIA practice, then the quality of Russia's exportables and nontradeables is usually significantly overstated, as is their global market worth. Contrary to Ivanov's assertion, Russia's unfavorable exchange rate confirms the low international value of its nonnatural resource exportables, and its low standard of living judged in terms of global preferences. The ruble is not 58 percent undervalued as he suggests. See Aleksei Ponomarenko, "Gross Regional Product for Russian Regions: Compilation Methods and Preliminary Results," Conference on "Regions: A Prism to View the Slavic–Eurasian World," Slavic Research Center, Hokkaido University, Sapporo, Japan, July 22–24, 1998; CIA, *Handbook of International Economic Statistics*, CPAS92–10005, September 1992; Steven Rosefielde, "Unlocking Northeast Asia's Development Potential: The Russian Paradox," in Kimitaka Matsuzato, *Regions: A Prism to View the Slavic World, Slavic Research Center*, Hokkaido University Press, 2000, pp. 278–92. Ivanov cites Gertrude Schroeder's finding that "During the years 1951–1990, per capita consumption in the USSR rose at an average annual rate of 2.8 percent, compared with 2.1 percent in the US. As a result, the relative level increased from one-fifth in 1950 to 27 percent in 1990." He believes her estimate, which is respectively 19 percent and 12 percent below her prior estimates reported in 1979 and 1981 for the year 1976, extrapolated to 1990, corroborates his. Her latest estimate for 1976 is 30 percent. But the CIA statistics she

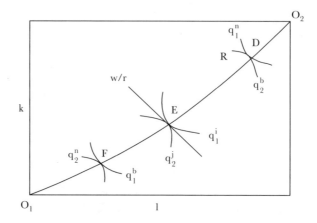

Figure 11.1   Russian factor allocation

levels during the Soviet era) and labor unemployment is in the high double digits. The isoquant levels within the production space also have been reduced because capital and labor are misincentivized and inadequately rewarded.

Factor prices are distorted by entry barriers and economic disorder, and an extraordinarily large share of all intermediate inputs are bartered.[12] This, together with insider abuses, has depressed production from point E'' on the Russia's pre-crises imperfectly competitive production feasible frontier to point R on a drastically lower feasibility frontier in figure 11.2.

employs are not dollars. They are geometric means of separate ruble and dollar estimates. The dollar figures are in the vicinity of 40 percent. Also note that Schroeder's latest estimate is based partly on an upward revision in the US growth rate, and a series of subsequent studies comparing Eastern European, Soviet, and Russian figures on comparative size. See Gertrude Schroeder, "Comparative Levels of Consumer Expenditures in Russia and the Former Soviet Union, 1950–1990s," The Groningen Center for Growth and Development, Conference papers, 2000. She never carried out this computation in detail. The US raised its figure for personal consumption expenditures in 1976 by 5 percent (confirmed in personal correspondence); Imogene Edwards, Margaret Hughes and James Noren, "US and USSR: Comparisons of GNP," in *Soviet Economy in a Time of Change*, US Congress, Joint Economic Committee, Washington, US Government Printing Office, 1976, Vol. 1, p. 379; and Gertrude Schroeder and Imogene Edwards, *Consumption in the USSR: An International Comparison*, Joint Economic Committee, Congress of the United States, Washington DC, US Government Printing Office, 1981. Also see UN, *International Comparison of Gross Domestic Product in Europe*, 1990, p. 71. OECD, *Purchasing Power Parities and Real Expenditures*, 1990, EKS Results, Vol. 1, p. 49; Goskomstat RF, *International Comparisons of Gross Domestic Product*, 1993, pp. 114–17, 123–6.

[10]   Stefan Hedlund, "Path Dependence in Russian Policy Making: Constraints on Putin's Economic Choice," *Post-Communist Economics*, Vol. 12, No. 4, 2000, pp. 289–407.

[11]   Stefan Hedlund, "Will the Russian Economy Revive under Putin?" *Problems of Post-Communism*, March/April 2000, pp. 54–62.

[12]   Personal conversation with Valerii Makarov, January 4, 1999. Cf. V.I. Makarov and G.B. Kleiner, "Barter v Rossiiskoi ekonomike: osobennosti i tendentsii perekhodnovo perioda," Tsentral'nyi ekonomiko-matematicheskii institut, preprint, WP/96/006, Moscow 1996; V. Makarov, and G. Kleiner, "Barter v Rossii: institutional'nyi etap, "(Barter in Russia: Institutional Stage), *Voprosy ekonomiki*, No. 4, April 1999, pp. 79–101; A. Iakovlev, "Prichinakh bartera, neplatezhei i ukloneniia ot nalogov v rossiiskoe ekonomike," (On Reasons for Barter, Arrears and Tax Evasion in the Russian Economy), *Voprosy ekonomiki*, No. 4, April 1999, pp. 102–16.

This shortfall, the gap between what Russia could have achieved and what it has accomplished, is aggravated by the inferior characteristics of its goods and technologies. The same preoccupations which divert managers from profit-maximizing and diminish the volume of output also make them inattentive to quality, which can be expressed in figure 11.2 by converting inferior goods into smaller quantities of standard products at the competitive marginal rate of transformation, and contracting the production feasibility frontier further, with production occurring beneath point R.

There is no way to put a happy face on these inefficiencies. They are caused by Russia's authoritarian market system, not the vanishing legacy of Soviet administrative command planning. But adherents of universalistic Anglo-American rationalism remain hopeful that competitive entrepreneurship or state modernization programs will transform Russia's economic culture, mechanisms, and institutions. Perhaps they are right, but the task will not be easy because authorities, agents, cronies, and tycoons will fiercely resist. The task is further complicated by Russia's disordered financial markets.

The collapse of Russia's financial system in August/September 1998 speaks for itself. The state and favored private banks had been complicitous in one financial fraud or another from the outset.[13] During the first two years after Yeltsin came to power, the government resorted to un-collateralized currency printing to pay its bills, wiping out the personal savings of ordinary people and diverting vast sums to the elites.[14] This was then followed by a new scam in which banking became primarily a business of lending overnight deposits to the government at above competitive rates, instead of making productive loans to commerce and industry. The government covered these disguised

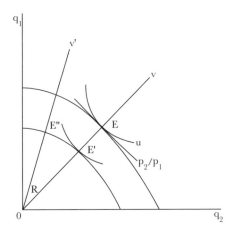

Figure 11.2 Russian efficiency possibilities

[13] During 1997 the state-owned Russian Central Bank (CBR) earned about three billion dollars from trade in high-yield government securities, but only 250 million dollars was transferred to the budget. The rest was "misappropriated." See Vladimir Ivanov, "Crisis in Russia: As Bad As It Gets," *Erina Report*, Vol. 25, December 1998, p. 28. The Central Bank is now under investigation for embezzling an additional billion dollars.

[14] Steven Rosefielde, "Klepto-banking: Systemic Sources of Russia's Failed Industrial Recovery," in Howard Stein, Alu Ajakaiye and Peter Lewis, *Deregulation and the Banking Crisis in Nigeria: A Comparative Study*, Basingstoke, Palgrave, 2001.

transfers by floating dollar denominated paper in the West at rates in the vicinity of 100 percent per annum that can not be sustained, leading directly to default and the subsequent collapse of the entire financial system. Although some of these tactics have been applauded for curbing inflation, Russia's financial sector is a fiasco. The government and its cronies not only mismanaged the supply of credit, and the allocation of loanable funds, starving traditional industrial enterprises of operating capital, but manipulated interest and foreign exchange rates, compounding the nation's underproductivity and inefficiency.

Russia's production woes are aggravated by corresponding distributional inefficiencies. The collapse of the Soviet Union disorganized retail distribution and concentrated wealth and income in relatively few hands, impoverishing large segments of the population. These transfers never would have been tolerated in a consumer sovereign regime, or in the imperfectly competitive economies of the mature West, even though some interpret gross inequity as a sign of progress in Russia's post-communist transition. The disorganization of the retail market exemplified by widespread barter, Mafia control over small vendors, and oligopolistic trade and distribution, illustrated by point D' in figure 11.3, all indicate that Russia's consumer sector is inefficient. The standard of living for most of the population is poor not just because supplies are inadequate, but also because the retail sector is badly organized in Moscow and across the nation's regions, and is unjust. Figure 11.4, which arrays kleptocrats on the ordinate and the common man on the abscissa, depicts this outcome by comparing the achieved Russian social utility frontier at D with the competitive ideal. It suggests that the average quality of Russian life is much lower than its competitive potential, with the kleptocrats faring well compared with ordinary people.[15]

It follows directly from the foregoing survey that Russia's authoritarian market system is extraordinarily inefficient, compounding the harm inflicted by routine governmental inefficiency with theft and criminal compulsion. It is designed to serve the anti-productive interests of authorities, agents, cronies, tycoons, and the Mafia, and will not prosper until business is competitively disciplined under the rule of law.

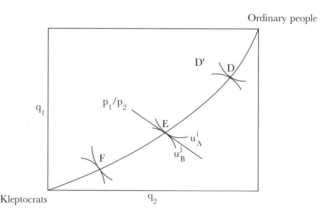

Figure 11.3 Russian retail distribution

[15]   Elizabeth Brainerd, "Winners and Losers in Russia's Economic Transition," *American Economic Review*, Vol. 88, No. 5, 1998; Michal Rutkowski, "Russia's Social Protection Malaise: Key Reform Priorities as a Response to the Present Crisis," Social Protection Discussion Paper No. 9909, World Bank, April 1999.

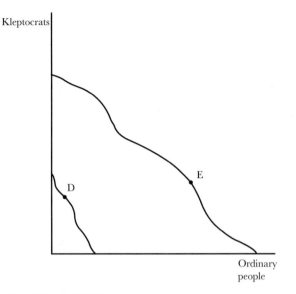

Figure 11.4   Russian utility possibilities

Review

Main Features of the Russian Economic System

Culture: Authoritarian/anti-authoritarian. The mentality has deep historical roots in the Tatar occupation, Czarism, and Soviet despotism. Anti-authoritarianism is a mix of passivity, opportunism, immoralism, Utopian idealism, and Byzantine intrigue.

Motivation: Klepto-authoritarian privilege, rent- and asset-seeking.

Mechanisms: Natural resources, land, and a substantial share of the industrial means of production remain partly or wholly state-owned, providing a basis for state power. Private markets are preferential, and imperfectly competitive. The old Soviet industrial sector is repressed by financial industrial groups. Managers in state and semiprivate enterprises misappropriate revenues, and spin off valuable assets to themselves with impunity. Workers, although often majority shareholders, are powerless. Criminal compulsion is rampant. The Red Mafia is frequently in league with the police and the security services.

    The state disdains the public interest, and authorities are self-seeking. Their programs, controls, and regulations have hindered more than assisted free competition.

| Institutions: | State ownership, worker majority shareholding, financial industrial groups, kleptocracy, Red Mafia, police, security services, military. |

Main Inefficiencies

Law of demand:	Widespread forced substitution.
Law of supply:	Worker supply curves are weak functions of wages, because of mass involuntary unemployment. Managerial supply curves are more functions of rent-seeking and asset-grabbing than wages. Enterprises respond to these corrupt incentives.
Law of equilibration:	Markets are imperfectly competitive. Distribution to some private entities and the state, including the security services and the Ministry of Defense, is often on a nonnegotiated basis. Distribution to the rest of the economy is dominated by Walrasian barter because the monetary system is in ruins. Labor mobility, especially into Moscow, is municipally controlled. Marshallian production equilibration is disordered by criminal rent-seeking and asset-grabbing, without concern for worker welfare. Keynesian macro-equilibration is impaired by criminal self-seeking. Money emission, credit, expenditure programs, controls, and regulations are aimed at enriching authorities, not stimulating aggregate effective demand.

The state sets the rules of the market.

Tactics of Klepocratic Economic Management

Topic	Problem	State Response
Partial and full state ownership	Curtails normal individual utility-seeking	Unfettered insider discretionary use of revenue and assets
Majority worker shareholding	Encourages under-remunerating managers and outside shareholders, including the state	Vest absolute insider discretionary authority with managers
Unfettered managerial control	Rent-seeking and asset-grabbing, anti-productive mentality, apathy	Booty sharing with state administrative elite, and Mafia – this includes

		toward worker welfare	misappropriation of state-owned natural resources
	Institutionalized depression	Resource demobilization	Seek mis-appropriable assistance from the IMF, other governmental institutions, and Western investors lured into the criminal rent-seeking, asset-grabbing game

Systemic Structure

	Share of GDP	Productivity (Destructiveness)	Coercion
Markets			
Perfect markets	0	–	–
Inefficient markets	15	Very low	High
Collusive markets	20	Low	High
Government	50	Low	High
Obligation			
Criminal disservices	15	(Extremely high)	–

Systems Characteristics

	Degree/Intensity
State macro-regulation	Low
State micro-regulation	
Pro-competitive	Low
Elite	High
Welfare/security	Low/medium
State spending programs	
Privileged contracting	High
Misappropriation	Extremely high
Cronyism	Extremely high
Criminal disservices	
Asset seizure and embezzlement	Extremely high
Addiction/vice	High
Repression, extortion, and murder	Extremely high
Subjugation and servitude	Medium

Causes of macroeconomic disequilibria

Sticky wages	Low
Sticky prices	Low
Investment avoidance	Extremely high
Capital flight	Extremely high
Misinvestment	Extremely high
Liquidity preference	Extremely high
Insecure private property rights	Extremely high
State property rights	High
Foreign capital flows	High
Fear of criminality	Extremely high
Anticompetitive business repression	Extremely high
General business repression	Medium
Labor subjugation	Medium
Judicial risk	Extremely high
State corruption	Extremely high
Macropolicy mismanagement	Extremely high
Class conflict	Incipient

Main Performance Indicators

Per capita GDP 1998 (US = 100)	15
Per capita GDP growth 1990–99 (compound annual rate)	−5
Per capita GDP growth 1960–99 (compound annual rate)	0?
Inflation 1990–99	Triple digit
Unemployment 1999 Share of labor force	
International definition	14
Including discouraged workers	25
Retirement support burden	Low
Nonworking mothers and wives	Low

Present Direction of Reforms

Rationalizing the mechanisms of authoritarian privilege by using the secret police as a tax police to curb the political power of tycoons and subordinate regions to the center, while building foundations for the rule of law that somehow enhance competition without curtailing authoritarian privilege.

Review Questions

1. To what extent does Russia still retain state ownership?
2. Neither Russia nor China operate under the rule of contract law, even though Russia's Communist party no longer rules. Why does not contract law prevail in Russia?
3. In what ways do Russia's state agents have more independence than China's?
4. In what sense are Russia and China "collectivist"?
5. What are the unique features of Russia's historical culture?
6. Is Yeltsin's version of laissez-faire authoritarianism a radical departure from Czarist arrangements?
7. Who are Russia's kleptocrats?
8. What are the special features of Russian property? How do Russian property rights differ from those assumed in perfect competition?
9. Why do not Russian workers assert their property rights? Why do not they organize to change the law? Is the problem cultural or political?
10. How did the Soviets control moral hazard?
11. How did Boris Yeltsin transform administrative command planning into a market system?
12. Why did not Yeltsin's market reforms attract foreign investors lured by new opportunities and cheap skilled labor?
13. What was shock therapy, and why was it destructive?
14. What are "asset-grabbing," "asset-stripping," and "rent-seeking"?
15. Is there historical precedent for Russia's business corruption?
16. Who are Russia's economic sovereigns? How did they obtain their power?
17. How does Russia's kleptocratic market mechanism differ from the American managed market system?
18. Is obligation a significant Russian economic mechanism? If so, what role does it play?
19. What is forced substitution? How does it modify the law of demand in Russia?
20. How do fraud and misappropriation distort the law of supply in Russia? Explain.
21. Why do egalitarian labor-managed firms sometimes underemploy managers?
22. Why do not Russian firms properly profit maximize?
23. How does state market management in Russia differ from the American approach?
24. Why is the Russian system productively demobilized?
25. Why is Russia's Walrasian adjustment mechanism disordered?
26. Why is Russia's Marshallian adjustment mechanism disordered?
27. Why is Russia's Keynesian adjustment mechanism disordered?
28. What are the special features of Russia's system structure?
29. Is Russia's economic system transitory? Explain.
30. Is Russia's factor supply and allocation Pareto efficient? Use the Edgeworth–Bowley production box in figure 11.1 to explain.
31. Is Russia's production Pareto ideal? Use figure 11.2 to explain.
32. Is Russia's retailing efficient? Use figure 11.3 to explain.
33. Is the Russian system socially just? Use figure 11.4 to explain.

CHAPTER 12

TRANSITION

The economic systems of America, Continental Europe, Japan, China, and Russia are likely to endure for generations because culture changes slowly and institutions are often path dependent. But this does not mean that systems are static. They evolve and devolve in response to shifting tastes, attitudes, politics, technology, and exogenous shocks. The process of moving from one system to another is called transition. It can take many forms, and applies to both real and ideal economies at all stages of development. During the 1990s, after the collapse of the Soviet Union the sub-problem of transitioning from command to market systems has been in the limelight. Strategies and tactics were derived from market theory on the universalist premise that the nations of Eastern Europe and the former Soviet Union did, or soon would behave like efficient competitors operating under the rule of law. Although there have been some modest successes, the approach has largely failed because these former socialist systems violated universalist premises, including adherence to the rule of law. China by contrast, rejecting "shock therapy," fared much better by adopting cautious, carefully tested, and tightly controlled market reforms tailored to the special requirements of its communist system. There is a danger that the transition strategies of Eastern Europe and the former Soviet Union are more than false starts; that their reforms have become path dependent and will play an important negative role in shaping the future configuration of global wealth and power.

It would "be childish" to think that the "triumph of civilization in the singular" would lead to the end of the plurality of cultures embodied for centuries in the world's great civilizations.
Fernand Braudel, *On History*, University of Chicago Press, 1980, pp. 212–13.

Comparative systems traditionally have focused on exploring the properties of ideal and real economies. The collapse and dismemberment of the Soviet Union, restoration of independence in Eastern Europe, and the marketization of China have shifted attention recently toward a sub-field called "transition," which analyzes the process of dismantling existing economies and efficiently constructing better ones. This task and the larger problem of Third World transition (not discussed in this text) have always seemed simple to those who imagined a frictionless reform process where institutions are forged on demand. Vladimir Lenin believed that socialism could be constructed instantaneously from the ashes of Czarist capitalism by replacing private ownership, money, and voluntary exchange with a central "post office"; that is, a planning agency which placed and filled orders. Joseph Stalin took a similar approach, supplemented with forced agricultural collectivization, a strategy widely emulated by other "development states" in Eastern Europe and many Third World countries.

Market proponents also have been incautious, urging less developed nations to hastily shed their traditional institutions, and socialist economies to replace their planning bureaus with state price boards charged with managing prices and wages instead of physical production. In the early 1990s economists like Stanislav Shatalin, Jeffrey Sachs, and Stanley Fischer advocated "shock therapy," the abrupt demolition of Soviet command institutions to jump start free enterprise, predicting that transition could be accomplished in 500 days.

The naivete of these transition schemes is seldom conceded. Proponents try to hide their impracticality by suggesting that success turns on resolving a few key political and economic problems. Marxists propose "liquidating" their enemies "as a class," and perfecting administrative command planning. Advocates of market globalization adopt the same position, but switch villains and ideals. They call for the destruction of communism, and prescribe market competition.

Both approaches are essentially the same. Transition is conceived as a process of overcoming technical impediments to attain perfect outcomes, or second bests. But the possibility that universalist transition strategies could be misapplied, or backfire is never considered. This is unrealistic. Reforms appropriate for well-functioning planning and market economies are unlikely to work when core axioms are flagrantly violated in real systems.[1]

STAGES OF TRANSITION

Transition is usually portrayed as a four-stage process beginning with a convulsive event like the Bolshevik revolution, or the collapse of communism, followed by periods of stabilization, institution building, and globalization. Stabilization is needed to douse the flames of inflation, to halt plummeting production, and to arrest the spread of unemployment caused by radical change. Institution building fills the vacuum created by the destruction of the old economic order. And globalization exports the system to other nations.

Monetary reform is a prominent feature of stabilization. Old currencies are withdrawn, or re-denominated, and replaced by new ones, backed by stringent cash emission and credit controls. This occurred after the Bolshevik revolution, and again after Boris Yeltsin took power in the 1990s. The strategy and tactics of stabilization sometimes are generic,

[1]   Olivier Blanchard, *The Economics of Post-Communist Transition*, Oxford University Press, 1998; Joseph Stiglitz, "Whither Reform? Ten Years of Transition," Keynote Address, Annual World Bank Conference on Development Economics, April 28–30, 1999; Martin Feldstein, "Refocusing the IMF," *Foreign Affairs*, Vol. 77, No. 2, March/April 1998, pp. 20–33.

applying interchangeably in market, planned, collectivist, communalist, and managed economies, but often they are systems specific.

The institutions appropriate for one system are seldom compatible with others. Having rid the nation of markets, Russia's Bolsheviks nationalized the means of production, and then gradually erected a complex administrative command planning mechanism. They established centralized and decentralized planning agencies, economic ministries, sectoral departments, construction and investment agencies, a system of enterprise management, a military industrial complex, a foreign trade monopoly, agricultural collectives, cooperatives, state wholesale and retail networks, a state bank network, a system of direct Communist party supervision, a plan compliance inspectorate, state price- and wage-fixing committees, state committees for norms, bonus setting, and technology, and courts for the enforcement of state contracts.

Boris Yeltsin's institution building strategy was just the reverse. Privatization replaced nationalization; free enterprise supplanted state command, and competition was substituted for price and quantity controls. This means that planning, ministerial, and regulatory institutions like the state bank which remained had to be redesigned so that they served the market in accordance with the rule of contract law, instead of being its master.

In both instances political leaders believed that their aspirations were progressive, and expected other nations to emulate their examples. Lenin and Stalin sought to "globalize" command communism through class struggle; Yeltsin by returning to the "West" and encouraging other members of the former Soviet Union to follow suit. Although neither transition was successful in achieving perfect, or even second best, planning or markets, this did not deter Stalin or Yeltsin from declaring victory. The Soviet Union and Russia did transition, but the transformations were not the desirable ones predicted.

SUCCESS INDICATORS

Russia's transitionary woes, and those of others, are invariably concealed by mislabeling, and the misuse of indicators which superficially suggest that the new systems correspond closely with ideals. The Soviet constitution of 1936 declared that the USSR had achieved "socialism," implying that whatever distortions blemished the Soviet Union's planned economy were not serious enough to thwart prosperity, equality, social justice, and harmony. Putin's description of the Russian system as market capitalism under the "dictatorship of law" similarly suggests that transition has made the economy equitable and competitively efficient.

Some economists support these empty claims with reams of statistics. During the Soviet period, plan directives were cited as proof that managers passively obeyed commands, despite the importance of the bonus-contracting mechanism. Official wage scales were accepted as proof of income leveling, and official purchasing power parities that Soviet per capita incomes were close to the Western European mean. More recently, statistics are being marshaled to suggest that Russia has privatized in a perfectly competitive sense even though workers own the majority of their firms' insider shares. Mass unemployment is treated as a sign of market building, and rent-seeking as evidence of free competition. Change of any kind in this way is misconstrued as evidence of ideal transition.

FEASIBILITY AND DESIGN

None of this means that transition is impossible. If any economy is inefficient, performance can be improved by perfecting it with better markets, plans or both. When this is accomplished in market economies by expanding choice without fundamentally altering institutions and mechanisms, the process is called liberalization. The same basic process becomes transition when institutions, mechanisms, and their interplay are significantly altered. Optimization theory also suggests that as barriers to choice crumble, efficiency should always sequentially improve. Liberalization and market transition should be one-way streets. They should be beneficial, unless – as is too often the case – reforms themselves are faulty.

Transition strategies can be misdesigned in many ways. Restraints and controls on economic activities can be eliminated, or imposed without providing safeguards against abuse. When Yeltsin sanctioned laissez faire before establishing the rule of law he expanded people's choices, but did not deter them from stealing state assets, rent-seeking, and exerting monopoly power. His initiative failed because negative effects outweighed positive influences.

Transition may also go awry because new institutions are ill-conceived. The privatization plan devised by Anatoly Chubais, Russia's privatization czar, pitted workers against managers, the government and outsiders instead of supporting competitive profit-maximizing. And transition may be destabilizing if it undermines public confidence. Fearing the worst, managers may disinvest, and capital may flee the country. Realistic transition theories and programs must take all these factors into account. They must begin with the establishment of an effective rule of law or functional planning. They must be carefully designed so that new institutions are productive, robust, stabilizing, and resistant to abuse. And they must be adroitly implemented to maintain confidence and deter adverse selection. These principles are generally applicable, but the details must be tailored to suit each circumstance and introduced warily with strict controls.

SHOCK VERSUS GRADUALISM

The post-Soviet Russian and Chinese experiences underscore the superiority of caution over zeal. The Russians and their Western advisors were hasty, persuading themselves that dismantling the old order would shock competitive free enterprise into existence. They did not fret about the costs, leaving the people to pay the piper. Deng Xiaoping was wiser. He had learned first hand from China's "Great Peoples' Proletarian Cultural Revolution" that shock methods were disastrous, so he set the Red Dragon on a gradualist transition path that has transformed the Maoist system and accelerated growth without catastrophic repercussions. If Russia's or China's communist economies had been plug-compatible with perfect competition, and opposition quelled, then speed would have been a virtue. But this is wishful thinking. Russia and China had shunned free enterprise in the first place because they were reluctant to play by competitive market rules, and powerful political forces favored other systemic arrangements. Whenever this is the case, gradualism is likely to be best.[2]

SYSTEMS THEORY

This insight can all be easily encompassed in an expanded transition theory which adds cultural pluralism to the Newtonian core, and recognizes the potential importance of unique historical events that often make change path dependent. Institutions like keiretsu, or chaebols in South Korea in this approach, instead of being viewed merely as barriers to market efficiency, reflect cultural priorities that must be accommodated, not unthinkingly disregarded. Likewise, systems cannot be reduced to a single universal principle such as governance, game, or stabilization theory. These concepts illuminate aspects of systems. They do not define them. Sensitivity to these concerns avoids many otherwise unexpected dysfunctions, and provides outcomes nations prefer.

Transition theory can also be improved by clarifying objectives. All economic systems are in flux. Their institutions and mechanisms are constantly being reformed in response to advances in knowledge, shifting attitudes, partisan wrangling, and exogenous shocks. Every economy in this sense is transitional. This is important to grasp because it shows that societies do not always know where their economic systems are heading, or if they do, how best to get there. Gradual systemic evolution and devolution provide a living laboratory where nations learn what they want, and how to achieve it through doing and controlled experimentation. Contemporary transition theory, especially applied to Russia, non-Russian members of the Commonwealth of Independent States, and Eastern Europe, is more activistly inclined. Like Bolshevist dogma, it tries to artificially impose preconceived ideals, shunning the benefits of learning by doing, and patient institutional experimentation. The development of a complete concept of transition would make today's over-zealous practitioners more aware of their bias, and produce more effective strategies of managing change and transition.

---

[2]   P. Boone, S. Gomulka and R. Layard, eds., *Emerging From communism: Lessons From Russia, China and Eastern Europe*, MIT Press, Cambridge, 1998. Cf., Jean Francois Huchet and Xavier Richet, "Between Bureaucracy and the Market: Chinese Industrial Groups in Search of New Forms of Corporate Governance," paper prepared for the American Economics meetings, New Orleans, January 7, 2001; Ronald McKinnon, *The Order of Economic Liberalization: Financial Control in the Transition to a Market Economy,* Johns Hopkins, Baltimore, MD, 1991; Josef Brada and Arthur King, "Is there a J-Curve for the Economic Transition from Socialism to Capitalism?" *Economics of Planning*, 25, 1, 1992 pp. 37–53; Michael Ellman, "Transformation, Depression, and Economics: Some Lessons," *Journal of Comparative Economics*, 19, 1, 1994 pp. 1–21; Stanley Fischer and Alan Gelb, "The Process of Socialist Economic Transformation," *Economic Perspectives*, 5, 4, 1991 pp. 91–105. Stanley Fischer, Ratna Sahay and Carlos Vegh, "Stabilization and Growth in Transition Economies: The Early Experience," *The Journal of Economic Perspectives*, 10, 2, 1996 pp. 45–66; Stanislaw Gomulka, "The Cause of Recession Following Stabilization," *Comparative Economic Studies*, 33, 2, 1991 pp. 71–89; Stefan Hedlund, *Russia's "Market" Economy: A Bad Case of Predatory Capitalism*, UCL Press, London, 1999; Janos Kornai, "Transformational Recession: The Main Causes," *Journal of Comparative Economics*, 19, 1, 1991 pp. 39–63; Kevin Murphy, Andrei Shleifer and Robert Vishny, "The Transition to a Market Economy: Pitfalls of Partial Reform," *Quarterly Journal of Economics*, 107, 3, 1992 pp. 889–906; Andrei Rapaczynski, "The Role of the State and the Market in Establishing Property Rights," *The Journal of Economic Perspectives*, 10, 2, 1996 pp. 87–104. Lance Taylor, "The Market Met its Match: Lessons for the Future from the Transition's Initial Years," *Journal of Comparative Economics*, 19, 1, 1994 pp. 64–87.

THE POST-SOVIET EXPERIENCE

A net assessment of the successes and failures of contemporary transition theory, strategies, and tactics, is beyond the scope of this text. Nonetheless, tables 12.1 and 12.2, which summarize the GDP and inflation experiences of 12 Eastern European and 15 former Soviet nations, provide a vivid impression of the transition experience of these former communist regimes. They show that all suffered sharp declines in their GDP, and were plagued by skyrocketing inflation. After a decade some are on the road to recovery, but others are still mired in depression and inflation. And the data suggest that there is a danger that this mistransition may not be easily reversed. Many contend that these results are satisfactory, arguing that revolutionary change always comes at a high price.[3] But China stands out as a salutary counter-example. It has succeeded better than any of its peers in smoothly shifting from a command to a market economy, and achieved nearly double digit rates of growth without adopting the shock methods prescribed by Western transitology. As a consequence, its future is better defined and more promising.

Review Questions

1. What is "transition"?
2. How does "transition" differ from liberalization?
3. Should the evolution and devolution of institutions and mechanism be considered "transition?"
4. Transitologists have traditionally concentrated on discontinuous systemic transition. The Bolshevik revolution compelled the Soviets to study the best way to construct socialism. The Soviet collapse gave market advocates an opportunity to reverse the process. Has this created a "universalist" analytic bias, where historical, cultural, political, and ethical aspects of systems are disregarded, or insuffiently taken into account?
5. Has a "universalist" analytic bias had adverse consequences for the transition states of Eastern Europe and the former Soviet Union? Explain.
6. What are the four stages of discontinuous transition? Elaborate.
7. Universalist theories tend to be reductionist, allowing transitologists to claim that satisfying some simple condition like monetary stabilization is sufficient to initiate a self-sustaining transformation. Give some examples.
8. How do economists try to make it appear that failed transition polices have been successful?
9. How might transition strategies be misdesigned? Give three examples.
10. What are the pros and cons of "shock therapy"?

---

[3] Stanislaw Gomulka, "Macroeconomic Policies and Achievements in Transition Economies, 1989–1999," *Economic Survey of Europe*, March 3, 2000, UN, Economic Commission for Europe.

Table 12.1 Real GDP/NMP in the ECE transition economies, 1980, 1986–99

	1980	1986	1987	1988	1989	1990	1991	1992	1993	1994	1995	1996	1997	1998	1999
Eastern Europe	88.7	97.8	99.4	100.8	100.0	93.2	82.9	79.3	79.0	82.1	86.9	90.3	92.2	93.9	95.2
Albania	79.4	93.1	92.4	91.0	100.0	90.0	64.8	60.1	65.9	71.4	80.9	88.2	82.0	88.6	95.7
Bosnia–Herzegovina	–	–	–	–	–	–	–	–	–	–	–	–	–	–	–
Bulgaria	76.2	93.6	99.3	101.9	100.0	90.9	83.3	77.2	76.1	77.5	79.7	71.6	66.6	68.9	70.7
Croatia	99.0	102.6	102.5	101.6	100.0	92.9	73.3	64.7	59.5	63.0	67.3	71.3	76.2	78.1	77.9
Czech Republic	–	93.2	93.7	95.7	100.0	98.8	87.3	86.9	86.9	88.8	94.1	98.7	97.7	95.5	95.3
Hungary	86.3	95.5	99.4	99.3	100.0	96.5	85.0	82.4	81.9	84.4	85.6	86.8	90.7	95.2	99.4
Poland	91.1	94.1	95.9	99.8	100.0	88.4	82.2	84.4	87.6	92.1	98.6	104.5	111.7	117.1	121.8
Romania	88.5	105.8	106.7	106.2	100.0	94.4	82.2	75.0	76.2	79.2	84.8	88.2	82.8	78.3	75.8
Slovakia	–	94.8	97.1	99.0	100.0	97.5	83.3	77.9	75.1	78.7	84.2	89.7	95.6	99.8	101.7
Slovenia	98.9	104.1	103.5	100.5	100.0	91.9	83.7	79.1	81.4	85.7	89.3	92.4	96.6	100.4	105.3
The former Yugoslav Republic of Macedonia	93.3	102.7	101.4	98.1	100.0	89.8	84.3	78.7	72.8	71.6	70.8	71.6	72.6	74.8	76.8
Yugoslavia	95.7	101.4	100.2	98.8	100.0	92.1	81.4	58.7	40.6	41.7	44.2	46.8	50.3	51.5	41.6
Baltic states	67.8	85.6	89.0	96.0	100.0	97.8	89.9	67.9	58.2	55.2	56.4	58.8	63.7	66.6	65.4

Estonia	74.5	88.2	89.2	93.8	100.0	91.9	82.7	71.0	65.0	63.7	66.4	69.0	76.3	79.4	78.3
Latvia	68.5	85.1	89.0	93.6	100.0	102.9	92.2	60.1	51.1	51.1	51.0	52.7	57.3	59.5	59.6
Lithuania	64.7	84.9	88.9	98.4	100.0	96.7	91.2	71.8	60.2	54.3	56.1	58.7	63.0	66.2	64.2
CIS	77.5	92.4	93.9	98.1	100.0	96.8	90.9	78.0	70.4	60.3	56.9	55.0	55.6	53.9	55.5
Armenia	73.5	97.7	94.5	92.2	100.0	94.5	83.4	48.6	44.3	46.7	49.9	52.8	54.6	58.5	60.3
Azerbaijan	79.6	100.6	105.1	109.7	100.0	88.3	87.7	67.9	52.2	41.9	37.0	37.4	39.6	43.6	46.8
Belarus	65.7	88.9	91.3	92.4	100.0	98.1	96.9	87.6	81.0	70.8	63.4	65.2	72.6	78.7	81.4
Georgia	79.4	98.8	96.8	103.6	100.0	84.9	67.0	36.9	26.1	23.4	24.0	26.7	29.7	30.6	31.5
Kazakhstan	87.0	92.3	92.1	100.1	100.0	99.0	88.1	83.4	75.8	66.2	60.8	61.1	62.1	60.9	62.0
Kyrgyzstan	69.1	83.6	84.7	95.6	100.0	104.8	96.5	83.2	70.3	56.2	53.1	56.9	62.5	63.9	66.2
Republic of Moldova	72.1	89.2	90.3	91.9	100.0	97.6	80.5	57.2	56.5	39.0	38.3	35.3	35.9	32.8	31.3
Russian Federation	78.1	92.9	94.2	98.4	100.0	97.0	92.2	78.8	71.9	62.8	60.2	58.2	58.7	55.8	57.6
Tajikistan	80.7	93.4	97.1	107.5	100.0	101.8	97.0	82.5	83.7	69.2	64.2	68.5	60.7	63.8	74.0
Turkmenistan	80.7	93.4	97.1	107.5	100.0	101.8	97.0	82.5	83.7	69.2	64.2	68.5	60.7	63.8	74.0
Ukraine	75.0	90.0	93.4	95.2	100.0	96.4	88.0	79.2	68.0	52.4	46.0	41.4	40.2	39.5	39.3
Uzbekistan	76.0	88.0	88.4	97.0	100.0	99.2	98.7	87.7	85.7	81.2	80.5	81.9	86.1	89.9	93.9
Total above	**80.3**	**93.7**	**95.2**	**98.7**	**100.0**	**95.9**	**88.8**	**78.1**	**72.4**	**65.9**	**64.8**	**64.3**	**65.4**	**64.7**	**66.1**

Source: United Nations Economic Commission for Europe, *Economic Survey of Europe, 2000*, No. 1, New York, 2000, p. 225.

Table 12.2 Consumer prices in the ECE transition economies, 1990–99 (annual average, percentage change over preceding year)

	1990	1991	1992	1993	1994	1995	1996	1997	1998	1999
Albania	–	35.5	193.1	85.0	21.5	8.0	12.7	33.1	20.3	–0.1
Bosnia–Herzegovina	594.0	116.2	64,218.3	8,825.1	553.5	–12.1	–21.2	11.8	4.9	–0.6
Bulgaria	23.8	338.5	91.3	72.9	96.2	62.1	123.1	1,082.6	22.2	0.4
Croatia	609.5	123.1	663.6	1,516.6	97.5	2.0	3.6	3.7	5.9	4.3
Czech Republic	9.9	56.7	11.1	20.8	10.0	9.1	8.9	8.4	10.6	2.1
Hungary	28.9	35.0	23.0	22.6	19.1	28.5	23.6	18.4	14.2	10.1
Poland	585.8	70.3	45.3	36.9	33.2	28.1	19.8	15.1	11.7	7.4
Romania	5.1	170.2	210.7	256.2	137.1	32.2	38.8	154.9	59.3	45.9
Slovakia	10.4	61.2	10.2	23.1	13.4	10.0	6.1	6.1	6.7	10.6
Slovenia	551.6	115.0	207.3	31.7	21.0	13.5	9.9	8.4	7.9	6.2
The former Yugoslav Republic of Macedonia	608.4	114.9	1,505.5	353.1	121.0	16.9	4.1	3.6	1.0	–1.3
Yugoslavia	580.0	12.0	8,926.0	2.2E+14	7.9E+10	71.8	90.5	23.2	30.4	44.1
Estonia	18.0	202.0	1,078.2	89.6	47.9	28.9	23.1	11.1	10.6	3.5
Latvia	10.9	172.2	951.2	109.1	35.7	25.0	17.7	8.5	4.7	2.4
Lithuania	9.1	216.4	1,020.5	410.1	72.0	39.5	24.7	8.8	5.1	0.8
Armenia	6.9	174.1	728.7	3,731.8	4,964.0	175.5	18.7	13.8	8.7	0.7
Azerbaijan	6.1	106.6	912.6	1,129.7	1,663.9	411.5	19.8	3.6	–0.8	–8.6
Belarus	4.7	94.1	971.2	1,190.9	2,219.6	709.3	52.7	63.9	73.2	293.7
Georgia	4.2	78.7	1,176.9	4,084.9	22,470.6	177.6	39.4	6.9	3.6	19.3
Kazakhstan	5.6	114.5	1,504.3	1,662.7	1,879.5	175.9	39.1	17.4	7.3	8.4
Kyrgyzstan	5.5	113.9	854.6	1,208.7	278.1	42.9	30.3	25.5	12.1	36.7
Republic of Moldova	5.7	114.4	1,308.0	1,751.0	489.4	29.9	23.5	11.8	7.7	39.3
Russian Federation	–	160.0	1,528.7	875.0	309.0	197.4	47.8	14.7	27.8	85.9
Tajikistan	5.9	112.9	822.0	2,884.8	350.3	682.1	422.4	85.4	43.1	27.5
Turkmenistan	5.7	88.5	483.2	3,128.4	2,562.1	1,105.3	714.0	83.7	16.8	–
Ukraine	5.4	94.0	1,209.6	4,734.9	891.2	376.7	80.2	15.9	10.6	22.7
Uzbekistan	5.8	97.3	414.5	1,231.8	1,550.0	315.5	56.3	73.2	17.7	–

Source: United Nations Economic Commission for Europe, *Economic Survey of Europe, 2000*, No. 1, New York, 2000, p. 231.

CHAPTER 13

COMPARATIVE POTENTIAL

All great power systems are second best. They are inferior to self-regulating, generally competitive regimes, and are inefficient with respect to their cultural ideals. But this does not mean that their performance prospects are the same. There is a clear hierarchy of economic potential measured in terms of achieved living standards, GDP growth rates, employment, and price stability. The Anglo-American system seems best on these criteria. Despite flaws, America is likely to enjoy higher growth, lower unemployment, and greater price stability than Continental Europe and Russia, because of its superior entrepreneurship, competitiveness, and the high stature of its contract law.

These virtues are the fountainhead of Anglo-American prosperity and security. Continental Europe and Japan are less vigorous, and show distinct signs of sclerosis despite their liberalization. Continental Europe is burdened by its corporatist obligations and leisure ethic, while Japan is disoriented by the waning effectiveness of communalism and by the discordance between communalist and individualist values.

These problems, however, pale in comparison with Russia, where Putin continues to resist committing to either free enterprise, under the rule of contract law, or authoritarian economic mobilization. Although Russia's natural resource wealth, and under-utilized capacities could support a substantial economic recovery, the deficiencies of its authoritarian market system assure that its performance will be subpar. The gap between its living standard and its affluent competitors must widen as long as the present system endures.

China also possesses an authoritarian market system that in the long run is destined to underperform. But its intermediate-term prospects are bright because the Communist party has thus far succeeded in containing moral hazards, and mobilizing domestic and foreign capital for rapid economic development. This asymmetric model, which sacrifices current consumption for "catch-up" growth, should allow Beijing to climb from the fourth to the second development tier in the next few decades. Systems theory alone cannot predict how this will precisely reconfigure global wealth and power in 2025, but it does largely explain why America, Continental Europe, Japan, China, and Russia will not converge to a common high frontier, and why – despite globalization – relative and absolute poverty in some countries will intensify.

Contemporary great power systems are alike in two senses. They all harness markets, government, and custom for the benefit of their economic sovereigns, and violate generally competitive efficiency requirements. Some of these distortions are technical. Others are attributable to misgovernance, collectivism, communalism, criminal misconduct, obligation, faulty property rights, moral hazard, juridical misrule, and disregard for the rule of law.

The losses inflicted by these shortcomings are not easily measured across systems, allowing many analysts to infer that market economies are broadly alike and have similar potentials. This relativism sometimes is extended to command economies to justify the belief that all economies will achieve the same living standard in the long run.

These popular attitudes are incompatible with competitive market and optimal planning theory, which teach that the degree to which outcomes deviate from the equilibrium ideal should be positively correlated with anticompetitive distortions. From this perspective, America should be the economic front runner in the 21st century, followed by Continental Europe, Japan, China, and Russia, subject to various compensation effects. Japan, for example, might outpace Continental Europe because of its superior adaptivity, and China might outdistance everyone for some period because of its extreme underdevelopment.

The particulars elaborated in chapters 7–11 enable us to probe more deeply beneath these generalities, portraying new millennium performance prospects as a contest among four distinct systemic strategies: constituent managed markets, corporatist–elite managed collectivism, communalism, and authoritarian laissez faire. These alternatives correspond with the Anglo-American, Continental European, Japanese, and Russian–Chinese economic models. While all are inefficient, their performance potential can be conveniently discussed in terms of these concepts.

The primary cause of America's underperformance from a generally competitive standpoint is its cultural schizophrenia; that is, enlightenment sanctioned, golden rule abiding, frontier individualism on one hand, and collectivist state dependency on the other. The individualist aspect promotes competitively efficient outcomes including charitable transfers insofar as participants adhere to the golden rule; a condition too often honored in the breach. Under the best circumstances, individualist competition produces general equilibrium. More often outcomes are less favorable, either because laissez faire is interpreted to permit conspiracies in restraint of trade and predatory misconduct, or succumbs to destructive macroeconomic disorders. Advocates of competitive individualism try to combat these distortions through education, moral appeals, the rule of law, and minimally interventionist micro- and macroeconomic regulation. If the response is proportionate to perceived lapses then American economic performance should closely approximate the ideal, driven not only by the invisible hand, but by conscious renewal of purpose, commitment to the golden rule, vigorous antitrust enforcement, adherence to the rule of contract law, and neutral macroeconomic stabilization.

The collectivist "shadow" side of American culture, including assaults on the rule of law through judicial activism and executive decrees, however, hampers these initiatives. Calls for better education, moral renewal, minimalist microeconomic regulation, and macroeconomic equilibration serve as a guise for a myriad of interventionist programs which cannot be reconciled with charitable individualism because they reflect alien collectivist values.

The essence of these distortions does not lie so much in particular programs, or even excessive reliance on bureaucratic administration, but in the disparity between what people democratically want and what their representatives give them. Broadly speaking, Continental European and American economic sovereigns transfer income and perks to themselves at the expense of the public through privileged contracting, misregulation, mislegislation, and mistransfers at enormous cost calculated not just in terms of tax burdens, but in hidden compliance expenses, unnecessary product characteristic mandates, oligopoly rents, impeded competition, stultified innovation, effort disincentives, the emergence of a culture of dependency, and social injustice.

America's "spotlight" individualist culture diverts attention from these costs by insisting that they are socially justified and by misequating national welfare with the level and growth of GDP regardless of its composition, waste, and inequities. All sorts of "bads" like pornography in this way are treated as value added, but denial and mischaracterization do not alleviate the problem. The unpalatable truth is that a constellation of minor collectivist infringements of general individualistic competition ramify and cumulate through America's culturally regulated market system, significantly degrading education, training, labor conditions, factor allocation, product design, innovation, management, production, finance, investment, distribution, transfers, public services, the environment, macroeconomic stability, growth, and the quality of existence.

The magnitude of these distortions is further blurred by fluctuations in underlying rates of technological progress, and conjunctural and entrepreneurial forces which ameliorate, or aggravate, adaptive processes. When the winds of change are blowing America's way, playing to its strengths in informational entrepreneurship, marketing, and finance, aggregate performance can be astonishingly robust for a mature economy as it is today. It also can be appallingly bad, as it was during the Great Depression. However, the most striking feature of the American economy over the long run has been its stability. The net effect of a host of ever changing factors has been a steady expansion of per capita aggregate activity at a 1.5 percent annual clip. During the last decade of the 20th century, American growth was far more robust, driven by aggressive entrepreneurship, rapid innovations, especially in communications technologies, and a huge financial bubble. This *fin de siècle* exuberance cannot last because the bubble and the merger mania it has entailed must burst, leaving a legacy of intensified oligopoly, accompanied by a new wave of collectivism. The first decade of the 21st century will surely disappoint the bulls, but on balance America is probably well placed to outperform its historical norm because various aspects of individualist culture, including labor mobility, fungibility, and entrepreneurship, appear well suited to capitalize on the efficiency and mass marketing potential of the informational, technological revolution sweeping the globe.

The same conclusion does not apply to the other great powers because the positive impact of American-style individualistic liberalization, entrepreneurship, and technological progress is likely to be countervailed by the accumulating corrosive forces of statism, corporatism, authoritarian laissez faire, and communalism. The exact prognosis varies from case to case. The per capita income growth trend in Continental Europe has been adverse for decades despite relatively rapid global technological progress, reduced socialist militancy, and persistent efforts to reverse growth retardation through denationalization, deregulation, liberalization, and European integration. Although Continental European attitudes toward general competition have mellowed, and the traumas of the industrial revolution receded, corresponding statist and corporatist adaptations either dampened or negated their impact. Even the speculative asset valuation bubble of the late 1990s occasioned by global merger mania has not halted Continental Europe's aggregate devitalization, suggesting that when the boom ends, average per capita growth is likely to lag behind both the feeble performance of the 1990s and the postwar mean. Perhaps Continental Europe will converge to the Anglo-American model, or monetary union will save the day, but the initial dismal reception of the Euro can hardly be heartening.

Japan's postwar per capita growth trajectory closely tracks Continental Europe's, persistently decelerating despite numerous positive developments. It has gradually opened its markets to imports and foreign investment including mergers and acquisitions. It has downsized the state sector, diminished coercive planning, deregulated, introduced Western management practices, globalized, increased the flexibility of human resource management, promoted entrepreneurship, and lavishly financed research and development. It has even fostered the spread of pro-productive individualist values, all to no obvious avail. This suggests that the pronounced underperformance of Japan's economy in the 1990s will persist due to the conjuncture of a variety of cultural, competitive, and demographic factors. On the technical front, Japan is facing increasingly aggressive export competition to Western markets from South Korea, China, and other Asian developing economies, pressuring profit margins at the very time that its rapidly aging population threatens to diminish labor productivity and reduce per capita living standards. But the deeper problem confronting the nation is what to do with communalism. Should it be reinvigorated by attacking the divisive aspects of Japan's burgeoning individualism? Should it be consciously reengineered to preserve and enhance the positive aspects Aoki praises, while embedding entrepreneurial individualism? Should it be jettisoned, embracing Western guilt culture, individualism, and the welfare state? Are any of these ideals feasible? Various arguments easily can be marshaled supporting such propositions, but of course the jury is still out. Under the circumstances, therefore, it is appropriate to emphasize the difficulty of the undertaking. As the Russians discovered to their dismay, it is easier to pontificate about rapid efficient cultural adaptation in a time of intensive global competition than it is to do it. While the Japanese may once again confound the experts, the odds against their outpacing the postwar norm, and even the disappointing performance of the 1990s seem extremely high.

This brings us to Russia and China, both of which have embarked on the perilous path of authoritarian laissez faire, trying to capture the static and dynamic efficiencies of managerial decontrol, while retaining the preeminent authority of the state (Chinese Communist party) through government ownership and discipline. Both nations also have a history of radical, often cataclysmic, social change. Therefore it is essential to preface any assessment of their prospects by assuming that they will retain some version of authoritarian laissez faire, rather than embracing Anglo-American free enterprise, Continental European corporatism, Japanese communalism, or golden rule abiding perfect competition.

Additionally, it needs to be appreciated that the experience of both nations with authoritarian laissez faire has been bipolar. Russia has been ravaged by what sometimes has been called "katastroika" (catastrophic radical reform). Its GDP and industrial capacity utilization have sunk so low that it is difficult to imagine Russian per capita growth declining more precipitously in the first decade of the 21st century than the last decade of the 20th century. Likewise, it is equally hard to believe that China could achieve the double digit per capita GDP growth claimed after Tiananmen Square in perpetuity. A more useful approach is to inquire whether either country can achieve anything more than a meager improvement in its respective living standards in the 21st century. Holding a large number of variables *ceteris paribus*, the answer appears to depend on whether the prevailing Russian and Chinese authoritarian laissez-faire mechanisms are frozen in place, or each moves toward the other.

If they are frozen, then Russia will be fortunate indeed to achieve subpar per capita GDP growth, and even this accomplishment may not improve living standards for the majority because demand will remain under the thrall of kleptocratic sovereignty. China reciprocally will be lucky to avert a sharp deceleration in its growth as the economic toll of severe moral hazard diminishes efficiency, work, and investment incentives. Alternatively, if Russia disciplines its officials, and restores proprietary and administrative supervisory control over its minority manager co-owners, it will probably experience a rapid recovery in its industrial capacity utilization, which will translate into an aggregate growth spurt for several years in the high single digits. This probably will be hailed as a triumph of transition, but will not last because officials and minority manager co-owners will soon develop potent counter-measures. Reciprocally, if China succumbs to the Russian disease – that is, a deterioration of government discipline – it will suffer a prolonged bout of negative economic growth. Better outcomes, of course, can be conceived by shifting from a category B to a category A model, where officials perfectly administrate and owner–agents perfectly profit-maximize to generate competitive consumer sovereignty. But Soviet Marxists who rejected this course during the Stalinist period may be right. The temptations to abuse are too great in the Russian and Chinese cultural contexts to produce satisfactory long-term growth.

If this is correct, then Russian and Chinese authoritarian laissez faire will not provide a turnpike to sustainable modernization. Statistical deception and partisan fanfare may temporarily give a contrary impression but, like Stalin's and Mao's much ballyhooed command resource mobilization strategies, they will fail.

Review Questions

1. What are the four main contemporary systems strategies?
2. Rank these systems in terms of their inclusiveness and social protection. Treat Russia and China as separate systems. Explain your ranking.
3. Rank the five great power systems in terms of civic obligation.
4. Rank the five great power systems in terms of the importance of the rule of contract law.
5. Three of the five great power systems do not depend heavily on the rule of contract law. How have two of them succeeded despite this handicap?
6. Why is culture more powerful than institutions in explaining the behavior of the five great power systems?
7. Why is crime more destructive in some systems than others?
8. Why is workaholism a key element of three of the four successful great power systems? Does the leisure ethic pose a threat to Continental European prosperity?
9. How does the need to put a positive face on all systems encourage an erroneous belief in market universalism? Explain.
10. What is the main virtue of each system? What is each's major demerit? Rank the desirability of the five great power systems.
11. Why have liberalization and globalization failed to reverse the negative effects of Continental European, Japanese, Chinese, and Russian systemic inefficiencies?

PART IV

PERFORMANCE

CHAPTER 14

MEASUREMENT

The comparative theoretical merit of the five great power systems analyzed in part III can be tested empirically. The most widely used measure for appraising comparative economic performance is "gross domestic product." It represents the sum of all goods and services produced by a nation for sale during the course of a year, including unsold inventories and exports. Some readily marketable goods intended for personal use, like food produced by farmers, and do-it-yourself construction projects, are also counted. The quantities of these goods and services are valued and aggregated at prevailing market prices.

Chores like household work, leisure activities, and charitable activities, which are not intended to provide people's livelihoods, as well as criminal disservices like illegal gambling, bootlegging, and prostitution, are excluded from national income.

GDP thus does not measure total utility. It is an indicator of the market value of purchased, and saleable goods and services generated from "work," omitting the utility derived from "leisure." This makes it a measure of production potential: the ability of a nation to produce consumer, government, investment, and export goods, and it is useful more for evaluating national economic potential than welfare.

For those who understand the conceptual limitations of GDP this poses no problems, but there is an unfortunate tendency for people to assume that because GDP statistics are compiled according to a standard international methodology, all national income statistics are basically alike, regardless of how much systems diverge from the generally competitive ideal. This is fallacious. A detailed examination of this problem is provided in this chapter in preparation for later statistical comparisons. The more systems depart from category A self-regulating generally competitive norms, the more their production statistics valued in domestic or foreign currencies overstate real economic performance and potential. This needs to be borne in mind when evaluating comparative economic merit and prospects.

The theories of great power economic systems behavior elaborated in chapters 7–11 can be tested with GDP time-series data, but assessment is complicated by problems of measurement. Prices used to value inputs seldom reflect general competitive scarcity values as they should for valid comparisons (see figure 2.11, point E). Data can be adjusted but the improvement is frequently cosmetic. It is therefore essential, in trying to accurately appraise the future, to understand how standard GDP statistics may mischaracterize real achievements and causality. GDP data valued at imperfectly (non)competitive prices misrepresent ideal (real) utilitarian and technological relationships. Reported transactions do not tell us how much indicated utility deviates from the ideal (figure 7.6), or whether goods are exchanged at their marginal rates of substitution (figure 2.4). They do not tell us if factors are combined at their marginal technical rates of substitution (figure 2.6), are efficiently employed (figure 7.1), or if technologies are best. In short, they do not inform us whether people receive what they want, and whether what they get is efficiently supplied.

The severity of the problem depends on how culture, politics, ethics, mechanisms, and institutions cause prices to depart from their category A ideal under culturally regulated constituentism, collectivism, communalism Frederich and authoritarianism.

Consider the case Friedrich von Hayek described as "planned chaos," where prices are random numbers assigned to "things" with a bundle of characteristics arbitrarily designed and produced without regard for cost by state authorities. Products created in this way may be goods (positive utility), indifferents (zero utility), or bads (disutility), and none will have the characteristics anyone most desires except by coincidence. Assume further that households buy only goods, and the state purchases everything the people do not acquire; retaining these things, or distributing them on a compulsory basis. The sum of these transactions just as under perfect competition will comprise the gross domestic product. The arithmetic product obtained by multiplying arbitrary prices (p) by equally arbitrary "things" (q) could yield a number of great magnitude, misinterpretable as "value," when in fact the figure is literally "absurd" (meaningless), or utility (u) is negative as shown in the following example:

$$
\begin{aligned}
GDP &= p_1 q_1 + p_2 q_2 \\
&= 5(10) + 10(20) \\
&= \$250,
\end{aligned}
\tag{14.1}
$$

$$
\begin{aligned}
Utility &= -u_1 q_1 + -u_2 q_2 \\
&= -5(10) + -10(20) \\
&= -\$250.
\end{aligned}
\tag{14.2}
$$

GROWTH

The same difficulties obscure the measurement of growth. Statisticians in our mystery country could honestly report that the nation produced more "bads" this year than last, creating an illusion of progress, when in fact the only accomplishment was worsened living standards. Of course, this is extreme. If all production is of some use to recipients then it would seem to follow that the growth of "things" implies some gain. But this does not mean that there will be a perceptible improvement in well-being. Additional goods could be concentrated in the creation of war mobilization capacities and materiel that will never be used, civilian equivalents, or cause disgruntlement because of the disparity between the things desired and received. The accumulation of shoddy goods, or products with inferior characteristics, can diminish a community's sense of well-being even though it appears to be statistically better off.

These anomalies can occur when growth is slow or fast. The true standard of aggregate economic performance is the optimal category A rate, or some efficient category B analog, not its highest magnitude. If more output means undesired curtailments in leisure, faster is worse, not better. Category B economies often give false impressions of rapid development because the state overinvests, or misinvests, public funds, or concentrates on the production of goods with unwanted characteristics that are amenable to rapid expansion, such as no-frills construction. And, of course, these distortions are exacerbated if the competitive component of GDP growth is declining. Growth thus is best understood by assessing the degree to which quantitative increases need to be discounted for demand inefficiencies and qualitative distortions. There is not any unique way of balancing these factors because individual qualitative judgments differ, but some rough corrections can be made by studying demand and supply efficiency, crisis behavior, stages of economic development, and global marketability.

The best proxy for the latter is to choose a large relatively efficient category B economy which produces a full range of globally marketed products as the standard. The characteristics of these goods are known to be desirable because they are widely sold on a competitive basis. Consequently, prices on the demand side should closely approximate marginal rates of substitution, while those on the supply side represent domestic rates of marginal transformation, including competitively acquired foreign components.

America usually serves in this capacity because it is a large, open, competitive nation, although, as previously explained, prices often are distorted by various forms of market power. The valuation of other nation's GDP in dollars can be accomplished in two ways: through exchange rates, or a technique called purchasing power parity. The former is the simplest. A single exchange rate can be employed in computing aggregate GDP, or its components. The technique is satisfactory for comparisons with other large open economies unperturbed by speculative distortions like rampant inflation, politically misinspired capital movements, or transitory imbalances in payments for foreign goods and services. But its usefulness is problematic otherwise, especially where exchange rates are noncompetitively, or discriminatorily, fixed by foreign governments, and domestic prices are similarly controlled. Dollar values computed from such exchange rates provide misleading impressions of comparative GDP size and relative product values. Political authorities in closed societies can always try to delude naive outsiders into believing that they are prosperous by overvaluing their currencies.

PURCHASING POWER PARITY

Economists try to remedy this problem, as well as other distortions, by bypassing exchange rates, pricing individual foreign goods directly in dollars. This is easily accomplished for exports and imports described collectively as tradeables by assembling the requisite price data. The domestic dollar value of American products sold in Japan and the prices of Japanese products sold in America can be used directly, or for close substitutes to compute aggregate GDP.[1] And the technique can be supplemented by valuing nontraded goods at their American production cost. Construction, including housing, factories, government facilities, and weapons, is often estimated in this way.

Purchasing power parity, however, is not a panacea. It is vulnerable to misjudgments about the qualitative value of foreign substitutes with thin markets, or nontradeables. This problem is especially acute for closed economies, or partially open economies like Russia with noncompetitive exportables, where there are large disparities between supply cost and demand value. Russian nontradeables computed at American factor cost (capital and labor value added) may be large, but their value in the global market is negligible. This explains the wild divergences in estimated dollar purchasing power parities which sometimes place Russian per capita GDP at the mean of the developed West, and at other times rank it as an underdeveloped nation with a standard of living only a fifth the optimistic assessment. There is room for legitimate differences of opinion in such circumstances, but large divergences should be interpreted as telltale indicators of immense distortions which seriously overstate the economic efficiency of closed, and miscontrolled, systems.[2]

PRODUCTIVITY

A parallel set of difficulties beset international productivity comparisons computed in dollars, which tacitly assumes that foreign and American factor values are the same. The inability of closed economies to globally market their products demonstrates the foolishness of this assumption. Likewise, the marginal rates of factor substitution which govern factor prices in open, competitive economies do not coincide with those elsewhere, and therefore misrepresent the production potential of closed systems. And, of course, if GDP and factor costs in closed economies have no clear normative or efficiency significance measured either in dollars, or domestic currencies, then productivity computed as output–input ratios cannot be unambiguously interpreted.

The following formula for the comparative coefficient of factor productivity illustrates the point:

$$P = (y_i/y_j)/[(k_i/k_j)^{\alpha}(l_i/l_j)^{(1-\alpha)}], \tag{14.3}$$

where y_i, k_i, and l_i, represent the GDP, capital, and labor of a specific country like America or the Soviet Union, and α and $1 - \alpha$ are the elasticities of factor substitution which apply if the production functions for the economies being compared are identically Cobb–Douglas.

---

[1]   The technique is extended to nonclose substitutes, and sub-aggregates by forming dollar yen parities for the prices directly collected, and applying these ratios as "sub-exchange rates" to omitted products.
[2]   Steven Rosefielde and Ralph W. Pfouts, "The Mis-specification of Soviet Production Potential: Adjusted Factor Costing and Bergson's Efficiency Standard," in Rosefielde, ed., *Efficiency and Russia's Economic Recovery Potential to the Year 2000 and Beyond*, Ashgate, Aldersgate, 1998, pp. 11–32; Abram Bergson, "Neoclassical Norms and the Valuation of National Product in the Soviet Union and Its Postcommunist Successor States: Comment," *Journal of Comparative Economics*, Vol. 21, No. 3, December 1995, pp. 390–93. Cf., Anders Aslund, *The Myth of Output Collapse after Communism*, Carnegie Endowment for International Peace, Working Paper 18, March 2001.

Table 14.1   Coefficients of factor productivity (US = 100) Gross material product per unit of factor (labor and reproducible capital) inputs

	1960	1975
United States	100	100
United Kingdom	64	73
USSR		
Official	41	73
Bergson	41	55
Belkin/Shukhgal'ter	13	18
Rosefielde	10	15

Source: Steven Rosefielde, ed., *Efficiency and Russia's Economic Recovery Potential to the Year 2000 and Beyond*, Ashgate, Aldersgate, 1998, p. 114. The entry for Rosefielde above is impressionistic, and has not been precisely calculated.

The ratios of output–input ratios in equation (14.3) (America compared with the USSR) under ideal circumstances should indicate the degree to which the productivities in a large, open economy like America exceed those of closed, controlled rivals like the Soviet Union. But this can only be so if the dollar value of Soviet output y_j and capital k_j reflect the prices they fetch on the global market; the value added of labor in both countries is proportional to labor inputs in man–hours, and American dollar Cobb–Douglas factor income share weights approximate those in the Soviet Union.

None of these assumptions is true, and all greatly bias estimates of Soviet relative productivity upward. The example in table 14.1 illustrates the depth of the potential distortion. When Soviet data are converted to dollars using official or adjusted statistics that fail to take detailed account of the impaired marketability of the Kremlin's manufactures, the USSR's productivity performance appears good in light of historical backwardness. But when further adjustment is made for impaired marketability, validated after Russia introduced semicompetitive foreign exchange rates, comparative Soviet productivity falls drastically (even though the capital component of weighted inputs is downscaled). Clearly, the performance of inefficient systems can be significantly overstated by unwittingly adopting statistical conventions which imply that they are efficient.

INDEX NUMBER RELATIVITY

Although the kind of independent sampling data needed to judge the extent to which standard compilations exaggerate the performance of closed and controlled economies are occasionally undertaken, the task is time-consuming and expensive. A cheaper, interesting, but oblique alternative therefore frequently has been preferred. Instead of comprehensively adjusting official statistics, the reliability and sensitivity of GDP size, growth, and productivity estimates have been evaluated by pricing quantities in both dollars and the national currencies of closed and controlled economies. In the Soviet case, dollar valuation generated comparative size and productivity estimates, casting the Kremlin's performance in a relatively favorable light, while ruble valuation favored America.

The rationale for this technique, known as index number relativity, does not lie in the behavioral properties of closed and controlled economies but, rather, in well-documented price disparities that distinguish industrial from pre-industrial economies. The phenomenon has two interesting aspects. First, the relative price of manufactures in advanced countries compared with agrarian products tends to be low because of technological progress, economies of scale, and learning. This means that when dollar prices are used to weight production in less developed controlled economies like the Soviet Union they impose low values on manufactures the Kremlin produces in small quantities, and high values on abundant agricultural outputs, giving the impression that Soviet GDP is comparatively large.[3] Conversely, because Soviet prices display reciprocal properties, ruble estimates of American GDP overstate its size. Second, the price structure in most industrializing countries, including the Soviet Union, tend to shift toward the pattern of advanced nations as manufactures expand with the result that growth measured at base year ruble prices (high prices for rapidly expanding manufactures) is faster than when measured at final year ruble prices (low prices for rapidly expanding manufactures).

There is nothing that requires these outcomes in closed, controlled economies, but they were validated in the Soviet case because Goskomtsen (the Soviet Price Committee) fixed prices in accordance with their embodied labor input, causing ruble prices for manufactures to fall as productivity rose, mimicking the competitive market. Moreover, analysts discovered that it was possible to illuminate matters further by taking account of planners' preferences. Since the declared purpose of Stalin's rapid industrialization policy was to industrialize, Moorsteen correctly pointed out that base year ruble prices which produced relatively high rates of GDP growth better measured changes in the production potential Stalin desired than final year prices, and so were more appropriate.[4] This concept is best understood with the aid of figure 14.1, which depicts the Soviet Union's production possibilities (feasibilities) frontier at the start of industrialization in 1929 and at the end of the second Five Year Plan in 1937. According to official claims the 1937 frontier not only lies above the 1929 frontier, but structural potential drastically shifted in favor of manufactures. The change in agricultural potential measured along the 1929 expansion path is small, but industrial potential burgeoned along Stalin's preferred 1937 expansion path. This shift in manufacturing potential turns out to be best measured with base year prices. This is easily seen by drawing the 1929 price ratio through 1937 GDP at point B following the line until it intersects the 1929 expansion path, and observing that the ratio of growth measured AA' closely approximates the true change in production potential BB'.[5] A similar case can be made that dollars provide a better impression than rubles of the value of Soviet GDP from the perspective of global market demand.

---

[3]   The same principle held after the Soviet Union's initial industrialization, even though agriculture's contribution to GDP declined because advanced industrial products produced inexpensively in America were scarce in the USSR, while obsolete goods produced in abundance in the Soviet Union were scarce and expensive in the USA.

[4]   Richard Moorsteen, "On Measuring Productive Potential and Relative Efficiency," *Quarterly Journal of Economics*, Vol. LXXV, No. 6, August 1961, pp. 451–67.

[5]   Because Soviet prices were fixed in 1927–8, they were in force in 1929, and it is these price relatives which are usually employed to measure production potential for the economic structure Stalin preferred.

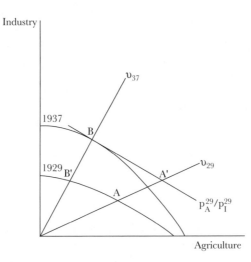

Figure 14.1 Soviet economic potential interpreted from the standpoint of index number relativity

Index number relativity analysis thus provides scholars with a tool for claiming that, despite the ambiguities of the data Soviet growth, comparative size and productivity were greater than most observers understood. These assertions have some limited merit. The structure of post-industrialization outputs no doubt reflect Stalin's preferences more accurately than those prevailing in 1929, and ruble prices were linked to changing nominal productivities, but these virtues do not negate the fact that relative prices were not correlated with marginal utilities, and purchasing power parity dollar estimates disregard the impaired marketability of Soviet manufactures. While base year ruble prices probably did more accurately measure the change in production potential Stalin preferred, the magnitude of that change nonetheless is exaggerated by the accumulation of things with characteristics few really wanted. Likewise, valuing the Kremlin's manufactures in dollars on the false premise that they were marketable at conventional purchasing power parities is misleading. Claims made by both Goskomstat and the CIA that Soviet GDP in the 1980s, computed in dollars, was two thirds of America's, or that its per capita living standards were at the Western European mean, have proved after decontrol to be preposterous. The usefulness of index number relativity as a device for analyzing comparative economic performance, like all other indicators, thus depends fundamentally on the degree to which countries being compared satisfy efficiency principles: the greater the degree of inefficiency, the less the merit of index number relativity assessments.

EXPLANATION

Measurement errors associated with economic inefficiency have another unfortunate consequence. They obscure causality. Misvalued economic statistics which do not satisfy efficiency axioms cannot be used to accurately identify the relative importance of various real causal influences, or the causality that would apply if the economy were competitively efficient. They can only identify nominal relationships misimplied by misvalued statistics. Students should be aware that econometric discoveries about the determinants of growth and other phenomena in relatively efficient, open economies which may appear to apply in closed, controlled economies could well be illusory. This means that the road to transition and convergence is intrinsically more statistically obscure than analysts are sometimes prepared to acknowledge, and that forecasts regarding the future configuration of wealth and power must be correspondingly qualified. While today's leaders can be overtaken by tomorrow's stars, it is probably wise to discount their challenge unless it is clear that the performance of upstarts like China, which seem so vital, are founded on efficient economic processes.

Review Questions

1. Markets are essential for generating knowledge about the characteristics of general equilibrium. Without them, economists can only guess the structure of Pareto efficient supply and demand. What does this imply about the limitations of data adjustment? Explain.

2. What is "planned chaos"? Can GDP be computed with meaningless state fixed prices? Elaborate.

3. Many eminent economists insist that if growth statistics are positive, social welfare must be increasing. Are they right?

4. Can the substitution of American market prices for arbitrary planning prices overcome this ambiguity, if products and characteristics are correctly matched? In what sense?

5. What are the competing merits of revaluing the GDP of other countries through the market foreign exchange rate, and purchasing power parity?

6. Do planning and misgovernance obscure value added, national income, and the assessment of factor allocational efficiency? Explain.

7. Why do "coefficients of factor productivity" calculations tend to overstate the relative performance of controlled economies?

8. What is index number relativity, and why is it a useful tool of comparative analysis?

9. What are the inferential limitations of index number relativity analysis?

10. Does econometric analysis using data from controlled and mismanaged economies run the danger of misconstruing causality? Explain. Does this problem extend to research on the American economy?

CHAPTER 15

GLOBAL PERFORMANCE

The past provides a baseline for the future. Systems theory suggests that after the initial growth spurt following the Second World War, the performance of the American, Japanese, Continental European, Russian, and Chinese economies should have gradually decelerated as reconstruction waned, and moral hazards became more pronounced. The evidence appears to confirm this expectation even though all five systems liberalized (America abandoned New Deal regulations, Europe integrated, and Japan, Russia, and China increased their reliance on markets), embraced globalization, and freely borrowed elements from each other, so that by the turn of the millennium they were more alike than ever before.

Per capita GDP growth has trended down, with the United States during the 1990s performing best, followed by Japan, Continental Europe, and Russia, despite what appear to be robust advances in technology. The only enigma is China. The data suggest that it is following the trajectory of a variety of systems like Japan, South Korea, Malaysia, and Thailand emerging from extreme initial backwardness.

These patterns are echoed in the global data with the least developed countries, Eastern Europe, and the Commonwealth of Independent States which deviate furthest from the generally competitive norm, faring worst. The big picture divides the globe into three separate worlds: winners, challengers, and also-rans. The First World, with 16 percent of the population, includes America, Canada, the European Union, Japan, Australia, New Zealand, Israel, Iceland, Malta, Norway, and Switzerland. The Second World features eight Asian tigers: China, Hong Kong, Taiwan, Singapore, South Korea, Malaysia, Indonesia, and Thailand. The new "Third World," which contains 57 percent of the planetary population, is represented by the least developed countries, the CIS, and Eastern Europe, other poor countries classified by the UNDP as medium and low "human development," and a miscellany of nonindustrial, high human development states like Brunei and Mexico.

The growth retardation that has gripped the globe for the last three decades has not been unremitting. There have been subcycles and counter-tendencies. Some members of the Third World spurted raising hopes for global convergence, but soon were winded. Likewise, some nations have drastically underperformed the mean, while a few countries like the Asian tigers have mounted a sustained ascent. Fluctuations in resource and commodity prices, and the shift from engineering to information-based innovation, provide partial explanations of these sub-trends, as each culture and political system coped as it could with global change. The rise of multinational national corporations, merger mania, and swings in international capital flows are other important elements in the story, all refracted through the prism of systems.

The future will surely bring new challenges and discontinuities. Few cultures are all weather. It is probably safe to infer that the dual process of gradual devitalization and reconfiguration, rather than growth acceleration and convergence, will predominate. This means that in the first quarter of the 21st century the gap between winners and also-rans will widen, with the United States pulling further ahead of the European Union and Japan. Russia will wither, while China might just become the consummate "Asian tiger."

RECONFIGURATION OF WEALTH AND POWER

The reconfiguration of global wealth and power predicted by systems theory augers an era of selective prosperity for some great powers, coupled with increasing social injustice, inequality, and conflict. The quantitative dimensions of these trends can be discerned from the statistical record. This chapter focuses on systemic aspects of economic performance, chapter 17 on military power, and chapter 18 on the implications for international relations.

Data compiled on 174 countries in table 15.1 by the United Nations Development Program for the benchmark year 1995 provide an instructive point of departure. The UNDP divides this universe into two worlds, industrially developed, and other developing

Table 15.1   Indicators of comparative systemic performance population, GDP, growth and inflation

	World	TWO-WORLD MODEL			
		Developed, including transition	Developing		
			All developing	Least developed	Transition
Number of countries	174	50	124	48	25
Population millions (1995)[a]	5,627	1,233	4,394	543	335
GNP millions (1995)[b] dollars: exchange rate	27,077	22,332	4,745	100	587
GDP millions (1995)[c] dollars: purchasing power parity	33,706	20,144	13,481	547	1,334

GNP per capita (1995)[d]:					
exchange rate	4,812	18,158	1,141	215	1,750
GDP per capita (1995)[e]:					
purchasing power parity	5,990	16,337	3,068	1,008	3,982

GNP growth per capita: annual rate, exchange rate[f]

1965–80	–	3.3	3.0	–	–
1980–95	0.9	1.6	2.1	–	–

GDP growth per capita: 1987 dollars, annual rate[g]

1960–70	3.1	2.8	3.7	1.1	–
1970–80	1.6	1.8	3.8	−0.6	(5.4)
1980–90	0.6	1.0	0.7	−0.1	1.2
1990–95	0.7	0.7	3.3	−1.7	−5.4
1980–95	0.6	0.9	1.8	−0.6	−1.3

GNP growth per capita: annual rate, weighted[h]

1960–80	4.0
1980–92	1.9
1993–96	1.5

	THREE-WORLD MODEL		
	First World	**Second World** **Rapidly**	**Third World** **Low per**
	Developed	**developing**	**capita GDP**
Number of countries	25	6	115
Least developed			48
Transition (EE + CIS)			25
Other poor nations			42
Population millions (1995)[a]	831	1,544	3,252
GNP millions (1995)[b] dollars: exchange rate	22,071	1,688	3,955
GDP millions (1995)[c] dollars: purchasing power parity	18,434	5,604	9,666
GNP per capita (1995)[d]: exchange rate	26,560	1,093	1,216
GDP per capita (1995)[e]: purchasing power parity	22,183	3,629	2,975
GNP growth per capita: annual rate, exchange rate[f]			
1965–80	3.4	5.7	2.3
1980–95	2.2	6.2	0
GDP growth per capita: 1987 dollars, annual rate[g] 1980–95			
Least developed			−0.6
Transition (EE + CIS)			−1.3

Source: United Nations, *Human Development Report 1998*, Oxford University Press, New York, 1998. United Nations, *Human Development Report 1995*, Oxford University Press, New York, 1995.
[a–h] For derivation, see appendix B.

nations, with two sub-components: post-communist transition economies (Eastern Europe and the Commonwealth of Independent States) and least developed countries. The former communist economies are categorized as industrially advanced; the least developed countries as developing. Each is the poorest performing element in its respective group. Using this classification, America, Europe (defined as the European Union plus Norway and Switzerland), Japan, and Russia are industrially advanced, and China is rapidly developing.

The four industrially developed great powers, with 16 percent of the world's population, surveyed in table 15.2, generated roughly 60–80 percent of the planetary GDP computed in dollars respectively through the exchange rate, and purchasing power parities in 1995 (see chapter 14 for a discussion of these valuation conventions). Russia's contribution to the four was minute. China, with 22 percent of the world population, contributed 3–11 percent of global GDP calculated alternatively via the exchange rate or purchasing power parities. Its purchasing power parity GDP was approximately half America's and exceeded Japan's, with Russia lagging far behind. Living standards and economic potential indicated by the GDP statistics display a similar pattern. The "big three" industrial advanced countries (American, Japan, and Europe including the United Kingdom and Ireland) enjoy living standards four to 12 times greater than Russia, and more than 29 times that of the least developed countries, with no sign of the widely heralded catch-up effect. Living standards in the least developed countries have been declining absolutely and relatively compared with the rich industrial nations for three decades. Russian per capita growth according to

Table 15.2 Indicators of comparative systemic performance population, GDP, growth, and inflation

	America	Japan	Europe	Russia	China
Population millions (1995)[a,1]	267	125	383	149	1,220
GNP millions (1995)[b] dollars: exchange rate	7,100	4,964	8,913	332	745
GDP millions (1995)[c] dollars: purchasing power parity	7,100	2,741	7,437	675	3,581
GNP per capita (1995)[d]: exchange rate	26,980	39,640	23,272	2,240	620
GDP per capita (1995)[e,2]: purchasing power parity	26,977	21,930	19,418	4,531	2,935
GDP growth per capita: annual rate[f]					
1965–80	1.8	5.1	3.2	(6.5)	4.1
1980–95	1.5	3.6	1.6	−3.3	8.6
GDP growth per capita: 1987 dollars, annual rate[g]					
1960–70	2.7	9.7	3.9	–	2.1
1970–80	1.6	3.3	2.5	6.5	4.1
1980–90	1.7	3.4	2.1	0	7.5
1990–95	1.3	1.0	1.0	−6.6	11.0
Inflation					
1985–95	3.2	1.4	4.6	149	9.3
1995	2.5	−0.6	3.1	191	12.8

Source: United Nations, *Human Development Report 1998*, Oxford University Press, New York, 1998.
[a–g, 1, 2] For derivation, see appendix C.

the UN's estimates was stagnant in the 1980s, falling precipitously thereafter.[1] Although the rate of material progress has been diminishing for all categories since 1970, America, Europe, and Japan have performed relatively well compared with the former Soviet Union, Eastern Europe, and the least developed countries.

Only China seems to have bucked the trend among the great powers, joining a select group of developing countries exhibiting high and accelerating rates of aggregate economic growth over the decades, like South Korea. The importance of this phenomenon can be made more apparent by revising the UN's classification from two to three categories, separating those developing countries on a fast track, and shifting Russia, the non-Russian CIS, and Eastern Europe to the ranks of the low per capita GDP nations in the Third World.

The second panel in table 15.1 provides this breakdown for the First, Second, and Third Worlds. The First World is dominated by the "big three" industrially developed nations; but also includes Canada, Australia, New Zealand, Israel, and Iceland. The Second World is comprised of a surprisingly few industrializing nations that have managed to sustain unusually high rates of per capita growth for more than 35 years, and succeeded in exporting their manufactures to the West. Only eight countries qualify: China, Hong Kong, Taiwan, Singapore, South Korea, Malaysia, Indonesia, and Thailand.[2] The Third World is composed of three distinct subgroups: least developed countries, the former communist countries of Eastern Europe and the CIS, and 42 other poor nations. Twenty-eight countries with mixed characteristics are lumped in with the Third World statistics on population, GDP, and per capita GDP, but are excluded from the growth rate statistics in order to isolate the potential of the medium and low human development component. The 28-country nonindustrial, high human development group is composed of rich nations like Brunei, and low and medium per capita GDP states classified by the UNDP as nonindustrial "high human development."[3]

All the countries in the First World possess workably competitive market systems with predominantly private ownership of the means of production. They broadly uphold the golden rule, and adhere to the rule of law. America, Canada, the United Kingdom, Ireland, Australia, and New Zealand rely on the Anglo-American model, while the rest save Japan are collectivist. The Second World is conspicuously Asian, with various British,

---

[1] The official Soviet per capita GSP (gross social product) growth rates were:

	1960–70	1970–80	1980–90	1990–95
Official (Soviet)	5.3	4.3	3.2	–
United Nations (Russia)	–	6.6	0	−6.6

The United Nations apparently accepts official Soviet rates for the 1970s, but not the 1980s.
Sources: *Narodnoye khoziaistvo SSSR 1990*, Moscow 1990; *Narodnoye khoziaistvo za 70 let*, Moscow, 1987; and table 15.2.

[2] The subcalculations for the Second World in table 15.1 exclude Taiwan because the UNDP does not report them. Hong Kong is excluded because it federated with China in 1997.

[3] The countries in the residual category are Cyprus, Barbados, Antigua and Barbuda, Bahamas, Belize, Brunei Darussalam, Argentina, Bahrain, United Arab Emirates, Kuwait, Qatar, Chile, Costa Rica, Uruguay, Trinidad and Tobago, Dominica, Fiji, Panama, Venezuela, Mexico, Saint Kitts and Nevis, Grenada, Columbia, Saint Vincent, Seychelles, Saint Lucia, Mauritius, Brazil, and Libyan Arab Jamahiriya. Hong Kong, which belongs in the Second World, is also excluded because it merged with China. The population of these 28 states is 382.3 million. Their combined GDP is 1.547 trillion dollars, and per capita GDP 4,478 dollars.

European, and American cultural overlays. The state plays a prominent role either in regulating the market or strictly enforcing the golden rule. All can be characterized as some variant of authoritarian laissez faire. The group is primarily ethnically Chinese, with strong Confucian influences extending to South Korea. The Thai and Indonesian cultures have some Chinese elements, with a large Indian admixture. Islam is a factor in Malaysia and Indonesia. None of these nations are communalist in the Japanese shame cultural sense, but all except perhaps Indonesia seem capable of managing the contradictions of authoritarian laissez faire.

Third World systems tend to be illiberal and corrupt compared with the First World, and unruly compared with the Second World. They are vulnerable to foreign exploitation. Their persistent backwardness can be partly attributed to their traditional cultures, selected state ownership of the means of production, excessive regulations and controls, pervasive institutional and moral hazards, and abusive foreign intrusions. But it is also ascribable in strong measure to their refusal to play by rules applied either in the First or the Second World. Culture, politics, and ethics prevent them from emulating Anglo-American constituentism, Continental European collectivism, Japanese communalism, and successful variants of Asian authoritarian laissez faire.

The consequences of these systems preferences seem stark. Nations adhering to the Anglo-American, Continental European, and Japanese models can expect to achieve rapid per capita growth during the early phase of their ascent to prosperity, followed by a long period of growth retardation, perhaps converging to a low growth or steady state asymptote. Singapore, Hong Kong, and Taiwan suggest a similar pattern for the Second World, perhaps with a higher asymptote, although the future performances of China, South Korea, Malaysia, Indonesia, and Thailand appear more problematic. Prospects for nations with systems further removed from the generally competitive paradigm appear dull, or grim. Some Third World nations will surely achieve gradual improvements in their living standards, but others like the least developed countries, the CIS, and Eastern Europe could become increasingly impoverished.

The reconfiguration of great power economic and military might in the first quarter of the 21st century is best appreciated in this perspective. If, as the trends of the 1990s suggest, America pulls further ahead of Continental Europe and Japan, it will also do so with respect to the Third World. Its prosperity will stand in glaring opposition to the plight of 57 percent of the world, especially the 73 least developed and non-Chinese post-communist states. The dominant motif will be divergence, not convergence, except for the Tigers in the Second World. Their good fortune will enhance the influence of South Korea, Thailand, Malyasia, Taiwan, and Indonesia, with a combined population roughly that of the European Union, but of course the most striking transformation may occur in China. Its GDP could quickly surpass America's, creating a new global bipolarity against a background of flagging Japanese and Continental European power, Russian marginalization, and Third World discontent, far different from the future envisioned by Samuel Huntington.[4] And if anticompetitive category B market, governmental, and criminal forces intensify in the First and Third Worlds, the global reconfiguration of wealth and power could become acutely destabilizing.

---

[4]   Samuel Huntington, "The Lonely Superpower," *Foreign Affairs*, Vol. 78, No. 2(March/April 1999), pp. 35–49; Huntington, *The Clash of Civilizations and the Remaking of World Order*, New York, Simon and Schuster, 1996.

FORECASTS

Tables 15.3 and 15.4 provide benchmarks for quantifying these possibilities. The estimates presented are projections of recent trends intended for illustrative purposes, not scientific prediction. The baseline estimates assume that the First, Second, and Third Worlds will grow at their respective 1980–95 means during the first quarter of the 21st century. Estimates for the least developed countries, the CIS and Eastern Europe are computed the same way, but the great power country estimates rely on the 1995–99 trend. Varying the reference end periods allows us to consider different scenarios.

Table 15.3 forecasts per capita GDP growth for 1995–2025. Panel I suggests that while planetary per capita GDP will increase by nearly a third, living standards in the First World will nearly double, and increase sixfold for the authoritarian Asian tigers. The Third World by contrast will endure the same level of poverty it does today, with living standards in the least developed countries, and the CIS–Eastern European group, falling by 16 and 32 percent respectively. As a consequence of these transformations, the planetary mean per capita income will fall by a third compared with the First World. There will be a compression of inequality between the First and Second Worlds, with the Asian Tigers' per capita GDP rising from 16 percent to more than half the level of the First World, but inequality will drastically widen between the riches and nouveaux riches on one hand, and nearly five billion people classified as low and medium material and human development on the other.

Table 15.3   Per capita GDP growth projections 1995–2025

	Per capita GDP 1995 (dollars)	Per capita GDP growth	Per capita GDP 2025 (dollars)	Index 1995	Index 2025
Panel I (indexes: First World = 100) (growth trend period 1980–95)					
Planetary	5,990	0.9	7,837	27	18
First World	22,183	2.2	42,613	100	100
Second World	3,629	6.2	22,056	16	52
Third World	2,975	0	2,975	13	7
Least developed	1,008	−0.6	843	5	2
CIS + EE	1,750	−1.3	1,193	8	3
Panel II (indexes: America = 100) (growth trend period: 1995–99)					
America	26,977	1.5	42,167	100	100
Japan	21,939	0	21,939	81	52
Europe	19,418	0.8	24,662	72	58
Russia	4,531	−1.0	3,372	17	8
China	2,935	8.0	29,534	11	70

Sources: tables 15.1 and 15.2.

Assumption: Panel I per capita GDP will grow at the trend rate 1980–95. Panel II per capita GDP will grow at the trend rate 1995–99.

Table 15.4   GDP growth projections 1995–2025

	GDP 1995 ($billions)	Population growth trend	GDP 2025 ($billions)	Index 1995	Index 2025
Panel I (indexes: First World = 100) (population growth trends 1995–2015)					
Planetary	33,706	1.2	93,505	100	100
First World	18,434	0.2	37,599	55	40
Second World	5,604	0.8	43,256	17	46
Third World	9,666	1.5	12,650	29	14
Least developed	547	2.4	760	2	1
CIS + EE	1,334	0	1,334	7	1
Panel II 1995 (indexes: total = 100) (population growth trends 1995–2015)					
Great powers	21,534	0.7	71,149	100	100
America	7,100	0.8	14,095	33	20
Japan	2,741	0	2,741	13	4
Europe	7,437	0	9,445	35	13
Russia	675	−0.4	446	3	1
China	3,581	0.7	44,422	16	62

Sources: tables 15.1, 15.2, 15.3, *United Nations, Human Development Report 1995*, Oxford University Press, New York, 1995, Table 22, pp. 176–77, Table 41, p. 200.

Method: The planetary figure for 2025 is computed by summing the First, Second, and Third World projections.

Projections are computed by multiplying the per capita growth rates in table 15.3 by the population growth rates in table 15.4, compounded 30 years from 1995–2025.

Note: Population projections are provided for 1995–2015 by the UNDP. These have been extended an additional ten years. The population growth forecast for the Second World has been calculated by summing the UNDP's population estimates for 1995 and 2015 for China, Singapore, South Korea, Malaysia, Indonesia, and Thailand.

Panel II in table 15.2 addresses the same issues from the standpoint of the great powers, redefined here by including the United Kingdom and Ireland in the new composite called Europe. The pattern is broadly the same for America, China, and Russia as it is for the First, Second, and Third World, although China's ascent is faster, and Russia's decline more gradual. The lackluster performance of Japan and Europe in 1995–99, however, has an adverse impact on their extrapolated relative standings. China's per capita GDP surpasses Japan's and Europe's by a considerable margin in 2025, reaching 70 percent of the American benchmark.

Table 15.4 continues the exercise by examining GDP growth. The estimates contain several important surprises, because while population growth forecast by the UNDP is rapid for the planet as a whole, the Second and Third Worlds, the least developed countries, America, and China; it is zero in the CIS, Eastern Europe, Japan, and Western Europe, with substantial declines in Russia. The estimates in panel I imply that while per capita planetary GDP will increase less than a third, GDP will nearly treble. National income in the First World will double, but this achievement will be dwarfed by an eightfold gain in the Second World. At the end of the first quarter of the 21st century, GDP generated in the Second World will exceed the First's by 15 percent, resulting in co-equal bipolarity. The Third World will make a small gain in aggregate production, but its relative share will fall from 29 to 14 percent, with the deterioration concentrated in the least developed countries, the CIS, and Eastern Europe. The once mighty former Soviet bloc will dwindle into economic oblivion.

Panel II in table 15.4 mirrors these patterns for the great powers, with Japan and Europe once again faring badly, this time because the UNDP expects them to experience zero population growth. Their combined share of great power GDP is projected to decline from 48 to 17 percent, displaced partly by America, but most astonishingly by China. Thanks to its rapid rate of growth in 1995–99, China's GDP in 2025 is forecast to be treble America's. At first glance, this seems preposterous, but the driving force is plausible. If China manages to reach only 70 percent of America's living standard, its vastly larger population arithmetically necessitates its becoming the world's largest economy.

As initially cautioned, these estimates are only illustrative. Japan and Continental Europe may become revitalized despite their systemic vulnerabilities. Russia could trans-form its culture and join the West, and of course China could falter. The historical record and systems theory both suggest that Beijing may not realize its rosy potential, even if the statistics used to gauge that potential are reliable. The economy of Asia's first and preeminent Tiger, Japan has become dyspeptic despite its continued discipline, hard work, and forced saving, and some like Paul Krugman dispute the reality of the Asian miracle.[5] Nonetheless, 30 years of sustained high rates of GDP growth in the Second World is significant, suggesting that China and the Tigers should be taken seriously.[6]

Figures 15.1 and 15.2 graph these trends and forecasts. They are worth pondering. But it should also be recalled that GDP and per capita GDP statistics are better interpreted as measures of economic potential than living standards or utility, because their components are not easily interpreted. Investment is only significant if it provides a valuable stream of future consumption. Often, expected payoffs do not materialize. The Soviets routinely invested 35 percent of their GDP which might have increased economic potential, but the UNDP's revised growth estimates for 1980–95 indicate that these outlays were squan-dered. Government services are notoriously difficult to evaluate, and consumption only measures the purchase of inputs intended to provide utility, not the level of utilities actually derived. The quality of life, economic merit, social justice, and other factors affecting international relations and security may not be adequately correlated with GDP, per capita GDP, and growth, requiring a closer microeconomic inquiry.[7]

---

[5]   Paul Krugman, "The Myth of Asia's Miracle," *Foreign Affairs*, Vol. 73, No. 6, 1994, pp. 62–78.

[6]   Krugman correctly argues that Asian productivity gains were not phenomenal, but he misses the deeper point that "Asian values" facilitated globally market-oriented resource mobilization that has eluded the rest of the Third World.

[7]   Bart van Ark and Robert McGuckin, "International Comparisons of Labor Productivity and Per Capita Income," *Monthly Labor Review*, July 1999, pp. 33–41. Estimates of comparative international productivity are more complicated than many suppose. In addition to the familiar purchasing power parity problem (see chapter 14), data on hours worked as distinct from hours employed vary greatly in coverage and quality from country to country, as do levels of involuntary unemployment. These subtleties are important because if hours worked are relatively low in some countries, productivity (measured as per capita GDP) will be understated because the

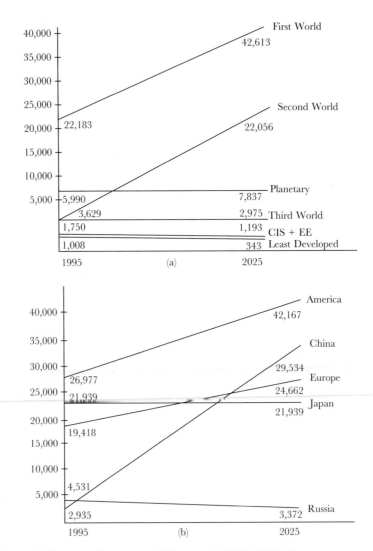

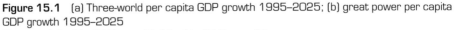

Figure 15.1   (a) Three-world per capita GDP growth 1995–2025; (b) great power per capita GDP growth 1995–2025
Sources: (a) table 15.3, panel I; (b) table 15.3, panel II

"leisure" income implicitly earned by workers is not being taken into account. Likewise, countries operating near full employment will appear more productive, when they are merely exhibiting higher labor force participation rates. The performance of the American economy is particularly sensitive to these and other adjustments. Hours worked per person in 1997 were estimated at 1,966 using the OECD's method derived from the Current Population Survey, but only 1,628 according to Angus Maddison's component method which takes account of vacations, holidays, absences due to sickness, and part-time work. The OECD approach yields results which place nine countries ahead of the United States in GDP per hour worked, with disparities as large as 30 percent. Maddison's preferred statistics reduce this number to four countries and the maximum disparity to 7 percent. Without these adjustment, America is number one in GDP per person employed. See table 15.1

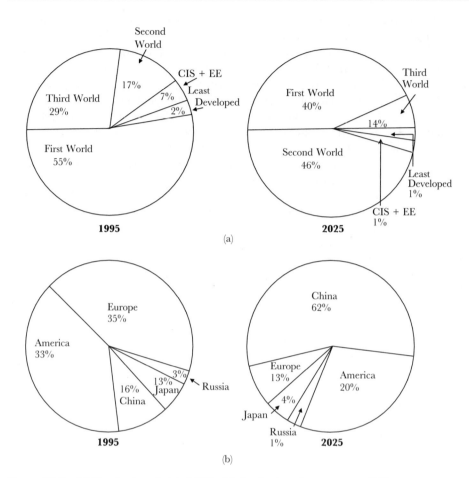

Figure 15.2   (a) Distribution of global GDP; (b) distribution of great power GDP
Sources: (a) table 15.4, panel I; (b) table 15.4, panel II

WELFARE

The UNDP has tried to accomplish welfare by devising various indicators of "human development." Its human development index uses a complex formula that weights the relative importance of life expectancy, adult literacy, educational attainment, and adjusted real GDP per capita ($PPP) to rank the performance of 174 countries. A gender-related development index, gender empowerment measure, and poverty index focusing on longevity, knowledge, and a decent standard of living are employed as supplementary indicators. The criteria utilized in the poverty index are the percentage of people expected to die before age 40, adult illiteracy, access to safe water, and health services, and the weight deficit of children less than five.[8]

These indicators increase our appreciation of what a Third World experience means, and form the basis for the UNDP's action program aimed at alleviating poverty, malnutrition, energy shortages, environmental abuse, deficient water supplies, inadequate access to health services, substandard housing, and transportation, but they do not illuminate the underlying causes of low human development.[9] The challenge for the Third World, and the other worlds, is not the lack of resources, knowledge, and technologies to solve these maladies, but systemic barriers to their utilization. Markets have become ubiquitous, and there are pockets of prosperity and modernity in most contemporary societies, yet the statistics show that 73 nations are backpedaling, most are treading water, and only a few are gaining ground, while the leaders themselves are flagging. This suggests that although it should be easy to emulate the constituent and collectivist market institutions of the First World under the rule of law, or even to substitute missing prerequisites with authoritarian resource mobilization, as Gerschenkron surmised,[10] cultural, political, and ethical barriers to imitation are formidable, and remain sources of degeneration for those who succeed, including today's front-runners. The deep conceptual roots of this double jeopardy have already been identified in chapters 5 and 6, which demonstrated the virtual impossibility of perfect competition and perfect planning, and of course are confirmed less tidily in the historical record of the rise and fall of civilizations.

There appears to be a perpetual battle in all societies between forces that favor generalized prosperity, and those concentrating wealth, curtailing equal opportunity, and sometimes fostering decline. Macropolicy variables and microdiagnostics seldom reflect this clearly, because indicators can be interpreted in many ways. For example, rising profits and stagnant wages either may be associated with vibrant entrepreneurship and accelerated growth, or intensified oligopoly power. Nonetheless, selected macropolicy and microstatistics do illuminate the culture driven systems strategies currently being pursued, and their consequences.

MACROSTRUCTURE

Table 15.5 highlights some profound differences in macro-management strategies adopted by constituent, communalist, corporatist, and authoritarian laissez-faire systems. The Continental European central governments, constrained by their collectivist cultural convictions, spend 43 percent of GDP to regulate aggregate economic activity and redistribute income. Japan, by contrast, placing more faith in community than state administration, restricts the share of central government expenditures to only a third the collectivist European level. The same pattern is replicated in the unemployment benefit statistics. Japan

[8]   United Nations, *Human Development Report 1998*, Oxford University Press, New York, 1998, p. 107.
[9]   Ibid., pp. 88–9.
[10]   Alexander Gerschenkron, *Economic Backwardness in Historical Perspective*, Harvard University Press, Cambridge, MA, 1961.

Table 15.5   Indicators of comparative systemic performance: macropolicy

	America	Japan	Europe	Russia	China
Central government expenditure as a share of GDP (1995)[a]	23	(14)	43	27	–
Budget deficit (%GDP)[b]					
1980	2.8	7.0	4.9	–	–
1995	–	(.)	4.8	10.5	11.9
Unemployment benefit expenditures as % of government expenditure (1991)[c]	1.5	0.7	2.9	–	–
Unemployment benefit expenditures per capita by the central government (1995) dollars[d]	92	2	250		

Source: United Nations, *Human Development Report 1998*, Oxford University Press, 1998.

References:
   a. Table 25, p. 182; Table 45, p. 204. See derivation of bracketed entry in the note below.
   b. Table 26, p. 184; Table 46, p. 205.
   c. Table 33, p. 192.
   d. Table 33, p. 192, Table 45, p. 204.

Note: 1995 per capita central government expenditures on employment benefits, given 1991 expenditure share weights are shown below. Japanese central government expenditures as a share of GDP are not reported in Table 45, p. 204. They have been estimated by taking the ratio of Japanese/America government GDP shares 10/16 (Table 45, p. 204) and multiplying it by the American central government expenditures as a share of GDP, 23.

spends only a hundredth of what the Europeans do per capita to alleviate the social burden of unemployment, because the Japanese are opposed to work ethic eroding entitlements.

Statistics on the composition of GDP presented in table 15.6 illuminate other important systemic differences. American culture is more present-oriented than the other great powers. Its consumption share of GDP is 10 percent higher than the rest of the First World, and its investment share conspicuously less. Yet due to entrepreneurial efficiency, America's per capita GDP growth rate has surpassed Japan's and Europe's, a pattern replicated in the defense data reported in table 15.7. According to some theorists, America's comparatively large per capita defense expenditures should have impaired its growth relative to the Japanese and European mean, but has not.

Table 15.8 provides important insights into systemic employment patterns and conditions of labor. American competitiveness has been associated with high labor mobility and diminishing trade unionization. This has resulted in a service sector intensive employment structure, low levels of long-term unemployment, and glacially rising real earnings (including fringe benefits) over the past 30 years. These characteristics stand in stark contrast to Continental Europe, where strong unions have helped labor earnings rise faster than per capita GDP, but at the cost of entrenched high levels of long-term employment and reduced rates of aggregate economic growth.

Table 15.6 Indicators of comparative economic structure

	America	Japan	Europe	Russia	China
Composition of GDP (1992)[a]					
Consumption	67	57	59	40	–
Government	18	9	19	23	–
Investment	16	31	19	32	–
Composition of GDP (1995)[b]					
Consumption	66	60	60	58	46
Government	16	10	19	16	12
Investment	16	29	19	32	40

Sources: United Nations, *Human Development Report 1995*, Oxford University Press, New York, 1995. United Nations, *Human Development Report 1998*, Oxford University Press, New York, 1998.

References:
  a. Human Development Report 1995, Table 19, p. 192, Table 37, p. 212.
  b. Human Development Report 1998, Table 23, p. 182, Table 45, p. 204.

Table 15.7 Indicators of comparative systemic performance: military activities

	America	Japan	Europe	Russia	China
Military expenditures percent 1992 GDP					
1992 prices	5.3	1.0	2.7	–	5.0
Per capita (1992) dollar prices	964	136	251	–	19
Troops (1992) thousands	1,914	246	2,320	–	3,030.7
Arms exports millions (1992) dollars	4,607	376	–	–	–
Military expenditures percent 1995 GDP					
1995 prices	3.6	1.0	2.5	6.5	5.7
Per capita (1995) dollars	1,001	348	493	470	29
Troops (1996) thousands	1,483	236	2,044	1,270	2,935
Arms exports millions of dollars	10,288	–	6,390	4,512	–
Arms imports millions of dollars	–	–	–	–	1,957

Note: Russian and Chinese defense expenditure and troop data understate the real figures.

References:
  Human Development Report 1995, Table 14, p. 182; Table 31, p. 206.
  Human Development Report 1998, Table 19, p. 170; Table 45, p. 204.

SOCIAL INDICATORS

Table 15.9 underscores these correspondences by highlighting the extraordinary levels of American poverty and income inequality, akin to those of kleptocratic Russia. Europe and Japan by contrast, although less affluent, have less poverty and greater egalitarianism, especially when account is taken of the fact that Japan's poor are protected by family and communitarian obligation. The dark side of American individualistic affluence is

Table 15.8   Indicators of comparative systemic performance: employment structure and labor conditions

	America	Japan	Europe	Russia	China
Employment structure (1990–92)[a]					
Agriculture	3	7	6	20	72
Industry	25	34	29	46	24
Services	72	59	65	34	13
Employment structure (1990)[b]					
Agriculture	3	7	6	14	72
Industry	26	34	32	42	14
Services	71	59	62	45	13
Employment (1995) as percent of total population[c]	51	53	47	52	60
Labor force unionized (1995)[d], percent	14	24	32	75	–
Labor force unionized percent change (1985–95)[e]	−22	−17	−3	–	–
Weekly hours worked in manufacturing per person (1993–96)[f]	42	38	39	30	–
Unemployment (1996) percent[g]	5.4	3.4	11.5	3.5	–
Long term unemployment as percent of labor force (1995)[h]	0.5	0.6	4.0	–	–
Involuntary part-time workers as a percent of labor force (1992)[i]	5.0	1.9	2.9	–	–
Real earnings per employee 1980–92 annual growth[j]	0.4	1.9	2.6	–	–

References:
   a. Human Development Report 1995, Table 11, p. 176; Table 26, p. 201.
   b. Human Development Report 1998, Table 16, p. 164; Table 32, p. 191.
   c. Human Development Report 1998, Table 32, p. 191.
   d. Human Development Report 1998, Table 32, p. 191.
   e. Human Development Report 1998, Table 32, p. 191.
   f. Human Development Report 1998, Table 32, p. 191.
   g. Human Development Report 1998, Table 33, p. 192.
   h. Human Development Report 1998, Table 33, p. 192.
   i. Human Development Report 1998, Table 33, p. 192.
   j. Human Development Report 1998, Table 32, p. 191.
Note: All entries for Europe refer to the European Union, except for long-term unemployment, which includes Switzerland, Norway and Malta. See table A15.2.

   The employment figures as a share of the total population for the United States is inconsistent with official estimate of 67.

   The weekly hours worked in manufacturing excludes unpaid overtime. Japanese laborers work much longer hours than Americans, Europeans, and Russians.

Table 15.9   Indicators of comparative systemic performance: poverty and inequality

	America	Japan	Europe	Russia	China
Poverty[a]					
Population below EU/OECD poverty line, percent (1989–94)	19.1	11.8	7.7	22.1	–
Inequality[b]					
Income inequity, ratio of highest to lowest 0 percent, 1980–94	8.9	4.3	6.2	14.5	7.1
Social pathology					
Homicides by men per 100,000 (1980–86)[c]	12.4	0.9	1.7	9.0	–
Suicides per 100,000 (1989–94)[d] males	20	23	20	74	–
females	5	11	7	13	–
Drug crimes per 100,000 (1980–86)[e]	234	32	–	–	–
Reported adult rapes, thousands (1986)[f]	90.4	1.8	9.5	–	–
AIDS cases per 100,000 (1996)[g]	13.8	0.2	5.0	(.)	–
Life expectancy at birth (1995)[h]	76.4	79.9	77.0	65.5	69.2
People not expected to survive to age 60 as percent of population (1995)[i]	13	8	10	32	–
Maternal mortality (1990)[j] per 100,000	–	18	13	75	95
Infant mortality (1996)[k] per 1,000	5	4	6	20	38
Births to mothers aged 15–19 (1992–95)[l]	12.8	–	3.6	14.3	–
Divorces as percent of marriages (1992–95)[m]	50	–	35	62	–
Single female parent homes, percent (1985–91)[n]	8	5	–	35	–

Sources: United Nations, *Human Development Report 1998*, Oxford University Press, New York, 1998.

References:

    a.   Table 27, p. 186.
    b.   Table 27, p. 186.
    c.   Table 36, p. 195.
    d.   Table 36, p. 195.
    e.   Table 36, p. 195.
    f.   Table 36, p. 195.
    g.   Table 36, p. 195.
    h.   Table 1, p. 128; Table 8, p. 148.
    i.   Table 12, p. 156; Table 27, p. 186.
    j.   Table 12, p. 156; Table 27, p. 186.
    k.   Table 12, p. 156; Table 27, p. 186.
    l.   Table 36, p. 195.
    m. Table 36, p. 195.
    n.   Table 36, p. 195.

Note: Europe refers to the European Union, except for the entry for life expectancy which includes Norway, Malta and Switzerland.

manifested further in statistics on social pathology. American males commit more than ten times as many murders per capita, and 50 times as many rapes, than the Japanese. The incidence of AIDS in the United States is 70 times greater. America's divorce rates, and births to (mostly single) mothers aged 15–19 are also disproportionately high compared with Europe.

Clearly, the affluence and dynamism associated with the American form of managed market system is not ideal from the standpoint of social welfare and economic justice, and may eventually become self-limiting as privilege becomes institutionalized. The Japanese and European systems likewise have glaring deficiencies. Despite decades of liberalization, their root communalist and collectivist cultures have also begun to ossify. Although there is ceaseless talk of impending revitalization, further degeneration may still be in the cards. Culture, politics, and ethics therefore are likely to play a greater role in shaping the future of the First, Second, and Third Worlds than technological progress. Economists who ignore systems cannot see this. Their category A theories focus on improving the quality of capital and labor inputs, innovation, and sound macroeconomic policy making without sufficiently taking account of systemically embedded market power, government misregulation, business misconduct, and disregard for the rule of law.

Review Questions

1. Generally competitive theory predicts a convergence in living standards among the great powers and the rest of the world. Do UN data confirm the prediction? Explain.
2. Systems theory suggests that there should be a correspondence between performance and the degree to which economies approach the perfectly competitive ideal. Do UN data confirm this prediction? Is the superior performance of China explicable on other competitive principles like the "catch-up" effect?
3. Does the superior performance of the Second World, Chinese zone lend credence to the importance of culture? Explain.
4. Market economies which honor the rule of contract law can be found in the First and Third Worlds. What does this suggest about the importance of culture and the adverse side effects of globalization?
5. How has wealth and income been globally reconfigured during the last 40 years?
6. How are they likely to be further reconfigured during the next quarter century? Explain.
7. Will the anticipated reconfiguration of wealth and income correspond with universalist market theory? Could it be destabilizing?
8. Have the material costs of Continental European corporatism and Japanese communalism, judged from the American standard, been sufficient to clearly outweigh their respective cultural benefits? Explain.

Appendix A: Supplementary Tables

Table A15.1 Eastern Europe and the Commonwealth of Independent States: per capita income 1995

Purchasing power parity (dollars)	
Albania	2,853
Armenia	2,208
Azerbaijan	1,463
Belarus	4,398
Bulgaria	4,604
Croatia	3,972
Czech Republic	9,775
Estonia	4,062
Georgia	1,389
Hungary	6,793
Kazakhstan	3,037
Kyrgyzstan	1,927
Latvia	3,273
Lithuania	3,843
Macedonia	4,058
Moldavia	1,547
Poland	5,442
Romania	4,431
Russian Federation	4,531
Slovakia	7,320
Slovenia	10,594
Tajikistan	943
Turkmenistan	2,345
Ukraine	2,361
Uzbekistan	2,376
Total	99,545
Countries	25
Average per capita income	3,982
Population	335,000,000
GDP billions (1995) dollars: purchasing power parity (millions)	1,334

Source: United Nations, *Human Development Report* 1998, Oxford University Press, New York, 1998.
References:
   Table 1, pp. 128, 129; Table 41, p. 200.

Table A15.2   Europe: GDP, per capita income, and other selected indicators (1995)

	Population (Millions)	GNP $X	GDP $PPP	GNP/N $X	GDP/N $PPP	Unemp., long (%)	Poverty line (%)	Life (years)
France	58.1	1,451	1,230	24,990	21,176	4.9	7.5	78.7
Norway	4.3	136	96	31,250	33,427	1.3	6.6	77.6
Finland	5.1	105	95	20,580	18,547	6.1	6.2	76.4
Netherlands	15.5	371	308	24,000	19,876	3.2	6.7	77.5
Sweden	8.8	210	170	23,750	19,297	1.5	6.7	78.4
Spain	39.6	532	586	13,580	14,789	13.0	10.4	77.7
Belgium	10.1	251	218	24,710	21,548	6.2	5.5	76.9
Austria	8.0	217	171	26,890	21,322	1.1	76.7	–
UK	58.1	1,095	1,121	18,700	19,302	3.8	13.5	76.8
Switzerland	7.2	286	179	40,630	24,881	1.1	–	78.2
Ireland	3.5	53	62	14,710	17,590	7.6	11.1	76.4
Denmark	5.2	156	114	29,890	21,983	2.0	7.5	75.3
Germany	81.6	2,252	1,662	27,510	20,370	4.0	5.9	76.4
Greece	10.5	86	122	8,210	11,636	–	–	77.9
Italy	57.2	1,088	1,154	19,020	20,174	7.6	6.5	78.0
Luxembourg	0.4	17	14	41,210	34,004	3.7	5.4	76.1
Portugal	9.8	97	124	9,740	12,674	0.7	–	74.8
Malta	0.4	–	5	–	13,316	–	–	76.5
Totals	383.0	8,913	7,437	399,370	354,912	67.8	99.5	13,863
Entries				17	18	16	13	18
Average				23,492	20,877	4.2	7.7	77.0

Source: United Nations, *Human Development Report* 1998, Oxford University Press, New York, 1998.

References:
Table 1, p. 128; Table 27, p. 186; Table 41, p. 200; Table 46, p. 205.

Definitions:
GNP: billions of dollars (exchange rate)
GDP: billions of dollars (purchasing power parity)
GNP/N: per capita income (exchange rate)
GDP/N: per capita income (purchasing power parity)
Long-term unemployment: 12 months or more
Poverty line: percent below the EU/OECD standard 1989–94 (below 50 percent of median disposable personal income)
Life expectancy: at birth

Table A15.3   Europe: GDP per capita and growth (dollars and percent)

GDP per capita	1960	1970	1980	1990	1995
France	7,219	11,166	14,564	17,485	18,069
Norway	7,895	11,926	17,856	21,914	25,390
Finland	7,351	11,376	15,140	19,576	18,460
Netherlands	7,943	11,279	13,855	16,283	17,325
Sweden	9,873	14,389	16,903	20,018	19,521
Spain	2,828	5,207	6,657	8,618	9,141
Belgium	6,363	9,770	13,170	15,679	16,428
Austria	6,727	10,101	14,160	17,090	18,109
United Kingdom	6,795	8,463	10,161	12,899	14,440
Switzerland	15,779	21,412	24,027	27,820	26,721
Ireland	3,904	5,656	7,791	10,656	13,134
Denmark	9,835	14,049	16,858	20,511	22,247
Germany	–	–	–	–	–
Greece	1,570	3,228	4,568	4,794	5,020
Italy	5,296	8,562	11,821	14,642	15,392
Luxembourg	9,704	12,942	15,606	21,187	21,851
Portugal	1,402	2,533	3,728	4,930	5,175
Malta	989	1,535	3,713	5,583	–
Totals	111,473	163,594	210,578	259,685	266,420
Entries	17	17	17	17	16
Average	6,557	9,623	12,387	15,276	16,651
Excluding Malta	6,905	10,129	12,929	15,881	16,651

GDP per capita growth	1960–70	1970–80	1980–90	1990–95
Europe	3.9	2.6	2.1	1.7
Europe excluding Malta	3.9	2.5	2.1	1.0

Source: United Nations, *Human Development Report 1998*, Oxford University Press, New York, 1998, Table 5, p. 140.

Table A15.4   Eastern Europe and the CIS: GDP per capita and growth (dollars and percent)

	GDP per capita				
	1960	1970	1980	1990	1995
Former USSR					
Armenia	2,043	887	1,483	1,759	587
Azerbaijan	–	–	–	1,020	355
Belarus	–	–	–	2,724	1,712
Estonia	–	–	3,354	3,693	2,530
Georgia	715	1,181	1,966	1,760	433
Kazakhstan	793	–	–	1,741	961
Kyrgyzstan				1,072	501
Latvia	1,020	1,777	2,689	3,530	1,912
Lithuania	–	–	–	2,684	1,683
Moldavia	–	–	–	–	–
Russia	–	1,700	3,204	3,193	1,988
Tajikistan	384	–	–	718	255
Turkmenistan	–	–	–	–	–

Ukraine	–	–	–	2,072	999
Uzbekistan	–	–	–	–	–
Subtotal Armenia, Georgia, Latvia, Russia		5,545	9,342	10,242	4,920
Entries		4	4	4	4
Average		1,386	2,336	2,561	1,230
Subtotal All except Moldova Turkmenistan, Uzbekistan				25,248	12,004
Entries				12	12
Average				2,104	1,000
Eastern Europe					
Albania	–	–	698	908	887
Bulgaria	–	–	2,344	3,176	2,605
Croatia	–	–	–	–	–
Czech Rep.	–	–	–	3,680	3,164
Hungary	742	1,350	2,059	2,456	2,334
Macedonia FYR	–	–	–	–	–
Poland	–	–	1,682	1,559	1,701
Romania	–	–	1,511	1,452	1,358
Slovakia	–	–	–	3,622	3,054
Slovenia	–	–	–	–	–
Subtotals All less Czech, Slovakia, Croatia, Macedonia, Slovenia	–	–	8,294	9,551	8,885
Entries			5	5	5
Average			1,659	1,910	1,777
Subtotals All less Croatia, Macedonia, Slovenia				16,853	15,103
Entries				7	7
Average				2,408	2,157
EE + CIS subtotals			17,636	19,793	13,805
Entries			9	9	9
Average			1,960	2,199	1,534

	GDP per capita growth (percent)			
	1960–70	1970–80	1980–90	1990–95
CIS (4) Armenia, Georgia, Latvia, Russia	–	5.4	0.9	−8.7
CIS (12)	–	–	–	−8.8
EE (5) Albania, Bulgaria, Hungary, Poland, Romania	–	–	1.4	−1.3
EE (7) (5) plus Czech and Slovenia	–	–	–	−2.0
EE + CIS (9)	–	–	1.0	−5.4

Sources: United Nations, *Human Development Report 1998*, Oxford University Press, New York, 1998, Table 5, pp. 140–141.

Table A15.5   GDP per capita and growth (dollars and percent): selected cases from the
Second and Third Worlds

| | GDP per capita | | | | |
	1960	1970	1980	1990	1995
Second World					
Singapore	1,510	3,067	5,907	9,877	13,451
Chile	1,162	1,397	1,580	1,912	2,532
Indonesia	190	211	349	537	720
South Korea	520	967	1,953	4,132	5,663
Kuwait	–	35,866	18,431	–	17,016
Thailand	300	487	718	1,291	1,843
Malaysia	708	1,001	1,688	2,301	3,108
China	75	92	138	285	481
India?	206	245	262	274	381
Third World					
Thailand	300	487	718	1,291	1,843
Malaysia	708	1,001	1,688	2,301	3,108
China	75	92	138	285	481
India?	206	245	262	274	381
Argentina	2,701	3,533	3,996	3,150	3,793
Venezuela	2,815	3,298	3,067	2,560	2,648
Mexico	938	1,363	1,949	1,839	1,724
Iran	–	–	2,980	2,667	2,389
Syria	1,988	2,096	2,683	2,624	2,389
South Africa	1,808	2,296	2,593	2,342	2,165
Philippines	418	495	679	628	630
Egypt	237	338	590	745	726
Mali	217	225	279	260	256
Pakistan	135	223	259	350	381

| | GDP per capita growth | | | |
	1960–70	1970–80	1980–90	1990–95
Second World				
Singapore	7.3	6.8	5.3	6.4
Chile	1.9	1.2	1.9	5.7
Indonesia	1.1	5.2	4.4	5.8
South Korea	6.4	7.2	7.8	6.5
Thailand	5.0	4.0	6.0	7.4
Malaysia	3.5	5.4	3.1	6.2
China	2.1	4.1	7.5	11.0
India?	1.7	0.6	0.4	6.8
Third World				
Argentina	2.7	1.2	−1.9	3.8
Venezuela	1.6	−0.7	−1.5	0.7
Mexico	3.8	3.6	−0.5	−1.2
Iran	–	–	−1.0	−2.0

Syria	0.5	2.5	−0.2	−0.9
South Africa	2.4	1.2	−0.9	−1.4
Philippines	1.7	3.2	−0.7	−0.1
Egypt	3.6	5.7	2.4	−0.5
Mali	0.4	2.1	−0.7	−0.3
Pakistan	5.1	1.5	3.1	1.7

Appendix B: Table 15.1 Sources and Derivation

References:

a. Table 22, p. 176; Table 41, p. 200.

b. Table 26, p. 184; Table 46, p. 205.

c. Derived from Table 22, p. 176; Table 41, p. 200; Table 1, pp. 128.

d. Table 26, p. 184; Table 46, p. 205. The entry for World is computed by dividing the GNP figure by the population shown above. The entry in the source, substitutes a 1997 World Bank estimate for 1995 of $4,880.

e. Table 1, pp. 128, 129. The figure for Eastern Europe and the CIS is estimated directly by multiplying the unweighted per capita income figures for these countries by their combined population. See table A15.1.

f. Table 46, p. 205. The discorrespondence between the World growth rates and those of the components suggests the World figures are weighted, and the components are not.

g. Table 5, p. 140. There is no indication as to whether the figures are computed through the exchange rate or purchasing power parity. Judging by the scale, the estimates have been computed through the exchange rate. The discorrespondence between the World growth rates and those of the components suggests that the World figures are weighted, and components are not. The entries for EE + CIS are computed in table A15.4. The estimate for 1970–80 only represents for CIS countries: Russia, Armenia, Georgia, and Latvia. The other entries cover these countries plus: Albania, Bulgaria, Hungary, Poland, and Romania.

h. Derived from the United Nations' Human Development Report, 1995. The growth rate of each country is weighted by its volume of economic activity. The USA has a heavy weighting. If calculations are made using population weights instead, the overall world growth rate changes very little. Also, growth figures after 1996 show a substantial slowing because of the financial crisis which afflicted Asia and Latin America and the former Soviet Union from mid-1997 to early 1999.

Definitions World: All countries, but excludes Sikhim, Serbia, and probably Taiwan. Hong Kong is listed separately from China.

Developed:	All industrial countries, including Australia, Israel, Japan, New Zealand, North America, Canada, and the USA; Eastern Europe and the Commonwealth of Independent States, Albania, Armenia, Azerbaijan, Belarus, Bulgaria, Croatia, Czech Republic, Estonia, Georgia, Hungary, Kazakhstan, Kyrgyzstan, Latvia, Lithuania, Macedonia, Moldova, Poland, Romania, Russia, Slovakia, Slovenia, Tajikistan, Turkmenistan, Ukraine, Uzbekistan, West and South Europe, Austria, Belgium, Denmark, Finland, Germany, Greece, Iceland, Ireland, Italy, Luxembourg, Malta, Netherlands, Norway, Portugal, Spain, and Sweden.
Other:	The rest including Hong Kong, but not Sikhim, and Taiwan.
Least Developed Countries:	Afghanistan, Angola, Bangladesh, Benin, Bhutan, Burkina Faso, Burundi, Cambodia, Cape Verde, Central African Republic, Chad, Comoros, Democratic Rep of Congo, Djibouti, Equatorial Guinea, Eritrea, Ethiopia, Gambia, Guinea, Guinea-Bissau, Haiti, Kirbati, Lao People's Democratic Republic, Lesotho, Liberia, Madagascar, Malawi, Maldives, Mali, Mauritania, Mozambique, Myanmar, Nepal, Niger, Rwanda, Samoa (Western), Sao Tomé and Principe, Sierra Leone, Solomon Islands, Somalia, Sudan, United Republic of Tanzania, Togo, Tuvalu, Uganda, Vanatu, Yemen, and Zimbabwe.
Transition EE and CIS (East Europe and the Commonwealth of Independent States):	The countries following are treated by the UN as being "industrialized" despite their low per capita GDPs. They are better classified as "misindustrialized" or "misdeveloped": Albania, Armenia, Azerbaizan, Belarus, Bulgaria, Croatia, Czech Republich, Estonia, Georgia, Hungary, Kazakhstan, Kyrgyzstan, Latvia, Lithuania, Fed Yugoslav Rep of Macedonia, Rep of Moldava, Poland, Romania, Russian Federation, Slovakia, Slovenia, Tajikistan, Turkmenistan, Ukraine, and Uzbekistan.
Note:	The United Nations does not list information on Taiwan separately, and probably excludes it from its data on China, and the World.
	A significant part of the explanation for the disparity between the World growth statistics reported in panels g and h is the replacement of Soviet-era official growth rates for Eastern Europe and the Soviet Union with new EE and CIS series showing virtually no growth.

Also, the East European and CIS statistics do not belong in the "industrially developed" category. The United Nations does not explain its weighting system for the per capita GDP aggregates in panel e. If purchasing power parity GDP weights are applied from panel c, the developed estimate increases to 1.1, and the other category declines to 2.4 for the period 1990–95.

Subcalculations:
First World:

The "big three," America, Japan, and the European Union, plus Norway, Switzerland, Malta, Iceland, Australia, New Zealand, Canada, and Israel, are defined by the UN as industrially developed countries. The data are taken from table 15.2, supplemented by statistics for Australia, New Zealand, Canada, Israel, and Ireland.

The growth rates are averages solely of the big three.

Countries with relative high per capita GDP which have been either included in the Second World, and Third World, or are not classified as industrial by the UN are: Slovenia, Czech Republic, Slovakia, Hungary, Poland, the rest of Eastern Europe and the CIS, Cyprus, Hong Kong, Singapore, Antigua and Barbuda, South Korea, Bahamas, Brunei Darussalam, Argentina, Bahrain, United Arab Emirates, Kuwait, and Quatar.

Second World:

	Pop.	GNP (X)	GDP (PPP)	GNP/N	GDP/N	GNP/N 1965–80	GNP/N 1980–95
	(1)	(2)	(3)	(4)	(5)	(6)	(7)
Singapore	3	80	75	22,730	22,604	8.3	6.0
South Korea	45	435	521	9,700	1,594	7.3	7.5
Thailand	59	160	451	2,740	7,742	4.4	6.3
Malaysia	21	78	192	3,890	9,572	4.7	4.0
China	1,220	745	3,581	620	2,935	4.1	8.6
Indonesia	198	190	784	980	3,971	5.2	4.9
Hong Kong	6	142	144	22,990	22,950	6.2	4.8
Taiwan[a]	21	260	–	12,404	–	–	5.3
Totals (excluding Hong Kong and Taiwan)	1,544	1,688	5,604				
World Share (excluding Hong Kong and Taiwan) (percent)	27.0	6.2	16.6				
Weighted average				1,093	3,629		
Unweighted Average						5.9	6.2

NB: the weighted averages are computed by dividing columns 2 and 3 by column 1.
[a]The data for Taiwan are from the Economist Intelligence Unit, Second Quarter, 1999 Report (record 1 of 2), Country Reports: Asia Pacific, and report 9-1-94.

		Taiwanese Growth			

Real GDP (percent)

1988	1989	1990	1991	1992	1993
7.3	7.6	4.9	7.2	6.5	6.2

1994	1995	1996	1997	1998	1988–98
6.5	6.0	5.7	6.8	4.8	6.3

Real GDP per capita (percent)

1988	1989	1990	1991	1992	1993
6.1	6.5	3.6	6.3	5.4	5.2

1994	1995	1996	1997	1998	1988–98
5.5	5.0	4.8	5.9	3.9	5.3

Third World: Global totals, less the First and Second Worlds. The growth rates for the Third World are computed by averaging the United Nations estimates for medium human development excluding China; low human development (Human Development Report 1998, Table 26), Eastern Europe and the CIS (table A15.4). This includes 134 less developed countries, excluding Chile, Costa Rica, Uruguay, Trinidad and Tobago, Dominica, Fiji, Panama, Venezuela, Mexico, Saint Kitts and Nevis, Grenada, Columbia, Saint Vincent, Seychelles, Saint Lucia, Mauritius, Brazil and Libyan Arab Jamahiriya, all with relatively poor growth records. The bias from their omission should not be significant.

Appendix C: Table 15.2 Sources and Derivation

References:

a. Table 22, p. 176; Table 41, p. 200.
b. Table 26, p. 184; Table 46, p. 205.
c. Derived from Table 22, p. 176; Table 41, p. 20; Table 1, pp. 128, 129.
d. Table 26, p. 184; Table 46, p. 205.
e. Table 1, pp. 128, 129.
f. Table 26, p. 184; Table 46, p. 205. The bracketed figure represents GDP per capita (probably purchasing power parity) expressed in 1987 dollar prices for the period 1970–80. See Table 5, p. 141. The figure for 1980–90 is zero, and 1980–95 is −3.2. The estimate for the 1980s differs sharply from the official Soviet figures.
g. Table 5, pp. 140–141. The Europe entry refers to the EU less Germany, plus Switzerland and Norway. See table 15.3. The estimates are derived from composite per capita GDP statistics for Europe divided by 16, the number of countries sampled. This growth is unweighted for comparative GDP size or population. The

underlying data have probably been computed through the exchange rate, but this is not explicitly stated in the source.

h.   Table 26, p. 184; Table 46, p. 205.

Notes:

1.   Some estimate China's population at 1.5 billion. See Robert Kaplan, "China: A World Power Again," *Atlantic Monthly*, Vol. 284, No. 2, August 1999, pp. 16–18. It is unclear whether Kaplan's statistics or those provided by the United Nations include Taiwan.

2.   Iu. Ivanov, "mezhdunarodnykh sopostavlenniakh VVP," (On International Comparisons of GDP), *Voprosy ekonomiki*, No. 3, March 1999, pp. 112–127 argues that dollar purchasing power parities, "experimentally" derived according to methods employed in a 1996 OECD study indicated that Russia's per capita GDP in 1996 was 27 percent of the US figure. This estimate is 35 percent greater than the figure derived in a Goskomstat RF study undertaken in conjunction with the OECD in 1993. Applying these coefficients to the purchasing power parity estimate for 1995 above places Ivanov's figure at $7,263 and Goskomstat's at $5,395. Alternative estimates for 1995 by Aleksei Ponomarov, Deputy Chief of the Department of National Accounts (Goskomstat RF) presented in 1998 based on regional data place per capita GDP at $3,750. See Aleksei Ponomarenko, "Gross Regional Product for Russian Regions: A Prism to View the Slavic Eurasian World," Slavic Research Center, Hokkaido University, Sapporo Japan, July 22–24. All of these various estimates can be instructively compared to the CIA's and Goskomstat SSSR estimates circa 1991 of $13,137 in 1991 prices. CIA, *Handbook of International Economic Statistics*, CPAS92–1005, September 1992. Cf. Steven Rosefielde, "Unlocking Northeast Asia's Development Potential: The Russian Paradox," in Kimitaka Matsuzato, *Regions: A Prism to View the Slavic World*, Slavic Research Center, Hokkaido University, 2000.

Territorial Coverage:

Europe includes all the developed continental states, plus the United Kingdom and Malta, excluding Cyprus and Crete, and the former communist nations (Poland, Hungary, the Czech Republic, Romania, Bulgaria, Yugoslavia, Slovenia, Croatia, Bosnia, and Albania) for the population, GNP, GDP, and per capita statistics. The growth and inflation series refer to the European Union: Austria, Belgium, Denmark, Finland, France, Germany, Greece, Ireland, Italy, Luxembourg, Netherlands, Portugal, Spain, Sweden, and the United Kingdom. The non-EU members included in the first category are Malta, Norway, and Switzerland.

The per capita GDP growth rates for the United Kingdom computed in 1987 dollars are as follows:

	1960–70	1970–80	1980–90	1990–95	1980–95
United Kingdom	2.2	1.8	2.4	2.3	2.4
Europe	3.9	2.5	2.1	1.0	1.7

See table A15.3.

PART V

INTERNATIONAL RELATIONS

CHAPTER 16

SECURITY

Asymmetries in systems performance and potential are radically reconfiguring global wealth and power, raising profound questions about their impact on international security. A clear grasp of the relationships between economics and power-seeking that Samuel Huntington contends drives international relations is essential for appraising future offensive and defensive military prospects, patterns of economic domination, and the belief that globalism will set everything right.

Theory reveals that the pursuit of security and power are economic activities to the extent that they are guided by rational utility-seeking under conditions of scarcity. Optimal security and power are governed by the laws of demand, supply, and equilibration, and depend on striking a balance between perceived needs and costs. These correspondences, however, do not mean that security and power are goods in the normal generally competitive sense, because their purpose is to deter potential adversaries, or dominate them. In either instance, purchases of security and power services (both economic and military) imply an intention to violate the golden rule by influencing, coercing, or compelling others to alter their behavior instead of treating them as arm's-length competitors. Economic relationships between adversaries consequently are incompatible with a self-regulating, category A global general competitive system. Adversaries can employ efficient category A systems domestically to achieve all their economic objectives, but if security and power are at stake their external relations must be conducted at least in part on other principles. If these principles are not rational – if, for example, they are based on political passions – then the cause of external category A inefficiency is noneconomic.

The degree to which deterrence and compellence optimally displace mutually advantageous, golden rule competition will depend on the populace's security and power preferences where systems are self-regulating, and on other sovereigns where they are not. Broadly speaking, culturally regulated category B systems should be less efficient in providing security and power services because market power, misgovernance, and obligation typically prevent factors from being allocated to best use. But there are no theoretical reasons that preclude illiberal and authoritarian regimes indifferent to consumer welfare from building superior military forces or exploitive economic capabilities, when the priority their leaders place on security and power exceeds that in self-regulating, category A democracies. Democratic free enterprise is not sufficient to assure deterrence or compellence against an authoritarian foe. And, of course, this indeterminism is stronger if democratic market economies are culturally regulated, category B systems.

Globalist commerce by itself from this perspective cannot secure peace as long as some nations seek power, and others security from external domination.

"Global politics is always about power and the struggle for power, and today international relations is changing along that crucial dimension. The global structure of power in the Cold War was basically bipolar; the emerging structure is very different."
Samuel Huntington, "The Lonely Superpower," *Foreign Affairs*, Vol. 78, No. 2, March/April 1999, pp. 35–49.

PRINCIPLES OF INTERNATIONAL SECURITY

The divergent economic prospects of the great powers analyzed in chapters 13 and 15 suggest that both per capita GDP and welfare evaluated from an individualistic, general competitive perspective will become increasingly stratified during the early years of the 21st century, with America at the apex and Russia at the bottom of the heap. This does not mean that the quality of life will change correspondingly from collectivist and communalist perspectives, but America probably will fare relatively well on most measures. It might seem to follow that the outlook for global peace is enhanced by America's economic ascendancy. America's growing economic power will give pause to those Washington considers aggressors. But relations among the great powers are more complicated. All possess declared or virtual nuclear forces, and exhibit large disparities in resources, population, and commitment to defense activities. The military might of individual great powers may not be correlated with per capita GDP, and increases in America's relative economic strength may not deter bad behavior by other great powers. An air campaign which succeeded in Yugoslavia is unlikely to work in Russia or China.

Prospects for great power conflict depend on a host of technical variables like the relative efficiency of the military machine building sector in specific countries, and diverse cultural and political factors. Just as the behavior of economies is strongly influenced by culturally regulated category B systems variables, these same forces also may affect the security of individual nations. Broadly speaking, peace is strengthened by democracy, especially in international commerce, and golden rule abiding general competition, while some alternative cultural and political goals increase the risks of conflict. This no doubt explains why many advocates of liberalized free enterprise intuitively associate its global diffusion with the achievement of a golden age of peace and prosperity.

But is this intuition correct? Should security-optimizing be equated with efficiency, international affluence, and social justice? And if, as will be shown, the market for security everywhere is inefficient and anticompetitive, does this provide some advantages to collectivist and communalist systems over American managed markets, or even general competition?

The answers to these questions are not obvious, and require a grasp of the formal relationship between security and economic utility-seeking. This is best accomplished by delineating the correspondences between ideal security and economic demand and supply; by explaining why security optimization is intrinsically less efficient than other aspects of utility-seeking, followed by a thorough discussion of systemic differences and their implications. For the sake of symmetry, let us begin by classifying security regimes according to the same criteria used in chapter 2 to analyze economic systems (figure 2.1).

The apex of the security systems hierarchy depicted in table 16.1 is a class of Utopias which allow society to fully realize its potential in a secure and peaceful environment. These models are Utopian because they claim to eliminate all human conflict, and assume that nothing is scarce.

The economic versions of these harmonist regimes recognize scarcity and the possibility of international conflict, but assert that economic efficiency and peace can be secured with perfect markets or plans, and international good will. The community of nations in this vision adheres to the golden rule in its economic and foreign relations. The solution is unrealistic, because the appeal to good will does not guarantee that people will voluntarily uphold the golden rule, or honor their commitments.

Category A theorists believe that the danger of bad faith can be disposed of "scientifically" with competition and democracy, assuming that if the people's voices are heard everyone will universally abide by principles of impartiality and fairness. Category B theorists do not accept this approach because many nations are authoritarian, and democracy does not preclude power-seeking. They insist that the best strategy is to devise culturally and politically sensitive economic and security regimes, buttressed by optimal defense programs that deter aggression at least cost.

Table 16.1   Security systems: main concepts

Harmonist		
	Comprehensive Diverse Utopias	
	Economic Perfect markets or plans and international good will	
Scientific		
Category A self-regulating		Category B culturally regulated
Universalistic		Nationally or culturally specific
	Focused on	
Building efficient markets, democracy		Building culturally appropriate security regimes combined with optimal defense

DEMAND

The volume of security services sought is governed by the law of demand. People purchase them up to the point where their marginal utility is equal to price. For this to occur they must be able to discern utility, rank different utility experiences, reconcile differences in personal and group judgments about what constitutes utility, and utility must be diminishing everywhere in the domain of choice. Just like any consumer good, the demand curve is negatively sloped because the sacrifice (prices) people are willing to make (pay) for security services depends on the marginal utility of foregone consumption goods. If the utility of butter is high, people buy few guns, and vice versa. Demand prices fall in tandem with marginal utilities as security services consumed rise. People's ability to optimize their consumption of security services and other goods can be depicted with utility indifference curves indicating the compensation required to maintain a constant level of utility when units of another product are reduced (figure 2.4). If people have well-defined nested sets of utility indifference curves, it is easily shown that they can utility maximize by choosing the assortment of security services and other goods where their budget constraints are tangent to their highest indifference curves. Perfect governments in the ideal category A security model will demand precisely this amount. Comparativists accept this logic where governments actually adhere to the requirements of category A models, but caution that security decisions are often made noneconomically (without adequately considering relative marginal utilities), or are unduly influenced by the preferences of insiders. If governments are impassioned with a cause; if demand is distorted by politics, or communitarian pressures, procurement programs may be detrimental.

SUPPLY

The law of security supply is the complementary belief that people can and will elaborate production programs which allow them to determine best product and service assortments for all states of demand. This requires suppliers to figure out the optimal cost-minimizing and revenue-maximizing requirements for all potential levels of security service production, hiring factors until the value they add is equal to their marginal costs, in proportions determined by marginal rates of factor substitution. For the law of supply to hold in this sense, producers must appreciate the necessity of profit-maximizing, cope effectively with external intrusions in their businesses, and the marginal productivity (cost) of at least one factor, in at least one activity must be diminishing (increasing) somewhere in the production set.

Factor supply for security services in the ideal case is depicted as a positive function of input compensation because the marginal utility of leisure increases as employment expands. Just as with any other good, in equilibrium factor prices are set at the intersection of their respective supply and demand curves, and are used by producers to determine the marginal rate of factor substitution, where these factor prices (w/r) are tangent to enterprise isoquants (figure 2.6). The sets of these tangencies for all levels of production determine every security service firm's marginal cost curve. Proprietors are able to augment their command over consumption by maximizing profits, producing to the point where the product price is equal to marginal cost in the perfectly competitive case (see figure 2.7).

Comparativists accept these principles where supply actually adheres to the requirements of category A models, but note that decisions regarding the production and distribution of security services are often political or may be unduly influenced by secrecy.

DEMAND AND SUPPLY EQUILIBRATION

The law of security services demand and the law of their supply are both indeterminate in the sense that neither identify ideal consumption and supply programs in isolation, because consumers do not know which assortment of security services and other goods is best until they discover the terms upon which their demands can be supplied; and, vice versa, suppliers cannot maximize profits until they find out what people desire, and the terms upon which they are willing to offer their services. The existence and attainability of a general individualist utility security equilibrium hinges on the theoretical possibility of constructing one or more mechanisms that can solve this problem by establishing mutually agreeable, voluntary terms of exchange for every transaction, where each participant freely utility seeks within the possibilities of bounded rationality. The body of knowledge which attempts to analyze category A utility-seeking solution mechanisms for security services is called equilibrium theory, and its guiding principles are called the *law of security services supply and demand equilibration*.

This law is often thought of as being universal, but varies from system to system. It asserts that people are capable of discerning which configuration of security services they desire (consumption program), and wish to supply (supply program) at any arbitrary set of prices from among their portfolios of feasible programs, and then search interactively for better solutions by negotiating more agreeable terms of exchange until no one is willing to alter their choices in response to new terms others are prepared to offer. The process can be visualized as movements along fixed demand and supply curves as conventionally derived searching for a point of equilibrium (figure 2.9), but these curves will also shift as the changing structure of supply affects wage–rental ratios, marginal costs, and the distribution of income. Changes in preferences and technologies provide additional reasons why these schedules may sometimes shift.

The conditions for achieving a category A security services supply and demand equilibrium are the same as those for the general economic case. People must efficiently compile portfolios of security service consumption and supply programs; they must be able to recognize discordances between these plans, and discover ways of bringing about a resolution of all discrepancies; and they must be capable of efficiently coping with external intrusions. These problems can be dealt with by utilizing conventional Walrasian, Marshallian, and Keynesian adjustment processes, or their analogs in the case of perfect planning.

Comparativists accept this logic where Walrasian, Marshallian, and Keynesian adjustment processes adhere to the requirements of category A models, but insist that security service decisions are often made noneconomically, and that supply programs are frequently subordinated to the dictates of anticompetitive insiders. The law of security demand and supply equilibration, when it works, should lead individuals and governments to choose rationally, given their preferences, but otherwise results may be systematically distorted by extraneous motives and insider moral hazard. These risks are particularly acute in closed, authoritarian societies, which permit leaders to manipulate public perception and maintain unduly large military–industrial capabilities, despite their supply side inefficiencies.

AUTHORITARIAN COMPARATIVE SUPPLY ADVANTAGE

This danger is increased if civilian and uniformed security service providers can be convinced on patriotic or other related grounds to work for low, or even subsistence wages, as draftees. No-frills militaries like the Soviet's, supported by no-frills military–industrial enterprises, were able to equal or surpass American weapon procurements and fighting forces despite the Kremlin's relatively small GDP, at least in part because of conscription, requisitioning, and state wage-fixing. Weak international competitiveness and low-quality domestic consumption goods may also make it easier for many countries to sustain higher defense burdens than commonly imagined. If Iraq's domestic manufactures fetch little on the international market, and are not prized at home, the sacrifice of figs for guns is more bearable. And, of course, the temptation to over-procure security services may be intensified further if the productivity of embodied technology in the military–industrial sector surpasses the economy-wide average; there are economies of scale in mass weapons production, and technology exhibits increasing returns over a long stretch of stage II.

Compensatory factors like conscription, cheap military–industrial labor services, economies of scale, and increasing returns are not associated exclusively with particular systems. They are just as compatible with general competition as authoritarian laissez faire. But they do tend to unduly benefit collectivist, communalist, and authoritarian regimes whenever they are inclined to over-procure security services judged from the competitive perspective. This can be seen most vividly in the case of Russia which, due to its Soviet legacy, has the capacity to easily out-procure the United States in many types of defense services, even in its present decrepit state, if Putin or his successors desire. It follows directly that while generally competitive, domestically golden rule abiding systems should be economically and security efficient, security calculus in the real world is more complex. Power-seeking, competitively efficient systems necessarily disregard the golden rule in dealing with foreigners; and the entire array of less efficient collectivist, communalist and authoritarian systems could challenge competitively efficient regimes which misappraise their security requirements. Economic superiority and power are not necessarily complementary. America could economically outpace its rivals and still find itself vulnerable.

GREAT POWER SECURITY TRAITS

This was an essential aspect of the Cold War. The United States and its advanced market-oriented industrial allies including Japan, despite their collectivist and communalist features, were more economically efficient than their authoritarian adversaries in the Soviet bloc, yet were unable to apply force outside their sphere of influence, as NATO did in Milosovich's Yugoslavia, because cost asymmetries allowed the communists to build a credible military deterrent and conduct successful offensive operations, most notably in Korea and Vietnam. The West had the economic capacity to do better, but opted for nuclear deterrence, containment, and a "prosperity" offensive called "engagement" for a host of complicated political reasons, including a reluctance to accept large cuts in real wages and incomes.

After a ragged start, and decades of inconclusive skirmishes in the Third World, these policies gradually bore fruit as Western affluence gave pause to those who previously saw Soviet-style socialism as the road to a better world, culminating in Gorbachev's capitulation. Although the Soviet Union could not have been vanquished militarily in 1989, and could have hung on to its empire for generations, introducing reforms that would have slowly improved living standards, it succumbed to the leadership's loss of confidence and domestic opportunism.

This ended an important chapter in international security relations, which began after the First World War with the rise of fascist and communist challenges to democratic free enterprise. Many celebrated the triumph of general competition, and predicted that armed conflict between great powers had become obsolete because all nations were well down the path toward becoming golden rule abiding, open, free enterprise systems, concerned only with material prosperity. In this universe security primarily depended on low-cost confidence building and anti-terrorist initiatives. Relative affluence, and even boundaries, hardly mattered because globalism promised to improve everyone's lot within the constraints imposed by resource endowments, culture, and politics. On this logic, it really did not matter that Russia as the chief partner in the Soviet Union had lost 40 percent of its territory, and all its satellites. Nor should the prospective incorporation of all these peoples and lands into NATO pose any abiding concern. The same arguments moreover applied to China, so that barring some form of ideologically enthused authoritarian revanche, the world seemed poised on the brink of durable peace and prosperity.

The wars in Rwanda, Iraq, and the Balkans during the 1990s were treated as exceptions that proved the rule. They were interpreted as the atavistic reflexes of a vanishing order destined to quickly fade. Peace among the great powers, and between the great powers and newly emerging nuclear forces like India were thought to be assured regardless of whether the distribution of wealth and power in the world converged, or diverged; or whether the 21st century would usher in a millennium of good or bad times.

Lost in this idealist turn of thought is the reality that none of the great powers are generally competitive, or reliably golden rule abiding. They are all engaged in economic power-seeking, and some in military competition as well, contradicting the assumption that the benefits of fair trade will eventually deter nations from taking economic and military advantage of their partners. Authoritarianism is alive and well in Russia and China, albeit discreetly veiled and ingratiating, while constituentism, collectivism, and communalism continue to hold sway in varying degrees in America, Continental Europe, and Japan. If the 21st century as advertised proves to be harmonious, this will not be attributable to the forces of economic and security utopianism, but to other factors like self-restraint and nonprovocative deterrence. The strong will have to bridle those elements in their societies seeking foreign domination, and avoid giving the misimpression of hostile intent through the size, structure, and posture of defense forces, and the conduct of international policy. The weak will have to shun the temptation to compensate for economic shortcomings by conscriptive militarization or foreign adventures. Of course, it is also conceivable that peace and prosperity might be achieved in a less seemly way. The strong could adopt strategies of domination, deliberately using their economic and military might to achieve maximum material advantage for themselves, as Marxists frequently allege is the hidden agenda of capitalist great powers. This approach is esteemed in the shadow culture as tough-minded *"realpolitik"* and may occasionally work, but involves assuming inordinate risk for small and ephemeral gains.

Since, on the basis of economic systems theory, America is likely to remain the strongest of the great powers for most of the first quarter of the 21st century, it will bear most of the responsibility for creating a peaceful, just, and prosperous international order, preferably through nonprovocative restraint rather than hegemonic, national utility-maximizing domination, while Russia, China, and any newly aspiring great powers like India or Iraq must resist the impulse to wager on defense. Continental Europe and Japan almost certainly will play constructive roles, if the strongest and weak great powers adhere to a confidence building script, but they could be drawn into a destabilizing interplay if the present cooperative environment turns adversarial. Likewise, special consideration needs to be given to China's gargantuan population. Any significant improvement in its economic productivity will give Beijing enormous control over security resources. Although handicapped by an inferior economic system, the benefits of economic backwardness are sufficiently large that China's GDP could eclipse America's in absolute size, shifting it from the category of weak to the category of a strong great power well before 2025.

There are two persuasive reasons for all parties acting responsibly even though none of the great powers are generally competitive, nor scrupulously abide by the golden rule: war aversion and social cost. The human and political risks of armed hostilities are high, even without considering the dangers of nuclear, chemical, and biological warfare; and the economic consequences could be similarly daunting. Military operations in high per capita income nations are extraordinarily expensive in terms of foregone current consumption, while prosperity-seeking authoritarian systems like Russia and China should be concerned about undermining their commercial modernization. Nonetheless, as cogent as these reasons should be, systemic factors enmeshed in culture and politics often supercede material calculus. NATO and China, for example, paid scant attention to operational costs or the misery inflicted on those they purportedly sought to help from their respective operations in Yugoslavia and Tibet. Once politicians convince themselves that they must do something, sober assessments of costs and benefits become the first casualties of war.

The systemic, cultural, and political factors which put security at risk among the great powers in the 21st century are not difficult to identify. Rational security decision-making under the Anglo-American market system is particularly vulnerable to the vagaries of constituent sparring, causing a mismatch between force capabilities and political aspirations. Defense spending as a share of gross domestic product has fallen continuously (even during the so-called Reagan buildup) since 1967, when outlays for the Vietnamese war peaked; a decline driven above all by the need to manage Cold War rivalries, and a post-communist resolve for mutual, balanced force reductions. But at the same time, especially during the 1990s as America began to economically pull away from the rest of the pack, leaders gradually became more interventionist in support of the new global order. American forces were employed in Haiti, Somalia, Iraq, Croatia, Bosnia, Herzegovina, Serbia, and Kosovo. America used NATO to detach Poland, Hungary, and the Czech Republic from the Russian sphere of influence; is seriously contemplating extending the process to the Ukraine and beyond, and employs international organizations like the IMF and World Bank to collectivistly coordinate global economic activity. If the trend persists under the banners of spreading democracy and general competition, one-sidedly pressing American commercial and political advantage at the expense of foreign interests, hegemonic bullying could trigger a destabilizing military response among some great powers for which America is ill prepared to cope. Plausible rationales can be made for these actions. The exercise of superpower could promote global law and order by compelling would-be renegades to heel. But the risks are worrisome.

Russia for its part during the 1990s has validated America's assertiveness. Boris Yeltsin acquiesced to America's version of the new global order in return for embezzle-able Western assistance.[1] He acceded to NATO expansion among Russia's former Eastern European satellites, and seemed prepared to accept Western absorption of most former Soviet republics. He tolerated the air war against Yugoslavia and NATO's occupation of Kosovo. But this behavior, veiled by insincere liberalism, could change abruptly in various unpleasant ways. Kremlin leaders may find it convenient to draw a line in the sand, and start modernizing Russia's armed forces in earnest with an eye toward halting and reversing NATO's advance. The cost will not be prohibitive. In the Soviet tradition, modernization could proceed on a prioritized basis, retaining conscription, but concentrating resources on elite troops needed for preserving domestic authority and expanding influence in the "near abroad" (independent republics of the former Soviet Union). Idle military industrial capacities can be reopened, workers paid a pittance, and RDT & E redirected toward countering the West's "smart" conventional weapons and stealth technologies. Indeed, the process may already have begun. Military industrial production in 1999 and 2000 grew at roughly 30 percent per annum.[2] Russia already possesses massive nuclear deterrent forces, and has the luxury of modernizing them at its convenience. These actions would not be enough to turn the tide in Western Europe, but they would allow Russia to test

[1] In early August 1999, the French newspaper *Le Monde* printed an expose describing the massive embezzlement of foreign assistance to Russia, and accusing the IMF of tacit complicity. Michel Camdessus, the Director of the IMF, responded that the institution was blameless, because it had hired the Price Waterhouse accounting firm, which found no irregularities in Russia's IMF accounts. The *Wall Street Journal* contacted Price Waterhouse, which stated that the Russians prevented it from conducting a meaningful audit (*Wall Street Journal*, August 24, 1999, p. A19. Also see Bob Davis, "IMF Doesn't Watch Fund Disbursement," *Wall Street Journal*, August 24, 1999, p. A2). Further rounds of accusations and denials followed, punctuated by an investigation of the Bank of New York's money laundering operations of these and other embezzled funds. See Paul Beckett, "Authorities Study Bank of New York's Ties to Inkombank," *Wall Street Journal* August 14, 1999, p. A2; "Siphoning of Russian Funds may be on a Scale not Previously Imagined," *Wall Street Journal*, August 26, 1999, p. 1; "Brash Russian Banker and his Tangled Deals Intrigue Investigators," *Wall Street Journal*, August 26, 1999, p. 1; Bob Davis, "Laundering Probe Could Mean Trouble for Gore," *Wall Street Journal*, August 26, 1999, p. A20. Separately, a series of articles has appeared on the theme "Who Lost Russia?", tying Russia's criminality to its failed transition. See George Melloan, "Who Lost Russia?" *Wall Street Journal*, August 24, 1999, p. A19; John Lloyd, "The Russian Devolution," *New York Times Magazine*, August 13, 1999.
[2] Julian Cooper, "The Russian Military Industrial Complex: Current Problems and Future Prospects," seminar on "Russia's Potential in the 21st Century," House of Estates, Helsinki, Finland, March 23, 2001. Russia's economy according to Vitaly Shlykov is "structurally militarized." For more on this concept, see Steven Rosefielde, "Economic Foundations of Russian Military Modernization: Putin's Dilemma," in Col. Michael Crutcher, ed., *The Russian Armed Forces at the Dawn of the New Millennium*, US Army War College, Carlisle Barracks, Pennsylvania, 2001, pp. 101–17. Cf., Lennart Samuelson, *Plans for Stalin's War Machine, Tukhachevskii and Military-Economic Planning*, 1925–1941, Macmillan Press, London, 2000.

NATO's resolve on the margins of the continent. The Kremlin's options beyond this are limited until the leadership confronts and surmounts the contradictions of authoritarian laissez faire and its destructive moral hazards. There is no evidence that they will do so any time soon, but unwise American pressure could badger them into it. And once the paradigm is reversed, and disciplined authoritarian markets installed, Russia's vast resources and engineering culture could transform it once again into a formidable adversary.

The pro-security advantages of authoritarian collectivism, especially in a disciplined market that keeps moral hazard within bounds, applies doubly to China. Many Western security analysts dismiss the risk by assuming that collectivist societies on a turnpike toward rapid market-driven modernization will not allow themselves to be detoured by developing huge military forces to right perceived past wrongs, or to seek unfair advantage from foreigners. But countries which refuse to abide by the golden rule internally can hardly be expected to stay their hands when they are empowered by brisk economic growth, rapid military industrial technology transfer, and are challenged by aspiring nuclear powers like India. China is in a position to control its security labor costs for the foreseeable future and therefore can exert substantial undue influence at its discretion.[3]

Continental Europe is more tautly constrained by the high cost of its defense services. It could follow America's bad example by increasingly leveraging security forces in pursuit of various coercive advantages, but after Milosovich there are few obvious targets of opportunity to justify the expense. Perhaps sometime in the next few decades the European Union will decide to distance itself from American tutelage, but this is not likely to amount to much, and will leave the continent vulnerable to Russian resurgence.

Finally, there is Japan, the country which confounds all conventional wisdom because its communalist shame culture is perfectly capable of reconciling export-oriented market commercialism with foreign domination, and high per capita living standards with low-cost military expansion. These behavioral propensities, characteristic of prewar Imperial arrangements, have been held in check by Japan's American-imposed postwar constitution, the US–Japan security treaty, and the absence of any credible challenge before the advent of Chinese authoritarian laissez faire, but here as elsewhere, beneath the veneer of stability, global security is being buffeted by the winds of change.

RECONFIGURATION OF WEALTH AND POWER

Attitudes toward these emergent conflicts vary widely. Those who misequate contemporary economic and security behavior with general competition and golden rule abiding, of course, are optimistic. Happy endings are predetermined by their premises. But realists disagree. The increasing economic ascendance of America, or even its supersession by China, could arguably be benevolent or malign. They could merely amount to a rotation among winners and losers, the usual ebb and flow of fortunes, or could be catalysts for strife and mass suffering. Systems theory provides useful insights into why collectivist,

---

[3]   Richard Bernstein and Ross Munro, "China I: The Coming Conflict With America," *Foreign Affairs*, Vol. 76, No. 2, March/April 1997, pp. 18–32; Steven Mosher, *Hegemon*, Encounter Press, San Francisco, 2000.

communalist, and authoritarian economic and security systems create the risk of conflict, and the possibility that David might vanquish Goliath, but are not deterministic. If economic power becomes extremely asymmetric, weak nations can always accept their fate and sub-optimize through conciliation, tribute, and guile, while biding their time, deceiving, and plotting revenge. Or they can take immediate defensive/offensive counter-measures if the leadership of economically weak great powers are able to arouse, or coerce their populations into a no-frills arms race. The reconfiguration of economic wealth and power prefigured in the 21st century by systems theory thus is best understood as a manageable problem that could get out of hand if denied, ignored, or mishandled.

Review Questions

1. Why is it plausible to suppose that American military security is positively correlated with the relative size of its GDP?
2. Why have some argued that global security depends on the relative size of America's GDP?
3. Why has Samuel Huntington argued that global security depends on a narrow dispersion of national GDPs?
4. Why does Huntington believe that a common standard of living is sufficient to overcome what he calls the "clash of civilizations"?
5. What are the distinctive features of "harmonist" concepts of ideal security?
6. Why is there a fundamental contradiction between rational power and security seeking and the premises of category A economic globalism and its promise of universal prosperity?
7. The purchase of national security services is usually a collective governmental decision. Does moral hazard complicate the determination of the demand for national defense? Explain.
8. The supply of defense services should be determined by profit-maximizing. But sometimes the state prefers to set the competitive process aside in order to be sure of receiving the goods it desires. Why are commands sometimes preferred to paying suppliers prices that will get the job done? Is this a case of governments wanting to eat their cake and have it too?
9. Are the conditions for achieving a category A security services supply and demand equilibrium the same as those of the general economic case?
10. For these conditions to be satisfied policy-makers must dispassionately evaluate choices, and suppliers must not succumb to moral hazards. Why are these conditions likely to be more difficult in the market for defense services?
11. How does security secrecy complicate matters?
12. Is it paradoxical that the most efficient way of defending against adversaries is to behave competitively at home, and coercively abroad? Explain.
13. Does the optimal level of security expenditures depend on culture and social priorities? Does this give authoritarian laissez-faire systems like China an advantage?
14. Why do the low opportunity costs of authoritarian dual economies provide them with a comparative advantage in producing weapons and maintaining large military forces?
15. Should this advantage disappear if democracies correctly perceive the threats confronting them?

16. International security can be increased, and defense costs reduced if national leaders can be persuaded that trade and cooperation are more beneficial than power-seeking. Why is it difficult to abide by this insight when the world is populated with category B economic systems, with divergent growth?

17. What are the two primary reasons for cooperating in a world where divergence is the norm?

18. Why has Samuel Huntington described America as a rogue superpower? What are the dangers associated with this behavior?

19. Why might Russia, China, Japan, and Continental Europe decide to change their security postures in the not too distant future?

20. Is the 21st century security problem manageable?

CHAPTER 17

MILITARY BALANCE

From the dawn of the thermonuclear age to the dismemberment of the Soviet Union, the world was bipolar. Two superpowers, the United States and the USSR, possessed 95 percent of the global strategic nuclear arsenal, and deployed ballistic missile delivery systems to make them credible deterrents. These forces served their purpose. While both superpowers sparred on the periphery, neither dared threaten the other's territorial integrity. The disintegration of the Soviet Union, and its traumatic aftermath, combined with the rapid economic emergence of China, have profoundly altered the strategic equation. Russia has drastically reduced its nuclear and conventional forces, and has almost ceased procuring new weapons for its troops. Its forces are rapidly becoming obsolete, a problem aggravated by poor maintenance. The West, for complex reasons, has drastically downsized its own arsenals, preserving rough strategic nuclear parity, but the status quo ante is being undermined by nuclear proliferation and China's resurgence. If current trends persist, the world is heading toward nuclear superpower tripolarity, because China is building up precisely at the time that its competitors are rushing for the exits.

This is not how early post-Cold War pundits imagined things would turn out. Samuel Huntington and Francis Fukuyama thought America would be the planet's lone superpower, and that globalization would curb power-seeking by creating a common high living standard. Instead, the world must cope with an unstable superpower threesome, other nuclear aspirants, and worsening economic divergence. Finding ways to cope with systems-based asymmetries in wealth and security is quickly becoming the central problem of the new millennium.

War, according to the Prussian strategist Karl von Clausewitz (1780–1831), is diplomacy by other means. It is the use of military force to achieve ends that cannot be accomplished with nonviolent methods like intimidation. Sometimes military strategists prefer to attack out of the blue, dispensing with diplomacy to achieve surprise, but most often war is viewed as a last recourse when an aggressor concludes that persuasion is futile.

The willingness to fight depends on policy-makers' assessments of benefits and costs to themselves and the nation. Their prospects for success hinge on the superiority of their weapons, troops, training, and tactics. Inferior military forces may also serve a useful purpose if they deter would-be aggressors, or elicit concessions. America's armed forces are better than Russia's; nonetheless, the Clinton administration indulged the Kremlin with billions in foreign assistance to encourage reduced nuclear deployments.

The design, creation, maintenance, and reform of military forces depends on the degree to which policy-makers wish to preserve the option of threatening or employing war (retaliation) as an instrument of utility-maximizing. Nations at substantial risk of aggression, or which see great benefit in wielding power will build large, potentially superior forces. Others will satisfice as conditions dictate. This means that the size, structure, technology, mobility, and readiness of national (alliance) militaries provides important clues about intentions.

Data on the comparative size and composition of military forces are traditionally divided into two components: conventional and nuclear. Figures refer to weapons that are actively deployed, or in operational reserves, excluding decommissioned older equipment in deep storage, or employed for other purposes like target practice. Confirmation of decommissioning is often difficult to obtain. Standard sources either take the declarations of military organizations at face value, or treat limits stipulated in arms control and disarmament agreements as accurate indicators of deployments, even when it is widely understood that such assumptions are erroneous. Soviet "spare" ballistic missiles, which were designed both as reloads and first strike weapons, were not counted in the SALT and START totals because the Soviets argued that silos could not be reused.

This means that measures of comparative military size can often gyrate wildly. Russia, for example, decommissioned 2,292 aircraft between 1996 and 1998. This might seem to imply that it would take the Kremlin a decade to re-achieve its earlier force levels. But, the task could be accomplished in a matter of weeks in the event of war, merely by re-commissioning equipment stashed in inactive inventory. The tables which follow should be interpreted accordingly. Most provide snapshots of reality, filtered through the lens of conventions which are sometimes meant to deceive.

Nonetheless, the big picture is broadly accurate. It shows that Russia and the United States are preeminent nuclear powers, both possessing the ability to reliably strike high-value targets anywhere in the world with thousands of strategic and tactical nuclear warheads. Together, they account for more than 95 percent of 20,000+ nuclear warheads in the operational inventories of the signatories to the Nuclear Non-proliferation Treaty (table 17.1). British, French, and Chinese nuclear forces are sufficient to provide a credible deterrent, but only China appears to have the political possibility of increasing its nuclear arsenal to the superpower standard.

Conventional forces display a similar pattern, but the preponderance of America and Russia is less pronounced and more variegated. Both maintain enormous tank, armored fighting vehicle, and artillery forces (table 17.2), that are roughly matched in quantitative terms, but China runs a close third (table 17.3). Moreover, even smaller countries like Japan possess formidable ground fighting capabilities (table 17.4), judged from the standpoint of their local defense requirements. The same reservations apply for combat aircraft, while the collapse of Russia's navy has allowed China and Japan to eclipse the Kremlin in major surface combatants.

Table 17.1   Aggregate number of strategic delivery vehicles (as of January 1, 1998)

	ICBM	SLBM	IRBM	Bombers	Warheads stockpile
US	701	464		321	7,770
Russia	756	648		80	8,527
Ukraine	66			44	?
China	17+	12	46+	some?	180
United Kingdom		64		96	296
France		64	48	86	512

Sources: IISS, *The Military Balance 1998/99*, Oxford University Press, 1999, p. 292. *SIPRI YEARBOOK 1995: Armaments, Disarmament and International Security*, Oxford University Press, London, 1995, pp. 328–333.

Notes: Ukraine's ICBMs are unarmed. The United States has several hundred tactical nuclear weapons; the Commonwealth of Independent States 2000–6000, and China 120.

This erosion of Russia's military power is symbolic of its broader decline. At the end of the Soviet era it could be plausibly argued on numeric grounds that Moscow's nuclear and conventional forces substantially exceeded America's, while Washington enjoyed qualitative superiority, especially in command, control, and communications essential for modern war fighting. But the decade of post-Soviet decline which followed has tilted the quantitative balance against Russia (excluding the rest of the CIS), despite substantial parallel force size reductions in the United States and Europe. Worse still, from the Kremlin's viewpoint America's advantage in technology, particularly microelectronics, has become cavernous, with no prospects for catch-up until Russia finds a formula for economic recovery.

However, the gradual emergence of America as the world's only military and economic superpower is more difficult to document than might be imagined, because during the Cold War the West found it politic to understate the comparative size of active Soviet forces. The arms control data which governed perceptions showed the United States with a substantial edge in strategic nuclear warheads in 1990, 12,718 to 10,779, which has been reversed. Russia today officially possesses approximately 750 more warheads than America,[1] misimplying that START I has given the Kremlin a margin of nuclear superiority it hadn't previously enjoyed. Moscow had, and continues to have, substantial nuclear superiority when account is properly taken of ballistic missile "spares."[2] Data on commissioned conventional forces also tend to understate Russia's capabilities past and present, implying parity when the Soviet deployments were numerically superior in the 1980s, and exaggerating decommissionings in the 1990s.[3]

[1]   *SIPRI Yearbook 1995: Armaments, Disarmament and International Security*, Oxford University Press, London 1995, p. 642.
[2]   Viktor Mikhailov, former Russian Minister of Atomic Energy, confided that Russia had 42,000 nuclear weapons circa 1997. He was quoted earlier as stating that the Soviet Union had more than 50,000 nuclear weapons in 1991. Official Western estimates never exceeded 20,000 nuclear weapons.
[3]   Most of the former republics of the Soviet Union are members of the Commonwealth of Independent States (CIS), which maintains a unified defense system under the control of Russia. For some comparative purposes it may be appropriate to add weapons held in the non-Russian CIS to the Kremlin's totals.

Table 17.2   Russian and US military equipment arsenals 1998

Tanks	
Russia	16,210
USA	8,369
AFV/APC	
Russia	28,530
USA	27,627
Artillery/MRLS	
Russia	16,453
USA	7,225
Combat aircraft	
Russia	2,868
USA	4,475
Major surface warships	
Russia	44
USA	134
Attack submarines	
Russia	72
USA	66
Strategic submarines	
Russia	26
USA	18
Strategic ballistic missiles	
Russia	180 SS-18 (10 MIRV)
	188 SS-19 (6 MIRV)
	92 SS-24 (10 MIRV)
	360 SS-25 (1 warhead)
USA	590 Minuteman III
	50 Peacekeeper MX
	115 Minuteman II silos (START accountable)
Strategic bombers	
Russia	28 TU95H (with ALCM) plus 5 in Ukraine
	32 TU-95H16 (with ALCM) plus 20 in Ukraine
	6 TU-160 (with ALCM) plus 19 in Ukraine
USA	95 B-1B
	66 B-52H
	13 B-2

Source: IISS, *The Military Balance 1998/99*, Oxford University Press, London, 1999, pp. 20–7, 108–12.

Nonetheless, the real deterioration in Russia's relative military standing is readily discerned in the post-Soviet weapons production statistics. In 1990, the Soviet Union produced 1,600 main battle tanks, more than Japan's entire current tank force. It produced 40 strategic bombers, 115 ICBMs and SLBMs, and 430 combat fighters

Table 17.3   China's force structure: 1998 armed forces personnel (active)

2,820,000	Regulars
1,200,000	Reserves
?	Paramilitary
	Air force
46	Su-27SK
180	J-8
566	J-7 (MiG-21)
2,095	J-6 (MiG-17)
142	H-6 (Tu-16)
200	H-5
440	Q-5
	Navy
18	DDG
35	Frigates (FFG)
1	Nuclear ballistic missile submarine (SSBN)
5	Nuclear attack submarines (SSN)
1	Guided missile submarine (SSG)
56	Diesel submarines (SS)
163	Missile craft (SSM)
17	Landing ship-tank (LST)
50	Landing ship-men (LSM)
	Strategic forces
17+	Intercontinental ballistic missiles
12	Submarine-launched ballistic missiles (SLBM)
46+	Intermediate-range ballistic missiles (IRBM)
	Nuclear weapons
280	Strategic nuclear weapons
120	Tactical nuclear weapons

Sources: Source: IISS, *The Military Balance 1998/99*, Oxford University Press, London, 1999, pp. 178–80.

(table 17.5). About 80 percent of these totals were manufactured in Russia.[4] In the waning years of Gorbachev's presidency, mass weapons production was the preferred strategy for modernizing the force, and striving for superiority. A decade later, Russia is procuring just a few percent of these weapons, and has ceased building major surface ships, bombers, and transport aircraft entirely. Although it retains formidable capabilities, its weapons stock is rapidly aging. This needn't be disastrous. The United States makes do with much lower

[4]   Aleksei Ponomarenko, *The Historical National Accounts of Russia 1961–1990*, Institute of Economic Research, Hitotsubashi University, Tokyo, January 2001.

Table 17.4 Japan's force structure: 1998 armed forces personnel

242,600		Regulars
48,600		Reserves
	Air force	
50		F-1
20		F-4EJ
180		F-15J/DJ
49		F-4EJ
	Navy	
9		Destroyers
48		Frigates
16		Submarines
	Army	
5		Army regional commands
1,090		Main battle tanks
60		Armored fighting vehicles
870		Armored personnel carriers
480		Towed artillery
310		Self-propelled artillery

Source: IISS, *The Military Balance 1998/99*, Oxford University Press, London, 1999, pp. 182–5.

Table 17.5 Estimated production of major weapon systems, Russia 1990–97

	1990 USSR	1991 USSR	1992	1993	1994	1995	1996	1997
Main battle tanks	1,600	850	500	200	40	30	5	5
Inf. fighting vehicles	3,400	3,000	7,005	300	380	400	250	350
SP artillery	500	300	200	100	85	15	20	10
Bombers	40	30	20	10	2	1	1	0
Fighters/FGA	430	250	150	100	50	20	25	35
Transport aircraft	120	60	5	5	5	4	3	0
Helicopters	450	350	155	150	100	95	*75*	*70*
Submarines	12	6	6	4	4	3	2	2
Major surface shops	2	3	1	1	0	1	1	0
ICBMs/SLBMs	115	100	55	35	25	10	10	2
SRBMs	0	0	80	105	55	45	35	30

Source: IISS, *The Military Balance 1998/1999*, Oxford University Press, London, 1999, p. 106.

levels of arms acquisition, but Russian maintenance during its great depression has been inadequate. A large part of its arsenal is in a state of acute decay, underscoring the negative impression conveyed by the production data. Economic statistics tell a similar tale. CIA figures computed just prior to the fall of communism put American and Soviet military spending at parity. Today, the picture is completely different. The International

Institute of Strategic Studies and NATO estimate that America outspends Russia militarily by four to one, while the IMF and SIPRI believe the disparity is twice as disadvantageous.[5] All these estimates understate Russia's defense activities, just as they did during the Cold War (table 17.6), but not enough to alter the image of pronounced decline.[6]

This is true whether the norm is America or the rest of the world. During the 1990s, India and Pakistan joined the nuclear club, and China has gradually increased its nuclear forces. Beijing has maintained a standing army of 2.8 million, and is modernizing its ground, air, and sea forces. Its defense spending is estimated to have grown 10–15 percent annually throughout the decade.[7] As a consequence, China's global military position has necessarily improved in every dimension relative to Russia's, and in most aspects compared with America and Europe. While China has been forging ahead, Russian–CIS defense activities have fallen approximately 75 percent, and American expenditures by a third (table 17.7).

Should these trends persist into the next century, China is likely to join the club of super, and near-super, powers. The unratified START II treaty signed January 3, 1993 commits America and Russia to reduce their strategic nuclear arsenals to 3,500 each, with additional cuts under discussion for START III; levels well within Beijing's grasp.

Table 17.6 Comparative size estimates of Russian and American defense activities (billions of 1978 dollars)

	1992	**1996**
Russia	75.9	55.7
America	108.9	97.3
Comparative size (index: US = 100)	69.7	57.2

Sources: Steven Rosefielde, *Forgotten Superpower: Russia's Military Revival and the New Global Order*, February 1998, draft. CIA, *Handbook of International Economic Statistics*, CPAS92–10005, September 1992, Tables 7 and 21, pp. 23, 29, Vitaly Shlykov. Cf., Noel Firth and James Noren, *Soviet Defense Spending: An History of CIA Estimates*, 1950–1990, Texas A&M University Press, 1997; and William Lee, "Review of Noel Firth and James Noren, Soviet Defense Spending: An History of CIA Estimates," *Slavic Review*, Vol. 58, No. 1, Spring 1999, pp. 262–63.

NB: The estimates above have not been corrected for learning curve bias, and therefore accord with the CIA's official purchasing power parities. For a discussion of this important issue, see Steven Rosefielde, *Forgotten Superpower*. Proper adjustment raises Russia's comparative size. The nonprocurement component of Russian defense activities has been adjusted 40 percent due to territorial change. See CIA, Handbook of International Economic Statistics, CPAS 92–10005, September 1992, Table 7, p. 24. The Russian component of the Soviet population was 51.5, and GDP 78 percent circa 1991. See Aleksei Ponomarenko, The Historical National Accounts of Russia 1961–1990, Institute of Economic Research Hitotsubashi University, Tokyo, January, 2001.

[5] IISS, *The Military Balance, 1998–1999*, Oxford University Press, London 1999, pp. 15, 105.
[6] Ponmarenko's reconstruction of Soviet GDP from NMP data demonstrates that Russia achieved moderate rates of GDP growth during the 1980s, and that its high levels of weapons production were not an illusion. The main outstanding issue remains where weapons are concealed in official NMP statistics. The logical place is in the capital account, but these values are too low to accommodate all the arms produced.
[7] Charles Wolf, Jr., K.C. Yeh, Anil Bamezai, Donald Henry, and Michael Kennedy, *Long-Term Economic and Military Trends, 1994–2015: The United States and Asia*, Rand, Santa Monica, CA, 1995, pp. xii, xiv.

Table 17.7   Department of Defense: total obligational authority (billions of 1998 dollars)

	Army	Navy	Air Force	Total
1985	108.2	135.8	128.7	302.3
1990	99.8	122.8	115.8	363.4
1998	62.7	82.8	76.3	262.0
1999	64.3	81.5	77.1	258.6
2003	64.9	80.3	78.6	260.7
% change 1990–98	−37.4	−32.5	−45.0	−35.0
1998–2003	3.9	−3.1	3.0	−0.5

Source: IISS, *The Military Balance 1998–1999*, Oxford University Press, 1999, p. 16.

Continued double digit growth in military expenditures should also allow the Chinese to close the conventional gap, especially in the Asian area of military operations.[8]

Both Russia and America could reverse fields, matching China's advances, but this does not appear likely. Vladimir Putin and his entourage are preoccupied with consolidating the privileges of the new elites, and Washington tacitly operates under the assumption that its superior production capabilities deter as effectively as its standing forces. Leading specialists within the defense establishment do not believe that Beijing will shoulder the cost of constructing a superior arsenal, and assume that should push come to shove America can quickly make the futility of the endeavor clear by rapidly procuring whatever additional weapons might be required. This attitude has some technological substance, and rests on the premise that since a nuclear conflagration is improbable, geography will always give America the time needed to counter any foreign conventional arms buildup. It is also compatible with the notion cogently articulated by advocates of arms control and disarmament that the West and Russia can safely and should substantially downsize their forces well below current levels. This could happen, but for the moment at least the United States is planning to hold its defense spending constant or increase it slowly in real terms for the foreseeable future.

Absent Beijing's own self-restraint, it seems therefore that the world is moving toward a tripolar nuclear superpower system, with two relatively unstable actors. Declared strategic nuclear warheads under START II, if extended to China, will stabilize in the vicinity of 10,000, with Russia secretly reserving an additional 3,500 strategic warheads, using past norms of deception to gauge the future. The good news is that these totals excluding tens of thousands of tactical nuclear warheads will be about a third those prevailing during the Cold War, but the addition of the China factor could well aggravate the risk of miscalculation. Awareness of this danger has not crystalized yet, but is a tacit element in the emerging debate over national ballistic missile defense (NMD). Opponents have carried the day on this issue for more than three decades by insisting that it was technologically infeasible, ruinously costly, and would prompt the Soviets to augment their strategic nuclear arsenal to overwhelm ballistic missile defenses. The Kremlin's acquisition of some 12,000 dual anti-aircraft/anti-ballistic missile SA10s, SA12s, and now SA20s was

---

[8]   Steven Mosher, *Hegemon*, Encounter Books, San Francisco, 2000.

either denied (insisting they only had an anti-aircraft mission) or disregarded as being technologically ineffectual.[9] However, advances in technology combined with proliferation of threats (North Korea, Iran, India, and Pakistan), the parlous state of the Russian economy, Putin's endorsement of nuclear employment when circumstances warrant,[10] and likely further reductions in America's nuclear deterrent appear to be making the adoption of ballistic missile defense probable. Russian threats to re-MIRV (add multiple warheads to its ICBMs), and fears that a sense of invulnerability will make Washington too aggressive are keeping the final resolution in doubt,[11] but this still seems to be the course of least resistance, because insiders believe that technology is America's ace in the hole, and doubt that Russia can retaliate.[12]

The attraction of building superpower nuclear arsenals, and perhaps ballistic missile defenses, in a universe where no sane leader should seriously contemplate nuclear war on its face is difficult to fathom. Why squander fortunes on systems no one intends to use, when the same result can be obtained by everyone agreeing to pare nuclear weapons to the bone, or abolish them altogether? The answer lies in the concept of sovereignty. Nuclear weapons place boundaries on the degree to which foreign powers can intrude on domestic policy-making, and on the authority of hegemons over their tributaries. During the Cold War, nuclear weapons divided the world into two camps, and complemented other forms of authority within each bloc. After the fall of communism, they have become more important than ever for this purpose, because globalization is eroding other lines of defense. Nations are being pressured into surrendering domestic political and economic control to international rules, and a case is being made for powerful and "morally superior" countries like America to disregard the sovereign claims of countries like Yugoslavia, Indonesia, and Rwanda whenever "human rights" are jeopardized. Whatever the rationalization, nations today are at greater risk of external intervention by adversaries than any time in the recent past, and can do little to defend themselves against concerted superpower conventional attack. They have to rely on a nuclear deterrent.

The rules of the new game have not been codified. Russia's nuclear forces did not give it a veto over American actions in Kosovo, but did allow the Kremlin to deploy occupation forces after the event. And, as is obvious, Washington has completely acquiesced to Moscow's operations in Chechnya, going so far as to declare that its foreign assistance was not linked to Russian military operations within Russia's sphere of influence.[13] Likewise, China is immunized from American incursions by its nuclear prowess.

[9]   William Lee, *The ABM Charade: A Study in Elite Illusion and Delusion* Council of Social, Political, and Economic Studies, Washington, DC 1997; William Lee, "Soviet Violation of Article I of the ABM Treaty and Its Implications: Update of the ABM Treaty Charad," Senate, Foreign Relations Committee, Hearing on the ABM Treaty, START II, and Missile Defense Testimony, May 13, 1999.

[10]   BBC, January 13, 2000.

[11]   Bruce Blair, *The Nuclear Turning Point: A Blueprint for Deep Cuts and De-Alerting of Nuclear Weapons*, Brookings Institution Press, Washington, DC, January 1999; De-Alerting Strategic Forces, Brookings Institution Press, Washington, DC, October 1998.

[12]   Keith Payne, "National Missile Defense: Why Now?" *Foreign Policy Research Institute WIRE A Catalyst for Ideas*, Vol. 8, No. 1, January 2000. The full version will appear in *Orbis*, Spring 2000; Paul Bracken, *Fire in the East: The Rise of Asian Military Power and the Second Nuclear Age.*

[13]   Joseph Kahn, "US Backs Away From Bid to Cut Off Aid To Russia," *New York Times*, December 29, 1999, p. A 8.

The temptation for nuclear proliferation is further increased by the cost of high-tech conventional competition. The commercialization of space, and diffusion of missile technology, makes it relatively cheap for nations like North Korea to create a credible nuclear deterrent countering American conventional military technologies. As a consequence, the military component of the global power rivalry is apt to change dramatically in the 21st century in ways that will surely raise catastrophic risks and increase lethality. Nuclear powers will find themselves secure from most unwelcome external intervention, but vulnerable to surprise attack if they reduce their forces, and susceptible to a multipolar arms race if China or India seek nuclear parity. Nonnuclear states outside the NATO umbrella are likely to experience a steady erosion of sovereignty as their conventional deterrents are marginalized by high technology, but may be compelled to modernize as rapidly as they can to counter regional rivals. Thus, despite the appearance of stability, the global military balance in many ways sits on the razor's edge. The world seems to be simultaneously at risk from excessive denuclearization, nuclear proliferation, and the resumption of conventional arms races. Armaments and technology of course do not condemn nations to war, nor assure peace, but they do determine the structure of costs and benefits as power-seekers struggle for tactical and strategic advantage, and in this way influence the trajectory of international relations.

Review Questions

1. Are nuclear forces concentrated in a few nations or are they dispersed?
2. Have arms control agreements and depression reduced Russia's conventional warfighting capabilities since 1991?
3. Why should Russian weapons production figures for the 1990s worry Kremlin leaders?
4. Why do the START agreements provide a strategic opportunity for China?
5. Why do American defense officials believe that superior US production capabilities are just as effective a deterrent as standing forces?
6. Is the world moving toward a tripolar military superpower regime with two relatively unstable actors?
7. Why is American ballistic missile defense the path of least resistance?
8. Why don't nations abolish their nuclear weapons?
9. How does America's tolerance of the Chechen war validate the utility of nuclear weapons?
10. Is the world becoming more militarily secure after the conclusion of the Cold War?

CHAPTER 18

INTERPLAY OF SYSTEMS: EFFICIENCY AND POWER

During the first quarter of the 21st century, the divergence in living standards between the First and Third Worlds which has been increasing since the 1960s is likely to widen as forecast in chapter 16. Disparities in international political power will follow the same pattern. The Second World will continue rapidly converging to the First, if the Chinese economic system does not come unglued. James Fallows' prediction that the Asian systems of the Second World will supercede America's is probably wrong, but this will not prevent them from achieving a combined GDP many times larger than the United States' by 2025.

Instead of the multi-polarity many assume will characterize the new world order, international relations will revolve around three superpowers: America, China, and Russia. This tripolarity will be reminiscent of the Cold War, but more dangerous because of destabilizing rivalries among various nuclear states including America, China, Russia, India, Pakistan, Japan, and Iran. Persistent economic divergence will encourage superpowers to be increasingly aggressive, compelling weaker nations to devote excessive resources to national defense.

These outcomes are systems driven, and are not likely to be altered by emulation, systemic innovation, technology, demography, global governance, or revolution, because individual and group behavior are dominated by power-seeking instead of efficiency. While statesmen can use reason to figure out optimal economic and defense policies for the public good, they seldom do. Ideals are sacrificed to ulterior motives. Likewise, while the invisible hand could generate the right outcomes under the rule of law, governments invariably interfere in the marketplace, tolerate oligopoly, and even use it to prosper at the expense of other nations. Misgovernance and oligopoly have been intensifying for decades, albeit under a "liberalizing" guise enabling power seeking to gain ascendancy over efficiency and welfare. The interplay of forces which advocates of general competition and rational world governance believe will reverse the divergence between rich and poor, and ensure global peace, therefore is unlikely to set things right, because it does not accurately represent the real shadow rules of the game.

INTERPLAY OF SYSTEMS

Economic systems are macrocosms of the cultures, politics, and personalities shaping individual utility-seeking under conditions of scarcity. Since forces are diverse, so too are national economic systems. Each shows the world two distinct faces: the spotlight ideals it professes, and a shadow reality where actions speak louder than words. No system lives up to its ideals. None are individually or collectively generally competitive. None are perfectly planned, or optimally consensual. Potentials and performance consequently are determined in the twilight zone where the rules of the game are difficult to decipher because motives and mechanisms are complex, and data inaccurate. Nonetheless, the distinctive principles of systems are readily discerned. They involve the prescriptive and proscriptive boundaries culture, ethics, and government place on individual freedom. The most flexible form is general competition which features markets, but does not preclude voluntary planning, collectivism, and group consensus building, all under the rule of law. Its outcomes approach the consumer sovereign ideal, and should exhibit rapid growth unless participants prefer gradual technological change. The entrepreneurial segment of the American managed market system comes closest to this standard.

Collectivist systems like those of Western Europe are also flexible, but their prescriptive and proscriptive requirements are more stringent. They mandate more generous social benefits, and anticompetitive work rules. Some conjecture that this sacrifice of competitive efficiency for social justice creates happier more productive workers, but the effect on productivity and growth over the long run is almost certainly negative. Communalist systems try to avoid these costs by consensus building, and under favorable circumstances succeed. But, as the Japanese example suggests, communalism tends to be weakly responsive to competitive pressures, limiting its attractiveness as an all weather strategy. Even authoritarianism has its merits whenever societies believe that threats make political and economic power more important than prosperity and compassion.

In general, competitive economic systems are superior, but still may be victimized by authoritarian regimes. Systems which respond constructively to the challenges of foreign entrepreneurship, or the threat of authoritarian power, should fare better than those which are inert. During the Cold War the deterrent capabilities that America mustered sufficed to fend off Soviet expansion, but the Kremlin failed to find an effective formula for winning the economic and technological competitions. What will be the result next time? How will America respond to the Chinese challenge, or Western Europe and Japan to the emerging competition from the Second World?

EFFICIENCY AND POWER

No one, of course, can fully foresee the end game, but by analogy with chess it is possible to analyze the future several moves deep using the concepts of efficiency and power. Efficiency in the general competitive, golden rule abiding sense represents the principle of fair competition. It embodies the faith that virtue will be rewarded. Hard work, self-improvement, foresight, prudence, creativity, and honesty will make everyone healthy, wealthy, and wise (spotlight culture).

Power is a reflection of the fact that competition is never general, and consequently people have a need to defend themselves against assault (also spotlight culture), and may if they choose play the role of assailant (shadow culture). The state serves both as a defensive and offensive mechanism against foreigners. In a nongenerally competitive world, power can be a force for good or evil. It is virtuous when it promotes efficiency, or protects us from aggression. It is vicious otherwise.

Future economic and security prospects for individual nations, and the world community, therefore can be conceived as a struggle between the forces of efficiency and abusive power. When efficient utility-seeking is in command, most people prosper. When it is not, the world's economies lose their vigor, stagnate, degenerate, and decline. The first step therefore in assessing the state of the global chess game is to evaluate trends in economic liberalization and abusive power.

The voices of the spotlight culture assure us that prospects are bright. In the aftermath of the Cold War, planning has given way to markets, state assets have been privatized, closed economies have been opened, and bipolar superpower confrontation has been replaced by unipolar–multipolar accommodation. As a consequence, America has experienced a decade of rapid economic growth, and the nuclear superpowers are no longer at each others' throats. But this misrepresents the larger reality. Anticompetitiveness and international power-seeking have been intensifying throughout most of the globe as withering economic controls and authoritarianism have been replaced by other forms of economic power and political aggressiveness. Efficiency on balance has been yielding to power. While America has prospered, most of the First and Third Worlds have not, despite the march of technological progress and possibilities for technological transfer. Rates of economic growth have steadily decelerated. Living standards in many cases have plummeted, and the world has been beset by escalating aggression, civil and foreign wars, and in some instances – like Rwanda – by genocide. The exact number of noncombatant civilian premature deaths has not been tallied, but where the calculations have been made the toll is shocking. More than 3.4 million Russians died prematurely in 1990–98 because political and economic power-seeking overrode competitive efficiency.[1]

Many have difficulty reconciling these facts with media happy talk, forgetting that political management of perceptions and attitudes is usually effective. Throughout the 1930s amid the catastrophe of Soviet-forced collectivization and the Great Terror, Stalin tirelessly proclaimed that black was white; that misery and destitution had made life truly joyous! Of course, the gulf today between golden age rhetoric and ebbing global economic vitality is not so extreme, but it is nonetheless important to appreciate that political self-congratulation is intended to disinform. Concepts like "liberalization" and "free enterprise" serve the same purpose when they misequate spotlight ideals with accomplishments. Both deceive people into believing that eliminating barriers to market entry enhances efficiency, even when it empowers oligopoly, monopoly, rent-seeking, and asset-grabbing. And, conversely, they call into question the very possibility of failure.

---

[1] Steven Rosefielde, "Premature Deaths: Russia's Post-Soviet Transition in Communist Perspective," *Europe-Asia Studies*, Vol. 53, No. 8, December 2001, pp. 1159–76.

How, it is sometimes rhetorically asked, could Russia's GDP have fallen in half, when administrative command planning has been abolished, property privatized, and markets enthroned? The correct answer is – easily, but this is only apparent if one appreciates that removing some barriers through liberalization does not preclude their replacement with institutions that are even more anti-productive and dysfunctional.

Americans have more difficulty grasping this than Russians, because global sclerosis has had little visible impact on the United States' economy during the 1990s. Its superior performance is partly conjunctural, and partly a consequence of its entrepreneurial ethic, but it also is due to America's increasing relative power. Although oligopoly and monopoly degrade national economic efficiency, they allow dominant players in the international market to accumulate anticompetitive rents, and accelerate their countries' growth at the expense of rivals. Rapid market penetration, coupled with burgeoning oligopoly power abroad, undoubtedly have fueled America's economic surge.

EMULATION

The losers in the global efficiency and power competition appear for the most part to grasp the essentials. They understand that private ownership of the means of production vested in competent hands, markets, entrepreneurship, and a semblance of the rule of law which subordinate power to efficiency are indispensable for improving living standards and exerting external influence, unless they gamble on authoritarianism. Gorbachev knew it. While lauding the "proven" superiority of communism in the late 1980s, he diligently pursued a program of radical economic reform and marketization. Even the French, who place so much stock in the state, fear that they will be compelled to embrace Anglo-American laissez faire.[2]

However, borrowing elements from other systems and successfully adapting them in an alien environment are entirely different matters. Sometimes, the institutions borrowed are antithetic. Central planning which commands managers to disregard consumer demand, cannot be reconciled with competitive, individual utility-seeking. Sometimes, their efficacy is diminished by other priorities. The French want managers to be bold innovators, but only in those instances where workers' security is not at risk, a restriction that reduces the scope for entrepreneurial gains. And, of course, before any fundamental change can occur, elites impose conditions that advance their interests. Boris Yeltsin's liberal supporters claimed to understand the virtues of fair and competitive privatization, but were not willing to tolerate it, preferring to steal the people's assets instead.

These three factors explain why all inferior economic systems do not emulate global best practices, and why some nations are likely to be more constructively adaptive than others. Japan, Western Europe, and the Second World in varying degrees have displayed an ability to effectively respond to competitive economic challenges that Russia and much of the Third World have not. This has enabled them to moderate their secular decline and keep the competitive efficiency option alive, while others have been drawn to authoritarianism.

[2]   Dominique Moisi, "The Trouble with France," *Foreign Affairs*, Vol. 77, No. 3, May/June 1998, p. 101.

SYSTEMIC INNOVATION

Similar considerations impair the ability of weak systems to respond by devising alternative mechanisms and policies that leapfrog existing best practice. Laggards in the First and Third Worlds sometimes try to make an end run on the global leaders by resuscitating planning and communalist consensus building, or by adopting radical innovations like egalitarian labor-managed firms, but seldom succeed because of the complexities and moral hazards entailed. Their efforts at resource mobilizing and institutional reform do not usually fare well for the same reasons, causing them to fall back on protectionism, and political–military forms of defense.

These defensive strategies are second best, even when poor nations are being exploited by foreign oligopolists. The ideal method for curbing such abuses is a vigorous domestic antitrust regime recommended by advocates of golden rule abiding liberalization. But the best is sometimes the enemy of the good. If foreign oligopoly cannot be rendered harmless by antitrust policies, protectionism may be the lesser of the two evils. This is why many market friendly economists like Paul Krugman sometimes support protectionism, even when it does not involve infant industries.[3] Although opponents are surely right that protectionism is a sub-optimal policy in a generally competitive world, and that it is liable to provoke trade-destroying retaliation, predatory risk may make protectionism the preferred course, especially when it is associated with foreign political domination.

For nations like Russia, which have boxed themselves in a corner by constructing a consumer unfriendly authoritarian economic system, the empowerment of its former superpower rival, and the rise of a dominating China, will probably lead to further revolutionary change. A neo-conservative, military-oriented regime could emerge, but it will not be either to Russia's or the world's long-term benefit, especially if it rekindles an arms race with America, Europe, China, Japan, the Koreas, India, Pakistan, and Iran.

LACK OF COMPETITIVE COMMITMENT

The tug-of-war between efficiency and power is further complicated by the maneuvers of aspiring economic and political factions. Sometimes fickle advocates of general competition champion laissez faire when the state is perceived as abusive, but change sides when oligopoly and monopoly are at issue. Likewise, power-seekers may support efficient competition among suppliers, or in consumer activities they do not control. Businessmen for obvious reasons are happy to assist employees' "right to work," curbing union power, and workers oppose business trusts. As a consequence, there are few governmental or private institutions that are committed to general competition, and the support which exists is episodic. This explains why fluctuations in the relative power of government and the private sector tend to have only a small impact on competitive efficiency, and global justice. Efficiency thrives in an environment where government primarily enforces the rule of law, and conspiracies in restraint of trade are prosecuted. When motives and policies are mixed, efficiency oscillates, and reconfigures around the primary trend.

[3]   Paul Krugman, "The Return of Depression Economics", *Foreign Affairs*, Vol. 78, No. 1, January/February 1999, pp. 56–74.

This means that even in periods of secular efficiency decline, efficiency may improve cyclically, or in response to governmental policies that are beneficial. Sometimes government and business cooperate to the detriment of unorganized labor, temporarily raising profits before the negative aspects of this anticompetitive behavior kick in. And sometimes governments create or improve institutions designed to expand markets and facilitate political cooperation. The United Nations, the World Bank, IMF, OSCE, EU, NAFTA, ASEAN, and regional defense pacts like NATO are all intended either to fight protectionism, or encourage power sharing as an alternative to aggressive international rivalry. But these institutions and other pro-competitive movements rarely provide a permanent solution to flagging productivity, or international aggression, unless the governments have the will to abide by the principles of fair competition. Otherwise, they only stimulate power-seekers to better conceal their quest for one-sided advantage; exacerbating matters by pressing for world economic and political governance in their own parochial interest. While it is comforting to believe that the invisible hand and responsible government assure the triumph of efficiency over power, it is difficult to see why either "carrots" (emulation and golden rule social welfare) or "sticks" (competition and threats) are likely to bring this about.[4]

THE ROAD TO 2025

The long-term postwar retardation in global economic growth, associated with the shift from government control to regulation, is likely to persist because "liberalization" has not done the job, and there are no Utopian mechanisms to arrest the process. State governance does not make societies economically efficient, politically just, or prudently self-protective. And nations cannot count on the "invisible hand" of market competition. The world in 2025 therefore is likely to look much as forecast in chapter 16, unless revolutionary changes or the epochal shifts in the characteristics of technology radically alter the paradigm.

The United States, contrary to the view of convergence theorists, will widen its lead over the weaker elements of the First World, and most of the Third World, as the advantages of backwardness arising from technology transfer continue to be overwhelmed by abusive power. The lower echelons of the First World will also outpace the Third World due to their adaptive advantage. The Second World, especially China and the four Tigers (Hong Kong, Singapore, Taiwan, and South Korea), will gain rapidly on America, although the fate of NIEs (newly industrializing Asian economies), Indonesia, Malaysia, and Thailand, after the financial crisis of 1997–98 are in doubt. As Paul Krugman has argued, there are good grounds for anticipating that the Second World will not constitute a superior system in the long run, after catch-up effects have been exhausted, but this should not prevent it from surpassing America's GDP by a wide margin.[5] The reconfiguration of wealth and power envisioned does not require Asian supermen, only perspiration and persistence.

[4]　C. Fred Bergsten, "Globalizing Free Trade", *Foreign Affairs*, Vol. 75, No. 3, May/June 1996, pp. 105–21.
[5]　Paul Krugman, "The Myth of Asia's Miracle," *Foreign Affairs*, Vol. 73, No. 6, November/December 1994, pp. 62–78. Krugman acknowledges that China's size implies that if it reaches only half America's productivity, its GDP will be more than twice as large. But he does not believe that its per capita GDP, or that of other Asian nations including Japan, can surpass the US standard because they are less entrepreneurially, and technologically proficient. He argues that their rapid growth is explained by "perspiration," not "inspiration," and their planning and cultures are not unique assets.

The declining fortunes of Continental Europe and Japan are likely to persist for other reasons as well. Both have to cope with rapidly graying populations, and falling fertility at sub-replacement levels. Populations at best will be stagnant, and are more likely to decline, despite immigration that is significantly altering ethnic and cultural compositions everywhere except Japan. The situation in the transition states of Eastern Europe, the Baltic States, and Russia is even more dire,[6] with one eminent specialist Murray Feshbach predicting a nearly 50 percent reduction in Russia's population by 2050. Stagnant and declining populations are usually associated with sluggish economic growth. Here the United States has distinct advantages over Continental Europe, Russia, Japan, and China.

A similar disparity exists with regard to information technology. For much of the postwar period, technological progress was concentrated in mechanical industries benefitting engineering cultures like Germany and Japan, but the new microelectronic, information-driven innovations appear to favor America's entrepreneurial temperament. Some argue that the sluggish adoption of the "communications" superhighway in Continental Europe and Japan augurs well for their catch-up potential in the first decade of the 21st century, but this is not an infallible rule of thumb. The catch-up potential of the Third World has been widening for decades without initiating a boom.

The gradual encroachment of world governance, epitomized by talk of creating a "super-IMF" to macro-coordinate the global economy, is another bad omen, especially for systems culturally predisposed toward statism, including the weaker members of the First World, the transition economies, and most of the rest of the Third World.

The interplay of global forces, including the probability of selected, radical systemic change therefore appears to support our forecasts. Although it is clearly within the capacities of human reason to constructively alter destinies by subordinating power to efficiency, and by mastering other political and social pathologies, the obstacles are monumental.

Review Questions

1. In what sense are economic potentials and performance determined in the twilight zone?
2. Can the future be usefully conceptualized as a struggle between the forces of efficiency and abusive power?
3. Why do optimists argue that liberalization is winning over the forces of abusive power?
4. Why do critics argue that liberalization is illusory; that authoritarianism has been replaced by other forms of economic power?
5. Has America's economic success during the 1990s been based solely on its superior competitiveness?
6. Why is emulation often ineffective?
7. Why do market-friendly economists like Paul Krugman sometimes support protectionism, even when it does not involve infant industries?
8. Why is there so little support for general competition?
9. Why do the positive effects of international institutional cooperation tend to diminish over time?

[6]   M. Macura, "Fertility Decline in the Transition Economies, 1982–1997: Political Economic and Social Factors," Chapter 4 in United Nations, *Economic Survey of Europe*, Economic Commission for Europe, 1999, No. 1, pp. 181–94.

GLOSSARY

administrative command planning
Three dominant principles of Soviet economic control: state administration, decrees, and national economic planning. A fourth regulatory principle, bonus-maximizing, was also important.

adverse selection
Cases where insiders make self-interested choices which degrade economic efficiency.

affirmative action
Preferences granted to selected minorities as compensation for past wrongs, or current handicaps.

Arrow's Paradox
The discovery that democratic voting almost always allows the preferences of losers to determine some policy decisions.

asset-grabbing
Illegal insider privatization of state assets.

asset-stripping
Selective seizure of valuable enterprise property like furniture and fixtures, or spinning off profitable activities to wholly owned firms at discount, leaving the state with the debt baby.

authoritarian laissez faire
An economic system with an authoritarian government of any persuasion which encourages unfettered free enterprise in some sectors.

automatic system of planning and management (ASUP)
Late Soviet era strategy of providing firms with real-time, interactive information including planning guidance needed for superior managerial decision-making.

bads
Products that generate negative utility, like pollutants.

business agent
An independent entity hired to represent and act on behalf of principals, granted more autonomy than state enterprise directors, but lacking an ownership stake often granted to senior Western managers. Agents serve themselves like entrepreneurs, but also address the needs of those employing them, including the Communist party of China, and the new Russian state.

capitalism
A loose term for a market economy where owners of real and financial capital are sovereign. The term is also indiscriminately applied to all market economies based on private ownership of the means of production. Critics portray capitalism as anarchic, internally contradictory, self-destructive, and exploitive. Advocates associate it with perfect competition, personal freedom, democracy, and consumer sovereignty.

cartels
Collusive associations of firms and banks designed to regulate business and exert monopoly power.

category A
Self-regulating, universalist systems.

category B	Culturally regulated systems.
Cold War	The contest between the West and the Soviet East for global hegemony without direct military hostilities. The struggle was played asymmetrically with the West relying on global economic engagement, and the Soviet bloc on military superiority. The causes of the Cold War remain contentious.
command	An authoritative order compelling recipients to obey directives instead of acting on their own volition.
communalism	Social, economic, and political systems designed to promote group well-being by subordinating individual rights and freedom when they cause inequality and disharmony. Worker-owned and -managed enterprises, kibbutzim, and Utopian communism are types of communalism.
communism	A Utopian scheme where private property is abolished, and members live communally, sharing work and income equally.
communist party	A political organization claiming to establish and secure a dictatorship of the proletariat, which abolishes private ownership of the means of production, runs the economy, and has a monopoly on social policy-making.
comparative coefficient of factor productivity	A formula used to compare factor productivities between and among countries, assuming constant Cobb–Douglas elasticities of factor substitution, and constant returns to scale.
comparative worth	A wage-fixing scheme intended to eliminate competitive differences in pay across professions by basing compensation on job similarities.
computopia	A Utopian state where ideal existence is achieved by computer calculation and assignment.
consensus building	The Japanese mechanism of determining employment, factor use, production, and distribution on the basis of continuous group and intergroup consultation.
constituentism	A system where lobbying makes special interest groups economically sovereign.
convergence	The theory that global living standards will equalize as nations develop, modernize, liberalize, and globalize.
corporatism	The use of professional, business, and labor groups (generic corporations) as the cornerstone of economic coordination. A form of group-managed market system.
culture	Durable attitudes and patterns of behavior approved by communities, which shape, underlie, supplement, and supercede transient public policies and edicts.
deterrence	A military force designed to dissuade foreign aggression, rather than seek offensive superiority. Deterrence is usually less costly than compellence.
duality theorem	The mathematical demonstration that perfect plans and perfect markets yield identical outcomes if technology, factor endowments, wealth and income distributions, and tastes are the same.
economic engagement	The interplay of economic actors seeking to exert power, or resist its exertion, and to control the rules of the utility-seeking game.

economic inefficiency	Producing the wrong goods mix at any level of activity.
economic sovereignty	The authority of individuals or groups to fix the rules of economic engagement, and control outcomes.
economic system	A set of motivations, mechanisms (markets, government, and obligation), institutions and rules of conduct shaping demand and supply, and responding to disequilibrium under conditions of scarcity.
Edgeworth–Bowley box	A diagrammatic apparatus used to derive production possibility frontiers, and the efficient distribution of goods along contract curves.
efficiency	The degree to which engineering or economic potential is realized.
egalitarian labor-managed firms	Worker-owned and -managed enterprises which pay equal dividends to members in lieu of wages. This convention overrides profit-maximizing and has complex behavioral effects.
egalitarianism	The principle of equal income distribution, regardless of differences in individual contributions to value added.
Euro-sclerosis	The ascription of European growth retardation to systemic rigidities, medically analogous to hardening of the arteries.
First World	Developed industrial nations.
Fisher equation	$MV = PQ$. An equality suggesting that money (M) is neutral: that variations in the money supply or velocity (V) only affects the price level (P), not aggregate economic activity (Q).
general competition	Unfettered competition that may fall short of perfect competition because of insider knowledge, product differentiation, increasing returns to scale, and other imperfections.
globalization	The hypothesis that universal, competitive market principles will govern economic behavior across the planet.
golden rule	The Christian and Confucian ethical principle of treating others as you wish they would treat you, which underlies the notion of fair market contracting essential for welfare-improving efficiency.
goods	Products that generate positive utility.
great powers	Countries considered militarily and economically superior to their competitors. America, Continental Europe, Japan, Russia, and China are usually classified as great powers.
gross domestic product	The annual national value of all marketable goods and services.
gross national income	The annual national income derived from producing all marketable goods and services.
guilt culture	Societies in which individual actions are autonomously governed by conscience, and misdeeds are deterred by guilt avoidance.
harmonism	The belief that there exists an ideal state where all human conflicts are reconcilable.
Hicks–Hansen neoclassical synthesis	A demonstration that government monetary and fiscal policy can be used to bring about a full employment equilibrium of diverse types.
hoarding	The withdrawal of money from circulation and storing it outside of the banking system.

idle cash balances	Money withheld from circulation and held outside of bank checking and savings accounts.
impartial systems	Regimes where the preferences of individual consumers determine outcomes without anticompetitive distortions. Consumers are "sovereign."
income effects	Changes in demand caused by income variations instead of price changes.
income multiplier	The sum of an initial incremental change in investment and additional consumption brought about through the reemployment of idle labor.
index number relativity	A disparity indicator of structural dissimilarity, or rapid economic transformation formed by either measuring GDP at domestic and foreign prices, or measuring growth using prices of different periods.
indicative planning	State-compiled economic plans which provide a framework for policy making and private profit-maximizing. Advocates believe these plans diminish market "anarchy."
indifferents	Products that generate no utility, either positive or negative.
invisible hand	Unobserved actions of markets which allocate factors, and produce and distribute goods and services.
institutions	Organizations which set the rules of various kinds of economic conduct.
job rights	Employment entitlements, benefits, and protections accorded by states or custom to labor.
katastroika	Catastrophic economic reform. The term refers to Gorbachev's failed perestroika (radical economic reform).
Keidanren	The Japanese business policy advocacy association.
keiretsu	A Japanese business affiliated group promoting economic coordination founded on cross-shareholding by related companies and their suppliers.
Keynesianism	The hypothesis that individual consumption and supply programs are competitively determined, but require government intervention from time to time due to hoarding, speculation, and pessimistic expectations.
kleptocracy	An economic system run by corrupt state officials and their cronies in the private sector.
law of demand	The principle that the desirability of goods and services are positive functions of utility and inversely dependent on prices.
law of supply	The principle that the volume of goods and services produced and distributed are positive functions of prices.
law of supply and demand equilibration	The axiom that supply and demand programs can be recomputed as prices are negotiated or varied until excess supplies or demands are eliminated and a stable equilibrium is established.
leisure	Nonwork activities of any type including pleasure-seeking and household maintenance, excluded from GDP.

Libermanism	A Khrushchev-era reform strategy which gave enterprise managers restricted opportunities to profit maximize subject to plan directives and bonus incentives.
lifetime employment	The Japanese industrial policy of retaining workers for life even when their wages exceed the revenue they generate.
linear programming	A mathematical technique for formulating and solving complex factor allocation, production, and output distribution problems where technology exhibits constant returns (is linear).
liquidity trap	The hypothesis that money will be hoarded as quickly as it is printed in a crisis, negating the stimulatory effect of monetary and interest policy.
LM–IS	The analysis of different kinds of nonfull employment joint equilibria in the money and investment markets. LM–IS and the Hicks–Hansen neoclassical synthesis are different terms for the same concept.
lump-sum dividends	Transfer payments paid without regard to work, based on a criterion like equal per capita distribution.
marginal propensity to consume	Consumption is a fixed proportion of personal disposable income.
market	An economic mechanism based on voluntary, negotiated, utility-seeking transactions.
market socialism	A socialist economy which relies on markets, but rejects private ownership. The economy is managed by marginal cost price-fixing rules instead of comprehensive state administration. The concept was first formally developed by Oscar Lange.
Marshallian adjustment mechanism	Excessively high or low prices cause profit-maximizing production levels to expand or contract.
material technical supply system	The Soviet-era system of administrative procurement and distribution.
mechanism	An economic procedure for performing activities including markets, government, and obligation.
MITI	The Japanese Ministry of International Trade and Industry. Renamed METI (Ministry of Economy, Trade and Industry) in January 2001.
MIRV	A ballistic missile "bus" capable of delivering warheads independently to several different targets (multiple independent reentry vehicle).
monopoly	A market structure where a single firm exerts market power.
moral hazard	The danger that economic participants will violate the golden rule.
net material product	A Marxist national product accounting concept, similar to GDP, but less comprehensive because it excludes "nonproductive" personnel services like haircuts, leisure, transportation, etc.
Newtonian core	The set of reversible economic relationships which yield efficient aggregate solutions before account is taken of historical shocks, cultural anomalies, psychology, and other behavioral imponderables.
oligopoly	A market structure where more than two firms exert market power.
one-man rule	The principle of absolute managerial authority. Workers and worker councils may have voice, but must obey managerial directives.

opportunity cost	The ratio of marginal outputs generated by a unit increase in inputs. The sacrifice entailed by allocating resources to one activity instead of another.
perfect competition	Competitive markets with homogeneous goods, full information, no barriers to entry, indivisibilities, or universally increasing returns that maximize individual welfare.
personal disposable income	Household income after taxes and transfers.
planned chaos	A term coined by Friedrich von Hayek to describe the futility of planning in nonmarket economies caused by discorrespondences between state-fixed prices and competitive equilibrium values.
power	The threat or exertion of force to obtain rents, excess profits, involuntary services, and assets precluded by unfettered competition.
preferential systems	Market power enables some individuals or groups to unfairly control outcomes.
productivity	The volume of output generated from unit bundles of inputs. Achieved levels of productivity may or may not be efficient.
production feasibility frontier	The set of constrained efficient supplies that can be generated from available factors.
production possibilities frontier	The set of efficient supplies that can be generated from available factors.
protectionism	The policy of impeding or denying foreigners access to domestic markets in order to shelter home industries, or to obtain excess returns.
purchasing power parity	The valuation of a nation's GDP using the market prices (purchase prices) of another country, bypassing the foreign exchange rate. The technique requires collecting export prices, and matching characteristics of nontradeables so that prices correspond accurately with products.
rent-seeking	The pursuit of privileged private use of state assets, or preferential government contracts.
rule of law	An ideal system where individuals freely utility maximize without arbitrary restraint, or assignment, and disputes are impartially adjudicated according to statute.
Second World	The Chinese cultural development zone, which has exhibited rapid, persistent economic growth.
shadow culture	Disreputable behavior tacitly condoned, or preferred to spotlight ideals.
shadow prices	Prices derived as solution values to linear or nonlinear programs as the inverses of marginal rates of product transformation.
shame culture	Societies of group-governed individuals ruled by fear of violating communal duty.
shock therapy	A liberalization strategy of radically dismantling existing mechanisms in order to jump start the market. In the Russian case this meant abolishing ministerial controls over enterprises, canceling state purchase contracts, freeing prices, and legalizing private ownership of the means of production.

shogun	The highest Japanese secular political ruler before the Meiji imperial restoration.
social democracy	A socialist-oriented democratic political economy that permits markets and partial private ownership of the means of production.
social utility frontier	A curve representing the highest levels of joint utility achievable as goods are redistributed between participants.
socialism	A loose term describing a wide variety of political and mechanistic arrangements where the state claims to restrict free enterprise in society's interest, with special attention paid to the welfare of workers and the poor.
socialist laissez faire	An economic system with a socialist government which selectively encourages unfettered free enterprise in some sectors.
spotlight culture	Laudable ideals showcased by cultural spokesmen.
stakeholders	Outsiders affected by business policies who claim a right to have their views count.
statism	Reliance on the state as the principal source of economic governance and social protection.
sticky prices/wages	An expression suggesting that Walrasian price adjustment is sluggish.
strategic parity	The rough balance of disparate kinds of nuclear and conventional global warfighting capabilities.
superpowers	The preeminent nuclear states. During the Cold War, America and the Soviet Union were considered superpowers because they possessed more than 90 percent of the planet's nuclear weapons, and were said to have rough strategic parity. China may soon join America and Russia. Some analysts insist that America is the only contemporary superpower because of its economic superiority.
systemic structure	The configuration of markets, governance, and obligation, and associated institutions.
tatemae	The Japanese cultural requirement to avoid personal conflict by telling people what they want to hear. This etiquette is an important aspect of consensus building.
technical inefficiency	The failure to optimally combine inputs, or realize full productivity, in some activity even when goods are produced in the right proportions.
tekhpromfinplany	Soviet-era enterprise technical, industrial, and financial plans.
Third World	Mostly poor nations which have not achieved rapid, sustained economic growth.
time preference	The desire to consume sooner rather than later unless compensated for waiting.
tradeoffs	Goods or services that must be provided as a quid pro quo. Similar to the concept of opportunity costs, but without an explicit connection to productivity.
transition	Literally, a movement from one state or system to another. But the term is usually employed to suggest that former planned economies inevitably will be transformed into generally competitive market systems.

universalism	The notion that there exist one or more economic principles which hold everywhere regardless of culture and politics.
utility	The perceived psychological benefit of consumption. These benefits are ordinal, ranking different experiences. Cardinal utility is additive, providing measures of aggregate well-being, but can only be calculated under restrictive conditions.
utility possibility frontier	The set of efficient utility outcomes, given various income and wealth redistributions.
Utopia	Any imaginary state where life is ideal.
visible hand	Governmental or obligational allocation, production and distribution of goods and services.
Walrasian adjustment mechanism	Excess demands or supplies cause prices to rise or fall until supply and demand are equilibrated.
welfare	A subjective judgment about the level of community utility, requiring judgments about the relative importance of different individuals.
welfare state	A state-regulated economy providing comprehensive social services for the protection and betterment of the population.
work	Income-generating activities, for own account or the market, included in GDP.
x-efficiency	Cultural sources of productivity like communal enthusiasm disregarded by classical economic theory.
zaibatsu	Captains of Japanese industry descended from the daimyo, or ruling feudal elite.

INDEX